ERICH RAEDER

Titles in This Series
(listed chronologically by date of publication)

LIBRARY OF NAVAL BIOGRAPHY

ERICH RAEDER

Admiral
of the
Third Reich

KEITH W. BIRD

Naval Institute Press
ANNAPOLIS, MARYLAND

Naval Institute Press
291 Wood Road
Annapolis, MD 21402

Library of Congress Cataloging-in-Publication Data

Bird, Keith W.
  Erich Raeder : Admiral of the Third Reich / Keith W. Bird.
      p.   cm. — (Library of naval biography)
  Includes bibliographical references and index.
  ISBN 1-55750-047-9 (alk. paper)
  1. Raeder, Erich, 1876–1960. 2. Admirals—Germany—Biography.
3. Germany—History, Naval—20th century. 4. Germany. Kriegsmarine—
Biography. I. Title. II. Series.
  DD231.R17B57 2006
  359.0092—dc22

                                                     2005037970

Printed in the United States of America on acid-free paper ∞

12 11 10 09 08 07 06   9 8 7 6 5 4 3 2
First printing

CONTENTS

FOREWORD

Erich Raeder is one of the most prominent admirals in German naval history. Born to a middle-class family near Hamburg, he entered the navy in 1894, served in the Far East from 1897 to 1898, and studied at the German Naval War College from 1903 to 1905. During World War I he served in staff billets, participated in mine-laying operations in the North Sea, and witnessed the Battle of the Dogger Bank and the Battle of Jutland as the chief of staff of Admiral von Hipper's battle cruiser scouting division of the High Seas Fleet. Raeder remained in the navy after the war and rose through a variety of positions to the rank of *General-admiral* (1935) and *Grossadmiral* (1939) while directing the expansion of the navy from a small coastal patrol force into a powerful blue-water fleet. In 1928 he became *Chef der Marineleitung,* that is, commander in chief of the navy, a position he held until January 1943.

When he was the senior officer, Raeder influenced every aspect of the navy while resisting what he considered interference in service affairs by civilian leaders, including Adolf Hitler. Raeder came to personify the German navy as no other officer, and he resigned his position rather than accept Hitler's plan to virtually abandon the surface navy in favor of a strategy based on U-boat operations. Raeder was convicted of war crimes at Nuremberg and was confined in Spandau Prison for a decade before his release, after which he spent his last four years in declining health.

Considering his service in three of the four German navies—the Imperial Navy, the *Reichsmarine,* and the *Kriegsmarine*—his command of the latter two, and his role in World War II, it is surprising that Raeder has not previously been the subject of a book-length, scholarly biography. Raeder published his memoirs, *Mein Leben,* in 1956. These were translated into English by Henry Drexel and published as *My Life* by the Naval Institute Press in 1960 and reprinted as *Grand Admiral* in 2001. Several studies of the German navies have been published, but no biography of the most important German naval leader of the twentieth century.

Keith Bird is superbly suited to produce this, the first, such study. Fluent in German, he is the author of *Weimar, the German Naval Officers*

Corps and the Rise of National Socialism (1977)—where he documented the navy and Raeder's support for Hitler and National Socialism—and numerous essays on Raeder and the German navy during World War II. He is also the compiler of *German Naval History: A Guide to the Literature* (1985). Bird not only describes the life of Raeder and analyzes his impact on German naval affairs, he also places Raeder in the context of the German political and military systems he served.

Thus, *Erich Raeder: Admiral of the Third Reich* is a welcome addition to the Library of Naval Biography, a series that provides accurate, informative, and interpretive biographies of influential naval figures—men and women who have shaped or reflected the naval affairs of their time.

James C. Bradford

ACKNOWLEDGMENTS

This book began in 1966 as an undergraduate honors thesis that introduced me to the extensive records of the German naval archives, which had been captured at the end of the war at Schloss Tambach. In the course of locating documents written after the war by German naval officers for the Allies, I was assisted by the U.S. Department of Naval History, whose staff provided me with copies of these classified studies. Years later, the good offices of the Naval Historical Center at the Washington Navy Yard supported my research once again with access to intelligence files and translations of major German documents.

Before my first visit to Germany in 1969–1970, microfilming projects, notably those of the National Archives and Records Administration (NARA), were invaluable in providing me with an overview of the rich resources available from the German naval archives. Arriving in Freiburg in the spring of 1970, shortly after most of the naval archives had been returned to the West German government, I found myself working with an international group of scholars who subsequently published significant, groundbreaking studies of the German navy and the political, social, and military implications of a modern industrial state that aspired to become a major sea power. During my research, I had an opportunity to meet and correspond with a number of former *Kriegsmarine* officers, including Admiral Friedrich Ruge.

In concluding this seven-year project, I am again indebted to a number of individuals and organizations. My friends at the Naval Historical Center, Gary Weir and, in particular, Randy Papadopoulus, provided both support and information. Once again, Patrick Kelly offered his assistance in critiquing drafts and sharing new sources with me. Tim Mulligan, NARA, shared copies of documents and Rolf Güth's privately published study of Raeder. My close comrade in arms, Tobias Philbin, generously lent me resources from his library and document collections and edited various drafts of the manuscript. I am very appreciative of *Flottillenadmiral a. D.* Otto H. Ciliax, Carl Dreesen, Jörg Hillmann, Michael Salewski, and Werner Rahn for sending me copies of their important work. Dwight Wilder, my New England "editor," brought new insights from all the papers and articles I have written over the years. Doug Peifer also provided me with feedback and shared with me some of his research notes. Rolf Hobson shared with me a copy of his groundbreaking dissertation on German imperialism at sea and the influence of Tirpitz's sea power ideology that redefines the scholarly debate over the ultimate aims of Tirpitz's fleet building.

I also could not have completed this work without the patience and support of Paul Wilderson of the U.S. Naval Institute Press. Equally appreciated is the support of my colleagues and, in particular, Michael McCall, the president of the Kentucky Community and Technical College System, who have been instrumental in bringing this study to its conclusion. I also want to give special thanks to Vicky Nicholas for her friendship and support.

The author appreciates the assistance of E. C. Finney Jr., of the Naval Historical Center, and Thomas Weis, of the Bibliothek für Zeitgeschichte, Stuttgart, in securing the photographs for this biography.

To my colleagues whom I met through my many trips to Germany and ongoing correspondence, I cannot say enough about their willingness to share manuscripts, books, and critiques of my writing. I am honored to be able to draw upon their seminal research and, in the case of my British, Canadian, German, and Scandinavian colleagues, to draw more attention to their studies to a broader range of readers. Besides those already mentioned, this list includes Jost Dülffer, Carl-Axel Gemzell, Holger Herwig, Walter Hubatsch, Paul Kennedy, Jürgen Rohwer, Gerhard Schreiber, and Bernd Stegemann, as well as many other scholars too numerous to name here who provided assistance in my studies. I hope that this effort complements their outstanding contributions to our field, knowing that its critical review will deepen our understanding of Raeder and his navy.

As in previous publications, I want to express my gratitude to the many archives and libraries, particularly to the Militär-Archiv in Freiburg and the Militärgeschichtliches Forschungsamt (MGFA), now located in Potsdam, whose staffs have greatly facilitated my research.

This book is dedicated to Professor Dr. Jost Dülffer, who has been a colleague in assisting and inspiring my studies in German naval history

for over thirty years; the late Dr. Theodore Ropp, who played a significant role in my development as a scholar and teacher; and my wife,
Nancy Laprade, who provided editorial assistance, supported my passion
from the beginning, and created a new life for me.

INTRODUCTION

The German naval theorist Wolfgang Wegener postulated that "it is always ideas that govern the world."[1] Grand Admiral Erich Raeder took the ideas of navalism and world power, attached them to Adolf Hitler's ideology, and almost changed the world. One of the most important naval leaders of the twentieth century, Raeder had a career that spanned the development of the *Kaiserliche Marine* under Kaiser Wilhelm II's *Baumeister,* Alfred von Tirpitz, its role and fate in 1914–1919, the rebuilding of the Weimar *Reichsmarine,* and the development of Adolf Hitler's *Kriegsmarine.* The stern, autocratic Raeder led and drove his naval service from 1928 to 1943. He survived the turmoil of the Weimar Republic and then the whims of a dictator for a decade. He served Hitler longer than any other senior commander in the Third Reich's armed forces.

Contemporaries recognized his role as comparable to that of Grand Admiral von Tirpitz. His successor, Karl Dönitz, commander of the U-boat arm, was more controversial and attracted more attention. Dönitz's outspoken Nazi rhetoric and the notoriety of the U-boat war, as well as his brief tenure as the last *führer,* overshadowed Raeder and dominated much of the postwar literature. Raeder's stubborn belief in the battleship and his leadership of Hitler's Kriegsmarine as an "Imperial-Christian navy" made him appear "anachronistic" to Nazi leaders and to other historians and hagiographers of Dönitz's much-mythologized U-boats.

History's assessment of Raeder began with his conviction as a war criminal at Nuremberg. The prosecution contended that Raeder was a "prime mover" in transferring the loyalty of the navy to the National Socialist state. They accused him of being a "mendacious politician" and an active accessory in Hitler's conspiracy against peace.[2]

The publication of his two-volume autobiography, *Mein Leben,* in 1956–1957, represented a well-organized attempt to justify his policies, defending the navy and its conduct of the war at sea in World War II. Largely ghostwritten by a group of officers coordinated by Admiral Erich Förste, the memoirs followed selected themes to support Raeder, who signed off on the final drafts. *Mein Leben* assumed the mantle of "official history" to refute the Nuremberg charges point by point and rehabilitate his life work. Its writers challenged the claim that Raeder had directed the navy toward preparing for a future war and that it had been politicized by National Socialist ideology. Further, they distanced the service from the Nazi regime and the charge that Germany had waged an aggressive and inhumane naval war.

To some extent, Raeder's efforts to present a more sympathetic view of his and the navy's role succeeded, supporting his defense that he was "only a sailor and soldier, not a politician."[3] Although some labeled his memoirs as a "whitewash," the foreword to the 1960 American translation decried the conviction of Germany's military leaders (an "undesirable precedent"), who were "merely" carrying out the directives of superiors.[4] Subsequent interpretations of Raeder would range in extremes from the Nuremberg indictment ("one of this century's most accomplished liars" whose career "could serve in many ways for the leadership principle gone wrong") to his defense that he was a patriot who practiced his profession honorably.[5]

Using a theme similar to the postwar memoirs of Germany's other military leaders, Raeder sought to disassociate the service and his policies from Hitler's aggressive expansionism. Faced with the undeniable fact of a criminal genocidal regime, he perpetuated the image of himself, and therefore the navy, as "apolitical" and victims of Hitler and Germany's "continental-minded" leadership who failed to see the importance of sea power.[6] Yet, by his own admission, he was seduced by Hitler as an "extraordinary man born to lead" and only "too late" discovered Hitler's "fatal charm" and his ability to disguise his true intentions. Even so, Raeder claimed he had been successful in the early years with Hitler, who had given him a "completely free hand" in matters dealing with his service. His hubris led him to believe that he could use the same tactics that he had learned under Tirpitz and the Weimar Republic in dealing with Hitler and National Socialism.

The onset of the Cold War and the creation of the Federal Republic's new navy, the *Bundesmarine*, influenced other sanitized versions of events of 1933–1945 consistent with his autobiography. The numerous studies of the history of the German navy written by former German naval officers under the aegis of the U.S. Navy and the British Admiralty in the first postwar years supported Raeder's defense that the navy had "fought with unblemished standard." Many of these officers became the nucleus for the rebuilding of the new West German navy. They were anxious to preserve the positive aspects of the Kriegsmarine, reflecting Raeder's call in 1939 to create "the foundations for later reconstruction" through their courage and leadership ability that he had so strongly championed after 1918.[7]

Critical to the perpetuation of legitimate naval traditions was the recognition of the role of their former commanders as part of the old navy's spiritual heritage. Those who chose to serve the Western allies and create a new navy were, along with their former comrades, united in their opposition to the conviction and imprisonment of their commanders as war criminals; the convicted commanders' fate represented their "martyr-dom" to a "victor's justice" as well as a "defamation" of the Kriegsmarine. The naval officers' highly organized and persistent efforts to free Dönitz and Raeder, and their hopes of rehabilitating them as models for the new West German navy, relied on the admirals' defense at Nuremberg and called for a "united front," regardless of their differences (e.g., the empha-sis on battleships vs. the U-boats).[8] Veterans' organizations sought to bridge the divide between the two leaders—on the one hand, Dönitz's Nazi sympathies, and, on the other, Raeder's apparently more respect-able example.

However, conflict over the integration of the legacy of Raeder and Dönitz into the newly established Cold War navies (both East and West Germany had to deal with their legacy) during this period hindered the navy's leaders and its supporters in critically evaluating their past. Those who broke ranks with their comrades over the defense of Raeder and Dönitz and questioned the apolitical nature of the Kriegsmarine or its conduct of war were ostracized and denounced (another parallel between 1918 and 1945).[9] The successful deflection of the political-military aspects of the Nuremberg charges against the navy's leaders (and the *Wehrmacht* as a whole) obscured the moral implications of Raeder's leadership and his relationship with Hitler and National Socialism. Edmund Burke's proscription, "the only thing necessary for evil to flour-ish is for good men to do nothing," applies to the Raeder story.

Fritz Fischer's post-Nuremberg (1962) study of Germany's first bid for world power and the subsequent "preconceived theoretical frame-works" of the revisionist new school of *Sozialgeschichte* (social history), in the 1970s and 1980s, judged Raeder more as a product of the political and social structure of Wilhelmine Germany than as a shaper of "his" navy's destiny. Although Raeder was a prominent figure in the monographs of Jost Dülffer, Carl-Axel Gemzell, Holger Herwig, Werner Rahn, Gerhardt Schreiber, Michael Salewski, and Charles Thomas, as well as mine, these studies concentrated more on the strategic, military-technical, and political aims of the navy and its officer corps within the state as a social and political institution and as a "traditional, conservative leadership group," and less on Raeder's life and professional career as an officer and commander over the tumultuous period of German history in the years 1876–1960.[10]

The publication of these new studies fueled a vigorous debate—over the "continuity" (and discontinuity) between the policies of the three German navies under the Imperial, Republican, and National Socialist regimes—that continues even today. The nexus is the relationship of the navy's institutional "ideology of sea power" and its global ambitions to Hitler's racial and expansionist ambitions in the Third Reich. Viewed as an institution in continuum, the issue of whether 1933 represented a break in the navy's planning and goals became closely tied with assessments of the rise of National Socialism and the origins of World War II.

Documentary evidence, increasingly supplemented by private papers, has unraveled the "orthodoxy" perpetuated by Raeder. His alleged non-political role and his claim that he had insulated (or at least distanced) the navy from National Socialism have appeared in a new light, more consistent with contemporary National Socialist claims (as well as his own boasts) that Raeder had led the service "effortlessly" into the Third Reich.

The intellectual history of Raeder's involvement with the Nazi regime and its objectives has a long pedigree. Beginning with Volker Berghahn's 1971 study of the political and social implications of Tirpitz's naval race with the British in the period 1897–1914, the evidence of Raeder's (and the navy's) affinity with Hitler began with Jost Dülffer's 1973 detailed analysis of fleet-building in the Weimar and Third Reich periods. In 1978, Gerhard Schreiber demonstrated how the continuity of the navy's concepts of sea power, expressed in terms unique to German navalism —*Seemacht, Seeherrschaft, Seegeltung* (sea power, naval prestige, and control)—blended with the officer corps' visions of world power or "world power horizon," *Weltmachthorizonte*, that began with Tirpitz and formed the basis of its revisionism in Weimar and naval planning under Hitler and during World War II. Schreiber's studies of Germany's *Seemachtideologie* provided convincing documentation that the indoctrination of the naval service, with its traditions and culture and its willingness to embrace fascism, precluded any need to "reeducate" the officer corps after 1933.[11]

Despite a vigorous debate over the interpretations between the academic historians and those who argued that ambitious fleet plans and aggressive expressions of pursuing world power did not represent military reality, the record overwhelmingly supports a linkage between the Tirpitz-Raeder political ideology of *Seemacht* and the actual decisions and policies made during the period 1888–1945, which cannot be simply dismissed as "fantasies" or "utopian." This is even more evident in Rolf Hobson's watershed 2002 study of the political significance in the evolution of Tirpitz's sea power ideology, which demonstrates how the imperialism of the Second Reich and its naval policies mutated into the fascism of Raeder's generation. Hobson's *Imperialism at Sea* reveals the inherent contradiction in the attempts by both Tirpitz and Raeder to find a military rationale in the "Risk Theory" or the Z-Plan versus the persistence of claims made for the political value of a fleet for Germany's global ambitions.[12] *Seemachtideologie* "warped" operational doctrines and eventually "supplanted" them, contributing to the contradictory operational planning and orders in World War II.[13]

The controversy over the "real" Erich Raeder thus continues even to the present day, in large part because of the diversity of the research themes cited above and the clash between scholars and naval writers who reject the historical methodology of the academic historians. These authors disclaim the "psychological analysis" of the navy's *Seemacht* ideology or the "alleged" sociopolitical motives behind the building of a German navy in the period before two world wars and fail to see the catalyst role that the so-called English problem played in Tirpitz's formulation (and Raeder's interpretation of this legacy).[14]

That this debate persists was evident in the June 2004 seminar in Potsdam, held by the *Militärgeschichtliches Forschungsamt* (Military History Research Office), which focused on the *Weltmachthorizonte* of four

Imperial Navy officers: Tirpitz, Albert Hopman, Paul Hintze, and Raeder. Challenging Schreiber's concept that the interwar navy pursued both revisionism *and* a second attempt to become a world sea power, Jörg Hillmann argued that the idea of *Weltherrschaft* (global supremacy) was not part of the navy's "repertoire," given the domestic and international realities and the focus on national renewal. For Hillmann, Raeder's world power horizon was never that of Tirpitz and the kaiser. The global dimensions of the commerce war were more the result of the dynamics of World War II and not due to any world power orientation in planning or in its realization. Although it is important that historians place Raeder and his actions in the context of the navy's military dimensions and not in a construct completely oblivious to the structure of how naval forces are developed and deployed, it is equally critical, as Wilhelm Deist warned, to pay attention to the "general context, to the subordination of the individual aspect under the varied panorama of historical development."[15]

The quote from Wegener at the beginning of this introduction and Hobson's new documentation of the evolution into the expansionist ideology of sea power suggest that, as Jost Dülffer summed up the discussion at Potsdam, "Ideas matter." But ideas also require people to give them meaning, substance, and impact. Who did the indoctrinating, either by deed or example? Who taught the lessons? Who made the decisions? Who carried forward ideology, the arguments, and the program of global sea power? The truth satisfies neither ideologists nor theoretical historians, because it was Raeder who carried the covenant of sea power across political divides and revolution, Nazism and the fog of war. Raeder made a difference in the stern, Prussian magisterial way he drove history and his institution in the direction he wanted. He did not reach his goals or those of his political masters. But there can be no doubt about the direction and pace of his progress. This book takes the measure of his journey in its intellectual, political, military, and social context. Raeder, as did his predecessors, systematically nurtured the desire for a future renaissance at sea and the spiritual legacy of Tirpitz until Germany was ready to resume its pursuit of sea power.

The key to understanding Raeder's contribution both to naval history and German history lies in linking together the parts of his career that have been treated separately within the larger context of his leadership of the navy in World War II (1939–1943). Raeder's significant policy-making role in all three German navies is grounded in his first twenty years of as a naval officer. His naval and political views evolved under the tutelage of Tirpitz. They were further influenced by his wartime experiences and by the politically charged period prior to his appointment as head of the navy in 1928. Except for his version of events in the first volume of his memoirs and my first book, *Weimar, the German Naval Officer Corps, and the Rise of National Socialism* (which covered the period 1918–1933), little has been written about the direct and indirect influences on Raeder and the development of his leadership principles and strategies, which were to reveal themselves with fateful consequences after 1933. His story reveals a pattern of continuity in the policies and actions throughout his career and the period of his leadership of the navy. And it demonstrates how he recognized, more than Tirpitz, that there had to be a connection between German naval strategy and national political and foreign policy. Although Raeder remained frequently blinded by *Ressortegoismus*—the narrow interests of his department—and the dreams of a *Weltmachtflotte* that had haunted Tirpitz, he played a significant role as a bridge between the Empire and the Third Reich. He helped the navy assess its mistakes and planned for a fresh, more systematic attempt "to upset the international status quo and to put the clock back at home."[16]

Raeder was not a supporter of parliamentary government and a party state. The issue of his loyalty and obedience and role as a soldier has been seen as an explanation for his willingness to support Hitler throughout the entire twelve years of the Third Reich. In spite of their differences over issues of grand strategy, especially Hitler's decision to invade the Soviet Union when Raeder wanted all resources to be directed against England and to wage an aggressive U-boat war (even if it meant drawing the United States into the war before Hitler wanted that to happen), he always acquiesced in the end. He did not hesitate to exceed his authority to advance the cause of the navy, but he was determined throughout his relationship with Hitler to demonstrate his and the navy's loyalty.[17]

The issue of taking and breaking oaths presents a thornier one for an assessment of the *Grossadmiral's* motives. Raeder certainly saw no problem with swearing a personal oath to Hitler, as he had done with the kaiser. Raeder had, however, broken his oath to the Weimar Republic and its constitution, which had incorporated the obligations of the Versailles treaty (the issue of his role in the 1920 Kapp Putsch could also be referenced here). In fact, the violations of the treaty had become so frequent that, before the end of the Weimar Republic, the Defense Ministry became concerned about the moral consequences of oath breaking on the future attitude of the officer corps.[18]

Raeder deserves credit for his formulation of a concept of how Germany could defeat its maritime foes, taking into account its historic and geographic realities—for which he has not received his due.[19] Although he never had the opportunity to write a comprehensive study of his ideas, the continued evolution of his strategic and political thoughts is evident in his pre-1914 writings, speeches to his commanders and Germany's political and military leaders, briefings on war games and fleet exercises, and operational directives to the fleet. While he eventually obtained in 1940 the long-desired bases providing access to the Atlantic for his warships and U-boats, his vision of a naval war of sea denial against the enemy's sea-lanes was never fully realized. He tried to overcome this historical reality by changing the perception of history, in terms both of his legacy and of his view of Germany's maritime destiny. To Raeder, what would advance Germany's maritime destiny was clearly more important than the niceties of archival evidence or the unvarnished truth.

This work covers the major issues that influenced Raeder's actions, based on my 1985 study of the historiographical and research themes of German naval history. The war at sea, 1939–1945, is presented here as it relates to Raeder's decision-making process and his strategic and operational objectives for the navy and his focus on the navy's future within a victorious German Wehrmacht.

Despite Raeder's denials of seeking another war against England or the argument that he had simply acquiesced to Hitler's overwhelming personality and the Führer *Prinzip*—which he continued to admire to the end (as did many other "fellow travelers")—this study reveals a more activist interpretation of the *Grossadmiral*. Far from being nonpolitical, he sought, directly and indirectly, to influence the political environment of the Weimar Republic and Nazi Germany in order to further the interests of the navy. He interpreted Germany's national interests as synonymous with that of "his" navy. Even as early as 1918–1919, when, as a young captain, he served as the spokesperson for the officer corps with the leaders of the new Republic, he played a far more aggressive role in the political issues of the day and harbored ambitions that reflected his growing conviction that he had the same considerable political acumen as his mentor Tirpitz, if not more.

The evolution of a distinctive "German School of Naval Thought" (Hobson), which began with Tirpitz, continued with equal if not greater fervor under Raeder, modified by the experiences and lessons he learned from the failure of German naval leadership in World War I, the ignominious end of the High Seas Fleet in the naval mutinies, and the political miscalculations of the officer corps in the first ten years of the Weimar Republic. Raeder's ambition to be a "second Tirpitz" seemed to be on the verge of success when a revisionist, pro-military Hitler endorsed the idea of an expanded navy. Raeder's concept of the navy (the legacy of Tirpitz), the claims for its deterrence value and alliance "readiness," the need for a fleet to grow commensurately with an expansionist post-Versailles Germany, and the use of the fleet as "an instrument of political power" all resonated with the new führer's short- and long-term goals.

True, Hitler's increasing interference in the pace and scope of the navy's rearmament reflected his view of his navy chief as his *Werkzeug* (tool). Hitler complicated Raeder's life and made his work more difficult, and at times, Raeder had to justify his actions to his officers. He frequently deferred to the führer's directives or anticipated what Hitler wanted—a trend that would ultimately hamper his direction of naval operations during the war. Hitler would not tolerate any changes in his naval plans, even as relations with England deteriorated in 1938, and Raeder knew that a war would find the navy woefully ill-prepared. When war came, a resigned and bitter Raeder saw his mission as demonstrating the navy's "right to existence" through its loyalty and usefulness for the Third Reich's future wars.

Raeder's rigid control over all aspects of the navy and his review of virtually every document (a practice that he instituted in 1928, albeit with a much smaller organization than the navy of 1939–1943) became a Sisyphean role under the demands of a global and "total" war after 1941. The "congruence of facts" that aligned Hitler with the navy's traditional goals disappeared as early as 1940, and Raeder became increasingly estranged from the führer.[20] Yet, although he had few assets apart from his U-boats, he sought throughout the war to impose his ideas of grand strategy on Hitler. As Raeder admitted, this was particularly true in his attempts to divert Hitler's planning for Operation Barbarossa before the English question had been resolved.[21] His attempts to interpret Hitler's intentions as an extension of his own nationalistic, conservative conception of the German state had its origins in Bismarckian and Wilhelmine Germany. These were exercises in self-deception, if not deliberate attempts to avoid complicity.

Recent research into Hitler's practice of rewarding his senior officers with pay supplements, grants, and gifts—all of which Raeder willingly accepted—made the issue of his loyalty and service to Hitler and the Nazi state an uncomfortable subject for his supporters, who saw in him the embodiment of the values of service, duty, and Christianity, whose principles stood in stark contrast to a state and a leader whose policies and methods had been exposed as characterized by terror and an ideology of evil.[22]

The "selective process of coming to terms with the past," which Raeder and other high ranking officers applied to the issue of their knowledge of the Holocaust, also became more obvious under the weight of evidence and public controversy beginning in the second half of the 1990s with the publication of the controversial *Hitler's Willing Executioners* by Daniel Goldhagen and an exhibition produced by the Hamburg Institut für Sozialforschung, "War of Annihilation [*Vernichtungskrieg*]: Crimes of the Wehrmacht, 1941–1944." These events sparked a major debate, which renewed the issues first raised at Nuremberg regarding the military's relationship with National Socialism and the individual responsibility of the Wehrmacht's leadership. The conclusion from these confrontations with the past clearly revealed that the Wehrmacht had been a largely willing executioner of Hitler's policies (whose anti-Jewish policies had become state doctrine after 1933).[23]

By the time of Hitler's 22 August 1939 speech to his commanders, there certainly could be no mistake of the brutality he expected of his soldiers (which presaged the wartime Commando and *Laconia* orders) and the nature of what would clearly be *Vernichtungskrieg* in Poland and in the East. It is precisely Raeder's relationship to Hitler and National

Socialism, more than his preparation and conduct of the war, that casts a shadow over his and the navy's "honorableness." While no direct link between Raeder and the crimes against humanity has been established, it is unlikely that he was unaware of the consequences of the anti-Semitism preached by Hitler and carried out by the Nazi Party and by elements of the Wehrmacht, both directly and indirectly. As someone who maintained such a strict control over the naval service and zealously attacked any infringement on his authority, he must have been aware of what was going on in the East concerning the extermination of the Jews to the extent that such actions affected the navy. This raises more serious questions about Raeder's credibility—in spite of his statements that he had never known about any such actions. As Franz-Josef Strauss, West German defense minister from 1956 to 1962, wrote to Dönitz, it was hard to believe that someone like the former *Oberbefehlshaber der Kriegsmarine* (i.e., Dönitz) would know less than what others, in less important positions, like himself (who served on the Eastern front), knew.[24] Other indications of the senior officers' knowledge of events are found in statements by Admiral Ruge, who admitted that he had heard of the atrocities against the Jews in 1943, and in the postwar testimony of officers such as Vice Admiral Leopold Bürkner who, as leader of the "Foreign" Section in Admiral Canaris's *Abwehr*, the Wehrmacht's intelligence service, documented the handing over of Jews to the *Sicherheitsdienst* (SD), the security service of the *Schutzstaffel* (the notorious SS).[25]

Finally, the records of naval operations and policy cannot always reveal the interplay of personalities, their weaknesses or their strengths. The qualities of the leader play a critical role in determining victory or defeat, disappointment or fulfillment. In spite of the ample record of Raeder as an officer and leader, we find an equally remarkable lack of documentation of the man. To this date, none of his personal records have surfaced. Recent studies of Otto Diederichs, Albert Hopman, and Georg Alexander von Müller provide us with more details of the life of an Imperial Navy officer and the intrigues around the major issues of the Kaiserliche Marine in the Tirpitz era than Raeder reveals in his memoirs or his existing papers.[26] For the grand admiral who extolled the quality of camaraderie in his farewell address in 1943, the literature provides only a few glimpses of Raeder himself as a *Kamerad,* husband, or father. He remains largely unseen inside the uniform—aloof, uncomfortable in professional relationships, religious, authoritarian, puritanical, intolerant of individual initiative (while professing his deference to the judgment of the commander at sea), and extremely sensitive to criticism. He concentrated on but one thing—the creation of a German sea power on a global scale, reflecting his conviction that there could be no German world power without a strong navy.

The story of Erich Raeder is as complex as the times and issues he confronted. It is inseparable from the fate of the navy he served and shaped. For Raeder, the idea of struggle, shaped as much by his personality as his experiences in fighting for "his" service, represents a significant key to his worldview, equal to his concepts of duty, obedience, and patriotism. As he stated in the foreword to his memoirs, his life had brought him both "the beautiful and the difficult, exaltation and tragedy in rich, often too great abundance. It has been a life truly full of labor and toil."[27] Controversy followed him even to the grave, and it is not surprising that, at the end, he chose to have his coffin covered by the Imperial Navy flag, which represented to him—far more than his twelve years under the symbol of the swastika—the values that he and his navy had embodied for thirty-nine years.

ERICH RAEDER

The Imperial Navy had been a child of its time and
its surroundings.
—*Erich Raeder, 1956*

1

The Genesis of an Admiral

The Navy, the Middle Class, and the Development of German Navalism

Erich Hans Albert Raeder was born on 24 April 1876, in Wandsbek,
near Hamburg, the first of three sons of Hans Raeder, a teacher of
English and French at the Matthias Claudius Gymnasium. Having lost
his own father early in his own studies, Hans had supported himself by
offering private lessons and, according to Raeder, had tutored several of
the future leaders of the navy, helping them to prepare for the service's
entrance examination—foreshadowing his son's future role as the
"schoolmaster" of the navy. In 1889, the family moved to Grünberg in
Silesia after Hans was appointed as the headmaster of the Friedrich
Wilhelm Realgymnasium. Raeder's mother, Gertraudt (née Hartmann),
was the daughter of a Royal Court musician and encouraged his musi-
cal talents, which in addition to his intellectual achievements would
later bring him attention from his superiors as a young officer.[1]

Raeder was an exceptionally bright student and had an avid interest
in history, geography, modern politics, and foreign languages. His father
was a stern but just parent who enforced the principles of "discipline tempered with affection—fear of God, love of truth, and cleanliness, within
and without."[2] Deeply religious, Hans insisted on regular attendance at
church and led the family in communal prayers. He also instilled in his
sons a sense of thrift—all traits that Raeder would later seek to impress
upon the men under his command. Politics were not discussed at home.
If, by chance, friends broached subjects touching upon political matters, Raeder's father would end that line of conversation with the admonition "no politics." "Politics" in this context alluded to distaste for the

1

"party politics" of the new German Reichstag and, in particular, the growing strength of the Social Democrat Party. This aversion was also a characteristic of the naval officer corps, which, as a whole, expressed contempt for the parliamentary system. As Raeder argued throughout his career, he considered himself "above party"—*Staatspolitische* (i.e., concerned only for the nation)—and therefore "apolitical." Given the fractious nature of German political parties and the Imperial Navy's financial dependence on a parliament elected by universal manhood suffrage, however, the service's future was inexorably tied to the economic, social, and political issues of the day.[3]

As the archetypical German authoritarian father, Hans Raeder demanded and expected obedience—a principle that he firmly impressed on his son. This authoritarian upbringing represents an essential element in understanding Raeder's later practices as head of the navy. Raeder and his younger brothers also had to contend with the burden of being the "school director's sons," which placed them in the difficult position of defending their father against their classmates—a situation that may have contributed to Raeder's well-known sensitivity to personal or professional criticism.[4]

Middle-class families such as the Raeders could be expected to be strong advocates of a German navy, the symbol of a unified nation and, along with the Reichstag, the only truly imperial institution. The support for a navy had deep roots in Germany's social and intellectual history. The call for a "German" fleet, promoted by the economist Friedrich List as early as the 1830s, served as a catalyst for German nationalism and was widely supported as a progressive idea by the academic community. In the context of the imperialistic zeitgeist of the second half of the nineteenth century, the *Kaiserliche Marine* became both the expression of and the instrument for spreading Germanism throughout the world.[5]

By the 1890s the Imperial Navy had become a mirror of German society, a microcosm of the young German empire's political and social conditions, and a symbol of national unity and the middle class's "liberal" ideals. As a child, Raeder had experienced this fusion of national unity with the widespread, almost religious, faith in Germany's destiny at sea. Together they became a political philosophy of *Seemachtideologie* first fully articulated by Tirpitz in the early 1890s—the same years in which Raeder began his naval career.[6]

Given the new kaiser's devotion to the navy and the "liberal" appeal of the service as the "darling of the nation and the middle class," Raeder's "sudden" decision, as he referred to it, in 1894 to join the navy, and his father's eager support, were both unsurprising in the context of the empire and the values of its middle class.[7] Two weeks before his final examinations in school, he announced to his father that he no longer wanted to study medicine for a career as a military surgeon but instead wanted to enter the navy as a line officer. In spite of the fact that the deadline for application (1 October 1893) had passed, he was accepted; and on 1 April 1894 he reported to the *Marineschule* at Kiel.[8]

Raeder's first contact with the navy, seeing the training ship *Musquito*, an 1851 British sloop purchased by the Prussian navy in 1862, at Lübeck, left him "completely unimpressed." He later attributed his enthusiasm for a naval career to his having read a book describing the cadet cruise of Prince Heinrich of Prussia around the world. He was so fascinated by this story, which he had received as a prize for his academic achievements, that he read it until he "knew it by heart."[9] Such books, referred to as "naval cadet literature," were popular during this period and served as recruitment tools for the navy.[10]

Raeder's portrayal of his choice of a naval career as a result of "fate" and the influence of a popular account of the adventurous life at sea seems incongruous with his later practice of precise and calculated decision making. As a practical matter, Raeder and his father would have known that the high cost of cadet education would require significant financial support from his family; it was one of the ways by which the navy made sure that only applicants from the "proper background" could join.[11] Raeder's decision to join the navy may have been regarded as a calling, morally equivalent to being called to the clergy. His decision was made to satisfy his own ambitions and to provide a sense of purpose in the face of the physical and mental challenges that command at sea presented. Raeder's character fit the "nobility of outlook" that would qualify him as an officer. His family values, his sense of duty, personal loyalty, and sacrifice, and his love of the Fatherland were characteristic of many of the candidates who chose the opportunities the navy offered.[12] They complemented the context of shared values in a navy that would enforce ideological over social homogeneity, to the detriment of independent thinking. As Tirpitz noted in 1895, the officer corps had to share common views not just in "strategic thinking" but also "in all questions."[13] As navy chief, Raeder would later vigorously—and ruthlessly—continue this tradition.

Raeder possessed the mental aptitude for serious study, as demonstrated by his achieving the coveted *Abitur* (final examination for university studies). The typically high level of education of the middle class was a much-desired trait for future naval officers.[14] He also had the discipline and ability to learn subjects on his own. When his family moved to Silesia, Raeder had to make up a year and a half of instruction in English, which he accomplished within a month. (He later taught himself Spanish in order to study the history of the Philippines during his 1898 tour of duty with the Far East Squadron.) [15]

From the Marineschule in Kiel to the Far East with the First Cruiser Squadron, 1894–1899

Raeder's training as an officer began with six weeks of infantry drill conducted by army non-commissioned officers, whose hazing so offended him that he considered dropping out. Any doubts on his part, however, were forgotten when Wilhelm II came to Kiel to admit his son, Prince Adalbert, to the navy as one of Raeder's classmates. The kaiser attended a ceremony in which the new cadets swore a personal oath to him in the Navy Chapel. Reflecting the growing self-consciousness of the naval officer corps as "the kaiser's elite," Raeder later regarded these ceremonies and the naval parade in the emperor's honor as the "high point" of this first phase of his naval career.[16]

This short stint of shore duty was followed by service on the training ships SMS *Stosch* and *Stein* with the seventy cadets of the 1894 crew divided between them.[17] On board the SMS *Stosch*, Raeder learned basic seamanship, including handling sails, rowing, and sailing the ship's cutters and drills on the ship's obsolete 15-cm (5.9-inch) guns. His theoretical studies included navigation, seamanship, and mathematics, as well as English and French. Rather short in stature (5'6"), he was particularly proud of his assignment to the royals, the topmost of all the yards; the task was to go aloft and quickly lower the sails in the event of bad weather—a risky and physically challenging job. After two training cruises, first in the Baltic and then to the West Indies, Raeder's first year concluded with stiff theoretical and practical tests, upon passing which the sixty cadets were promoted to *Seekadetten*. He finished at the top of his "crew" (class), living up to his own expectations. Raeder, labeled as "the clever Hans" by his crew members, did not form any special or lasting relationships with them. He mentions only three crewmates in his memoirs; one of them was Wolfgang Wegener, a rival whose later writings on naval strategy Raeder suppressed.[18]

His class was then divided among four training ships in which they studied navigation and gunnery as well as watch-standing under both sail and steam. Most important, they received their first indoctrination in leadership, as each cadet was assigned a section of enlisted apprentices to train. The fall exercises of 1895 were particularly important because they practiced abstract tactical maneuvers based on Tirpitz's *Lineartaktik*, the revival of the traditional (from the age of sail) line-ahead battle formation for the capital ships. The results from these exercises formed the operational doctrines of Tirpitz's 1894 Service Memorandum IX and also the basis for the first navy bill in 1897. This document, which Raeder referred to as "the tactical 'bible' of the navy," solidified the primacy of the battle fleet (in home waters) as the "most important plank" of Germany's foreign policy, with cruiser warfare regarded as secondary in importance.[19]

In preparation for the examination at the end of the second year, the practical and theoretical subjects of engineering and seamanship were stressed along with navigation, torpedoes, and gunnery. The final year of training before being commissioned was back in Kiel at the Marineschule. There, as they completed their academic training, Raeder and the crew of 1894 had more opportunities to be officers and gentlemen, with free time for sailing, rowing, sports, and rounds of parties, theaters, and concerts. Raeder passed the final examination of a *Seeoffizier*, with the highest honors.[20]

On 1 October 1897, the newly promoted ensign reported on board the SMS *Sachsen*, one of Germany's early coal-powered, pre-dreadnought armored ships, as the ship's signal officer. Raeder's first duty assignment was opportune, given the growing importance of signaling (and later wireless) in a modern navy. It allowed him to gain valuable experience on the bridge, especially during maneuvers and training cruises. Such training allowed him to lay the foundation for his distinguished performance at the side of Admiral von Hipper at the battle of Jutland in

1916. Raeder's tenure on the *Sachsen* and temporary assignment to her sister ship SMS *Baden*, however, was cut short as a result of rising tensions over Germany's colonial ambitions. On 1 October 1897, he reported to the armored cruiser *Deutschland*, preparing for duty in the Far East.[21]

Laid down in London in 1872, the *Deutschland* reflected the transitional state of German naval technology, carrying both sail and steam. At this time German factories were unable to produce armor plate, leaving the navy dependent upon foreign sources. The *Deutschland* lacked the speed to function as a cruiser and also was prone to frequent engine breakdowns, which, as Raeder noted, were a constant source of anxiety. The classes of ships represented by the *Sachsen* and *Deutschland* reflected the pre-Tirpitz naval construction program of designing ships that were suitable for Baltic operations as well as projecting Germany's naval presence overseas. The result was a conglomerate of all possible ship types— a collection of partly or completely outdated ships for different tasks, far from a coherent fighting force, especially when compared to the British Royal Navy.[22]

Raeder's experiences in the Far East during the formative years of Germany's colonial and naval expansion were critical in the evolution of his career and naval strategy. His assignments brought him into contact with influential officers and provided him with opportunities to impress them with his skills as an officer and with his ambitions. He interacted on a daily basis with a number of key players in the development of the service, including the kaiser's brother, Prince Heinrich of Prussia, under whom he later served as a personal aide in Aden and Peking. Additionally, he had the opportunity to interact with Count Maximilian von Spee, whose leadership of cruiser warfare in World War I would later have an impact on Raeder's strategic thinking, and Georg Alexander von Müller, who later became the head of the Naval Cabinet (the office responsible for all personnel decisions). Raeder, who served as Müller's aide in 1898, regarded him as a "fatherly friend" and a personality who was "misunderstood" by the officer corps (including Tirpitz).[23]

The voyage to the Far East took Raeder to the Mediterranean and then, via the Suez Canal, to the Red Sea and Indian Ocean. Joined by several Russian warships upon leaving Ceylon, the squadron arrived in Singapore, which had a large ethnic German colony. His impressions from numerous trips to the major ports on the Chinese and Russian coasts, as well as Korea and Japan, gave him special "insight" into the "center of British world power." He also claimed to have gained "a better understanding of Japanese psychology and military operations." In Hong Kong, he met future adversaries, including Captain John Jellicoe, later commander in chief of the British Grand Fleet, and witnessed the growing tension between Germany and the British and Russians in their competition to lease bases in China.[24]

Raeder was also a firsthand witness to the increasing hostility between Germany and the United States. The deterioration of German-American relations, which had begun with the Samoan Crisis of 1889, now intensified with the mutual resurgence of overseas ambitions of both countries. Although Raeder did not believe the sending of German cruisers to the Philippines at the beginning of the conflict was a belligerent act, he acknowledged that German sympathies lay with Spain. Following Spain's defeat, Germany sought additional colonies and in 1899, acquired most of the Samoan Islands—a visible signal of Germany's rise to "world power" status.[25] Diederich's angry cables to Berlin denouncing the "Anglo-Saxon world" reflected a prevailing belief among the officer corps that the British and American resistance to Germany's "powerful overseas policy to secure worthwhile colonies" must inevitably lead to conflict.[26] This conviction that a showdown with England would "doubtless" come "in some part of the earth, be it out of economic rivalry or as a consequence of colonial disputes," fueled Tirpitz's fleet-building plans and the navy's war games.[27] Anticipating this scenario, Raeder participated in the first war game designed to determine the strategy of the cruiser squadron in the event of a sudden war with England. As one of the staff officers of the opposing "British Commander," Raeder took credit for predicting that the German squadron would rendezvous in the Mariana Islands and then disperse in the Pacific for the attack on enemy commerce—exactly what the German Cruiser Squadron did in 1914.[28] This represented the beginning of Raeder's study of the strategic and operational issues of cruiser warfare.

The Evolution of Raeder's Strategic Thought in the Tirpitz Era

In October 1899, Raeder was promoted to *Leutnant zur See* and assigned to the First Sailor Brigade. His responsibilities included the training of the navy's enlisted personnel and the preparation of a new training manual. He also took time at the *Marine-Akademie* (Naval War College) in Kiel to study Russian. He was assigned six months later (April 1900) as watch officer on board the SMS *Aegir*, an *Odin* class coastal battleship assigned to the reserve fleet. In the summer of 1901, he received orders to report to the SMS *Grille* as executive officer. This was a significant posting, because the *Grille* served as a fleet tender and communications support ship for the Admiralty Staff's summer cruises and fleet maneuvers, providing Raeder with an opportunity to work directly with the navy's senior leaders.[29]

After the 1901 fall fleet maneuvers, Raeder received an important promotion as watch officer aboard the new 11,100-ton battleship *Kaiser Wilhelm der Grosse,* the flagship of Prince Heinrich, commander of the First Battleship Squadron. For Raeder, this assignment was affirmation that he was on the track for promotion, since such duty was considered a prerequisite for appointment to the Marine-Akademie or for senior staff service. Raeder later reflected on his service on board the *Kaiser Wilhelm der Grosse* and subsequently the *Kaiser Friedrich III* to criticize the prewar navy's methods of conducting training and fleet exercises. He believed that there was too much emphasis devoted to battle readiness and training to the detriment of "division work" and ship routines. In his view, given his subsequent experience in World War I, the latter were more important in the development of discipline, which he regarded as the foundation for every aspect of duty. Moreover, the rigid training schedule that permitted no deviation destroyed, in Raeder's opinion, "any originality or independent thinking on the part of the commanding officers."[30]

Raeder attributed the unstable international situation as the justification for Tirpitz's doubling of the size of the fleet in 1890 over the navy bill of 1898. Reflecting a prevailing distrust of England's economic and political liberalism, Germany regarded the Royal Navy not only as the measure of its own naval ambitions, but also as an intractable foe, opposing German *Weltpolitik*. Raeder understood that resolving the "English question" was the true purpose, if not the final goal, of Germany's fleet building, consistent with Tirpitz's memorandum of June 1897, which declared England as the "most dangerous naval enemy *at the present time*."[31]

Although he quoted Mahan in his early writings, Raeder's memoirs omit any mention of Mahan or his influence on German naval thought. His efforts to disassociate himself from Mahan reflect one of the primary implications of the German interpretation of Mahan—the challenge to England's supremacy at sea. By the time Raeder joined the service in 1894, Mahan's *The Influence of Sea Power upon History* had become a "naval bible" and, as interpreted by German navalists, provided the theoretical foundations for an expanded fleet—the "missing link" between world power and naval policy.[32]

Mahan's primary value for Tirpitz and younger officers such as Raeder was not his analysis of international relations or naval strategy and military operations, but his advocacy of a philosophy of sea power that itself became a unique German naval ideology. This *Seemacht-ideologie* represented a political interpretation of the benefits of sea power divorced from the military and strategic considerations of Tirpitz's fleet-building plan incorporating a Social Darwinist defense of German navalism and its global aspirations.[33] Tirpitz's dictum (1894), "world power is inconceivable without a strong fleet," would become Raeder's slogan (1934), "the scale of a nation's world status is identical with the scale of its sea power."[34] The need for a fleet as a "political power factor" against England served Tirpitz and later Raeder as an argument for the building of as many ships as possible. Neither, however, was to have the time or resources required to build such a fleet.

One of Raeder's few references in his memoirs to any naval strategist was the French captain René Daveluy. Raeder translated Daveluy's *Study of Naval Tactics* into German during his second year at the Marine-Akademie (a remarkable achievement, considering his other studies) and maintained a correspondence with Daveluy for years. One of the leading French proponents of Mahan, Daveluy clearly reinforced Raeder's embrace of Mahan's principle of the primacy of the battle fleet and the "decisive battle" as the only way to achieve mastery of the sea.[35] Daveluy, however, also discussed viable alternatives for the weaker navy through the use of diversion against the weaknesses of a superior enemy. Stressing speed and endurance (range) and the rapid changing of operational areas, the weaker navy could choose the time and place of the battle and cause the enemy to disperse its forces or even withdraw forces from its main fleet, creating a more favorable opportunity to engage the enemy's fleet. He also saw the possibility of operating cruisers in "groups of two or three" to attack enemy cruisers sent out to hunt down the commerce raiders. These "battle groups" might further reduce the enemy's numbers and create a *Kräfteausgleich* (equalization of forces). This form of offensive cruiser warfare involved strategic and tactical risks and considerable initiative and energy on the part of the commanders. It was to be coordinated within the overall operations plan of the navy and thereby contribute to the ultimate battle between the main fleets.[36] These ideas would play a critical role in the development of Raeder's later strategic concepts and the building of the Kriegsmarine.

Tirpitz's strategic thought—his advocacy of an expanded fleet to defend Germany's interests and global ambitions in the period 1894–1914—had a profound impact on Raeder and the development of German strategy through two world wars. Raeder closely analyzed Tirpitz's conception of how to counter England's maritime supremacy, and he followed the arguments of Tirpitz's critics. He would later modify them on the basis of his own studies and subsequent experiences in World War I. Although historians argue over whether Tirpitz actually meant to achieve parity, much less superiority, with the British, it is clear that he expected the fleet to serve as a deterrent, to allow Germany to achieve *Weltpolitik*—a latent "cold war" against England.[37] Tirpitz understood very well the long-term nature of fleet building and was prepared to build the fleet in stages.

The military value of Tirpitz's 2:3 ratio in capital ships was never successfully translated into concrete operational plans by the Admiralty Staff, as a direct result of Tirpitz's efforts to limit the *Admiralstab* to theoretical studies "without any contact with, or influence upon, the fleet itself."[38] At the same time, Tirpitz would not openly admit the anti-British thrust of his "Plan" until 1903, when it no longer could be camouflaged.[39] The lessons learned from Tirpitz's contradictions between his political and military rationale for his fleet—indeed, what scholars regard as the inconsistencies if not the irrationality behind the Tirpitz Plan—were less about the legacy of unlimited expansion than about the power of force per se, which was itself a product of Mahan's "scientific law of sea power."[40] England could be forced to acquiesce to Germany's overseas ambitions only by the threat of a battle fleet prepared to challenge British naval superiority in a final "annihilation battle." Even if the German fleet were defeated, England's global naval supremacy would be at risk.

This *Risikogedanke* (Risk Theory) represented Tirpitz's strategic underpinning for Germany's bid for world power. At the same time, a strong fleet would provide Germany with *Bündnisfähigkeit,* the ability to attract allies, especially those who chafed under British maritime superiority. A battle fleet, argued Tirpitz, was "the first line against England" —a "dagger at the throat" of Germany's "likely enemy."[41] Tirpitz's decision to build a fleet to serve its imperialist ambitions ignored the close connection between the continental and maritime balance of power that England had consistently sought to maintain, and it represented a significant break from the Prussian and Bismarckian foreign and naval policies.

Although much has been made of the contradictions and illusions in German naval strategy and tactics as well as its construction program, Tirpitz, as Rolf Hobson's recent studies have documented, established a unique "German school" of naval thought that merged the Prussian-Clausewitzian influence and navalism of Mahan into a political and military ideology of sea power in which the "political" interpretation of the sea power "displaced the 'parallel' military approach"—the "belief in the power of sea power as a magical peacetime force."[42] The Risk Theory, for all of Tirpitz's emphasis on the offensive, presumed deterrence and a defensive status and totally contradicted the strategic offensive as expressed in his earlier Service Memorandum IX. As Hobson argues, the Risk Theory was explicitly based on the acceptance of a numerical inferiority that *"according to Tirpitz's own theory* implied submitting to the control of the enemy in war."[43] Neither technological and tactical superiority nor historical examples of an inferior fleet beating stronger opponents could resolve Germany's numerical inferiority (and poor geographic position).[44] Ultimately, the fleet proved too small to win a decisive battle and "not large enough to be squandered in offensive operations."[45] This was reflected in the operational planning before the war and the lack of offensive action at the start of the war. As a "fleet in being," the navy was to be held as a bargaining counter until the army determined the next course of German expansionism.[46]

The "atrophy of strategic thought" and strategic fallacies inherent in German naval planning were not the only consequences of Tirpitz's attempts to formulate a viable naval policy for Germany's *Weltmacht* ambitions.[47] Any officer who questioned the direction or basic tenets of Tirpitz's naval policy was quickly silenced. His ideas had now become official dogma—"inviolate and sacrosanct."[48]

Yet, although he did not give commerce war the emphasis he placed on the battle fleet in naval planning and its concentration in the North Sea, Tirpitz had begun to consider a role for commerce war to support his *Risikogedanke* in the event that an open blockade precluded the decisive battle between the fleets.[49] He opposed the idea of abolishing the right of capture in the negotiations over the laws of war at sea at the Second Hague Peace Conference in 1907 when Germany, as a weaker sea power, was clearly even more vulnerable and should have had a keen interest in restricting belligerent rights.[50] Even as part of his theory of deterrence, the idea that England had more to lose in the threat to its imports and would have to disperse its forces to defend its sea lanes (thereby weakening its concentration against the High Seas Fleet) appeared to justify an expanded role for a *guerre de course* and was perhaps the only way to force the British to sue for peace (even if there were a successful naval battle). These ideas were seen not only in the operational plans for the overseas Cruiser Squadron in the years 1905–1914, but also in Tirpitz's emphasis on increasing foreign cruises for training and "for a political effect of the navy globally."[51] Tirpitz had noted on several occasions that "a modern cruiser abroad will draw approximately twenty enemy cruisers after it when it is correctly commanded"—ideas that Raeder later highlighted when reading a description of one of Trotha's prewar cruises.[52] Foreign cruises and naval operations in the Atlantic would be major priorities when Trotha and his chief aide, Raeder, began to rebuild the new navy after 1919.

The other major influence on Raeder was Rear Admiral Curt *Freiherr* von Maltzahn, who published the first study of the development of German naval tactics. Although his ideas were attacked by Tirpitz, Maltzahn was as Mahanian as Tirpitz in his belief in the decisive battle between the battle fleets as the most important element of naval warfare. Their major difference was over how Germany would develop its battle fleet against England. Maltzahn believed Germany must first create a fleet of overseas cruisers to foster the growth of Germany's "sea interests," which would in turn cause Germany to increase its fleet "commensurately" until it could challenge the strongest sea power.[53]

Given the nationalistic, imperialistic, and racist theories of the age, Maltzahn's claims for the domestic political benefits of German navalism echoed those of Mahan and Tirpitz: Germany's future as a world power depended upon these peacetime activities. Maltzahn was also heavily influenced by the geographer Friedrich Ratzel, who, like Mahan, extolled the importance of the sea and the "geographical foundations of the command of the sea." The result of this mix of Tirpitz with Maltzahn's Social Darwinist ideas, combined with Ratzel's notion of the state as a biological organism, constituted a navalist formulation that justified Germany's economic expansion to accommodate its growing population, similar to Hitler's later demands for *Lebensraum*.[54] At the same time, Maltzahn saw the value of the strategic defense inherent in the Risk Theory: it could both deter the enemy and protect Germany's sea communications while the fleet was being expanded, and it could provide political cover. The idea that an inferior fleet operating defensively could be of value was not lost on Raeder. It reinforced the ideas of Daveluy, who had also suggested how a weaker fleet might make a contribution to victory.[55]

In 1903, Raeder began a two-year course of postgraduate study at the Marine-Akademie with a small group of officers who had demonstrated aptitude for higher leadership positions. Their studies included naval history, naval science, and tactics. In addition, professors from the university in Kiel, with whom Raeder was to develop a lifelong relationship, conducted courses in mathematics, physics, history, geography, international law, and foreign languages. He took on more personal responsibilities in 1903, receiving permission to marry, and in the following year his first child, Anita, was born. During 1904, he spent three months in Russia, living with Russian families to improve his fluency, and closely followed the conflict between Russia and Japan.[56]

His War College entrance thesis reflected his experiences with the 1902 and 1903 fall exercises of the First Squadron and the evolving battle tactics of the fleet as well as his interest in communications. It contained an analysis of visual signal communications in battle and the need for rapid execution of speed and course changes. Raeder also produced a study in international law, "War without Declaration," written presciently shortly before the surprise attack on the Russians by the Japanese. He concluded that the only protection against surprise was to develop a fleet during peacetime capable of carrying out its wartime tasks and possessing the bases necessary for successful operations. Raeder also wrote two additional papers at the Akademie dealing with the problems in establishing a naval blockade and an economic and political-military study of the United States in the Pacific. His early writings demonstrated Raeder's ability to study a wide range of technical, strategic, economic, political, and legal issues.[57]

Raeder and Tirpitz in the Imperial Naval Office's News Bureau

Raeder's literary activities and keen interest in strategic matters were rare for an officer of his time and played a role in bringing him to the attention of senior officers. On 1 April 1906, the thirty-year-old senior lieutenant reported to Tirpitz's News Bureau. Regarded as the forerunner of modern propaganda ministries, this office had been created by Tirpitz in 1897 to mobilize public opinion in support of the navy's expansion and win the support of industrialists and politicians to the cause of the service.[58] The timing of Raeder's new assignment coincided with major developments in Tirpitz's grand designs. The *Dreadnought* "leap" in 1905 along with the new British *Invincible* class, the "battle cruisers," had raised the naval arms race to a new level. Given the increased costs and pace of British construction, Tirpitz was forced to return to the Reichstag in 1906 and convince them of the need to pass a supplementary appropriations bill. Raeder witnessed the intense debates in the Reichstag and Tirpitz's ultimate success in securing a 35 percent increase over the 1900 Second Naval Bill (three battleships were to be laid down annually) as well as participating in the preparations for an even larger campaign for 1908 when the "four tempo" program (four battleships a year) was approved.[59]

Raeder's responsibility was to review and summarize foreign newspapers and magazines regarding naval affairs. He also edited the navy's semiofficial professional journal, *Marine Rundschau,* and *Nauticus,* the naval affairs annual. During this period, Raeder became well acquainted with the leading German journalists and scholars who were supporting the navy. More importantly, Raeder enjoyed a close and personal working relationship with Tirpitz. His role as editor required sound judgment and the ability to avoid disclosing too much detail regarding German naval policy or technical issues. Secrecy was critical in Tirpitz's plans, especially regarding the ultimate size and disposition of the fleet, and Raeder quickly earned his trust and that of his colleagues. He also had to defend his choice of topics personally with Tirpitz. When Raeder presented Kaiser Wilhelm with the 1907 edition of *Nauticus*, the kaiser presented him with his first decoration, the Order of the Red Eagle, Fourth Class.[60]

Raeder's three-year tour of duty in Berlin provided him with invaluable insights into Tirpitz's policies and practices. He observed firsthand the master's manipulation of the Reichstag. In 1907, Raeder accompanied Tirpitz on the first "inspection" visit by legislators aboard the flagship *Deutschland*—a tradition that Raeder would continue once he assumed command of the navy.[61] Raeder also hoped to emulate Tirpitz's success in limiting the control of the Reichstag over his plans by creating a long-term ship replacement program that would automatically establish how many battleships would be built each year and replaced (after twenty years of service). He appreciated Tirpitz's skills as a master bureaucratic infighter whose *Ressorteifer*—the defense of his departmental interests against both internal and external intrigues—was legendary.[62]

Although Tirpitz claimed that building a strong navy channeled political unrest toward overseas expansion and reduced the political pressures on the domestic status quo (providing a "strong palliative" against the Social Democrats), that was only one of many arguments he used to justify his fleet expansion.[63] Raeder, however, more than his mentor, regarded the system-stabilizing and integrative role of fleet building as an article of faith. The concept that national (and political) unity was a *sine qua non* for the building of German sea power became a powerful conviction (and a political goal) on the part of Raeder and the officer corps after the humiliating failure of the High Seas Fleet in World War I. Tirpitz's political and ideological vision for Germany would have a decisive impact on the navy's worldview across three regimes.

Tirpitz tolerated no rivals to his power and vigorously enforced a rigid adherence to his policies; above all else, he valued personal loyalty—another trait Raeder shared with Tirpitz. But Raeder was not the blind follower of Tirpitz often portrayed by his critics. He had recognized the problems inherent in Tirpitz's manipulation of the splintered organization of the Imperial Navy. It had a badly diffused chain of command consisting of the *Admiralstab*, the *Marinekabinett*, and Tirpitz's *Reichsmarineamt*, the Naval Office. In 1899, Tirpitz had convinced the kaiser to further decentralize the command structure and dissolve the

Oberkommando der Marine (OKM, the High Command), ostensibly to allow the kaiser to assert direct authority as supreme commander. This structure allowed Tirpitz to use his influence with the kaiser to assert his policies and eliminate any rivals—an arrangement that served his purposes before the war. In sharp contrast to his harsh private criticism regarding its impact on the navy in World War I, Raeder's memoirs only noted the danger that Tirpitz's Naval Office "might formulate its plans without taking into consideration the practical experiences of the operating commands at sea."[64] Although he expected to be given command in the event of war, Tirpitz was unable to exercise control as he had intended. When Raeder became navy chief, he was determined to avoid Tirpitz's fate and created a unified command structure for both internal naval affairs and naval operations.[65]

Return to the Fleet: Raeder, the Kaiser, and the Scouting Forces

After his three-year stint in Berlin, Raeder looked forward to returning to sea and increased opportunities for advancement. In the fall of 1908, he received orders as navigation officer to the armored cruiser SMS *Yorck* of the Scouting Forces. After *Yorck* he hoped to be assigned as navigation officer aboard one of the new battle cruisers or as fleet navigator aboard the flagship *Deutschland*. Instead, he received orders to report to duty as the navigation officer on board the kaiser's personal yacht, SMS *Hohenzollern*. Raeder had counted on his relationship with Prince Heinrich to gain a position with the fleet, but the new fleet commander, Admiral von Holtzendorff, preferred to pick his own staff.[66]

Raeder's memoirs underplay the significance of this appointment to the kaiser's yacht. It had implications far beyond Raeder's professional development and strengthened his opportunity for future promotion. Beyond seniority, officers were rated by their immediate superior each year in a *Qualifikationsbericht,* which assigned a points-ranking for promotion. Advancement to the higher ranks not only reflected this process, but was furthered by the opportunity to be brought to the attention of the kaiser and his circle, as well as the chief of the *Marinekabinett,* who was responsible for promotion decisions.[67] He was, in fact, being touted as one of the navy's bright stars, thrust into the foreground to remind the kaiser of the navy's talent and promise. It was a stellar endorsement of Raeder by his own service, and he was in very select company. The number of line officers in the navy had grown to barely over 2,300 by 1914, and most of them had to man the ships of the expanding navy. Only a select few went to Berlin to help Tirpitz chart the course for the service as Raeder had done in 1906. Even fewer, perhaps a dozen or so, served in direct contact with Germany's head of state and the royal family. Raeder's assignment to the kaiser's yacht provided him with access to the ruling elite of pre–World War I Germany and to many foreign leaders as well.[68]

Raeder later claimed that he had never desired "court duty," but he certainly knew that the captain of the *Hohenzollern* was chosen from officers well known to the kaiser and was always close to court circles. Raeder was familiar with court society and its rules from his days in Berlin. Raeder always looked back with pride on his personal relationship with the kaiser, whose views on political and military matters he found "soundly reasoned." Even after 1945, Raeder loyally professed his homage to the heritage of the Hohenzollern era and the kaiser, to whom he had sworn a personal oath. Raeder was not uncritical of Wilhelm II but recognized him as the symbol of the nation's will to global maritime power, and he continued to maintain contact with him until the kaiser's death in 1940.[69]

Promoted to lieutenant commander in 1911, Raeder's contacts and growing reputation led to an offer in 1912 from Admiral Gustav von Bachmann, commander of the Scouting Forces and a close confidant of Tirpitz, to serve as first admiralty staff officer in the Scouting Forces. The Scouting Forces were responsible for carrying out fleet reconnaissance as well as serving as a fast division at the head of the main battleship forces in a general engagement. As the senior member of the their commander's staff and the official superior of the other staff members, Raeder occupied a key operational post during the critical stage of the pre–World War I buildup of the Kaiserliche Marine as tensions grew between England and Germany. He was directly involved in the discussions of strategic and tactical options and observed firsthand the growing threat to a close blockade with new developments in mines, submarines, torpedoes, and long-range coastal artillery. He contended that by 1914 the Admiralty Staff considered a "distant" blockade by the British as a "certainty and the fleet had begun to design counters to distant blockades.[70] It was also apparent from his description of the final year before the war that the "front" needed more time to perfect new tactics and integrate the new ships, technologies, and weapons entering service, particularly the new battle cruisers and torpedo boat flotillas.[71] Professionally, Raeder could not have been in any better position than that which he occupied in August 1914.

Raeder and Naval Warfare, 1914–1918

When Admiral Franz von Hipper replaced Admiral Bachmann in October 1913 as commander of the Scouting Forces, he inherited Raeder as his first admiralty staff officer. Raeder viewed Hipper's appointment as positive and praised him as having "risen exclusively through performance in the fleet."[72] Hipper had made his reputation in Tirpitz's torpedo boats. His leadership, probably reflecting this background, was more improvised; "sheer theory" was not his forte. Raeder considered him as an "energetic and impulsive individual" who had no experience or inclination toward staff work or the politics of the naval bureaucracy. Hipper hated "paperwork," which he left to Raeder; and up to this point, he had never had a large staff.[73] Both men had worked under Prince Heinrich and had served in the same position on the *Hohenzollern*. Hipper's biographer (1930) noted that Raeder's background had prepared him to be "familiar with every sphere of the service both practical and theoretical" and his "special knowledge" acquired at the naval ministry in Berlin "supplemented excellently that of his admiral's."[74] As Hipper's chief advisor, he was witness to the intense debates over the navy's strategic options during the course of the war and the internal divisions that developed within the officer corps. The impact of these experiences would play a critical role on his subsequent leadership of the navy.

Raeder's position as first admiralty staff officer was unique in the fleet. Raeder outranked the other staff members and was not merely "the first among equals." This role suited Raeder's authoritarian personality and ensured what he considered to be the "strong leadership and unity" necessary to direct Hipper's forces. Although he was a "born Admiralty Staff officer," Raeder had limited experience in serving on a co-equal, collegial staff. His later lack of enthusiasm for the Admiralstab in the postwar navy not only reflected Tirpitz's treatment of the Admiralstab as a "stepchild," but also reflected Raeder's experience with Hipper, in which he saw the influence that a strong chief of staff could exert on a commander. After he became head of the navy in 1928, he opposed any administrative or command structure that might result in a strong second personality.[75]

Under Hipper, the Scouting Forces perfected the *Ran an der Feind*, the "battle cruiser charge," as a cover for the withdrawal of the main battle fleet from a possible envelopment. His ships also practiced repeatedly the "battle cruiser breakthrough," which would smash through the screen of the enemy fleet to ascertain the strength and deposition of the enemy. Both maneuvers were considered extremely difficult and dangerous and required, as Raeder noted, "quick judgment and sure execution" on the part of the commanding officers and their staffs.[76] Under these circumstances communications, both visual signaling and wireless, one of Raeder's responsibilities, were critical. At this stage radio communication was in its infancy and extremely fragile. Signals by flashing lights and flag hoists, although well developed, tended to fail in bad weather, smoke, and darkness, as well as in the usual confusion and violence attendant on combat at sea in that era. With the inadequate means of reconnaissance at the start of the war (aircraft, zeppelins, and U-boats were still in their infancy), the role of the battle cruisers was essential to any success of the main battle fleet.[77]

In spite of "frequent" studies and war games involving England as a potential foe, Raeder contended that "such a conflict in actuality had not been considered highly possible."[78] It was assumed that a quick and decisive land war would deter the British or, at the least, postpone the need for an immediate fleet offensive if the British declared war. Despite Tirpitz's inconsistent statements both before and during the war and his later attempts at self-justification, he did not want war, because the fleet was not complete and he ultimately believed in its deterrence role.[79] The war at hand was for Germany's continental position and not for the *Weltherrschaft* in which the navy would play the leading role. Victory would consolidate Germany's territorial position (and resources) in Europe; next would come the acquisition of appropriate naval bases around the world, which would serve as the foundation for future expansion overseas and future confrontation with the maritime powers.[80]

Raeder's view of the first stages of the war at sea reflects the fleet's frustration under the operational restrictions of Admiral Friedrich von Ingenohl, the commander in chief. Ingenohl, according to Raeder, was not a decisive or inspiring leader. Raeder also felt keenly that Ingenohl's decision to put Hipper in operational control for the defense of the entire Helgoland Bight posed difficult command problems that detracted from his primary task of being ready to put to sea whenever opportunities presented themselves. This responsibility for Helgoland was made even worse by Ingenohl's interference with the disposition of Hipper's security forces.

In early October 1914, Ingenohl's increased concern over the declining morale of the fleet and falling combat readiness led him to propose a major operation to mine and bombard the British coast, which Hipper and his staff helped to plan. The bombardment of Great Yarmouth was Hipper's and Raeder's first baptism of fire. Although the mission was judged a tactical success, both men initially refused to wear their Iron Cross First Class medals because they considered the results so meager.[81] As Raeder lamented, if the High Seas Fleet had carried out their role, they would have met Admiral Beatty's forces and then been joined by Hipper's battle cruisers with an overwhelming German advantage—and perhaps "decided the war."[82]

The sense of a lost opportunity and the intensifying rancor among the officers against Ingenohl now reached a new level. Several weeks after this engagement, Hipper found himself the target of a campaign to force him to retire on the basis of "ill health." At issue was the call for a more aggressive use of the High Seas Fleet, whatever the risk, favored by a cabal of junior officers, such as Magnus von Levetzow and Adolf von Trotha, who were closely allied with Tirpitz. On 15 January 1915, Levetzow informed Admiral Henning von Holtzendorff, chief of the Admiralty Staff, that Hipper was broken down "physically and psychologically" and had lost the confidence of his commanders.[83]

On 14 February 1915, Vice Admiral Bachmann observed that Hipper was, as Raeder had told him, "not at his best" but that he had improved after the Yarmouth operation in late January. Bachmann did not regard Hipper as a leader; noting "his staff [i.e., Raeder] provides the leadership."[84] Over the next eighteen months, Levetzow continued his unsuccessful efforts to have Hipper relieved, lobbying the new chief of the High Seas Fleet in January 1916, Admiral Reinhard Scheer, the head of the Naval Cabinet, Admiral Müller, and even Hipper's flag captain, Maurice von Egidy.[85]

On 24 January 1915, the controversy over Ingenohl's leadership culminated in the Battle of the Dogger Bank. Having been assured by Ingenohl that no major fleet offensives were planned for the near future, Hipper had detached one of his battle cruisers for routine Baltic Sea exercises when he was unexpectedly ordered to sea. Despite the loss of the battle cruiser *Blücher,* Raeder praised the performance of the Scouting Forces. Gunnery and communications had been excellent and, as the first participants in a battle involving capital ships flying the Imperial Navy ensign, the officers and crew felt "we could do even better next time."[86] For the first time, Raeder had witnessed the destructive force of modern naval warfare and had demonstrated courage under fire. Now both Raeder and Hipper chose to wear their Iron Cross First Class medals, awarded personally by the kaiser.[87] In a development that was to prove fateful for this war and the next, the Battle of Dogger Bank also revealed the growing importance of code-breaking when, to their "amazement" (Raeder), the German forces were intercepted the very morning they put to sea, confirming suspicions that the British were decoding their wireless messages.[88]

Although Hipper received criticism for positioning the older *Blücher* at the end of his battle line, it was Ingenohl who was relieved of command and replaced by Admiral Pohl. Raeder was not pleased by the selection of Pohl, because he believed Pohl too cautious and one who would only use the High Seas Fleet under the most favorable conditions. Hipper also agreed that a "more unfortunate choice could not have been made."[89] Moreover, Pohl's appointment did not satisfy Tirpitz and his allies, Levetzow and Trotha, who now directed their intrigues against him.

In the search to find a viable alternative naval strategy and believing that the fleet could achieve only "partial successes," Pohl continued to prefer the strategy of *Kleinkrieg,* a war of attrition conducted with light forces, especially U-boats and torpedo boats, over the possibilities of a fleet engagement. At the same time, the pressure for an expanded U-boat offensive intensified within the officer corps and the public. The expansion of the traditional *Kreuzerkrieg* (cruiser warfare), with U-boats attacking enemy shipping without warning, represented the first step toward Germany's fateful initiation of unrestricted submarine warfare. Raeder, who would find himself confronting similar political and diplomatic issues in World War II, supported unrestricted submarine warfare.[90] Despite claims that the U-boats could achieve a "decisive" victory, only a handful of U-boats were available and there was no way to measure success in the new "commerce war." The navy never caught up to the challenges of the U-boat war, and its decisions were influenced more by "psychological" considerations—concerns over the inactivity of the High Seas Fleet and the threat to the navy's existence after the war.[91]

After Dogger Bank, both Hipper and Raeder concluded that the Royal Navy had not entirely abandoned the North Sea and proposed that the U-boats "whittle down" the British navy. At the same time, the fleet would prepare for a decisive battle within German waters (not farther than fifty sea miles from Helgoland).[92] Pohl, however, continued to send the entire fleet on frequent but short-range and ineffective sorties. Raeder objected to these missions, arguing that they exposed the capital ships to unnecessary risks, particularly mine and torpedo losses, without any real opportunity to engage the enemy fleet.[93] He also believed that the morale of the fleet was continuing to deteriorate under Pohl—a situation that he reported was being communicated through "regular approved channels." In mid-July 1915, Trotha, citing the "flagging morale of the fleet which never goes into action," implored Admiral Müller to support the creation of a supreme commander of the navy and to consider Tirpitz for this new position. Pohl's poor health, however, solved these problems when, in February 1916, the admiral died of cancer; Raeder characterized his death as "kind fate."[94]

The culmination of these internal intrigues resulted in the appointment on 15 January 1916 of the widely admired and tactically astute Admiral von Scheer as the new commander in chief. He quickly appointed Trotha and Levetzow as his chief of staff and fleet operations officer, respectively. Scheer intended to implement a more aggressive strategy, but he did not want a battle forced on the fleet under unfavorable conditions. His policy favored instituting a systematic and continuous pressure on the vulnerable points of the enemy, using all the weapons available: the U-boat and surface trade war in the north and on the open seas, and aggressive sweeps by the fleet and light forces in the North Sea. These efforts were expected to provoke British countermeasures that would create opportunities for a fleet engagement. Unlike previous efforts, the High Seas Fleet would deploy in force and energetically push forward to engage the "important units of the enemy fleet."[95]

Raeder was optimistic because he felt Scheer possessed the offensive spirit so lacking in previous commanders in chief and embodied the complete repudiation of the "old defensive spirit." Raeder praised Trotha as the "calm and deliberative adviser" and characterized Levetzow as "impulsive."[96] Raeder apparently was unaware that Scheer's staff were continuing their attempts to relieve Hipper through Scheer; in any event, their efforts failed.[97]

When Hipper returned from sick leave in mid-May 1916, Raeder presented him with plans for a raid on Sunderland. This would be far more risky than the previous southern raids, given the proximity to the northern bases of the Royal Navy. The alternative was an attack on British shipping in the area of the Skagerrak (Jutland) and the Norwegian coast. According to Raeder, he was asked for his opinion of the raid by Trotha, and he "emphatically" argued for the more cautious Norwegian sortie if zeppelin reconnaissance were not available for the attack on Sunderland.[98] This story, as Raeder tells it, is ironic, considering Levetzow's previous criticism of his influence on Hipper; but with Scheer now in command, Raeder's good judgment and his key position were valued. With a forecast of bad weather after 20 May, Admiral Scheer decided in favor of the attack against shipping in the direction of the Skagerrak. Although the British did have advance knowledge of the plan through a radio intercept of Scheer's orders, they were unaware of the last-minute change of objective from Sunderland to the Norwegian coast.[99]

The ensuing Battle of Jutland (or Skagerrak, as the Germans called their "victory") continues to generate countless analyses and became a key part of the German naval mythology, justifying the past and a future fleet. Raeder believed that most accounts of Jutland reflected a tendency to second-guess the commanders on both sides and did not appreciate the limited information available during the battle or the decisions made by those in charge—many of which were made on the basis of completely "erroneous deductions." Raeder singled out the American commander Holloway H. Frost's 1936 *The Battle of Jutland* as "an objective and most impartial study." Significantly, Frost praised Hipper as the greatest of all the commanders involved in the battle and was highly critical of the British.[100]

After the Scouting Forces' first encounter with the British battle cruisers, heavy damage to the *Lützow* forced Hipper and his staff to transfer to a torpedo boat where, for two hours, in the midst of the heaviest fighting, they could do little but watch. Raeder later expressed surprise at Scheer's orders, given the damage suffered by Hipper's forces, to have the battle cruisers "charge" the British not once, but twice, to cover the retreat of Scheer's main battle fleet.[101] When they finally managed to transfer to the *Moltke*, which had radio problems, they spent most of the night trying to put Hipper's new flagship at the head of the main fleet, unaware of Scheer's message to the battle cruisers to take station as the rear guard of the High Seas Fleet. Raeder worked through the night to collect information on losses and damage both to his forces and to the enemy. He believed British losses were heavy, but he had no idea of the extent of losses the Royal Navy had actually suffered.

When the German forces returned to base, Raeder prepared Hipper's oral briefing, which Hipper at first refused to conduct. According to Raeder, Hipper declared that he would not give any report stating, "I led the battle—and that is that!" Raeder finally persuaded him to make use of the material he had prepared when Hipper reported to Scheer for the post-battle briefing.[102] Raeder was proud of his commander's leadership and his own role in Hipper's decision-making process. Raeder had shared the battle periscope on the bridge and had "exchanged views on every situation [with Hipper], and not until this was done, had a command been given."[103] Raeder had been responsible for providing Hipper with every tactical message along with suggested actions. Their close relationship and the value of his work were not lost on Hipper, who praised Raeder's "un-resting activity and clear sightedness" that enabled the battle cruisers to reach a high state of efficiency.[104] To Raeder he wrote, "Whatever was granted to me in this war, whatever I have received in the way of honors or distinction, I owe to your clear, energetic and sympathetic support. . . . You were my good star and it turned pale when you left me."[105]

The Scouting Forces had accomplished more at Jutland than any German naval force to date and the Imperial Navy had won an indisputable "quantitative" victory over the Royal Navy.[106] After the war, the navy honored its anniversary every 31 May as the most important feat of arms in its young history. More importantly, the navy and Raeder used the symbol and spirit of Skagerrak to justify the building of a new High Seas Fleet.

The German boast of victory, however, belied the major shift in German naval strategy that occurred after Jutland. Although Hipper still hoped for a clash of the battle fleets, Scheer reported to the kaiser (4 July 1916) that a decisive naval battle would not compel the British to make peace; only a vigorous U-boat campaign would force England to its knees.[107] The decision on 1 February 1917 to concentrate on the U-boat war and wage "unrestricted submarine warfare" marked a decisive turn in German naval strategy and led directly to the entry of the United States into the war. As they would do in both world wars, Germany's political and military leaders seriously underestimated the potential of the United States and overestimated the effect of unrestricted submarine warfare on the British.[108] Raeder supported the resumption of unrestricted submarine warfare in 1917 but, in light of the fateful provocation of the United States into declaring war, he blamed the failure of the "political government" to inform the navy of "promising" peace talks with the United States. If the government had given its reasons for "vetoing unrestricted warfare at this time," claimed Raeder, "the navy would have been better able to understand its orders."[109]

After February 1916, the fleet was relegated primarily to supporting the U-boat war. Unable to stage any major offensives, the surface fleet undertook escort duties for the minesweepers and U-boats and initiated only minor operations intended to disrupt enemy convoys.[110] The U-boat war began to drain off the best officers and crew, leading to what Raeder considered "staggering" reports of serious deterioration of discipline in the battleships.[111] Raeder is silent in his accounts of this phase of the war about the growing threat to the unity of the officer corps generated by the U-boat war. The supporters of those who hoped for a fleet engagement were jealous of the increased attention and resources being devoted to the U-boat war and were concerned over the fate of a postwar navy and the diminished role of the battleship. The junior officers who were fighting the war on the U-boats, destroyers, and light forces resented the idle High Seas Fleet. This conflict also became an unwelcome controversy between Tirpitz's supporters and critics. The acrimony between those who advocated the primacy of *Kreuzerkrieg* with the U-boat as the principal weapon of the navy and those who supported the battleships initiated a debate that would continue to plague Raeder and the navy throughout the interwar years and beyond.[112]

Raeder blamed the "so-called mutinies of 1917" on the High Seas Fleet's lack of offensive action and the "infiltration by many undesirable characters" among the workforce whose political propaganda had begun to affect the fleet's crews. The officers who replaced those who went to the smaller ships and the U-boats were not of the same quality and failed to maintain the discipline and closeness of officers in ships engaged in daily combat. Although Raeder recognized the need to correct the "few real grievances," he felt that the punishment of the ringleaders had restored discipline, which remained intact despite "continued socialist agitation"—an attitude shared by Berlin and the fleet command. Raeder's views reflect the officers' depiction of these "sailors' strikes" in 1917 (and the later mutinies in 1918) as the naval version of "the stab in the back theory" for Germany's defeat. Only later would he and the officers acknowledge, albeit privately, that the *Kastengeist* (caste-spirit) of the officer corps and the mistreatment of the enlisted men had been responsible for the outbreak of unrest in the fleet.[113]

As the war progressed, the old criticism of Hipper's tendency to turn "too much of the tactical work over to his staff" resurfaced—a reflection of his reliance on Raeder. Meanwhile, Raeder recognized that he needed to have his own sea command, "if I were to advance in my profession."[114] Hipper had repeatedly delayed Raeder's transfer because he did not want to lose his talented chief of staff. In July 1918, Raeder finally succeeded in receiving command of the new cruiser, *Cöln* II. The *Cöln* joined the Light Cruiser Group, whose duty it was to lay minefields and escort minesweepers and U-boats—a monotonous routine that Raeder attempted to relieve by reading Schiller on the bridge.[115]

Tirpitz, Hipper, and Wegener: The Lessons of Naval Policy and Combat, 1914–1918

In 1939, Raeder would confront the same conundrum as the navy faced in 1914—Germany's poor geographic position and its quantitative inferiority to the enemies' naval forces. After 1918, Raeder and the navy's strategists struggled with how they could address these fundamental disadvantages without discrediting the legacy of Tirpitz. Raeder's public defense of Tirpitz obscured the evolution of his naval strategy during this early period and contributed to his reputation as a blind follower of Tirpitz.[116]

His support of Tirpitz, especially when it came to defending his fleet building plan and his strategy, was always, however, cloaked by his desire to minimize any conflict within the naval officer corps or its supporters and present a solid front to the navy's critics. He remained silent on the role of Tirpitz in the politicization of naval warfare in World War I, as well as on his intrigues against the kaiser and efforts to establish a dictatorial government after he resigned in March 1916. Tirpitz's subsequent attempts to replace Bethmann Hollweg as chancellor and influence the policies of generals Hindenburg and Ludendorff were well known in the navy, as his correspondence with officers such as Trotha demonstrates. As the chairman of the right-wing Fatherland Party in the last year of the war, Tirpitz championed the navy's ambitious war aims and the continuation of the war, rejecting any negotiated peace that could lead to domestic political reform. Tirpitz's boast, that the navy could have won the war if it had been used aggressively at the outbreak, became an unshakeable belief among the officer corps, masking its "unavowed sense of failure." His continued espousal of the ideology of power politics and his insistence on national spirit and unity of will constituted a precondition for German *Weltpoltik* that would continue to resonate within the naval officer corps in the postwar era.[117]

Hipper's influence on Raeder has received little attention in spite of their close relationship during a period of intense debate over all aspects of German strategy, tactics, and technology. Raeder's observations and interaction with his commander on these issues can be inferred largely through an assessment of Hipper's private papers and official documents and by comparison with Raeder's later words and actions. One of the most intriguing discussions over the navy's strategic options early in the war was prompted by a proposal from one of Hipper's captains, Max Hahn, who advocated utilizing the newest battle cruisers for a commerce war in the Atlantic.[118] Hipper's endorsement of this idea can be compared to Raeder's 1939 Z-Plan, which envisioned a fleet composed of task forces to threaten England's vital sea communications. This connection between Raeder and Hipper has been virtually ignored in the aftermath of the controversy over Wolfgang Wegener's criticism of the Tirpitz fleet and its strategy in 1915 and his subsequent feud with Raeder over the direction of Germany's naval strategy.[119]

What is significant in the debate over the extent of Wegener's influence on Raeder is the fact that Hipper's "Atlantic vision" from November 1914 substantially paralleled and supported Wegener's ideas in several major ways (as would Raeder's later conception of naval strategy). Both recognized the British strategy of avoiding action and England's advantageous geographic position, as well as the opportunity for the Germans to interdict British trade. Although Hipper believed that the occupation of the Channel coast by the German army would expedite a cruiser war fought with battle cruisers, he argued that the war against commerce in the Atlantic remained "the one way in which our High Seas fighting ships can damage the enemy and thereby justify their existence."[120]

Hipper also advocated a strategy of destroying the British cruisers that were protecting its trade by hunting down the German merchant raiders. He believed that forces would need to be kept as intact as possible for the almost certain "inevitable decisive battle" with the British that could occur in theaters other than the Atlantic. He argued that the commerce war should be conducted in a large area with an extended deployment, in particular the West Indies and South Atlantic as the most suitable areas of operation. Acknowledging that the resupplying of coal would present difficulties, he proposed adding fuel blisters to the ships, as well as establishing coaling stations off Iceland or Canada or in one of the northern Norwegian fjords.[121] Such an operations plan would also have supported the East Asia Cruiser Squadron under Graf Spee —a missed opportunity, given the early successes of German surface raiders as compared to U-boats, and a failure that Raeder would criticize in his postwar study of the "cruiser war."[122]

After Jutland, Hipper was also particularly impressed by what he believed to be the development by the British of a "flying squadron" of battle cruisers, along with fast battleships. Such an enemy force could make it difficult to link up with the German main battle fleet while impeding Hipper's efforts to locate the enemy's main fleet. As a result, Hipper proposed the development of a German flying squadron, which, by combining the new fast German battleships with the battle cruisers, could create a force that could block an enemy escape and trap the enemy between his forces and the main battle fleet.[123] This concept presaged Raeder's later development of the "battle group" for the Atlantic commerce war.

In Hipper's writings on Germany's future naval needs, he argued for increased speed, armor, and a greater range for his battle cruisers to support their overseas operations. New, large capital ships were also required, especially "if we desire to bring the war into the Atlantic."

Unlike others, Hipper did not see the U-boat as a panacea for resolving Germany's strategic dilemmas but saw a strengthened U-boat force as part of a balanced fleet. His concern over the limitations of the U-boat and improvements in antisubmarine countermeasures mirrored Raeder's views that the submarine could never replace the battle fleet. He also felt that new counterdefenses and the increased speed of capital ships would cancel out the threat of the U-boat. Hipper's view of Tirpitz's fleet building was also quite critical, arguing that ships should be built on the principle of superiority, not equality, to their enemy counterparts.[124] The fact that financial and therefore political constraints were in many ways primarily responsible for the compromises in size, armor, and armament of the Imperial Navy was not lost on Raeder, nor on the future führer, Adolf Hitler, whose own views on the High Seas Fleet were quite in line with Hipper's.

Raeder was well versed in Wegener's proposals regarding an alternative naval strategy following the summer of 1915. Wegener later accused Raeder, in what he implies was professional jealousy, of persuading Hipper not to forward Wegener's three-part memorandum to the Admiralty Staff for evaluation.[125] In fact, Wegener's famous trilogy enjoyed a wide circulation and evoked considerable discussion and debate.[126] Dismissing Tirpitz's Risk Theory as "cant," he rejected the idea that the Royal Navy would attack the Helgoland Bight, where there was no threat to its sea communications, and criticized the focus on the decisive battle as a result of "continental" thinking without regard to geographic position or maritime commerce.[127] Since the navies of France, Russia, and Italy were already aligned against Germany, Tirpitz's concept of the fleet's alliance value was also an empty hope. To escape the "dead corner" of the North Sea, Wegener called for an Atlantic strategy to outflank the British in the North—from the Skagerrak, "the gate to the Atlantic," and the Faeroe Islands—and in the West, from the French ports on the Atlantic coast and the Portuguese islands (the Azores and Cape Verde Islands). This would enable Germany to undertake a strategic offensive against the vital British trade routes.[128]

Wegener believed sea power was a product of having the necessary fleet and geographic position—that one is essentially useless without the other. His extolling of power politics, however, did not match the strategic or material resources available to the navy in World War I and were too radical and aggressive to be openly embraced in the postwar era. For Wegener, "the state failed to understand that the entire World War was a naval war, that the decision lay on the sea." It was not a question of the fleet's operational plans or tactics, but "grand strategy" at the level of the general headquarters—a critique remarkably similar to Raeder's in World War II, as was his warning that Germany's naval strategy would lie latent until conditions became ripe for the rebuilding of the fleet and a renewed pursuit of *Weltpolitik*.[129]

The Navy! Arisen out of the arrogance of Weltmacht, ruined
our foreign policy for over 20 years, [and] did not fulfill its
promises in war and now kindles revolution!

—*Ernst von Weizsäcker, 5–6 November 1918*

The navy makes a devastating impression on everyone who
had known it before the outbreak of war. . . . In the public
the view is widely held that the navy exists not for the people
but for its own purposes.

—*Friedrich Voigt (SPD deputy), 3 May 1920*

2

Raeder and the Politics of the
Naval Command, 1918–1920

Defeat and Revolution

In October 1918, while his ship was undergoing repairs, Raeder participated in a special commission at Spa to study possible armistice conditions. Raeder later understated the significance of this assignment, saying
that he was chosen simply because he was available. Along with Admiral
Scheer and representatives of the new *Seekriegsleitung* (SKL), the Supreme
Army Command, and the Foreign Office, he learned firsthand of
Germany's precarious military situation. Although the commission
worked out what Raeder considered to be "honorable" armistice terms,
it was clear to him that defeat was imminent. During this period, Raeder
had the opportunity to work closely with the army leaders, Field Marshal
Paul von Hindenburg, the future Reich president, and General Erich
Ludendorff. Like other naval officers, Raeder expressed high regard
for Ludendorff, whose later dismissal "caused a deep despondency" in
the military.

On 14 October 1918, Raeder received orders to report to Berlin as
the deputy of the secretary of the *Reichsmarineamt* (RMA), Vice Admiral
Paul Behncke. Although he regretted leaving his ship, he considered
this opportunity an "honor." He was confident that the high morale of
his crew would keep "subversive elements" from making any headway.
Later, he reported with pride that only his former ship and the *Königsberg*
had remained at their stations—"our last ships with disciplined crews."[1]
Raeder's appointment to Berlin was a direct consequence of the creation

of the SKL, which the kaiser had reluctantly agreed to on 11 August 1918. Trotha had been one of the major advocates for this change and had demanded that younger officers be placed in leading positions.[2] Raeder's assignment to the RMA, which replaced the SKL after its dissolution in mid-November, placed him in a key position during Germany's collapse and revolution. His role, initially as staff to the chief of the RMA and, from 4 December 1918, as chief of the Central Department, assured his participation in deliberations that would have fateful implications for the development of a new navy—quite an opportunity for a young commander. He also witnessed the debates in the National Assembly at Weimar over the new constitution and the formation of the government. As an advisor to the naval and political leadership, he used every opportunity to influence important decisions, not only in the development of the legislation for a provisional navy bill, but also the navy's new organizational structure. He was also actively involved in personnel decisions and recruited former colleagues to serve in the new navy.

In the final weeks of the war, Raeder participated in Scheer's attempts to implement a massive U-boat construction program (450 U-boats). Although the serious lack of resources suggested that the Scheer Program was intended more for propaganda purposes, it reflected the state of mind in the SKL as it struggled to continue the war even as defeat loomed closer.[3] In spite of Scheer's argument that the U-boat war "could still save us" and his insistence that "the navy did not need an armistice," Germany's new government under Prince Max von Baden ended Germany's unrestricted submarine warfare on 21 October 1918.[4] In response, Scheer informed the government that the High Seas Fleet had "regained its operational freedom" and began to plan a major fleet engagement against the Flanders coast and the Thames estuary, hoping to draw out the Grand Fleet.[5] For Raeder, the proposed operation was "well planned" with "little risk" and would provide a morale boost to the "harbor bound crews" of the High Seas Fleet.[6]

The origins of this plan were not solely driven by military considerations. On Raeder's return from his meeting at Spa on 10 October 1918, he had shared with Hipper a draft of the possible armistice conditions for the navy—consisting of "ten difficult possibilities ranging from the favorable to the unacceptable."[7] Raeder later wrote that he had already come to the conclusion in October that the war would end "unfavorably" and that Germany would probably have a "considerably reduced" fleet.[8] In fact, there was a growing fear that the British would demand the handing over of the German fleet.[9] Although Hipper acknowledged in his diary that the navy's honor was at stake, he indicated that he had planned an operation that took every opportunity to maximize success and, at the worst, to leave the navy with sufficient forces to support a new U-boat war.[10] Critics of the operation, however, later characterized it as a "death ride" and as an "Admirals' rebellion" against the new government intended to disrupt armistice negotiations.[11] Notwithstanding Hipper's attempts to provide a well-thought-out military rationale (which culminated in Operations Plan No. 19, 24 October 1918), the decision to commit the fleet constituted a major miscalculation. Hipper was well aware of the significant unrest among the crews and the effects of the loss of the best officers to the U-boats and the smaller units of the navy.[12] The SKL was also well aware that even with a disruption of the armistice talks, the war could only last at the most four to six weeks and that any success in a fleet action would not change Germany's inevitable defeat.[13]

Ultimately, regardless of Hipper's attempts to justify his planning or Raeder's characterization of the operation as having "little risk," the navy's leaders regarded the mission as a question of the navy's "honor and existence," without which it would suffer a "shock of shame" if the fleet did nothing.[14] As Scheer argued, "It is impossible that the fleet remain uncommitted in the last battle which sooner or later precedes an armistice."[15] If the navy could inflict heavy losses, England as a sea power would be reduced to second rank behind the American navy, while the surviving units of the High Seas Fleet would constitute the *Kernflotte*, the core of the fleet, making the building of a new *Welt-machtflotte* easier.[16] Whatever its chances for success, argued Hipper, "an honorable fleet engagement, even if it should become a death battle, it would be the foundation for a new German fleet, a fleet [that] would be out of the question in the event of a dishonorable peace"—a sentiment Raeder himself would echo twenty-one years later as World War II began.[17] Behind the references to national and naval honor, this operation reflected an officer corps obsessed with maintaining its own prestige and future after the war. This last act of a *Verzweiflungskrieg,* "war of desperation," returned German naval strategy to Tirpitz's concept of the decisive battle "between the Thames and Helgoland."[18]

Hipper's careful preparations for the 30 October operation were for naught. Beginning on 28 October, the rebellious crews of the High Seas Fleet began to disobey orders and a full-scale mutiny was under way. On 2 November, Hipper used the word "revolution" for the first time in his diary to describe a "Bolshevist" uprising against the government.[19] Refusing to acknowledge that they had lost control over events, the SKL believed that it was still possible to restore the authority of the officers and continue operations. Concerned about communications security, Scheer sent Raeder to inform Hipper that "dependable" army units were being dispatched to Kiel and Wilhelmshaven to enforce discipline. Upon arriving in Wilhelmshaven, Raeder quickly ascertained that the situation had deteriorated to the point that not even additional forces would be able to handle the growing crisis. Raeder's return to Berlin took two days as his train was stopped repeatedly by authorities hoping to prevent the revolution from spreading in the event revolutionary sailors were on board. The train was allowed to enter Berlin only after Raeder and other officers insisted.[20] By the second week of November, the revolution reached Berlin, and on 9 November 1918, Admiral Scheer informed the kaiser that his navy could no longer be relied upon.[21]

The outbreak of revolution, beginning in the High Seas Fleet and spreading throughout Germany, came as a profound shock to Raeder and the officer corps that would have long-term consequences. The pervasive feeling of despair, characterized as a deep "trauma" affecting the officers, can be seen in Scheer's declaration that "a curse lies on the navy because out of its ranks revolution first spread . . . over the land."[22] In the words of Raeder, "the whole country was led to believe that the navy was the chief instigator and propagator of the Revolution; as a result, its reputation suffered terribly for years." In attempting to absolve themselves of blame, the officers utilized every opportunity to propagandize their cause—a task made more difficult by the supporters of the new government, who took delight in reminding the navy of its "contributions" to the birth of the Weimar Republic.[23] The officers vigorously counterattacked, condemning the mutineers as the tools of outside agitators who had insidiously infiltrated the ranks of the enlisted men. The mere appearance of blue uniforms in inland cities, they argued, attracted much more attention than their actual involvement in the revolution justified. Frequently, "criminal elements" donned naval uniforms, in order to play a role in the revolutionary movement such as the "People's Naval Division" in Berlin. In his memoirs, Raeder denied that the navy had any responsibility or blame for the revolution. The "real dissidents were the reserves and draftees of the army—citizen soldiers—who had swallowed the political propaganda of the Independent Socialist Party (USPD) and the Communists." These parties, charged Raeder, were in fact the chief instigators of a premeditated plot against the navy.[24]

Raeder's analysis of the causes of the mutinies of 1918 reflects the official party line of the officer corps and would reappear in the policies that he and the navy would adopt and follow in later years. He acknowledged that the massive breakdown of military discipline had resulted from the inactivity of the High Seas Fleet and the increased opportunity for sailors to spend off-duty hours in establishments that were "highly unsuitable for a soldierly, well-disciplined spirit." The large number of workers in the naval yards and the subsequent infiltration of the workforce by many "questionable elements" whose political propaganda was "not without effect" also contributed to the situation. Moreover, the fleet suffered from the deterioration in the quality of replacement officers after the better officers were assigned to more dangerous assignments (e.g., U-boats). Raeder also singled out the Deck Officers Association for conducting itself as a quasi-union, politically corrupting their active colleagues. (Not surprisingly, the deck officer grade was later phased out.)

As Raeder and the officers attempted to reestablish control, the establishment of sailors' councils in the naval ports and the creation of a supreme naval council (the Council of Fifty-three) in Berlin represented a significant threat against their authority. The latter attempted to establish itself as the socialist parliament of the navy responsible for all naval matters, including countersigning all orders issued from the RMA. In spite of Raeder's claim that the Council of Fifty-three never caused any problems with the conduct of official business, the navy made every attempt to rid itself of the council movement and found a willing ally in the new republican government.[25] Less than a month after the Council of Fifty-three was formed, the head of the RMA, Admiral Ernst Ritter von Mann, complained that it was seriously interfering with the work of the RMA and that a number of his officers had threatened to resign.[26] When Mann finally resigned in January 1919, the existence of the council made it difficult for the government to find a replacement. Along with the government's fateful decision to cooperate with the leadership of the military in the interests of stabilizing the new republic, the appointment of Gustav Noske as defense minister sealed the fate of the council movement. For Raeder, the defeat of the Council of Fifty-three was a result of its ongoing agitation against the government and its political activity, which followed the party lines of the USPD. In Noske, the military found a socialist who understood military matters and, in Raeder's words, showed "complete understanding" of the importance of military discipline.[27]

Reestablishing the Naval Command: From the Imperial Naval Office to the Admiralty

With its command prerogatives restored, the officer corps had survived the turbulent period of the collapse of the old order and the beginning of the new republic with its "political exclusiveness and homogeneity" intact.[28] The navy was finally in a position to concentrate on discipline and organizational matters. The armistice terms had directed the Admiralty Staff and the Naval Cabinet to be dissolved and their responsibilities incorporated into a new *Admiralität*. Raeder, who was directly involved in these efforts, recognized the need for the navy to have "capable and forceful leadership," especially since it would be under a "political minister," that is, civilian leadership. From his experiences, the Imperial Navy's organization had resulted in the lack of "any tight, unified naval leadership." He favored the organization of the navy as it was before 1888, when both the administrative and operational offices were combined under one chief of the Admiralty.

Until a more suitable replacement could be found for the new position of Chief of the Admiralty, Rear Admiral Maximilian Rogge served as the acting state secretary of the RMA. The chosen chief, according to Raeder, would face the difficult challenge of being acceptable to the government while maintaining the full confidence of the navy. Although Rogge enjoyed the respect of the officer corps for his firm stand against any interference from revolutionary elements, Raeder was not impressed with him because he "had never commanded a combat force at sea during the war" and was practically unknown to the navy outside of his department.[29] For the officer corps, combat experience and especially participation in the victory at Skagerrak remained a prerequisite for the navy's highest leadership position—qualifications which also matched Raeder's profile (and ambitions). His personal choice was Trotha, who also had the full support of Tirpitz.[30] Trotha's ability to retain the support of the followers of both Tirpitz and the kaiser, given the bitter feud between the two, was also critical to the unity of the officer corps and was a skill that Raeder also practiced.

As the self-appointed spokesman for the officer corps, Raeder used his access to political leaders to actively support Trotha's candidacy. He received permission from Rogge to speak to Noske regarding Trotha's qualifications. Noske concurred with his assessment of Trotha and directed him to discuss the matter personally with President Ebert. At their 11 January 1919 meeting, Raeder learned that Ebert was also in agreement. The only issue for Ebert was whether the appointment of an officer so closely associated with the High Seas Fleet would be acceptable to the rebellious sailors.[31] For tactical reasons, it was decided that Trotha's appointment would be postponed until after the council movement was defeated and the new government was formed.[32]

Although Raeder himself quickly adjusted to the new conditions of the Republic and tried to convince officers such as Levetzow to remain with the navy, the decision to serve was not an easy one.[33] The mutinies and the ensuing chaos had demonstrated the complete helplessness of the officer corps. Many of the officers quit in disgust and shame. Of those who stayed, the common denominator was the conviction "that the future of the German people lies on the water"—a belief that "must fix itself in the officer corps as a dogma of unshakeable faith."[34] Raeder also credited Trotha's address to the officers in Kiel regarding the oath of allegiance to the new Weimar Constitution as having overcome certain "objections" of the officers.[35] Although Trotha stressed that the "most important" support of the monarchy had been in the officer corps, he pointed out that "now the ideal middle point lies in the patriotic state, in the Fatherland itself."

> The person of the President, who is dependent on the votes of the people, cannot have the [same] importance as before. But the most important support for the form of the State remains with the officer. The culmination

of his profession is still the unselfish enlistment of his person for the good of the State at any time and any place.[36]

Raeder's former commander, Prince Heinrich of Prussia, also played a key role in encouraging others to serve in the new navy. Acknowledging the officers' hesitation about serving the new Republic, Prince Heinrich stressed the obligation to a higher duty—the preservation of the navy. Along with this sacred duty, the officers were expected to heed their patriotic consciousness: their work for the state was "national." The people were sorely in need of a reeducation in national feeling, and such reeducation would be an important role for the officers with the new form of government.[37] If the government could accept this self-appointed role of the officer corps, then the former Imperial Navy officers could accept their commissions regardless of their political convictions.

Those, like Raeder, who chose to serve in the new Reichsmarine assumed that Germany would someday be allowed to possess a fleet commensurate with its resources and needs, and its officers should be trained to be the nucleus of a much larger force. They regarded both the Reichsmarine and the Republic as transitions and considered their task as a stewardship to keep the dreams of *Seegeltung* and *Weltmachtflotte* alive until the navy and Germany had healed itself of its current "sickness" (i.e., *Parlamentarismus*).[38] For Raeder, the naval officers were the true "trustees of Germany"—a concept that justified the obligation of the officers to make decisions on the basis of "national interest" as they defined it.[39] This self-serving aggrandizement of power was to lead to a series of serious political miscalculations throughout the history of the Republic and, especially in the early years, was to threaten the very existence of the navy and Raeder's own career.

Raeder, in his role as chief of staff, was acutely aware of the "delicate problems" faced by the navy during this period of reorganization. He recalled how Trotha repeatedly had to issue personal proclamations to convince the officers of the necessity of accepting decisions brought about by the change of government. The questions of the national flag to be flown by the navy and even the national anthem were emotionally charged issues. In the end, President Ebert decided to retain *Deutschland, über Alles* as the national hymn—an act that Raeder contended "won" the president many sympathizers. The naval flag also was allowed to remain black-white-red.[40] Raeder noted the difficulty of carrying out the terms of the armistice, but what was particularly galling to the officers' sense of honor was the internment of the German fleet at Scapa Flow. The naval clauses of the Versailles treaty presented in May 1919 dealt the navy a blow even more severe than what had been expected. The new fleet was to consist of six pre-dreadnoughts, six light cruisers, twelve destroyers, twelve torpedo boats, and no U-boats or aircraft. Other stipulations demanded the destruction of uncompleted warships and the surrender of any remaining ships, which effectively doomed the navy to the status of a third-rate naval power as long as the treaty remained in force. Even more crippling were the restrictions on the size and armament for future construction (e.g., 10,000 tons displacement for battleships).[41] After the scuttling of the fleet at Scapa Flow on 21 June 1919, the Allies demanded additional reparations that included the five light cruisers of the *Regensburg* class—the navy's last modern units.[42] With a fleet consisting of the antiquated pre-dreadnought *Braunschweig* and *Deutschland* classes and the older cruisers of the *Nymphe* and *Hamburg* classes, Raeder concluded, along with many of his fellow officers, that with the "poor financial conditions in Germany," there was little chance that there would be funds for new construction for a long time.[43] The "Carthaginian peace" or the Versailles *Diktat* (dictated peace), as it came to be called, was a "crushing" blow which left Germany with "a pigmy fleet already obsolete . . . [and] insufficient to defend our waters."[44] The Allied demands were so severe that it took a "special plea" by Trotha to get his officers to view them as a "challenge rather than a death sentence."[45]

Beyond the implications for the size and composition of the fleet, a complete reorganization in all aspects of command, personnel, education, and training would be required to enable the navy to have any military value. While the naval clauses of the treaty forecast disaster enough for the future, Articles 227–231 demanded the prompt surrender of the kaiser and other "war criminals" for trial and declared Germany's guilt for starting the war. The officer corps was incensed by what became known as the "shame paragraphs." Trotha informed Noske of the "catastrophic consequences" of the treaty for the navy and the threat to discipline as a result of the charges of "war crimes."[46] In a show of support not seen since before the mutinies, the entire garrison of Kiel, officers and men, marched in protest against the "Treaty by Force" that would doom the German people to an "honor-less and miserable slavery," destroying its "sea and world power."[47] On 19 June 1919, General Walther Reinhardt and Noske called a meeting to discuss the possibility of armed resistance if the National Assembly accepted the treaty in its current form. Ominously, a number of officers felt that the time had come to play a political role. Trotha had already urged the government not to sign the treaty and informed the chancellor's office that if any officers were surrendered to the Allies, the officer corps would collapse.[48]

As the government struggled with the Versailles treaty, Admiral Ludwig von Reuter, the commander of the interned fleet at Scapa Flow, ordered its scuttling on 21 June 1919. Reuter assumed full responsibility, claiming that he was anticipating the resumption of hostilities with the expiration of the armistice at noon on 21 June and was merely following the kaiser's orders of 1914 stipulating that no German ships were to be surrendered to the enemy.[49] Raeder hailed the scuttling as "the one inspiring occurrence in that depressing spring of 1919." He justified the German action because the Admiralty had learned from the Paris negotiations that "we would not receive a single ship of the High Seas Fleet." Therefore, it became clear that preventing the ships from being divided up among the victors and "to save its [the navy's] honor," the ships had to be sunk. According to Raeder, although Trotha could "naturally" not issue such a command to scuttle from his position as chief of the Admiralty, Trotha had privately impressed upon Reuter that the ships must be scuttled "at all costs." Even without any evidence of written orders, Reuter did what all officers expected and, in Raeder's words, not only did Reuter restore the morale of the navy, "but also laid the foundations for the eventual reconstruction of the fleet."[50]

For active and inactive officers as well as the navy's supporters, the "grand scuttle" satisfied the honor of the officer corps and "wiped out the stain of surrender" and "proved that the spirit of the Fleet is not dead."[51] It was also an act of defiance against the government and further weakened Germany's bargaining power. In a period of twenty years, Raeder and his fellow officers had witnessed a spectacular ascent to a world naval power followed by an ignominious defeat amidst mutiny and revolution—a rise and fall unprecedented in naval history that was to be overcome through its rebirth in a glorious *Gotterdämmerung* of self-destruction at Scapa Flow.

When the government was finally compelled to sign the treaty, Trotha regarded the decision as a disaster and asked his officers to support him in refusing acceptance of the treaty. On 23 June 1919, Trotha informed Noske of his actions, expecting to be relieved of duty or arrested and convinced that, if he left, the navy would collapse.[52] At the same time, Trotha released an internal statement declaring his disavowal of the government's actions, but expressed his determination to stay on in "these dark hours of the Fatherland" and appealed to his officers to remain at their posts.[53] It was clear from his actions that he did not want to associate himself in any way with the "political decisions" of the government.[54] By distancing himself from the government's acquiescence to the Allies, Trotha believed he could maintain his authority and preserve the unity of the navy. Noske's failure to check Trotha's disavowal of the actions of the government and the development of the navy's authority and independence under the exclusive leadership of the chief of the Admiralty would lead to serious political consequences for the navy in March 1920.

On 3 February 1920, the Allies presented the Germans with a final list of the war criminals to be surrendered for trial, including a number of naval officers and U-boat captains. Raeder was included on the list for his role as Hipper's former chief of staff.[55] Levetzow, now station chief of the naval base at Kiel, recommended that the navy support whatever government rejected the surrender of any officers "whether it was 'this [government]' or another" and advocated preparations for a civil war in cooperation with the army.[56] Raeder also saw an opportunity for the navy to redeem itself and anticipated the possibility that a new government, probably a conservative government or a dictator, would be formed.[57] Raeder was also concerned that the inclusion of Trotha on the Allied list might influence the government to remove him from office. He was convinced that the navy's very existence was dependent upon Trotha's continued leadership and informed Ebert and Noske that the navy would not tolerate a dismissal of its chief.[58] The timing of the demand for the surrendering of "war criminals" further incensed the officers, who rallied against the powerlessness of the government. Raeder's later description of events, that "things were going smoothly," was ludicrous.[59] The stage was now set for a confrontation with the government in which the navy would once again play a prominent role.

The Navy and the Kapp Putsch, March 1920

In his memoirs, Raeder praises the role of the *Marine Freikorps* (volunteer naval brigades) who were to play an important role in the reestablishment of law and order in the immediate postwar era and a fateful role

in the subsequent history of the Republic and the navy.[60] Their anti-
revolutionary and nationalistic, conservative proclivities would ultimately involve the Admiralty in the ill-advised support of a right-wing
coup d'etat in March 1920 that seriously jeopardized the future of both
Raeder and the navy. Although the more rabid elements were eliminated by choice or by their overt antirepublican lapses over the course
of the 1920s, their continuing ties to the navy would contribute to the
suspicions of the supporters of the government that the navy's leadership was not loyal, if not reactionary. At the same time, their independence and the sense of elitism of those who joined the new navy
constituted a threat to the unity of the officer corps.[61]

The most notable of the naval brigades were the Ehrhardt Brigade
and the Loewenfeld Brigade, named after their commanders. These
units were formed, with the approval of Noske, to assist the government
in restoring order and were composed of "officers, midshipmen, petty
officers and enlisted men, with the latter being drawn almost entirely from
the well-disciplined crews of the torpedo boats and U-boats." Raeder
praised Captain Hermann Ehrhardt and Captain Wilfried Loewenfeld as
"highly respected officers" who knew how to instill "both spirit and discipline" in their men.[62] Not all officers, however, supported the formation of these brigades. The commander of the Kiel Naval Station, Rear
Admiral Hans Küsel, feared that he would lose his best officers to
Loewenfeld, hampering his efforts to reestablish discipline among the
"politically infected" sailors under his command. Others feared that the
focus on land operations, however temporary, would make the transition back to the navy's primary maritime role more difficult.[63]

The spirit of the Naval *Freikorps* reflected a high degree of patriotism and a burning hatred for the revolution, Jews, and Bolshevism.
Known for their ruthlessness in battle, they felt, as representatives of the
revolution-torn navy, that they had something to prove. Unlike their
"weak brothers" in the new officer corps who, they charged, oppor-
tunistically announced their republican sympathies, they had not
made concessions to anyone. Under the German-Prussian code of unselfish service, "no soldier could abandon the state because of a change
in government."[64]

The immediate cause of the abortive right-wing Kapp Putsch in
March 1920 was the government's attempt to disband the *Freikorps* or

include them in the 15,000 men allowed the navy by the treaty.[65] Although Raeder contended that Trotha refused to believe "rumors" that the Ehrhardt Brigade was disgruntled over its dissolution, Trotha did not want to assume responsibility for these troops. As an alternative, he suggested disbanding the brigades slowly by transfers or discharges as a much safer solution.[66] Raeder attempted to justify Trotha's actions, arguing later that no one had any idea that the brigades were "in any way involved in the Kapp movement."[67] By 12 March 1920, rumors of the approaching putsch, however, were so alarming that Noske sent Trotha to Ehrhardt's camp outside of Berlin. Having announced his impending visit by phone, Trotha arrived to find the camp quiet, with no signs of any preparations for a coup.[68]

On the same day, Trotha and Raeder met with the staff of the brigade's nominal commander, General Walther von Lüttwitz, who assured them that there were no grounds for concern, after which Raeder immediately left for Hamburg to deal with personal matters. After receiving an emergency phone call, Raeder returned to Berlin in the morning of 13 March, learning that Wolfgang Kapp, a former Reichstag deputy, with the support of Ehrhardt's troops, had seized control of the government offices and declared General Ludendorff chancellor.[69] While Trotha and Raeder claimed surprise, there is little doubt that they believed Ehrhardt was capable of such action. From the beginning, the Admiralty was implicated in the putsch because of Trotha's immediate decision to place the navy "entirely at the disposal of the Kapp-Lüttwitz government."[70] Raeder would argue later that Trotha and "the greater part" of the navy had no thought of anything but "complete loyalty to the government."[71]

Toward noon on 13 March, Lüttwitz met with Trotha and informed him that the government had fled to southern Germany but that President Ebert had remained in Berlin and would "immediately form a new government." According to Raeder, Lüttwitz stated that he had assumed the duties of acting defense minister and requested that Trotha remain at his post and ensure that the navy maintain order.[72] Afterwards, Trotha met with Raeder and four other officers who "unanimously concurred in the decision to place themselves at the disposal of the new government." Trotha declared that his most important task was to preserve "law and order" and thereby "bring the navy intact through these troubles."[73]

In spite of growing evidence that the government (now in Stuttgart) was very much in command and had called for a general strike, Trotha refused to change his position, denying that there was any political activity on the part of the Admiralty in supporting the Kapp government. His actions were necessary to maintain a united front against chaos and the "threat of Bolshevism." Trotha disingenuously interpreted the coup as "only a change of cabinets under the *constitutional president* even if [it took place] under the force of an outside power."[74] Trotha's declaration of "neutrality" in the early stages of the putsch was, in fact, a political act, since the viability of the Kapp government depended on maintaining "law and order." The communiqués supplied by the Admiralty to the naval stations and then to the public made no pretense of hiding where their true sympathies lay. As one of Trotha's confidants later wrote, "the majority of the officers . . . wanted to cause the collapse of the government and bring in its place a rightist government. In my opinion, the time was not quite right."[75] Noske himself was convinced that Trotha had "placed himself under Kapp" in the mistaken belief that this would "save the navy." Even the naval officers on Noske's staff sided with Kapp "without hesitation."[76]

Although the officers hoped to "turn back the clock," they had seriously underestimated the conditions in the fleet. The crews of the minesweepers were, for the most part, unreliable, and the naval ports were still under the influence of the former soldiers' councils (contrary to Raeder's later claims that the navy had successfully restored discipline in 1919–1920).[77] In Wilhelmshaven, the officers were quickly placed under arrest by non-commissioned officers and enlisted men, and the command of the station was turned over to an *Obermachinist*.[78] In Kiel, Levetzow struggled to maintain control, with some initial success, with threats of summary executions if civilians or sailors supported a general strike, carried arms, or disseminated any propaganda concerning the "previous" government. By 17 March, however, the workers had shut down the port and factories of Kiel and open fighting had begun. The local political leaders demanded the immediate dismissal of Levetzow in order to prevent a "civil war."[79] In a phone call with Levetzow, Raeder indicated Trotha was defending Levetzow's actions (the Kapp government at this point had collapsed) and expressed Berlin's amazement over his success in maintaining order in Kiel. Raeder warned Levetzow of the danger from the deck officers, who were "jealous" of the officers' successes in maintaining law and order and would surely strike back as soon as they discovered an opportunity. To support Levetzow's remaining in office, Raeder urged him to contact prominent citizens to intercede on his behalf with the government.[80]

On 18 March 1920, however, the Admiralty relieved Levetzow and appointed Admiral Ernst Ewers as his replacement. Ewers quickly found that he had no command. With heavy fighting breaking out between the Loewenfeld Brigade and armed workers, negotiations between the naval station and civil authorities collapsed after a call from Raeder to the station was intercepted. Reportedly, Raeder had asked Levetzow to take control over the military leadership in Kiel.[81] Raeder, given what he believed was Levetzow's success in Kiel and the reported resignation of Noske, proposed that the admiral should take control of the overall military authority in Berlin to prevent a total collapse of order. After having learned that Noske had not resigned, Raeder phoned back fearing that his call might have been "misunderstood" and told Levetzow to ignore his previous message. At this point, Levetzow, however, attempted to take over military leadership on his own authority, which appeared to the government's supporters as a second putsch attempt and led to the arrest or removal of the naval officers by their men.[82] With the naval stations in the hands of the NCOs and the Admiralty hopelessly compromised in Berlin, the officer corps collapsed for the second time in two years.

Raeder and his fellow officers in Berlin had completely underestimated the power of the organizations representing the deck officers, petty officers, and sailors. With the exception of Trotha, who was dismissed on 22 March, the officers in the Admiralty continued to serve, but only the two naval brigades and a torpedo boat flotilla reported directly to the Admiralty; all other units and ships functioned without officers.[83] For the navy, the situation was desperate. In the Reichstag, the navy was seen as "the bearer of all mutinies . . . at first from the left, now from the right." Even Tirpitz despaired, "Hands off the whole affair! It [the navy] is rotten from the base up! Nothing healthy will ever grow from it again."[84] In many circles, there was open and unabashed talk of abolishing the navy altogether or, at the least, subordinating the navy to the army.

Raeder himself was under suspicion for being a key player in supporting the putsch and was forced to turn over his position to his senior assistant while awaiting the results of a special committee to evaluate the conduct of the officers during the Kapp Putsch. Subsequently, the Reichstag passed a general amnesty on 4 August 1920.[85] As Raeder admitted, a great many officers now left the navy because of the "unfair treatment" they had been given by the public and their feeling that the service would never regain its former position in Germany's armed forces.[86] For his part, Raeder pocketed his "complete" exoneration and claimed that he was free to resume his former position but that the "strain" and recent events made him glad to accept a position in the naval archives to assist in writing the official history of the naval war.[87] It was obviously in his interest to assume a less conspicuous post if he were to continue his career. Raeder was well aware that the new head of the navy, Rear William Michaelis, did not intend to give him his old position back, but he also knew that the navy did not intend to lose such an energetic and capable leader.

After the debacle of Kapp and the failed putsch by Hitler in 1923, he had come to the conclusion that neither the leadership nor the timing had been right for an attempt to overthrow the "parliamentary system." He believed that a right-wing government or a "dictator" supported by the people would be necessary to free Germany from what most "nationally oriented" conservative circles regarded as a totally unsuitable form of government. [88] It appeared more desirable if a strong leader would come to power legally, appointed by the Reich president "constitutionally, so to say."[89] In a letter to Noske before he took his new post, Raeder attempted to defend himself from charges of being disloyal and to indicate his support for the former defense minister as a "powerful personality" whom "all good national groups" and "the elite of the officer corps" would follow if circumstances were to "bring [Noske] again to a position of leadership."

> I am convinced that the way we blazed was the only way to gather together national strength and that in the future there will be no other way to make the Fatherland bloom again than to act in the common interest without regard to miserable party politics. . . .[90]

As he did with the 1917–1918 mutinies, Raeder blamed outside political influences for the navy's involvement in the Kapp Putsch. The navy had allowed itself to be misused for political purposes. The bitter lessons learned from these experiences made it clear to all members of the navy that "there was only one straight path—the path of complete abstinence from every type of party politics, and of unconditional loyalty to the state and to the government chosen by its people."[91] In Raeder's defense of Trotha, he testified that his superior had repeatedly emphasized that he wanted to keep all politics away from the navy and remain in his post in order to maintain the discipline and ensure that the service would remain intact in the face of all the turmoil. If the "leftist elements," particularly the deck and petty officers, had not put their own economic and political interests before their military responsibilities, then "the navy would have remained totally unaffected by the Kapp Putsch and, after the government returned, would have again served unified behind it." [92] This claim that the naval leadership's motives were only for the preservation of law and order represented another serious misjudgment of their men, who rejected the idea that the military should be neutral in the face of a coup. The notion that the armed forces were indifferent as to who held political power would have fatal implications for the development of the military as a "state within the state" and the response of the Wehrmacht to Hitler's "seizure of power in 1933."[93]

Trotha's actions continued to reverberate within the officer corps. Initially Rear Admiral William Michaelis had been reluctant to relieve Trotha; however, on 23 March 1920, in a discussion with Ebert, he was reassured that the government did not support a "trade union navy" and would give him a "free hand" to overcome the "chaos" and create a reliable naval force.[94] Michaelis now faced the problem of restoring the officers' authority over the deck officers and other NCOs who were still in charge. At the same time, Michaelis faced the equally daunting challenge of resolving the serious internal dissension among the officers.[95] Raeder felt that Michaelis was, "regrettably," not the type of personality to unify the officer corps and defend the navy's independence.[96] More important, he did not think that Michaelis had the support of the new defense minister, Otto Gessler.[97]

Raeder, like others, had naively hoped for Trotha's "rehabilitation," but when it became apparent that this was not going to happen, he began actively to champion other candidates. At one point, Raeder supported Levetzow—a remarkable misjudgment of the political situation following the events of March. For Raeder and others, Admiral Scheer also emerged as a possible interim chief, but he was allegedly rejected because he was on the Allied list of "war criminals."[98] In June 1920, Raeder reported to Levetzow that he had learned that the members of the Loewenfeld Brigade supported *Kapitan z. See* Dietrich Meyer-Quittlingen, whose appointment as navy chief would, he believed, lead to the navy's being placed under the army—an indication of Raeder's future struggles with the integration of the unruly elements of the "grey" or "brown" navy with the "blue" navy.[99]

The day that Raeder reported to his new position in the naval archives (1 July 1920), he informed Levetzow that Michaelis was going to remain as head of the navy, at least temporarily. He also advised Levetzow that, for the moment, it would not be appropriate to promote Scheer's candidacy, but he would keep Levetzow informed if the situation changed. Raeder feared that if Levetzow did anything more at this time, it might "disturb" Michaelis's "circle" and apparently might have repercussions for him. He now felt that Michaelis's remaining, at least over the short term, would be the navy's best hope, especially considering the future budget debates and the still burning issue of the war crimes trials demanded by the Allies—both of which represented "life or death" issues for the naval officer corps and the future of the navy.[100]

With the appointment of Admiral Paul Behncke as *Chef der Marine-leitung* on 31 August 1920, the navy successfully maintained its independence and the symbolic change from *"Admiralty"* to *"Marineleitung"* (Naval Command) satisfied those critics who wanted a clear break from any vestiges of the Imperial Navy. Behncke understood the political realities that the officers must accept if they expected the navy to exist as more than just a small coastal force. His most important task was to make the navy an "unconditionally secure and unified tool in the service of the constitutional government . . ." and to ensure the loyalty to the constitution from the oldest officer to the youngest sailor.[101] With Behncke's appointment, Raeder began a period of internal withdrawal from the levers of power, although, as his correspondence with Levetzow demonstrates, he stayed in close contact with the politics of the right-wing movement in Germany.

The first warship Raeder saw when he was a young boy was the *Musquito*, built by the British in 1851 and acquired by the Prussian navy in 1863. The ship was used as a cadet training sloop in the new Imperial Navy.

—*Bibliothek für Zeitgeschichte,* Stuttgart

Raeder's cadet training ship in the years 1895 and 1896, the *Gneisenau* (1879).

—*Bibliothek für Zeitgeschichte,* Stuttgart

In 1900 Raeder served as watch officer on the coastal defense ship *Aegir* (1895).
—*Bibliothek für Zeitgeschichte*, Stuttgart

In the summer of 1901, Raeder was the first officer on the Admiralty staff's training ship,
the *Aviso Grille* (1857). —*Bibliothek für Zeitgeschichte*, Stuttgart

Raeder was watch officer in October 1901 on board the *Kaiser Wilhelm der Grosse* (1899). —*Bibliothek für Zeitgeschichte,* Stuttgart

In 1905–1906, Raeder was the navigation officer on the coastal armored ship the *Frithjof* (1891). —*Bibliothek für Zeitgeschichte,* Stuttgart

In 1908–1909, Raeder served as the navigation officer of the armored cruiser *Yorck* (1904). —*Bibliothek für Zeitgeschichte,* Stuttgart

During fall 1909 exercises, Raeder served as the squadron's navigation officer on the coastal defense ship *Hildebrand* (1892). —*Bibliothek für Zeitgeschichte,* Stuttgart

Raeder was navigation officer on the kaiser's yacht *Hohenzollern* (1892) from September 1910 to September 1912. —*Bibliothek für Zeitgeschichte,* Stuttgart

Raeder served as chief of staff to the commander of the scouting forces, Admiral von Hipper, on the battle cruiser *Seydlitz* (1912), which served as Hipper's flagship from 1914 to 1917 (with the notable exception of the battle of Jutland). —*Bibliothek für Zeitgeschichte,* Stuttgart

Admiral Graf von Spee's cruiser squadron leaves Valparaiso, Chile, several days after its victory over the British at Coronel (1 November 1914). The three ships under way in the background are the *Scharnhorst* (1906), *Gneisenau* (1906), and the light cruiser *Nürnberg* (1906). —Naval Historical Center

Raeder's first sea command—from January 1918 to November 1918—was on board the light cruiser *Cöln* (1916). —*Bibliothek für Zeitgeschichte,* Stuttgart

Led by *Seydlitz* and the battle cruisers, the final voyage (19–21 November 1918) of the High Seas Fleet on their way to internment at Scapa Flow. —Naval Historical Center

Two of the six pre-dreadnought *Deutschland*-class battleships—the *Schleswig-Holstein* and the *Schesien* (both launched in 1906)—that were permitted by the Versailles treaty after World War I. —Naval Historical Center

The first *Panzerschiff,* the *Deutschland* (1931), in the Kiel Canal.
—*Bibliothek für Zeitgeschichte,* Stuttgart

The construction of the 10,000 "pocket battleship" *Deutschland,* which pioneered new welding techniques to save weight. The ship was commissioned in April 1933. —*Bibliothek für Zeitgeschichte,* Stuttgart

The light cruiser *Köln*, launched in 1928. Note the Nazi eagle on the stern and the pre-swastika naval war flag (the Nazi war flag was not introduced until 1935).
—Naval Historical Center

A navy Heinkel 60 floatplane, also designed for shipboard reconnaissance, overflies the *Köln*. Slow and poorly armed, the floatplane represented Raeder's failure to secure a modern naval air arm. —Naval Historical Center

The battleship *Scharnhorst* (1936) welcomes the returning *U-47* after its successful sinking of the *Royal Oak* in Scapa Flow in October 1939. —Naval Historical Center

Raeder's first super battleship (1939), the *Bismarck*'s official displacement was 35,000 tons. —*Bibliothek für Zeitgeschichte*, Stuttgart

A stern view of the *Bismarck*. —Naval Historical Center

Germany's first aircraft carrier, the *Graf Zeppelin*, launched in December 1938 and was more than 85 percent complete in 1939. Construction was stopped in April 1940 and resumed in March 1942, but the carrier was never completed.
—*Bibliothek für Zeitgeschichte,* Stuttgart

I want to preserve the smallest seeds so that when the time
comes, a useful tree will grow from it.

—*Adolf von Trotha, 1920*

3

Rebuilding the Navy: Raeder and the Reichsmarine, 1920–1928

The Naval Archives, 1920–1922

Given his central role in the Admiralty and his close association with
Trotha, Raeder and his supporters hoped that his *untertauchen*, "submerg-
ing," in the naval archives would avoid any further public scrutiny and
allow him to continue his naval career.[1] Although he looked forward to
the opportunity to resume his writing for the official history of the war
at sea, Raeder also prepared for a possible return to civilian life. His personal life was stressful; his first marriage had ended in divorce (he would
remarry before the end of the year, wedding the fiancée of one of his
fallen brothers). Both of his younger brothers had died in the war, one
on the eastern front, the other on the western—a heavy sacrifice for the
patriotic Raeder family. Although Raeder remained close-mouthed on
details of his personal life, these events must have only hardened his
resolve and his belief that these sacrifices could not have been made in
vain and that there was still a larger role for him to play. He enrolled at
Humboldt University with the goal of earning a doctorate in political science. Always practical, he also took a course in bookkeeping.[2]

Unlike the official army history, which was under civilian control, the
navy's official history was prepared under the direction of Vice Admiral
(Ret.) Eberhard von Mantey, the director of the Naval Archives since 1916
and the overall editor of the series. Its purpose went far beyond mere
descriptions or analyses of the operations of the Kaiserliche Marine.
The authors intended to paint a heroic picture of the naval war and

49

enshrine the positive accomplishments of the navy for posterity, as well
as to justify its continued existence.[3] As Mantey confided privately:

> History should not be written for the purpose of tearing down but for
> building up. Therefore, with marked failures, much must be done to cover
> them with love, because history must be constructive. . . . History writing
> must therefore be conceived as a part of building one's character. Not intel-
> ligence but character plays the [critical] role in war.[4]

Forbidden by the Treaty of Versailles to establish a naval war college,
Mantey also hoped to utilize the writing to serve as staff officer training.[5] This substitution of historical studies also served, in the absence of
practical preparations for war planning, to "prepare for war theoretically."[6]
It is not surprising then, particularly during the early days of the Republic,
that the navy repeatedly emphasized the importance of the writing of
history. In seeking to reaffirm the status it had enjoyed prewar in
Germany's bid for *Weltmacht,* the critical role of ideas and the navy's goal
to be a sea power would keep alive its hopes to rebuild the fleet.

The task of the writers was complicated by Tirpitz's efforts to justify his policies. In his 1919 memoirs, Tirpitz asserted that the High Seas
Fleet had been handicapped by its orders and should have been allowed
to go into battle as soon as possible. Tirpitz's criticism of the kaiser and
individual senior officers led to an open rift among the retired officers—
the spiritual leaders for the new Reichsmarine. Raeder was fully aware
of this internecine dispute and the threat it posed to the value of the tradition and history of the Imperial Navy, which had to be preserved if
it were to be of use to the new navy and maintain the unity of the officer corps.[7]

The rigid adherence to Tirpitz, as well a reluctance to risk any confrontation with the grand admiral and his supporters, precluded any
critical investigations of the basic strategic problems of the naval war or
alternative strategies.[8] Although contemporaries decried the "cult of
Tirpitz" and claimed that criticism of Tirpitz, "upon which not the light-
est shadow could fall," was "taboo" for Raeder, in fact he had a more
objective view of his mentor's legacy.[9] Although he acknowledged those
who attempted to justify Tirpitz's rejection of a strong, unified leadership
of the prewar Imperial Navy, Raeder privately disagreed; Tirpitz's "false
organization" had led to the navy's poor wartime leadership and performance.[10] He was fully aware of Tirpitz's strategic and organizational

failures and the overspecialization of the ships of a "high seas" fleet, whose mission concentrated on a decisive battle in the "wet triangle" of the North Sea. These thoughts, expressed by Tirpitz's foes and, in particular by Raeder's crewmate, Wolfgang Wegener, could not be openly admitted in the context of the politics of the Weimar period or in the Third Reich. He was fully aware that the official history lacked a critical, capstone work on the strategic problems of the navy in World War I. He hoped to write this final volume himself, once circumstances permitted a more objective evaluation of the naval war.[11] For Raeder, the legacy of Tirpitz and his spirit were essential to providing tradition and continuity and therefore the legitimacy of his own fleet ambitions.

The Writing of *Kreuzerkrieg:* The Continuing Evolution of Raeder's Strategic Thinking

Raeder's study of cruiser warfare closely matched his experience. Most of his sea duty had been spent in cruisers or the Scouting Forces, and he had known Count von Spee, whom he had met during his overseas tour in 1897–1898. The first volume of his *Der Kreuzerkrieg in den ausländ-ischen Gewässern*, published in 1922, dealt with the operations of Spee's cruiser squadron, including the successful engagement at Coronel on 1 November 1914 and his defeat at the Falklands in December 1914. Volume II, published in 1923, described the commerce raids of the light cruisers *Emden, Königsberg, Karlsruhe,* and *Geier.*[12] Although the number of ships sunk by Spee's forces (six warships and forty-two merchant-men) was minor compared to the losses caused by U-boats after 1916, Raeder noted the major impact on morale and prestige as a result of the brief cruiser war. The victory at Coronel and the successes of the *Emden* helped to shatter the myth of the invincibility of the Royal Navy and gave the Imperial Navy a sense of confidence and pride, which helped to overcome its lack of tradition and experience.[13]

Raeder's description of the cruiser war was carefully crafted to pay homage to Tirpitz. As did other writers, he corresponded regularly with Tirpitz as his work progressed.[14] On 10 July 1921, Raeder wrote to Tirpitz asking him if he would review the proofs for the first volume. In particular, he sought Tirpitz's comments on the introductory chapters that referenced the navy's (i.e., Tirpitz's) strategic principles in World War I.[15] On 16 August 1921, Raeder thanked Tirpitz for his help

and declared that he had "endeavored to pay justice to you to the full
extent." He also echoed the pro-Tirpitz argument that it was not the
navy but the politicians (especially Chancellor Bethmann-Hollweg) who
were responsible for the failure of the navy. Raeder supported the primacy of the battle fleet and the importance of seeking the decisive
battle. He also agreed with Tirpitz's advocacy of a unified command
once the war began and observed that during the navy's reorganization
in 1919–1920 he had worked hard to establish a unified command.[16]
Later, he wrote Tirpitz that he had endeavored "to integrate the valuable insights, which you gave me. . . ." He specifically noted that both the
High Seas Fleet and the overseas cruisers could have been used quite dif-
ferently if they had been directed under a unified command and a coordinated operations plan.[17]

In spite of the obligatory obeisance to Tirpitz, Raeder's study demonstrated his wide grasp of the issues involved in modern cruiser warfare,
including the complex international legal issues regarding the rights and
obligations of neutrals and belligerents alike. He had studied them
before the war, and they were also prominent in the writings of several
theorists with whom he was acquainted, particularly Daveluy. He also
had the opportunity to draw upon Julian Corbett's works, including his
Some Principles of Maritime Strategy (1911) which emphasized the importance of control of enemy sea communications. Additionally, Raeder utilized Corbett's official British naval history (1920), which includes some
of Corbett's illustrations along with his battle descriptions.[18] Building on
such studies, combined with the experiences and lessons he had observed
firsthand with the Scouting Forces, Raeder's examination of cruiser war
led him to formulate a uniquely German formula that was not based on
the traditional "either/or" battle-fleet-or-cruiser-fleet option that had characterized previous debates. Although he dutifully quoted Mahan in the
opening pages of his first volume, citing the principle that cruiser warfare alone could not have a decisive impact on the outcome of a war, he
did not preclude the role that cruiser warfare could play in an overall
national and naval strategy.[19]

The key to Raeder's strategic vision was his conception of all potential theaters as one interconnected whole in which simultaneous operations in different areas created a diversionary effect. Foreshadowing Raoul
Castex (*Théories stratégiques,* 1929–1935), who argued that the concept of

maneouvre made it possible to conduct an operation to bring strength against the decisive point, Raeder envisioned how a "weaker sea power" could create "a favorable situation."[20] At the same time, the dispersion of enemy forces created opportunities for achieving *Kräfteausgleich*, an equalization of forces, against both the enemy battle fleet and the warships sent to hunt the commerce raiders. Therefore, both cruiser warfare and commerce war and the role of the battle fleet were seen as part of the overall national maritime strategy.[21] He still affirmed Tirpitz's doctrine that, without a strong fleet behind it, a cruiser war with surface ships could fulfill only a secondary role. The "decisive battle" (Mahan) was still the ultimate goal of naval warfare, and forces should not be drawn from the battle fleet to support the cruiser war. At the same time, he incorporated Daveluy's idea that a commerce war could create a "diversion" that could provide relief to the battle fleet, especially in the first months of the war.[22]

The lessons Raeder gleaned from his studies and the course of the war on land and at sea, however, led him to different conclusions about the role of commerce war in the modern era. Although World War I had demonstrated British naval supremacy, it also had revealed the Royal Navy's weakness—its dependence upon its vast global sea communications. With the British forced to protect its far-flung empire, the Germans had an opportunity to seize the initiative and conduct a "strategic offensive," picking the time and place with a concentration of forces to achieve local superiority. Even assuming Germany's traditional numerical inferiority, its forces could either destroy the enemy's ability to wage war economically through the disruption or destruction of commerce or wear down the enemy's naval forces by attrition, thereby creating the conditions for a decisive fleet engagement.[23] The formulation of these ideas would take more concrete form in Raeder's development of his strategy after 1928.

In calling for an offensive strategy that recognized Germany's material and geographic weaknesses, Raeder recognized that the changing nature of maritime warfare required all the resources of a modern state. Along with Germany's other political and military leaders, he believed that the British sea blockade, the "hunger blockade" and the food shortages in the Great War, had led directly to the breakdown of morale at the front and at home. The dependence of modern war on the economic and industrial strength of nations underscored Clausewitz's dictum that war is a continuation of politics by other means and confirmed Raeder's view (as he had written in 1904) that the strategic preparations for war must begin in peacetime.[24] It was the role of the political leadership to establish the goals and make preparations to reach them in peacetime, whether building ships or acquiring the necessary bases. The fact that all industrialized powers, whether maritime or continental, were now dependent upon their overseas communications required a national maritime strategy—a combined warfare with air, land, and sea forces under joint command. In this concept of *Gesamtkrieg*, total war, victory would come not necessarily from the destruction of the enemy's forces but from the collapse of the enemy's economy—by definition *Wirtschaftskrieg*, an economic war.[25]

From his experience and research, Raeder noted the disruption and dislocation of troop movements and Allied shipping caused by the threat posed by Spee's ships, as well as the large number of warships diverted to search for his squadron and the lone raiders such as the *Emden* and *Karlsruhe*. He also concluded that, had Spee divided his forces and kept his largest units, the *Scharnhorst* and *Gneisenau*, together as a battle group (Daveluy), the disruption to commerce might have been more extensive and sustained.[26] Significantly, he saw the potential interaction between the operations of the squadron and the High Seas Fleet that created an opportunity for fleet operations in home waters. When the Germans had detected the detachment of the two British battle cruisers and then a third to hunt Spee, they realized that Hipper's Scouting Forces were now equal if not superior to Beatty's battle cruisers.[27] As a result, they attempted to take advantage of this and planned a second bombardment of the English east coast. This operation almost led to a clash between the two fleets—a missed opportunity that Raeder felt could have resulted in a smashing German victory and whittled down the Royal Navy, thereby making it more vulnerable for a future fleet engagement.[28]

As Hipper's chief staff officer, Raeder was also well aware of the acrimonious wartime debates over "so-called *Grosskrieg*" or "*Kleinkrieg*" and the search for alternatives. Hipper's support for deploying capital ships in the Atlantic to attack British commerce in late 1914 was not lost on Raeder, who saw the opportunity for such forces to provide cover for cruiser operations. It was evident that the navy had failed to take advantage of what Spee's cruiser squadron had all too briefly demonstrated.

To compensate for the lack of ships and bases, Raeder also felt that a better network of *Etappen* (communications and supply system), especially fitted out for cruiser warfare, would have provided more opportunities by forcing the enemy to disperse their forces, thereby affecting the balance of naval forces in European waters.[29] Raeder was also caustic in his assessment of the failure of both the political and military leadership to coordinate plans before 1914. Not only did the navy not know of the army's plans to invade France through Belgium, it never had a chance to discuss the most important prerequisite for conducting naval operations against England—the occupation of the Atlantic and Channel bases.[30]

For a successful strategic offensive in the economic war, the ability to quickly change operational areas and to appear simultaneously in multiple theaters—range and speed—were essential. At the same time, the attacker was on the strategic defensive. Any combat with inferior or even equal enemy warships, argued Raeder, must be avoided to maintain the maneuverability and speed required in such warfare. Any losses or battle damage could effectively end or curtail operations. The main forces operating in home waters were to operate "tactically offensive" to bind the enemy forces to the North Sea and surrounding waters. To undertake this type of warfare, both the cruisers and the fleet operating from home waters demanded a high degree of mobility, initiative, offensive spirit, and the courage to take risks. Neither the *Admiralstab* nor Spee, charged Raeder, had understood the real purpose of cruiser war, which was to sink or, even better, disrupt shipping and create the illusion that England could not defend its maritime communications. Spee's strategic failure at the Falklands in seeking military success instead of avoiding combat was understandable to Raeder, given Spee's "personal predisposition and training which like [that of] the majority of officers sought to engage the enemy's warships instead of continuing to attack enemy commerce."[31] Although he called attention to the misunderstanding of the art of commerce war and the interaction between cruiser warfare and the war in the North Sea, he did not extend his criticism to the prewar leadership and to Tirpitz—where it belonged.[32]

Raeder carefully sought publicly to profess allegiance to the Tirpitz dogma. However, other astute readers of *Kreuzerkrieg*, especially Germany's potential naval adversaries, took equally careful notice, when Raeder began rebuilding the navy under Hitler, of his published studies on cruiser warfare. Given his penchant for being circumspect, only an expert in naval strategy would have detected his veiled criticism of Tirpitz, but in 1938 an article in the French naval journal *La Revue Maritime* revisited his studies of cruiser warfare and attempted to draw conclusions for the development of Raeder's naval strategy. An exasperated Raeder wrote that this was precisely why historical studies such as his should be suppressed (to a later period, presumably after Germany had achieved its goals) lest they offer too much insight into German strategy and tactics to potential foes.[33] A British Naval Intelligence report in 1940 pointedly noted Raeder's criticism of the failure of the High Seas Fleet for not undertaking operations that would support Spee's cruiser operations.[34]

Raeder has never received due credit for having developed an independent strategic vision—one that differed from Tirpitz as well as Daveluy. This was, in part, a result of his strict adherence to the Tirpitz school for the reasons described above and his well-known opposition to Wegener's sharp criticism of Tirpitz, but also because he deliberately sought to obscure his true conclusions. Moreover, he left no comprehensive corpus of work, compared to his rivals.[35] In a footnote to his work in the archives, a surprised Raeder received an honorary doctorate on 31 May 1926, the tenth anniversary of Jutland, for the "scholarly merit" of his work, from the Christian Albrechts University in Kiel.[36] Raeder was as proud of this accomplishment as he was of his rank and, subsequently, included "Dr. Phil. h.c." in his title.

Inspector of Naval Education, 1922–1924

Raeder's concern for his immediate future ended on 1 July 1922 with his appointment as inspector of naval education, with the rank of rear admiral. This promotion brought with it the potential for continued advancement. Although he later remarked that this assignment was unexpected, his selection for the post clearly reflected the recognition that he was the best choice to be the navy's "schoolmaster."[37] Raeder's responsibility as inspector of naval education included the naval schools at Flensburg-Mürwick (line officers) and Kiel-Wik (engineer officers); the training ship *Berlin*, and the navy's sailing training ship, the four-masted schooner *Niobe*. He faced a unique challenge in dealing with the enlistment terms imposed by the Versailles treaty, which restricted officers to serve no more than twenty-five years and NCOs and enlisted men, no more than twelve years. In addition to their military training, the navy had to develop career training for the NCOs and enlisted men to prepare them for civilian jobs after they left the service. Under Raeder's leadership, the navy established vocational schools, and he took a personal role in developing the indoctrination course for the new instructors. In spite of the limited opportunities for promotion, these efforts improved morale and discipline, and Raeder believed that this training was successfully integrated with the men's military training.

Until he arrived in Kiel, the officer training programs for the Reichsmarine had been in disarray, with the basic directions and instructions "made up from scratch." He established training regulations and developed the curriculum for the officer candidates. This assignment provided him with the opportunity to put his stamp on the rebuilding of the new navy's officer corps and ensured that the lessons learned from the officers' failure of leadership in World War I would be addressed.[38] Shortly after his appointment, he confided to Levetzow that the "success of a sound rebuilding" of the navy was, more than ever, dependent upon the proper training of the its new leaders.[39] Raeder also urged the immediate resumption of foreign cruises to "show the flag" and provide the officers with the broadened perspective of overseas duty.[40]

Raeder closely followed each officer candidate and insisted on personally investigating each request for dismissal before a final decision was made.[41] He was determined that the Wehrmacht had to be strengthened as the protector of the Fatherland and the source of "moral and spiritual strength for future generations."[42] The "national task" of the naval officer corps was the promotion of the idea of *Seegeltung,* naval prestige, "without which the navy would degenerate into a mere coastal navy."[43] It was a matter of faith that the restrictions of the Versailles treaty would not remain in force forever and that the Reichsmarine was only a transitional entity; its new leaders would serve as the core of a future *Weltmachtflotte.*[44] Recognizing that the current political and economic situation would not permit the kind of material gain that the navy had experienced in 1892–1914, it was the duty of the officers to "do everything in our power to maintain and further develop the intellectual heritage" from the early period of Germany's attempt to become a global naval power.[45]

In an early concession to the Republic's democratic principles, qualified NCOs were allowed to apply to the officer corps. Raeder never supported this opportunity, believing officers "were born not trained." He also did not agree with the government's attempt to provide more opportunities to open the officer corps to enlisted men by allowing officer candidates without the *Abitur*—the requisite graduation requirement from the highest level of high school (Gymnasium)—to be given three years of service in which to qualify for admission to the officer corps. Behncke had hoped this practice would provide future officers with an intimate knowledge of the needs of their crews and gain "practical impressions" for leading their men. Raeder, however, feared that too much interaction within the ranks would create issues among impressionable young men that would later require "some effort" to overcome, and he also opposed the practice of combining officer candidates and enlisted personnel during the initial recruit training.[46]

During the winter of 1922–1923, Raeder reestablished an admiralty staff training program (the Treaty of Versailles required the abolition of the *Marine-Akademie*).[47] Although Raeder, like Tirpitz, was "almost fanatical" against any general staff organization, he recognized the need for the continuing professional training of officers. As a "subterfuge," Raeder developed a series of short courses for executive officers assigned as *Führergehilfen* (assistants to commanding officers)—a program that was expanded after 1926 to focus on naval history, strategy and tactics, and war games. His goal was to create a "staff technician" focusing on tactics and operational leadership.[48] To initiate this program, Raeder used his lecture notes and other materials from his studies at the Marine-Akademie to make up for the lack of any published material.[49] Compared to the prewar admiralty staff training, the scope of this training was very limited—a situation that Raeder would continue, to the detriment of the officer corps in World War II.

Although the officers could not publicly acknowledge their shortcomings, Raeder and many of his colleagues recognized that they had been "primarily" at fault in the collapse of the navy.[50] As Raeder emphatically stated, "Every superior officer in the navy silently swore that there should never again be a *November 1918* in the navy."[51] In confidential reports circulated through the navy, it was pointed out that the officers had failed to establish personal authority with their men and had ignored problems, focusing only on developing the blind obedience of the crews.[52] In the future, every officer was to be responsible for developing a close relationship with his men and their morale, promoting a spirit of camaraderie that was expected to ensure cohesiveness even under the most difficult circumstances. At the same time, the officers recognized that the conduct of the officers after the 1918 mutinies was inexcusable. The inaction of the officers in the face of the mutinies demonstrated a "fear of responsibility" and weakness. In the future, breaches of discipline would be dealt with severely.[53]

Raeder's principles of officer training called for "a firm but friendly discipline" to achieve a high standard of efficiency in the crews. This required a "well disciplined corps of officers and petty officers," as well as an officer corps that possessed "a modest but certain 'style' commensurate with the officer's rank." He insisted that the enlisted men be treated humanely, with dignity, and those officers who disciplined their subordinates in a humiliating manner were subject to severe action, including dismissal. Only when the officers learned the meaning of discipline for themselves, however, could they expect it from their men. The spectacle of officers being arrested by their own men in 1918 and 1920 led Raeder to emphasize the importance of developing character, dependability, and a sense of duty in the enlisted men. Technical training was secondary. "Men fight, not ships," the old adage of Admiral Albrecht von Stosch, the Imperial Navy's first chief, was firmly embraced by Raeder.

For Raeder, merely imposing discipline was not enough. Leaders needed to explain *why* obedience was required, and to do so through their own exemplary conduct and firmness. Raeder believed the true leader must deny himself luxuries and hollow amusements in order to lead by example. He blamed the revolution and the new republican government for creating conditions that increased the challenges facing the officer. In addition to the economic dislocations of the war and postwar inflation, Raeder decried the "subsequent distortion of social life . . . in certain customs and manners alien to our German way of life." Jazz, modern dance, pacifism, Bolshevism, social liberalism, etc., were all aspects of a cultural revolution that Raeder abhorred. He often felt disappointed when he tried to emphasize the simpler life and its values to a generation for whom "glamour and fashion often outweighed my words."

Raeder's goal was to create a "distinctive esprit de corps"—what he referred to as an "outward and inward navy style" that included strong character building and a strict moral code, especially as it related to marriage—as vital parts of the officer's development. One of his basic tenets in developing a comprehensive training program was his emphasis on fostering a firm religious conviction. Since the Weimar constitution, as Raeder lamented, did not permit officers to require their men to attend church services, he set a personal example by attending church regularly and asking his officers to assist him in establishing this as a custom for all hands. His emphasis on wearing his uniform as much as possible and adhering rigidly to dress regulations contributed to his reputation as a stiff, old-school Prussian officer.[54] This distinct "Raeder style" and his attempt to create a "navy family" reflected his patriarchal and conservative tone that, after his appointment as navy chief in 1928, allowed him to impress his views on the entire service.

Raeder was also keenly aware of other tensions that threatened the unity of the officer corps. He acknowledged the "inequities" between the line officers, engineer officers, and other officer grades (e.g., the medical corps) that had existed in the Kaiserliche Marine and how these differences required "adjustment" to create a more unified officer corps (albeit not with the success he claimed).[55] The officers' loss of authority after the Kapp Putsch and the assimilation of former naval *Freikorps* also posed a considerable challenge to the re-establishment and maintenance of discipline. After 1920, two navies existed—the "blue" and the "gray" (or "brown"). The "blue" consisted of those sailors who had remained with the navy following the chaos of 1918–1920, while the "gray" included the shore-based units consisting of the naval brigades. The latter's lack of discipline contributed to poor relations with supporters of the new state, who regarded the navy as antirepublican, if not a hotbed of radical right-wing activists.[56] The need to provide a program to teach young officers their duties and obligations "in the new State" was as immediate a challenge to Raeder as the need to train personnel who had no shipboard experience. The behavior of some of the first officer candidates at the *Marineschule* (most of whom were former brigade members) resulted in a Reichstag investigation into allegations that the navy was making a deliberate attempt to instill the "old spirit" through dismissing former enlisted men who did not hold the correct political views (i.e., a right-wing nationalistic orientation).[57]

Although the navy sought to retain as many as possible of the nationally minded and right-wing oriented of the former brigade members who had demonstrated their military worth, there was no shortage of volunteers—in spite of the twelve-year service requirement. In the middle 1920s, Raeder noted that 30,000 to 40,000 men reported annually to the Kiel Naval Depot alone, "of whom barely 1,000 could be accepted." With these limitations and the intent to enlist only "politically reliable" candidates, the navy developed an extremely detailed selection process.[58] The Social Democrat Party complained that the navy rejected republican-minded candidates, as well as "systematically eliminating every republican from the navy," but the navy argued that this was an "absolute necessity" to keep the troops free from any "party" influences. Questions as to a candidate's political affiliations were necessary because of what the service claimed were ongoing communist attempts to infiltrate the armed forces.[59]

The ongoing antimilitary attacks of the left-wing parties and pacifist organizations reinforced the navy's belief that any applicant associated with these groups was not patriotic enough to serve. As Raeder explained after the war, "People who never again want war cannot possibly wish to become soldiers.[60] One-quarter of the officer candidates' fathers were navy or army personnel or civilian employees of the military, while the others consisted of those from the same solid upper-middle-class social strata that the Imperial Navy had sought to attract before World War I.[61] Under these circumstances, the navy was able to ensure the homogeneity of the officer corps and support Raeder's ideal of creating a "navy family."[62]

The initial importance assigned to the navy's land formations reflected the political unrest of the times and was regarded as a "necessary evil" that distracted the navy's leaders from the primary task of rebuilding a viable naval force. This became particularly acute after the French occupation of the Ruhr in 1923 and the devastating inflation that followed. It was during this period that the military secured secret funds from the government to build their forces against internal and external threats and enlisted the support of right-wing paramilitary organizations to supplement their forces.[63] In spite of his problems with the political indiscretions and independence of former brigade members (such as Loewenfeld), Raeder appreciated their discipline and fighting abilities.[64] On 30 November 1923, Raeder praised them for "saving" Kiel from a communist uprising.[65]

In 1923, following the collapse of Hitler's coup in Munich, Raeder believed that the chances of a civil war or a "national freedom struggle" against the Treaty of Versailles had become a remote possibility, as were his hopes for a dictator who would dissolve the republican constitution. He disapproved of the Hitler Putsch and Ludendorff's participation and believed that it had "sabotaged the building of a *Rechtsdirektorium*—a right-wing "directorship"—which he believed was already in process by legal means." The creation of a coalition of "national" forces and the achievement of a majority in the Reichstag was more likely to create the desired "constitutional revision" than another "illegal action" against the government.[66] A few months later in January 1924, Raeder confided to Levetzow (who kept Raeder up-to-date on the Right's political maneuverings) that he did not believe a dictatorship could bring about the "constitutional revision" as long as the "*economic* foundations for rebuilding were not created."[67] Raeder's political views at this time were not dissimilar to those of Tirpitz (and Trotha), who sought to collect all the forces on the right and create a dictatorship possibly under Tirpitz's leadership, or, at the least, with his participation in a new government.[68]

Raeder was supportive of Tirpitz's efforts in early 1924 to persuade the army chief, Hans von Seeckt, to form a nationalist dictatorship independent of the Reichstag. Raeder's hopes that the increased representation of the German National People's Party (DNVP) in the elections of spring 1924 (which won Tirpitz his seat in the Reichstag) would result in their taking over the government and "end the flirting" with the Social Democrats, went for naught as the DNVP decided to carry out a policy of parliamentary obstructionism rather than participate in forming a new cabinet.[69] In spite of his professed "non-political" role, Raeder closely followed the day-to-day political maneuverings whose outcome would determine the navy's ability to rebuild its forces once the economy stabilized.

Commander of the Light Naval Forces of the North Sea, 1924–1925, to Chief of the Baltic Naval Station, 1925–1928

In September 1924, Raeder assumed command of the Light Forces in the North Sea—an assignment that he regarded as an important step in his professional advancement. He also saw an opportunity to "save *Seefahrt*" (the navy's maritime mission) and thereby restore the inner solidarity of the navy that had been overly preoccupied with domestic issues.[70] Joining the fleet during its maneuvers, Raeder's command included the old light cruiser *Hamburg,* the obsolete small cruiser *Arcona,* and the Second Torpedo Boat Squadron. Raeder's second sea command, however, was to be short-lived. In January 1925, Raeder assumed command of the Baltic Naval Station at Kiel and a promotion to vice admiral. Initially, he was reluctant to take this position, concerned that his career reflected more of the experience of a "desk admiral" than some of his rivals who had held more sea commands.[71]

Raeder did not inherit an easy situation in Kiel. He had to face constant criticism from the left-wing parties, including the Communist Party, which had strong support among the workers. At the same time, the patriotic and nationalist parties watched Raeder closely for any actions that appeared to curry favor with those parties whom they blamed for Germany's defeat.[72] The SPD's control of the local government and Raeder's lifetime nemesis, the leftist, antimilitary *Schleswig-Holsteinische Volkszeitung,* led him to initiate a vigorous campaign to cultivate the navy's supporters while fending off the often virulent attacks of its critics. His success in this careful balancing act increased his confidence in his own political skills. Although the effects of the Kapp Putsch had "largely died away," Raeder acknowledged the tensions that remained in Kiel. Later, in spite of the many difficulties that he had to deal with "again and again," Raeder would reflect upon this assignment as "one of the most rewarding of my entire career."[73]

Raeder's predecessor, Vice Admiral Ernst von Gagern, had also struggled with those officers who had refused to adjust to the new state, as well as those critics who were quick to label them as reactionaries.[74] In addition to the all-too-frequent lapses of judgment on the part of some officers (e.g., celebrating the kaiser's birthday), the navy's relations with right-wing organizations such as the *Bund Deutscher Marineverein* (BDM), the *Kaiserliche Yacht Club* (KYC), and the *Marine-Offizier-Verband* (MOV) were a constant source of irritation to republican supporters. Immediately after assuming command, Raeder established strong relationships with these organizations (including the Skagerrak Club), hoping to provide "a common meeting place between the naval officers and civilian circles."[75] The BDM was the largest of the naval societies, with 225 chapters with over 32,500 members nationwide. As fervent advocates of

Germany's drive for sea power, they represented a propaganda vehicle for the Reichsmarine and, through their youth organizations, a source of patriotic young men. As carriers of the traditions of the Imperial Navy, Raeder saw these groups as the best possibility of erasing the service's tarnished reputation, in spite of criticism over their right-wing nationalistic sympathies.[76]

Raeder's support of the KYC led to charges that active officers were illegally members of an "openly" antirepublican organization. One of the more "unfortunate" (Raeder) incidents occurred in 1926, during the dedication ceremony for the KYC's new clubhouse, when the vice commodore of the club, Prince Heinrich of Prussia, proposed a toast to his brother, Kaiser Wilhelm II, and then ordered the navy band to play "Heil dir im Siegerkranz," the forbidden national hymn. As chief of the naval station, Raeder was held responsible for a violation of the navy's political neutrality. Raeder condemned the playing of the hymn but justified the toast for the kaiser with the argument that the ex-kaiser was still the honorary commodore of the KYC, and that the prince had not attacked the "present state" or promoted the monarchy. Raeder defended his decision not to leave the clubhouse with the excuse that the event was not public.[77] The Defense Ministry felt that the officers should have left but decided that it would be politically inadvisable to admit any infraction and refused to censure Raeder.[78] A year and a half later, the attacks against the KYC and its association with the navy were renewed, and the new defense minister, Wilhelm Groener, appointed in January 1928, demanded that the KYC change its name. When the club refused, he ordered Raeder to work out a financial settlement over its loss of membership.[79] Raeder then formed the navy's own yacht club—the *Marine-Regatta-Verein*—which, however, still maintained a sporting and social relationship with the KYC.[80]

Raeder also defended the navy's ties to the Marine-Offizier-Verband, founded in November 1918 to assist former officers and maintain contact between inactive and active officers. The MOV also claimed to be an "apolitical" organization serving its members' economic interests and the "preservation of tradition"; however, many of its members were closely involved with right-wing organizations and celebrated nationalist and monarchist events. The MOV also assumed the role of the guardian of the officer corps' integrity, prescribing standards of conduct and political views. The ostracizing of several officers who professed support for pro-republican parties brought the MOV into conflict with republicans who accused it of being a "political" organization.[81] Unlike the KYC, Raeder and the Defense Ministry were able to avoid a broader investigation of its association with right-wing organizations and involvement in political demonstrations, and active officers continued their membership.[82]

A more serious issue for Raeder was the navy's relationship with right-wing paramilitary groups. Although the government had initially sanctioned the secret recruitment and training of volunteers from these groups in the wake of the French occupation of the Ruhr in 1923, the government had ordered such contacts dissolved in 1926.[83] Raeder, however, regarded the navy's contacts with paramilitary groups as necessary to nourish the *Wehrhaftmachung,* "war spirit," and the "patriotic feeling of the people."[84] Shortly after he became station chief, the navy's use of short-term volunteers became public during a budget hearing. Since they were not receiving training for duty at sea, a Social Democratic deputy inquired as to the intended use of such forces, assuming that the "explanation [was] probably in the dark realm of internal politics, perhaps a future Putsch."[85] Although the navy managed to cover up the enlistment of these short-term volunteers, Raeder was now personally subjected to a major attack by the SPD. The SPD charged that there was a "growing influence" on the navy from these radical groups in Kiel and asked for an official investigation into the extent of the navy's and Raeder's association with them. In December 1926, the SPD accused a number of active officers (notably Captain Wilhelm Canaris and Captain Loewenfeld, Raeder's chief of staff at Kiel) of having supported Hitler's 1923 abortive Putsch and the illegal selling of government property in order to obtain funds for proscribed activities, and even of having plotted to assassinate the army chief, Hans Seeckt.[86]

Raeder was fully aware that his predecessor had negotiated with right-wing organizations in the summer and fall of 1923 (including Ehrhardt's notorious *Organisation Consul,* which had ties to Hitler's fledgling National Socialist party). Given the seriousness of these charges, he asked the Defense Ministry to intervene, admitting that the navy had been forced to rely on such outside organizations because the military was simply not strong enough to handle domestic conflicts, much less any external threats. He insisted that all formations were subordinated to military authority and closely supervised. He denied any involvement in a conspiracy against Seeckt but acknowledged that the navy had transported (but not sold) military equipment to Denmark in order to avoid the Allied Military Control Commission.

Raeder informed Berlin that he had initiated a letter-writing campaign with prominent Kiel citizens to protest that the anti-navy campaign was undermining the "confidence in the reliability of the *Reichswehr* . . . as a firm proven supporter of the state and its constitution." Any attempts to link him with any illegal activities were without foundation, and he failed to understand how the navy's "defensive measures" against a vigorous foreign espionage system and communist infiltration tactics "could be labeled as an activity [directed] against the interests of the Republic." He also declared that he had expressly forbidden any association with Ehrhardt. He personally guaranteed "from my deepest convictions that the Reichswehr in its present composition and situation is an especially reliable and firm supporter of the state." Raeder emphasized that the sole criterion in the selection of recruits and their training was the development of capable soldiers. "Questions of whether a soldier is monarchist or republican . . . play no role at all—quite contrary to the constant assertions of certain circles." Although he had informed his staff in January 1926 that he wanted no association with any of these groups, he was prepared to enlist individuals who would be required to swear an oath to the constitution. His troops, he remarked, were proud "in the knowledge of being the only really firm and reliable defenders of the state." The Reichswehr, he insisted, must rely on its own forces, which would be sufficient for any domestic unrest if all troops performed their duties. The soldier must remember his responsibility and avoid all words or actions that might possibly reflect on his readiness to defend the state.[87]

In early 1927, the high treason trial of the navy's former undercover agents exonerated Raeder and found no evidence to justify legal action against any naval officers or any proof of any association between the naval station and Ehrhardt.[88]

This publicity over ties with right-wing organizations came at a particularly inopportune time for the navy. In 1927, the Reichstag began an acrimonious debate over the navy's first major postwar construction program (the *Panzerschiff*)—and the SPD refused to appropriate one cent for the new ship until the navy was "cleaned of fascist elements." They refused to accept the results of the trial and published new evidence demonstrating that the government had been unable to stop the various right-wing activities of Ehrhardt and other reactionaries with the military.[89] Already reeling from a major scandal involving the navy's use of secret funds for illegal rearmament (see chapter 4), the navy now faced widespread mistrust. These complaints against Raeder and the navy would resurface in the autumn of 1928 during the debate over his appointment as navy chief and almost jeopardized his future as well as the rebuilding of the fleet.

As excellent as the state of the entire navy is today, so have I
unfortunately determined that as a result of the ill-fated
Lohmann-Affair . . . the navy is for almost everyone, even
those quite well disposed toward us, a red flag.

—*Erich Raeder, 10 October 1928*

4

Chief of the Republican Navy, 1928–1933

Raeder's Appointment as *Chef der Marineleitung*

Raeder's rise to the leadership of the navy was a direct result of the
aftermath of the Lohmann Affair, which exposed the navy's use of secret
funds to support clandestine rearmament. To its foes, this scandal reaf-
firmed mistrust of the navy's policies and its questionable support of the
Republic and threatened the building of its new capital ships. Factional
strife now threatened Raeder's final ascent to the pinnacle of command
—and his ambition to begin the navy's second attempt to become a sea
power. His eventual appointment and success in restoring the navy's
soiled reputation gave him a chance to establish his strict authority over
the *Marineleitung* (Naval Command) and a renewed sense of his political acumen.

The Lohmann Affair had its roots during the 1923 Ruhr Crisis, when
special funds were provided to the military for rearmament. The navy's
funds were under the direction of Captain Walter Lohmann, chief of the
Sea Transportation Division, who subsequently diverted them to other
projects that included weapons procurement and development. Among
his other enterprises, he founded or supported various sports clubs and
commercial and shipping companies, among them a film company.[1] In
early August of 1927, the press published accounts of alleged misuse of
government funds and treaty violations, and an official inquiry was
begun. Although the government and the Defense Ministry managed
to restrict the scope of the investigation and ultimately declared that

all funds and projects had been eliminated, the navy's critics sensed a cover-up and suspected that there were more sinister political purposes behind Lohmann's activities.[2]

This debacle had a number of significant consequences for the Republic and the navy. First, Otto Gessler, the defense minister, and then later the navy chief, Admiral Hans Zenker, were forced to resign their posts. The new defense minister, Wilhelm Groener, promised to extirpate all the remnants of the "Lohmann System" from the navy and asked that the Reichstag deputies not let "this business" affect their judgment of the navy. He also pledged that neither the navy nor the army would be involved in such activities again and gave his personal guarantee that no more secret funds existed.[3]

Much of Groener's damage control achieved its desired effect. Certain activities were allowed to secretly continue, including the development of U-boats, airplanes, and torpedo boats. Significantly, the exposure of Lohmann's rearmament activities led to a coalition between the defense minister, the chancellor, and the governmental bureaucracies responsible for military and budget affairs, who now regulated secret rearmament behind the back of the Reichstag.[4] From this point on, the military's antirepublican posture (i.e., the rejection of parliamentary control) and its revisionist goals were combined with the government's acceptance of the Reichswehr's overall ambitions to create a united front that would circumvent and ultimately free Germany from the Versailles *Diktat*.[5] For Raeder, the lessons of these "well meaning" attempts to evade the treaty restrictions were clear.

> I assumed my new office with the firm conviction to travel the road of unquestionable correctness, in an absolutely loyal and well defined relationship to the state and its government. Nor would I permit any deviation by any other member of the navy.[6]

Rumors of Zenker's potential successor as navy chief began to circulate early in 1928. In March, Levetzow heard rumors that Raeder and Hermann Bauer were the top choices. Levetzow wrote to Raeder, praising him for his vigorous leadership as chief of the Baltic naval station that had won him the confidence of the officer corps.[7] Raeder's response to Levetzow was coy and calculated. He doubted whether Zenker would resign and averred that this was unfortunate because, in spite of the avowed respect he had for him, he thought Zenker was not a "fighter by nature." A strong leader was necessary if the navy's interests were to be defended from the army. Moreover, his repeated efforts to convince Zenker of the need for "strong personalities" among his staff had only brought a "definitely unfriendly response." Raeder went on to claim that Zenker's staff was opposed to him [Raeder] since they were "quite aware" that his appointment would mean considerable changes. Thus, he was under no illusions over his chances of being appointed. "I know too well that if Admiral Zenker is asked, he will recommend Admiral Bauer as his successor."

Although it was clear that Raeder regarded himself as the most suitable candidate, he played down his interest, stating that he was satisfied with his current post, where he had the firm support of his officers and had made considerable progress among civilian circles. Raeder was well aware that these accomplishments were exactly the qualities required of the new navy chief.[8] Levetzow, as Raeder expected, began to lobby for Raeder, referring to him as the "best officer that the navy has . . . who can still bring the old schooling to the leadership of the navy."[9] By August, Raeder became concerned that too much "politicking" on his behalf might backfire, and he warned Levetzow not "to direct General Groener's attention to me once more." He felt that everything was progressing well and feared that Groener might "become suspicious if he were [again] reminded."[10]

At the beginning of September 1928, Groener met with Raeder to discuss his views on "political and military affairs."[11] After this meeting, Groener decided to choose Raeder. Although Groener had been advised that Zenker's resignation and Raeder's appointment could be settled "quietly," quite the opposite happened.[12] Even before the official announcement, the SPD's wire service announced Zenker's resignation, with Raeder as his probable successor. Immediately a number of newspapers began to criticize Raeder. The *Berliner Morgenpost* asked, "The Imperial Admiral, should he become Chief of the Republican Navy?"[13] The Communist *Rote Fahne* labeled Raeder as a "fascist," while the *Berliner Tageblatt* claimed that Raeder had been the real "*Spiritus Rector*" in the Admiralty's support of the Kapp Putsch. The press also rehashed the series of incidents in Kiel involving members of the imperial family as examples of Raeder's monarchist proclivities.[14] The earlier charges against Raeder as responsible for fostering ties with right-wing reactionary associations also resurfaced, arousing "serious misgivings" among those who were alarmed by what they regarded as the navy's lack of support, if not hostility, against the Republic.[15]

The intensity of these attacks led Groener to doubt whether Raeder's candidacy could be salvaged. According to Raeder, Zenker also decided that Raeder was too tainted with politics and should withdraw.[16] The Hermann Müller (SPD) government closely monitored the press and expressed concern over the potential political difficulties if the charges against Raeder were proved true.[17] Groener assured the chancellor's office that Raeder had been chosen because he was "politically, in every way, a very sensible and moderate man."[18] The question remains why the Defense Ministry had not anticipated the outcry against Raeder. His critics had anticipated his selection as navy chief and had vigorously denounced him as belonging to the antidemocratic clique of high-ranking naval officers who continually throttled any liberal tendencies among the younger officers. The naming of Raeder, they claimed, would be another setback for the "new [i.e., republican] direction" of the military and the need for "democratic-minded" younger officers in the navy.[19]

Raeder realized his precarious situation, but he was also aware of the intense pressure on Groener to support him. The conservative press had already criticized Groener's inability to oppose "the growth of republican arrogance" in June 1928, when he had forced officers to resign from the KYC.[20] In late September, Raeder decided to force the issue and informed the Defense Ministry that he intended to resign to spare the navy and Groener any further embarrassment. Groener's investigator, Captain Friedrich Götting, reassured Raeder that these attacks, which contained "only a little truth," would not change the minister's mind. Götting recommended that Groener emphasize that Raeder was not a monarchist, but a "thoroughly reliable supporter of the constitution who is, after the most careful consideration, its best possible choice for *Chef der Marineleitung.*"[21]

As evidence of Raeder's political suitability, Götting cited a speech in which Raeder acknowledged that the navy's nurturing of a positive attitude toward the Republic had involved "considerable effort" and, understandably, new changes could not be created overnight. In the turmoil that had swept Germany after the revolution, officers as well as enlisted men had failed to adjust to the new times. Many either chose to leave as a result of their personal convictions or were discharged after errors in judgment. Raeder admitted the mistakes in the military's secret rearmament. He realized that these activities had aroused much public suspicion against the military.[22] Under President Hindenburg's leadership, however, the Wehrmacht had made great strides in developing the "proper attitudes." The Reichswehr, he insisted,

> is today . . . an absolutely reliable instrument of power, which will do its duty, regardless of whether it is used to defend the border or to maintain law and order internally. *Who holds this instrument in his hands controls the power in the state.* But if the state is to exist, this power must only be exercised by the constitutional authorities. No one else must be allowed to wield it, not even the political parties; the Wehrmacht must be entirely non-political, composed only of solders that decline to take part in any political activity.[23]

Göttling's support did not completely satisfy Groener. He was concerned about Raeder's actions during an incident involving the use of the navy yacht *Nixe* (1886) for an "eel research" trip. This trip was, in fact, part of an Imperial Navy custom in which the station chief and guests would enjoy a cruise through the Kaiser Wilhelm Canal, highlighted by a party ashore to sample the eel cuisine of local restaurants. It was during one of these trips—which, by "coincidence," had been held on Prince Heinrich of Prussia's birthday—that one of the speakers called for a toast to the prince. The press criticized this as an example of Raeder's "blatant monarchism." Götting defended Raeder, arguing that "in this spontaneous moment, he naturally joined the others" in saluting a brother officer. Although Götting argued that Raeder was not serving in an "official capacity," Groener asked why he failed to ensure that no political demonstration would take place. The fact that the trip was held on the prince's birthday was further proof of what Groener regarded as an act of appalling indiscretion (a year later, Raeder planned another "eel research" cruise on Prince Heinrich's birthday that the Defense Ministry curtly told him was "politically insupportable").[24]

Raeder repeatedly denied any charges of political involvement on the part of himself and his staff, and he boasted that he had educated his officers and enlisted men to be loyal to the constitution, "so they now hold uniformly the correct views. That was not the case at the onset." In a more telling comment, he claimed that he considered himself a supporter of the state "a thousand times more valuable than all those loud propagandists, who in reality only intend to make us loathe the Republic." Raeder also initiated the support of prominent citizens to campaign on his behalf, which played a major role in Groener's support. A letter to the *Frankfurter Zeitung* on 30 September 1928 from a well-known university professor in Kiel and respected republican attested to Raeder's unquestionable loyalty and provided the Defense Ministry with the opportunity to point to Raeder's favorable reputation in "republican circles."[25] At the beginning of October 1928, Groener held a press conference to support Raeder's appointment. Although the reaction was generally favorable, the antimilitary factions remained unimpressed. His opponents still grumbled that the question of whether Raeder was a "convinced republican" or not was still open to question.[26] One newspaper printed Groener's defense of Raeder under the sarcastic headline, "Admiral Raeder Is Even Enamored with the Republic."[27]

The most important factor in Raeder's favor proved to be Groener's personal credibility. His appointment as defense minister had been popular with the Left, and he was regarded as a "professed republican" who was sincere in his efforts to purge the military of its "unsatisfactory elements."[28] Raeder acknowledged his debt to Groener, noting that Groener had fulfilled his promise to energetically intervene for him, declaring "that he would stand or fall with me."[29] Raeder, however, had no illusions about the challenges ahead. Asking Tirpitz for his blessing, he noted:

> It is perfectly clear to me what a monstrously difficult office I am undertaking, but I do not shrink from the challenge, since I spoke with Herr Minister [Groener] in great detail, and received the impression that I could work with him quite well, and that he was determined to represent forcefully the interests of the navy.[30]

As the new navy chief, Raeder faced an "unlimited mistrust by the entire government, and the Reichstag" as well as the press. The Lohmann Affair further reinforced the negative attitudes toward the navy from its early history in the Republic. The constant attacks on the navy and the military in general, justified or not, reinforced Raeder's conviction to exercise a strong, unified control over all aspects of naval policy and operations. He resolved to be "thick skinned" against the "vulgarities"

of the left-wing, antimilitary elements.[31] He was prepared to accommodate any situations or individuals as long as the navy's long-term interests were advanced. The critical issue, as he shared with Tirpitz, was
whether the SPD—motivated by "a great fear of the Communists"—
would be finally compelled to clarify their position vis-à-vis the military. Raeder assumed that the SPD would join the Communists in
opposing the building of the Panzerschiff, thus "dragging the question
of approval or disapproval into party politics."[32]

Tirpitz was pleased that the navy was in good hands, and he concurred that the present situation was especially unfavorable for the navy.
While public opinion favored the maintenance of the army within the
limits of the Treaty of Versailles, "it was quite different with the navy."
Raeder's most important task, emphasized Tirpitz, was to educate the
public. Germany must utilize all of its possibilities, however meager,
under the limitations of the Versailles treaty to rebuild its fleet. He concurred that it was not a question of whether the money expended for
the new Panzerschiff would be better spent on the army, but the principle of rearmament itself. Although the navy's new construction presented Germany's political foes with the best possible target to attack the
navy and the military in general, any weakening of the country's resolve
to build the Panzerschiff would mean an irreparable loss of respect
before the entire world.[33] A major political player in Weimar's right-
wing movements (and actively involved in efforts to overthrow the
Republic), Tirpitz offered political counsel that was not lost on Raeder,
who fully appreciated the prestige factor of naval policy.[34]

Raeder had been an active participant in Tirpitz's prewar propaganda campaign, and he believed that the restoration of the navy's prewar popularity was a precondition for any rebuilding of the fleet.
Germany's Seegeltung could not be accomplished without a fundamental reorganization of the navy. Until Raeder addressed what he regarded
as the glaring organizational issues that had hampered the Imperial
Navy, the navy would be unable to gain support for its new ships or
restore its tarnished reputation. "Only through the combining of all
energies could the required striking power of the navy be secured and
its interests forcefully represented with the government, the Defense
Ministry and the financial administration."[35]

Characterized as "a fanatic of correctness, absolute loyalty and sub-ordination," Raeder carried on the tradition of Tirpitz's *Ressortegoismus* to its culmination.[36] Like Tirpitz, who listened carefully to what his colleagues had to say and then imposed his decisions in an authoritarian manner, Raeder resisted the slightest internal or external challenge to his strict authority and leadership to the very end of his tenure in office. Raeder regarded anyone who disagreed with him as his personal enemy —another characteristic he shared with Tirpitz.[37]

Raeder had delineated his administration's "guiding principles" at his first meeting with Groener in September 1928. Foremost on his list had been the absolute necessity of a firm, unified, and unrestricted command of the Marineleitung over all operations and personnel. He reserved the right to participate personally in all Defense Ministry discussions involving naval affairs. He also demanded the independence of the navy from the army command in every aspect—"matters of command, dis-cipline, maintenance, and particularly personnel."[38] Within a year of taking command, he issued his "authoritarian" (by his own account) directives and guidelines for the navy's operations as well as officer train-ing. These official instructions were to remain in effect until 1943, even though by then the navy had increased dramatically in size and had been completely altered in structure and scope. A contributing factor to his strict administration may have been his lack of seagoing command. Except for his short sea commands in World War I and as commander of the Light Naval Forces of the North Sea (often overlooked by his-torians), his career had mostly been spent in staff positions, leading some to regard him as a "desk admiral."[39] Raeder's justification for his actions was "the commander alone is accountable for his actions to his superiors."[40] He held himself answerable only to the head of state and the defense minister. Raeder's personality, his assessment of the navy's failings since 1914, and the deplorable situation of the navy both polit-ically and militarily in the Weimar Republic demanded absolute loyalty and recognition of his authority.

Above all, Raeder sought to suppress any criticism of his policies or any aspect of Germany's naval history. The officer corps was to think as one; he alone would be responsible for all evaluations, decisions, and orders. Arguments, which were contrary to his views, were either modified—without discussion—to Raeder's way of thinking, or he would remove the person who differed from him from his office.[41] One of his close colleagues, Admiral Kurt Assmann, charged Raeder with being "ruthless" against officers who were too independent or opposed his opinions. Assmann argued that Raeder did not like the "free expression" of ideas, since he was inclined to order what he regarded as correct.[42] Raeder was also apt to regard outspoken criticism as a breach of naval discipline and personal trust.[43] Active officers, as well as retired officers, would quickly discover Raeder's wrath if they disobeyed or disagreed with him.[44]

Raeder later denied that he had tried to suppress dissent, contending he had "required" everyone to express their views openly. All differences of opinion, however, or even the manner in which debates were conducted, were to be kept strictly confidential. Once a decision had been made, Raeder demanded absolute loyalty. The importance of suppressing dissension in the officer corps was essential, because the navy, in Raeder's experience, had to face a hostile and suspicious group of politicians and press and must always present a united front.[45] His supporters, such as Admiral Friedrich Ruge, argued that Raeder's efforts to "foster cohesion and harmony" among the officers were successful to a "considerable extent."[46] This claim is only partially true, given the ongoing internal debate over Raeder's rearmament plans, both before and after 1939, and his heavy-handed treatment of the engineering officers when they sought equality of status with the line officers.

Raeder's values and concepts became those of the navy, and vice versa. The Reichsmarine was "his" navy and the stamp of his personality had an impact on every aspect of navy life.[47] Raeder's intelligence and strong intellectual capacity, his phenomenal memory and ability to concentrate, afforded him an "incomprehensible" ability to accomplish a prodigious amount of work in a limited period of time (which can be seen in his extensive green-penciled marginalia throughout his files).[48] Raeder's overbearing intellectual self-righteousness, strong evangelical religiosity, and personal aloofness, mingled with an inner and exterior stiffness and a lack of humor or wit, all combined to make many uncomfortable, if not afraid of him. Raeder was quite aware of how he was regarded and tried to temper his image by reviving such traditions as the officers' "gentleman's evening" at Kiel, where he noted he was a "prime target" for the amateur playwrights and was depicted, at one such occasion, as not even owning any civilian clothes.[49]

Cooperation with the Government and the Defense Ministry

One of the most compelling reasons for Raeder's imposing his strict authority was the need to restore the image of the navy and gain support for its rebuilding from the government and Reichstag from 1928 to 1933. Any future controversies would threaten the navy's new construction program. Without the new Panzerschiffe, the navy would never rise above the level of a "coast guard." Groener also recognized that only under the strong leadership of the Defense Ministry could he establish the military as an instrument of the political leadership—a precondition for the revision of the Versailles treaty and the buildup of the armed forces for national defense. To do this, Groener knew that he and the military had to establish an effective working relationship with the government by creating an atmosphere of mutual trust.[50]

On 18 October 1928, Groener called a special meeting in which Raeder and General Heye were instructed to officially inform the government of "all those things which were not in harmony with the principles of sound budgeting and political honesty."[51] Once Groener completed his review of the treaty violations, he determined which projects were to be continued and transferred the responsibility for further secret rearmament to the government. Groener "insisted absolutely" that nothing should be held from him and that only he had the authority to sanction any proposed secret project or funding. Even then, security concerns and lack of cooperation hindered a full disclosure of the navy's records until Groener issued Raeder a "last chance." Subsequently, noted Raeder, the government took full responsibility and exonerated the Reich's defense minister, who continued to be responsible for covert rearmament. "We had to report to the *Reichswehrminister* everything that happened in the future and were not allowed to undertake any steps alone." Only in this way, according to Raeder, did Groener feel he could "take the responsibility toward the Government."[52]

Beginning with the 1928 budget, the government established a committee to oversee a secret budget to fund rearmament activities. The existence of this committee and its purpose (which was outside the oversight of the Reichstag) represented a major blow to the parliamentary system and was, in fact, a violation of German law (which had adopted the Versailles treaty as law). The secret funds came from the inflated budgets of the Defense Ministry and other government offices. In five years, the navy was able to increase these funds from 6.8 million marks to 21 million marks—a deception that involved careful and coordinated planning on the part of the civilian and military leaders.[53] During debates over the budget in the Reichstag, Raeder had to answer probing questions evasively, "yet, at the same time, satisfy the questioner. [In this manner] many of the secret sums of vital importance for the navy were substantiated with innocent explanations."[54]

There was another reason to reorganize the program of secret rearmament. The publicity over the violations of the treaty and rumors of continuing transgressions had not escaped the attention of the Allies. To prepare for a surprise investigation, Raeder directed that any measures that violated the treaty were to be the responsibility of the Naval Command and the defense minister personally, and individual cases would be evaluated as to whether the benefits were worth the risk. Finally, high-risk items were to be disguised, along with appropriate cover-up statements to be issued along with preparations for removing these items if necessary. The deadline for reporting all violations was 1 January 1929, and Raeder admonished officers "to make sure that nothing was omitted from this list."[55] These procedures and Raeder's threat to monitor the effectiveness of all cover-up measures further bolstered the authority of the Marineleitung and Raeder's role as the final arbiter in all naval affairs.

Raeder also instituted a series of meetings with key government offices where he initially received a cold reception. He asked for their confidence and believed he had convinced officials that the navy was thoroughly "unpolitsch."[56] He believed that he had successfully overcome the distrust of the navy that existed among both the supporters and critics of the Republic. He later boasted that "shortly" after he had assumed office the political atmosphere toward the navy had "completely changed."[57] Raeder's aggressive defense of the independence of the navy and its interests vis-à-vis the army could only be maintained with what later he characterized as "unquestionable correctness" on his part and the navy's.[58]

At the same time, his *modus operandi* was expediency. The navy's interests must be forwarded at all costs, whatever the issues of the day. He recognized that his relationship with Groener was critical if the navy was to receive the support it needed for its rebuilding. Raeder complained that Groener and his "political advisor," Kurt von Schleicher, had a tendency to bypass him in matters concerning the various departments of the Marineleitung—which he considered was a result of their habitually interfering in the army bureaucracy. These issues boiled over in December 1928, resulting in a "sharp confrontation" between Raeder and Groener. Raeder declared his intention to resign if Groener did not apologize. Groener subsequently did, and the "unpleasant" relations between the two subsequently improved (Raeder continued to regard Schleicher as no friend of the navy). Groener, however, made it clear in November 1928 that the navy had to base its rearmament and planning on what it could realistically accomplish under existing conditions. Only then could it be determined how the navy and the Panzerschiffe fit into an overall defense policy.[59] There must be, he admonished, no illusionary assumptions.

In spring 1929, Groener asked Raeder to answer the question, "Does Germany need large warships?" Raeder's careful response demonstrates his reading of Groener and the tactical nature of his policy of dealing with his superiors. He assured Groener that the navy's primary mission focused on a potential conflict with France and Poland and expressly declared that the navy's strategy was not determined by any "wishful thinking to reestablish an outstanding naval power." The most important task of the navy was to prevent the enemy from interdicting German overseas commerce. The lessons of the World War had demonstrated that the "cutting off [of] our sea lanes is the simplest and safest way, without any bloodshed, of defeating us." Given the Royal Navy and England's favorable geographic position, any conflict with England was unthinkable ("We would be doomed to failure right from the start"). Even if they were freed from the restrictions of Versailles, the navy could only fight a second-class naval power, such as France.[60]

Raeder's reassurances aside, Groener remained skeptical. His studies of the navy's operational plans concluded that the navy had ambitions beyond mere coastal defense. He also recognized that these plans did not take into regard either the kind or number of ships needed for the navy's professed mission. Groener also noted the lack of any coordination with the army, with each service assuming that it would be able to fight its own war. Groener insisted that the navy's primary area of operations should be the Baltic and the defense of East Prussia.[61] Although he publicly supported the Panzerschiff, he was well aware that this ship was not the most suitable ship for the role of the navy he envisioned. Winning approval for the new ships was, however, part of Groener's attempt to create an unified national defense plan and the military-industrial infrastructure along with the funds to modernize the military (the navy claimed 30 percent of the military budget and the Panzerschiffe represented a long-term commitment of substantial funds).[62]

Given these high stakes, Groener insisted that Raeder follow the lead of the Defense Ministry in all issues of policy and established the *Ministeramt,* the Office of Ministerial Affairs, in March 1929 to defend the ministry's political interests and coordinate all rearmament issues. The head of this office, General Schleicher, insisted that the navy abstain from any independent lobbying and rejected Raeder's proposed campaign to "shoot away" press materials arguing the navy's case.[63] Schleicher reminded Raeder that the issue was a "purely political" one and wanted to save all propaganda for a more opportune moment. Schleicher later reported that Raeder had finally fallen in line.

> One [Raeder] makes the finest proposals to me about private conversations with prominent [people] or [Reichstag] deputies, or naval writers, etc. and was, I believe, disappointed over my unfeelingness. But now he has resigned himself and on my proposal busily collects material *pour le cas que!*[64]

Raeder and the Panzerschiff

Raeder, accustomed to using the methods that had served Tirpitz well, resented what he regarded as a loss of control to influence the debate over the Panzerschiff—a "life or death" issue for the navy's future. Groener's suspicions of the navy's intentions were correct. The navy extolled the value of the Panzerschiff as an alliance factor and a guarantee that it would not sink to the level of a "coast guard."[65] Ironically, Raeder had at first favored the more heavily armored monitor type over the other alternatives to replace Germany's pre-dreadnought battleships. His decision may at first have reflected his own interests as chief of the Baltic station, since the monitor would be more suitable for duty in the Baltic and defending Germany's sea communications to East Prussia—a role that reflected Groener's conception of the navy's primary mission.[66] It soon became apparent, however, that the new Panzerschiff design posed a threat to the international naval agreements and might assist Germany's efforts to participate in future naval negotiations— possibly leading to the end of the restrictions imposed by the Versailles treaty. The international community regarded the 10,000-ton "small battle cruisers" (or "pocket-battleships") as "raiders" intended for offensive operations on the open oceans and capable of outfighting any ship they could not outrun. The international balance of naval power, bound by limitations imposed on capital ships and the 10,000-ton "Washington cruisers," made the development of a modern German navy a threat to the aging fleets of the maritime powers.

It was not until the December 1927 fleet exercises, however, that the military worth of the Panzerschiff became more evident than its "prestige factor."[67] In a classified memorandum issued on 2 October 1928, the navy outlined the possibilities of operations involving the North Sea as well as the Baltic and the protection of Germany's trade against the most probable enemies in a future war—France and Poland.[68] The Panzerschiff reflected Raeder's determination to develop a strategy that concentrated on attacks on the enemy's sea lanes—to create a deterrent force of "world-political importance" that would have a "strategic impact far out of proportion to its numbers because of its mobility and operational flexibility."[69]

For the first time, the navy planned to defend Germany's imports in the Atlantic and not just the North Sea. Without modern forces and an offensive strategy, however, these "operational objectives" would be unrealizable.[70] Nevertheless, as far from the military and political reality as these ideas were, the navy did not regard them as "fantasies."[71] The navy's "romantic tendencies" and its presumptuous attitude that "foreign policy should serve naval planning and not the reverse" reflected the continuity of the naval leadership's goal since 1918 to reestablish German naval power—a reflection of their policy of revisionism against Versailles as a precondition for the navy's ascendancy to maritime Weltmacht.[72] The discrepancy between the naval command's global ambitions and plans and the actual means of accomplishing them—particularly during the Weimar years—reflects the "unreal reality" of German naval politics.[73]

Although the debate over the Panzerschiff dictated that that the strategic role for the new ship was defensive and critical for the defense of the Baltic, it was clear that the ship was designed to be part of a much larger fleet to be built around the ultimate symbol of sea power: the battleship. Until the restrictions of Versailles could be lifted, the naval leadership ignored the principle of *Similia similibus* and intended to operate with a greater number of relatively smaller capital ships (a decision Hitler criticized in 1928). The Panzerschiff represented only an interim solution. As Raeder told Groener in May 1929, as long as other nations continued to build battleships, no nation could forgo having powerful capital ships.[74] The Panzerschiff was less a "change to the future" than an expression of the navy's long-held ambition to return to its claims for the military-political role of a fleet and its demand for equality among the world's sea powers.[75] With these new ships, Raeder could now pursue the operational framework for an offensive Atlantic strategy—a concept that his own studies had helped to shape. To secure these goals and even more ambitious global aims would require an even higher level of the political and diplomatic skills than Raeder had successfully demonstrated at Kiel, and with much higher stakes.

Raeder and the Politics of Weimar

Raeder was thoroughly aware of his political role as navy chief and the political implications of many of his policies, but his derogatory references to "politics" were always those associated with "party politics— especially those on the Left." He was willing, however, to work with those parties who were prepared to accept the role of the armed forces as the "bearers of the state."[76] His interpretation of his policies as "non-political," "above party," or *staatspolitik* (state politics) reflected his experiences in both the *Kaiserreich* and Weimar, in which political parties represented the factional strife that threatened national unity.[77] Raeder's attitude toward political parties also stemmed from deep resentment against the left-wing parties whom he held responsible for the mutinies in the High Seas Fleet and the parliamentary system that had protected them. From Raeder's perspective, the major supporters of the new Republic were the same individuals and groups who, before 1918, represented the "internal enemy" that the building of a fleet was designed to overcome.[78] The failure of Social Democrats and the other leftist parties to recognize the military requirements of the nation and the need for a navy incensed Raeder. For years, the republican parties had handled problems in a dilettante fashion, "deciding things on a case-to-case [basis]" without offering or rejecting in principle "any military policy." Under these circumstances, he charged, "pacifistic tendencies" had found an influence in the three leading political parties, the Center, the Democratic Party, and the Social Democrats.[79]

Raeder's accommodation to the Weimar Republic was tactical. Raeder was no monarchist. His deference to the imperial period was more emotional and related to its value for "tradition." To be sure, the navy had close ties to Wilhelm II as the "initiator" and strongest advocate for the building of a fleet. The officers regarded the monarchy as the embodiment of the state and saw their role as one of the pillars of support for the monarchy.[80] Raeder regularly received news concerning the ex-kaiser from retired officers who were in regular contact with him and communicated through them his "true gratitude and respect" to Wilhelm II. Raeder also maintained a close relationship with Prince Heinrich and visited Heinrich's residence in Hemmelmark.[81] The election of Hindenburg in 1925 as president represented for Raeder not only the establishment of an ersatz kaiser but a portent of a potential change in the constitutional government. When Hindenburg visited Kiel in May 1927, Raeder could hardly control his emotions over the "leadership" change represented by the field marshal.[82]

Sustained by the memory of the nation's popular enthusiasm for a fleet—when the navy was "carried by the love and recognition of the entire people," Raeder was intent on reestablishing the navy's role as a means of national and social integration.[83] For Raeder, the military and the navy, in particular, could not have a firm foundation unless they were grounded in the people: "A military must stand in a close relationship with the people whom they serve and cannot lead its own existence."[84] A unified Germany represented the absolute precondition for the reestablishment of sea power, which, of course, assumed overcoming the restrictions of the Versailles treaty. Raeder's efforts to create a navy "family" and a distinctive navy style reflected a social if not socialistic orientation. These elements, along with the navy's long-term Anglophobia and antidemocratic posture and its belief that Germany's and the navy's defeat in World War I had been the result of a "stab in the back," formed its revisionist outlook from 1918 to 1933.

Raeder's obsession with fighting communism also reflected his frustration with the Weimar "System." The experiences of the naval mutinies and the threat of Bolshevism had conditioned Raeder to regard communism as the most dangerous enemy. The naval ports provided havens for communist subversion and propaganda, particularly in Kiel.[85] As station chief in Kiel, Raeder had tried to get the police more involved in investigating communist attempts to infiltrate the navy, but found the Prussian police and other local authorities more inclined to focus on the antirepublican attitudes of the navy and its association with right-wing organizations. He suspected that some of the objections to his appointment in 1928 were the result of his energetic anticommunist efforts.[86] Any of his officers who did not share his views were sharply reprimanded.[87] In 1929, he considered it "more important to protect the Wehrmacht from (internal) subversion than to gather intelligence reports abroad." With the coming of the Great Depression and growing radicalization of German political life, Raeder feared a communist putsch.[88] The cooperation of the National Socialists with the Communist Party in the summer of 1932 was also an alarming development to those who feared the "red radicals" in the Nazi Party, and officers in Kiel were instructed to carry revolvers while off duty.[89]

The growing influence of the National Socialist movement also threatened the navy's unity, especially among the young officers. Growing unemployment, especially among discharged sailors, raised concern about the politicizing of the navy.[90] The influence of the Nazis in the navy, especially among the former veterans of the radical naval *Freikorps,* became noticeable as early as 1929. When the new commander of the torpedo boat flotilla inspected his officers and crew in the fall of 1931, he discovered that the "greater part" sympathized with the National Socialists.[91] One lieutenant wrote to Schleicher in January 1930, protesting that the younger officers were pro-Nazi because they regarded the National Socialist Party as "an active force which fights the decline of the Reich" and do not see any goal, other than foreign policy, only the demand for obedience "but seldom co-operation," from their superiors.[92]

Even Raeder was not sacrosanct. During one *Herrenabend* (Gentlemen's Evening) the young officers daringly presented a skit showing Raeder as a "tacking staff officer" and a "clear weather sailor."[93]

This gulf between the younger and older officers widened in the final years before 1933. The younger officers regarded the Republic's position toward the military as intolerable and feared that the navy would be neglected as Germany began to define its rearmament priorities for a post-treaty era. The Nazi Party's support of the military in principle, and its demands that Germany must be freed from the chains of Versailles, found a strong response. One officer later suggested a formula for this development: "the younger the officer, the more National Socialist; the older the officer, the more reserved."[94] The political climate, moreover, made it impossible for the navy to remain "unperturbed," especially when the republican parties used election slogans such as "Panzerschiff or food for children."[95]

During the spring of 1932, Joseph Goebbels discussed politics with a number of the naval officers at Kiel and claimed, "Everyone, officers and crews, are entirely for us."[96] Later that year, Admiral Marschall reported to Raeder that his men at the Baltic Naval Station were "not certain" in the event of a Hitler putsch. Raeder, aware of the sympathies of many of his officers, assured Marschall that he would lead the navy in such a way that there would be no danger to the navy or its position.[97] Later, Raeder boasted that he had led the navy completely and smoothly into the Third Reich. The navy, he claimed, remained unified in 1933 and provided an "example" to the other members of the armed forces.[98] Although Raeder agreed that the military could not be a "state within a state," the needs of the nation as defined by his and the navy's long-term goals were distinct from those as defined by any governmental body, including the Defense Ministry or parliamentary representation—in spite of his lip service to Groener.

In spite of Schleicher's efforts to curtail Raeder's lobbying, he persisted in maintaining contacts with key government officials and members of the Reichstag and used his connections with the retired admirals to ensure that the navy's case was presented. With the rise of the NSDAP and the growing domestic tensions, Raeder sought to ensure that the navy would be "above party" and insulated from any developments that threatened its unity or rebuilding. Increasingly, Raeder sought to bypass unsympathetic leaders in the Defense Ministry, primarily Schleicher. Beginning with the Brüning government, Raeder met personally with the chancellor so as to sidestep the Defense Ministry in pursuing his agenda. His notes for a meeting with Brüning on 21 September 1931 demonstrate his willingness to present any argument that would assure support for the building of more Panzerschiffe. In statements similar to those he later used to reassure Hitler as to the navy's goals, he indicated the navy's de facto "disarmament" (i.e., of the sixteen ships permitted under the treaty, only eight would be built by 1946) and promoted the Tirpitz era concept of *Bündnisfähigkeit* (alliance value) that the modernization of the fleet would provide. He assured the Chancellor that the Panzerschiff was not a product of whim or an "end in itself" but represented military necessity to enable the navy to fulfill its objectives in the Baltic. Raeder secured Brüning's commitment to build the third Panzerschiff ("C") with a promise that the construction of the ship would not start before 1 January 1933 (given the international "building holiday"). When the 1932–1933 budget was published, this assurance was missing, but Brüning was no longer chancellor.[99]

The dissolution of the National Socialists' *Sturmabteilung* (SA), the "Storm Troopers," in April 1932 also demonstrates Raeder's involvement in Weimar's increasingly volatile politics. When Groener proposed a ban on the SA, Raeder opposed this as a threat to the stability of the military because it ignored the SPD's paramilitary organization, the *Reichsbanner*. In Raeder's opinion, this action constituted a "one-sided attack against the Right" that would strongly disturb the military and provide the Nazis an opportunity to agitate for a civil war.[100] Raeder believed that any action against the excesses of the extreme right must be "balanced" by a simultaneous step against similar leftist organizations. He ignored the fact that the major difference between the two organizations was that one supported the government while the other did not. Hindenburg's opposition to the ban also played a role in Raeder's decision. The close ties between the military and the Reich president also made any policy against Hindenburg "quite inconceivable" for Raeder.[101] When Raeder presented his argument to Groener, he quickly discovered the "atmosphere" so opposed to his view that "any further objection would be purposeless and could only endanger the interests of the navy."[102] His acquiescence to Groener was consistent with his conviction that loyalty to the political leadership must be demonstrated at least overtly to protect the navy's interests. Later, Raeder characterized his attempts to deal with the SA *Verbot* as "thoroughly correct," and Groener himself noted that there were no disturbances in the navy because Raeder had simply forbidden any open criticism of the government's actions.[103]

In the aftermath of Groener's anti-SA policy, Schleicher abandoned Groener and tried to pressure Raeder to inform Hindenburg that Groener must resign immediately in order to protect the interests of the military. Raeder declined, stating that this was not an appropriate role for him but was better suited to the head of the Defense Ministry's Ministeramt, namely, Schleicher.[104] Raeder refused to become involved in a "palace revolution" against Groener.[105] Raeder was also aware that Hindenburg had "repeatedly expressed" himself against any involvement of the military in the political sphere and rejected Schleicher's request that he inform the navy that the Ministeramt disavowed Groener's actions.[106] Although Raeder claimed it was "rank disloyalty" as well as a breach of military principles to repudiate the actions of his superior, a later report drawn up by Hindenburg's office noted that Schleicher and both the army (Hammerstein) and navy (Raeder) had confirmed to him that Groener no longer had the confidence of the Reichswehr.[107]

On 13 May 1932, Raeder was surprised to learn that he was being considered as the leading candidate to replace Groener. Raeder believed that Schleicher had turned against him and sought to implicate him in "political activity." He saw this as an "obvious" move to have him take Groener's place and "so sink along with the Brüning Cabinet when it inevitably fell."[108] He immediately issued a "strong denial" that he had any interest in being appointed Reichswehrminister.[109] In a confidential letter to Levetzow, however, Raeder openly revealed his political ambitions and belief in his political abilities. "If a strong Reich cabinet appears possible, I am potentially ready to participate." Raeder hereby signaled his willingness to resign as navy chief and to represent the interests of both services as defense minister. As Raeder was aware, in the context of domestic politics in the spring of 1932, a "strong cabinet" would have included the NSDAP.[110]

Raeder indicated to Levetzow that he had "quite definite" personal and objective demands before he would agree to undertake such a responsibility. He would insist on a strict control of the Defense Ministry as he had done with the navy and a thorough "nonpoliticizing" of the military similar to what he had imposed on the navy. The interests of the navy would also be served by the ending of the "accommodation" of the needs of the navy to a defense ministry dominated by the interests of the army.[111] From this position, Raeder believed he could directly challenge the antimilitary parties that he felt denied the Reichswehr's military and social role in the state. In short, Raeder's "navy style" and interpretation of "politics" would become the standards for the personal and professional conduct of the Wehrmacht.[112]

At the same time, Raeder recognized the dangers associated with Schleicher's political intrigues. He wrote to Chancellor Brüning to assure him that he did not "seek" the post of defense minister and that he expected that Hindenburg's confidence in him would protect him against any political maneuverings (a copy was also sent to Schleicher).[113] Shortly after this, Raeder learned through Levetzow that Schleicher had informed Hermann Göring "that [Raeder]was not suitable [anyway] for the post of defense minister because [he] stood far to the left." Subsequently, a number of articles appeared in "very radical" leftist newspapers describing Raeder as "entirely acceptable" to replace Groener.[114] Raeder believed Schleicher was responsible, resentful of the politically "strong position" he had achieved because of his "above party" leadership of the navy, and was determined to discredit him. Raeder was equally determined not to be drawn into politics, "out of which I have so far successfully kept myself much to the dismay of several people but to the good of the navy." He believed he had successfully avoided Schleicher's trap to involve him in Brüning's doomed and "patched-up" cabinet.[115]

Levetzow warned him against becoming defense minister at this time. However, he flattered Raeder, indicating his appointment "would be . . . the first time that the existing *System* would have a fully suitable personality. . . . I know of no one that I trust as much as you that will be able to bring us through the rocks and danger of the present *political* situation." Levetzow was hoping to influence Raeder's attitude toward the Nazi Party. If Raeder did succeed in becoming defense minister or at the least maintain his position as navy chief, Levetzow hoped that Raeder would recognize the "strong support" offered by the NSDAP and other "patriotic sources" outside the government. He urged Raeder to find a "diplomatic way of winning the support of the young, active and often too impetuous and wild national forces"—something which the "clumsiness" and "party political bigotry" of Groener had been unable to do. Although he knew that Raeder and many others feared Nazi extremism, Levetzow argued they could be "tamed" and brought "closer to the state and political responsibility."[116] The potential appeal of the Nazi movement as a broadly based national movement for a solution of Germany's domestic (and international) difficulties was shared by other political and military leaders who assumed that the nationalism and defense policies proclaimed by Hitler were akin to their own.[117] In spite of what he told Raeder, Levetzow believed that Schleicher had been successful in impressing his views upon a naive Raeder and expressed concern over whether he would be "clever enough" to escape Schleicher's intrigues.[118]

Raeder was not above playing the same political games as Schleicher. In May 1932, under the pretext of discussing the naval budget with the chancellor, he warned Brüning about Schleicher's activities. The situation in the Defense Ministry, as far as the navy was concerned, "could not be endured much longer." Raeder charged: "The leading *Herren* no longer work, but discuss. Everywhere there is intriguing and the building of parties." If Brüning did not secure Schleicher's support, he would be forced out. Raeder also used his meeting to assure Brüning of his loyalty. He praised both the chancellor and Groener as men who possessed the "full trust" of the navy and promised that the navy would "never forget" how the Brüning government had supported the navy's rebuilding program. This praise was disingenuous but convincing. Brüning and Groener believed that Raeder had been thoroughly loyal during the stormy period of their dismissals.[119] Raeder knew the officers were growing increasingly impatient, as he was with both the leadership of the Defense Ministry and the government. His purpose in seeing Brüning was not only to profess his "loyalty" and preserve the favorable position that he and the navy had developed since 1928, but also to ensure that his direct personal connection to the chancellor, without interference from the Defense Ministry, would remain unbroken.

On 30 May 1932, after Brüning resigned his office, Schleicher became defense minister under the new Franz von Papen government. At the same time, international disarmament negotiations, critical to Germany's future naval construction plans, became a factor in the domestic political situation. The Geneva Disarmament Conference presented an opportunity for the navy to press for the "equality of arms" and naval parity with France. Given this background, Raeder exhibited newfound enthusiasm for the Papen government. He wrote to Levetzow suggesting that the latter's "friends" (Hitler and Göring) support the new government in order that the "we [the navy] will rise [*Hochkommen*] again."[120]

At this time, Raeder was engaged in a classic resource battle with the army leaders, who he felt were all too ready to abandon the navy for concessions at the disarmament conference.[121] This competition intensified after the army unveiled its *Umbau* (rebuilding) program in early 1932 and attacked the navy's share in armaments as being too high, arguing that the emphasis must be placed on a land war.[122] The navy's November 1932 Umbau program represented a "modest" plan that did not represent its true ambitions but reflected the reality of its inadequate personnel resources and the inability to reach even the treaty-imposed force levels. Raeder's program caused a great deal of disappointment, if not outspoken criticism, among the naval officer corps, who believed that "after years of being hobbled, the present opportunity to satisfy our most urgent requests had not been exploited."[123] In December 1932, some officers insisted that the navy must energetically take advantage of the present opportunities and institute a rapid expansion of the officer corps. Otherwise, if the navy remained passive while the army pressed forward, the navy might not be able to recoup its losses.[124] In spite of the progress at Geneva during this time frame, which held some promise for relief from the naval restrictions of Versailles, the most pressing challenges for Raeder were in domestic politics. In December 1932, there existed a distinct possibility that the National Socialists would join the government, and even though Hitler was considered to be "national" and therefore supportive of the military, Raeder remained uneasy about Hitler's views toward the navy.

> I think you will agree with me that I succeeded in 1933 in
> leading the navy to the Führer and into the Third Reich
> unified and without friction. This was accomplished easily
> because the entire training of the navy in the *Systemzeit* . . .
> was directed toward an inner attitude which of itself resulted
> in a truly National Socialistic attitude.
>
> —*Raeder, 1 February 1943*

5

Raeder, Hitler, and the Nazi Party, 1928–1939

Raeder, Levetzow, and Hitler, 1928–1933

Throughout his career, Raeder and the navy closely followed people and organizations that could affect the navy.[1] In addition to regular briefings on domestic political issues, Raeder's source of information about the National Socialist Party and Hitler was Raeder's former colleague, Magnus von Levetzow, whom he credited with impressing the future führer as to the navy's reliability and solid military spirit "free from all party politics."[2] Levetzow's contacts with Hitler began in 1928 and led to an active discussion of Germany's past and future naval policy. Levetzow reported that Hitler showed a "lively attention" and "understanding" of naval issues and shared the "bitterness" over the fleet's ineffective leadership in 1914.[3] In 1931, Levetzow's contacts with the party led to an unofficial exchange between Hitler and Raeder on naval policy. When Hitler asked why the navy's new light cruisers would be armed with nine 15-cm guns compared to the six 21-cm guns of the Japanese *Aoba* class cruisers, Levetzow requested an explanation from "the chief of the naval command, Admiral Raeder," his "close confidant." Raeder responded that the "threatening objections" of the Allies had prevented the navy from increasing the size of the cruisers' armament.[4] This question was Raeder's first indication of Hitler's detailed knowledge of naval armaments and his view that ships should be armed as heavily as possible.[5]

Raeder remained wary of Hitler's attitude toward the navy. Hitler's criticism of Tirpitz and the navy's prewar policies had been detailed in his *Mein Kampf* in the mid-twenties. His rejection of Germany's sea power and colonial policies in favor of an alliance with England threatened Raeder's goals of winning the government over to the navy's conception of its long-range "world political" role and securing a large battleship program. Moreover, Hitler had condemned the naval leadership in World War I as "half-hearted" and criticized Tirpitz's construction policies, which had produced ships that were too slow and poorly armed. The failure of the Imperial Navy was the result of the "absolutely erroneous so-called idea of risk," which renounced attack and assumed the defensive. He accused the navy of succumbing to *Parliamentarismus* and its prewar dependence on its "better [than the army's] parliamentary representation." These tendencies had contributed to its "serious lack of logic" and "half-baked ideas" in leadership, strategy, ship construction, and organization. In his unpublished "Second Book," dictated in 1928, Hitler characterized the High Seas Fleet as a collection of "so-called battleships" at best fit only for the enemy's target practice. "In the end, our fleet was only a romantic plaything, a parade piece that was built for its own sake." Hitler also rejected "the perverse and calamitous statement" that "Our future lies on the water." Germany's fate would always be determined on land, in Europe, because of its "disastrous" military-geographic position.[6]

In naval circles meanwhile, anyone who spoke of a "false naval policy before 1914" failed to recognize that "the entire question" was not only historical but relevant to the discussion of future foreign policy when "Germany will again have the opportunity to be placed on the level of a world power" and confront similar questions of naval policy. Such critics "could so easily stand in the way of such a future" and their "frequently repeated and unchecked views" reflected a "psychosis . . . that stands in the way of a sound judgment (see *Herrn* Hittler! [*sic*])."[7] During the intense debates over the building of the first Panzerschiff in 1928, Hitler disparaged these ships ("with them we cannot command the seas"). His only reason for supporting them was that a period of "no rearmament" represented nothing more than a guaranteed fulfillment of the imposed "peace" treaty.[8]

Levetzow believed that Hitler was more sympathetic to a strong navy and shared with him in November 1931 a comment from a retired officer who decried the fact that "the National Socialists had no understanding and no interest in the sea"—a statement "which amused us."[9]

With the party's growing success, Hitler's attitude toward the navy became even more critical. In May 1932, Hitler visited the cruiser *Köln,* where he wrote in the ship's guest book of his hopes for the rebuilding of the German fleet.[10] Hitler also used the occasion to declare that he would rebuild the fleet within the limits of the Versailles treaty, noting that if a ship was said to be 10,000 tons, then it would be 10,000 tons, no matter how large it actually was.[11] Raeder was encouraged by these statements, especially given fears that Hitler might renounce a navy altogether.

In late October 1932, however, Hitler shocked Raeder with sharp criticism regarding the Papen government's support for his proposed naval program. The building of large battleships, Hitler argued, would adversely affect Anglo-German relations, and the high cost of construction would take money away from the army. The navy's focus should be in the Baltic, which did not require battleships. Characteristic of his attacks on the Imperial Navy, he faulted the navy for not sufficiently taking into account new technology. "Psychological reminiscences" more than technical considerations appeared to determine the navy's rearmament.[12] An angry Raeder complained to Levetzow, now a NSDAP deputy in the Reichstag, that Hitler's statements were:

> [the] silliest that he has uttered so far. How can the man in order to attack Papen disturb foreign policy in so criminal a manner and endanger all the threads that we have spun. I have not understood him for a long time. . . . What Hitler says about the Baltic and North Sea is really nonsense. If we were to follow him, we would build a coastal navy and should never be capable of defending [ourselves] against the French. Our mission will very soon be again in the North Sea. The navy, however, cannot [like the army] be remodeled overnight. He [Hitler] should leave the negotiations with England to us and not be like a bull in a china shop. As for the rest [of his statements], he had expressed himself quite differently on board the *Cöln* [*Köln*].

Raeder warned that Hitler's "party political" maneuverings were losing him support from the younger officers in the army and navy, who were now "fully healed" from his influence. Recently, Raeder had heard only negative comments from Hitler, nothing positive.[13] Nevertheless, Raeder still expressed his hope that the National Socialists would join the government after the November elections. The appeal of Hitler's nationalistic, pro-defense, and revisionist policies had attracted the sympathy of many officers, including Raeder, who hoped to utilize the more "positive" elements of the movement for their own agendas. But Raeder still feared that the extremists of the party under Gregor Strasser would push the "leftist tendencies" agenda of the NSDAP at the expense of its "nationalism."[14]

Levetzow attempted to reassure Raeder about Hitler's support in spite of the latter's "unreasonable" comments.[15] In early January 1933, Raeder informed Levetzow that he would welcome the NSDAP's participation in the government. He believed that Hitler's party leadership was now secure—a guarantee that the left wing of the NSDAP would not prevail. At the same time, Raeder did not understand the Hitler-Papen coalition—"when men fight in such a filthy manner, they cannot later sit back down at the same table." He asserted that Papen and Hitler were ambitious intriguers who had no concern for the "well-being of the Fatherland." He declared to Levetzow that he had "given up trying to understand "party politics" and hoped that the New Year would finally resolve Germany's domestic politics.[16]

Nevertheless, Raeder continued to recognize the potential of the Nazi movement for rearmament and shared other military and political leaders' desire that the Nazis not collapse. He saw the potential of a nationally minded mass movement for the future rebuilding of the fleet. As a former Imperial Navy officer, Raeder supported the call for a "unified *Volk*" and a strong leader who would undertake the responsibility "to protect the interests of all classes and occupations"—the essential prerequisites for a strong navy and victory in war.[17] His rabid anticommunism also influenced his support for Hitler. In the midst of the Great Depression and increasing communist support, Raeder, like others, regarded the Nazis as the final bulwark against Bolshevism.

The growing influence of National Socialism also compelled Raeder to adopt a more pro-Nazi attitude in spite of his own reservations about Hitler's views on the navy. Raeder personally supported a number of former naval officers who had become members of the party. This earned him, according to Levetzow, a "strong trust" with the party.[18] When the Skagerrak Club nominated Captain (Ret.) Wilhelm Busse as its national chairman in April 1932, Busse was concerned that his Nazi affiliation might cause difficulties for the navy. Raeder, however, reassured him that his election would be "extraordinarily" welcome because of his ties to the party.[19]

The eagerness on the part of Raeder and his officers to integrate what they regarded as the positive aspects of Hitler and his movement was genuine, reflecting the navy's "affinity for Fascism."[20] With Hitler's appointment as chancellor, the officers celebrated the rekindled enthusiasm of the masses, which they had not witnessed since 1914, and regarded Hitler as the culmination of the work of Bismarck, Kaiser Wilhelm II, and Tirpitz.[21] The Nazis' "national" goals resonated with the navy's *Seemacht* ideology and its traditions as well as its bitter experiences with *Parliamentarismus* and democracy. It reflected their relationship with the Weimar Republic and the "cultural Bolshevism" and moral decay that revolution had brought to Germany. The "social" goals of National Socialism—the promised creation of a true *Volksgemeinschaft*, a "people's community"—were compatible with the belief in the navy's role in social integration and the "national feeling" required to support fleet building. As the leader of the navy's officer staff training expressed it, echoing Trotha's prophecy in 1920:

> We can only build a navy . . . on the foundations which the National Revolution has begun to create. Now the forces, which in the last 14 years were splintered through struggles in the parliament, are free to overcome . . . all of the infamous sabotage attempts of Social Democratic doctrinaires and pacifists. . . .[22]

Raeder's concept of an "outward and inward navy style," with its emphasis on leadership and discipline, conformance to "traditional" German values, and a strict moral code, reflected a patriarchal and conservative tone that also conformed to the goals of the NSDAP. The emphasis on patriotism and a belief in the national mission of the officer corps strengthened the compatibility with the *pseudosoldatische* aspects of National Socialism, as did the officer's concept of *Innere Führung* (inner leadership), favoring teamwork and tolerance among officers and men.[23] The officers saw the opportunity to end the navy's self-imposed isolation from the state and intensify its mission to educate the people of the need for sea power.

At the launching of the *Admiral Scheer* and the commissioning of the *Deutschland*, on 1 April 1933, Raeder expressed his optimism in Germany's naval rebirth. The "government of the national revolution" would lead "a unified people filled with the national feeling in the spirit of the great Chancellor [Bismarck] to a new era." He utilized the juxtaposition between the *Deutschland*, Germany's first capital ship construction under the Versailles treaty, and the *Admiral Scheer*, named after the "victor of Jutland," to highlight the need to break the heavy bonds of the treaty restrictions and focus on the symbol of the German sea power—the Battle of Jutland: the "life source, the presupposition for the rebuilding [of] the navy," for the re-establishing, "even if in a moderate way for the time being, of German *Seegeltung*."[24] Within the navy, as well as to Hitler, Raeder's message of support for the party was clear. These ships represented only a temporary solution until larger ships could be built. With a unified navy firmly under his leadership, his only remaining obstacle was to convince Hitler of the navy's value as a power factor in Germany's foreign policy as well as its role in Germany's long-term domestic political integration—a legacy of Tirpitz's claim for his fleet building.

Lobbying for Sea Power and the Fleet

Raeder's first meeting with Hitler occurred on 3 February 1933, shortly after Hitler became chancellor. Hitler used this occasion to outline his foreign and domestic policy and goals for the leaders of the Wehrmacht. He emphasized that he was taking over the leadership of both domestic and foreign policy and that the armed forces would no longer be involved in domestic policy. He declared that he would ensure a period of undisturbed development for the army and navy and assured the military that there would be no competition with the party's paramilitary forces, the SA, or the SS. In addition to Hitler's political-military aims— the freeing of Germany from the shackles of the Versailles treaty—he proclaimed his social goals, namely, the creation of a true *Volksgemein-schaft* and the elimination of unemployment. His call for the reestablishment of the "military spirit" of the German people met with an enthusiastic response from the assembled officers, especially Raeder. They also appreciated Hitler's deference to the absent President Hindenburg. Raeder's account of this meeting reflects his efforts to present a "moderate" Hitler whose more aggressive policies he would learn of only later. Others present, however, noted that the new chancellor spoke of "the conquest" of "*Lebensraum* and its ruthless Germanization."[25]

Although Raeder could find many positives in Hitler's policies, he remained concerned over the navy's role in defense priorities. In his mind there was still a lingering concern that Hitler might abolish the fleet or at least not enlarge it. The officers were also anxious about Hitler's knowledge of naval matters, given his background in Austria and southern Germany, and questioned whether Raeder had any opportunity to acquaint him with the "purpose and necessity" of the navy.[26] Raeder agreed that Hitler would have to be "educated" in naval affairs and won over, whether in the short run or longer term, to the navy's conception of its "world-political" role, or at least to granting the navy a "fair share" in Germany's rearmament. He emphasized that he would never propose or support any policy "because of political reasons" that would forestall the building of battleships once Germany was freed from the Versailles treaty.[27] By now Raeder was also aware that he had a powerful rival in Göring. In addition to his influential position in the party, Göring was the new *Reichskommissar* for aviation and a threat to Raeder's development of naval aviation as well as a rival for resources once Göring became head of the Four Year Plan.

At his first official meeting in late March 1933, Raeder began cautiously to inform Hitler of the military-political aspects of the navy's current expansion programs and to gain his support. His primary mission was to familiarize Hitler with naval issues and show how the navy's interests did not interfere or contradict Hitler's goals as he understood them. He addressed Hitler's concern that any naval rearmament might endanger Hitler's policy toward England. Raeder declared up front that the navy had no intention of having England as an enemy. In his later descriptions of this meeting, Raeder characterized Hitler's foreign policy at this stage as moderate, arguing that the führer never mentioned possible opponents, emphasizing his "firm resolve" to live in peace with England, Italy, and Japan. Hitler, neither "at this time nor later, spoke of preparation for even the possibility of war against either France or Russia." Raeder reinforced the führer's view that the "German fleet's role lies within the framework of its responsibilities toward European continental policy" and observed that the only possible country against which the German fleet could be measured was France, given the insignificance of the Soviet navy.[28]

Raeder sought to impress upon Hitler the provisional target of the navy's rebuilding and the modesty of its expansion. He declared himself in complete agreement with the number of ships permitted by the

Versailles treaty, although, anticipating relief from its restrictions, he cited the need to build U-boats and an aircraft carrier as included in the 1932 Umbau plan. In addition to reassuring Hitler of the "reasonableness" of his naval aims, Raeder sought to convince Hitler that the navy should be free to decide the tonnage of the new Panzerschiff "D" in accordance with the agreement that had been reached on the "equality of status" in Geneva in 1932. This would allow the German navy to match the tonnage and armament of the new French battle cruisers of the *Dunkerque* class. Raeder maintained (as he had done with Groener) that the navy's role in national defense was the defense of trade and merchant traffic in both the Baltic and North Seas. He also emphasized the necessity of long-term planning and "navy buildup: twenty years in advance. Not for today, but the total situation." Fleet building was measured by decades and not from one day to the next—a fact that Tirpitz had repeatedly observed. Raeder took pains to point out Germany had actually "disarmed" its navy, in light of the numbers permitted under the treaty. The planned construction of three Panzerschiffe at 10,000 tons each and one new 26,000-ton ship would represent only 56,000 tons, against England's 525,000 tons of battleships.

Although Hitler did not agree to build a 26,000-ton "anti-*Dunkerque*," Raeder received authorization to build the fourth Panzerschiff before 1936, regardless of the outcome of any international negotiations. He believed he had successfully overcome Hitler's previous criticism of battleship building and had convinced Hitler that his construction plans were no threat to England. Whether he got a glimpse into Hitler's long-term goals may be inferred from Raeder's noting the "alliance factor" of the fleet at the end of the meeting.[29] In this case the navy's *Bündnisfähigkeit* was seen in concert with England and not, as Tirpitz had proposed, in allying with the lesser naval powers against England. An Anglo-German coalition would presumably set the stage for global hegemony against the emerging world power of the United States. Although Raeder later sought to characterize this idea as "entirely utopian," this was true only in that it was beyond the capacity of the German fleet for the foreseeable future.[30] Raeder's immediate concern was to establish his support for Hitler's foreign policy and military priorities and demonstrate the navy's absolute loyalty and obedience to the new regime. Henceforth, Raeder would seize every opportunity to educate Germany's new leader of the value of the navy as a political instrument, beginning with Hitler's three-day visit in Kiel in May 1933, culminating in a dramatic night-time fleet review featuring the new *Deutschland*.[31]

Raeder's strategy, in addition to demonstrating the navy's loyalty to Hitler, was to emphasize repeatedly the case for sea power. which he felt complemented Hitler's plans. In speeches to the party leaders, Raeder and his senior officers presented the formula that they felt resonated with the führer's political goals: (1) a small coastal navy had no worth as an alliance factor; (2) a strong navy was needed to represent German interests overseas; and (3) if a navy (even if limited in numbers) was well organized and integrated with all types of ships, it could serve as the nucleus for later development. Raeder's understanding of Hitler's long-term program at this stage, if he was aware of it to any degree, did not influence him as much as did his concern for the continuity of the navy's tradition and its future goals. Reflecting the Tirpitz legacy, Raeder and his officers envisioned the steps by which Germany would achieve its global ambitions in which sea power would be both the cause and effect of *Weltmacht*. As one of his senior officers told Nazi leaders in spring 1933, the navy must plan now "for a future in which, after a solidification of our strategic position on land, German sea and world power [*See- und Weltgeltung*] would be established again and would be securely protected [by the fleet]."[32]

Unlike the army, the navy had to wait until Hitler's leadership created the necessary conditions for Germany's rise to *Seegeltung*. This would allow Germany to "again awake and strengthen the *understanding,* the *love* of the sea and the *will* of the nation and never again allow the life veins to be cut which for a *free great* people lie on the *free oceans*."[33] With Hitler, Raeder's goals appeared within reach. Hitler had overcome the domestic conflicts that had caused the Germans to lose their global ambitions, and the collective strength of the German people could now be harnessed in support of Germany's rebid for *Weltmacht*.

Raeder utilized every opportunity to lobby directly with Hitler for the navy's rearmament and to bypass the defense minister. He regarded Hitler as being easier to deal with than Blomberg (who saw issues only from the perspective of the army) and found Hitler's knowledge of naval affairs remarkable—"In some respects he was even superior to supposed experts." And, in the early years, Raeder maintained that Hitler was always receptive to his suggestions and plans.[34] In his visit to Kiel in May 1933, Hitler spoke of the desire of Germany to achieve "its place in the sun" peacefully, if possible. But, if necessary, it would be ready for the struggle to win Germany's "honor and freedom" and "for that purpose we need the fleet." Departing from his earlier criticism, Hitler praised the navy's achievements, within only a few decades, to instill in the "entire German people its pride in its bluejackets."[35] His acknowledgment that time, not purpose, had been a factor in the short history of the Imperial Navy reinforced Raeder's confidence that the navy would play a role in the führer's plans. The navy reciprocated Hitler's support with an enthusiasm that prompted one observer to write: " [Hitler] can be sure, that the German fleet is true to him as surely no one else in the entire Reich could be."[36]

Raeder spared no effort to demonstrate the navy's integration into the Third Reich. He promoted, for example, the mingling of the SA at naval functions and the navy's involvement at party-sponsored programs (e.g., "People's Track Day). On 28 August 1933, he ordered that the navy could respond in kind to the greeting "Heil Hitler." This was shortly followed by orders to use the National Socialist salute in certain situations.[37] He also did not tolerate any criticism of the new political leadership or its representatives. He sacked the fleet chief, Vice Admiral Walter Gladisch, who had made disparaging comments about the "brown party bosses" during Kiel Week in 1933, and warned that he would punish without reservation any officer who did not treat Nazi officials with the proper respect.[38]

In the fall of 1933, Raeder sharply warned his officers about the need for secrecy in the navy. Carelessness not only threatened the navy's plans but, above all, threatened the "great domestic reconstruction work of the Führer."[39] To Raeder's contemporaries, it appeared that the admirals stood closer to the National Socialist leadership than the army generals.[40]

In addition to utilizing every official occasion (e.g., launchings and commissionings) to demonstrate the navy's loyalty, Raeder took every opportunity to link the navy's history and traditions with Hitler and National Socialism through special events such as the dedication of the navy memorial at Laboe on 30 May 1936 (the twentieth anniversary of Jutland), which was carefully staged to commemorate the sacrifice of the navy's heroes in 1914–1918 and the rebirth of their spirit and honor under Hitler. In Raeder's emotional keynote speech, he compared the navy's struggles after 1918 to Hitler's "long years of the most difficult and bitter fight in history" to lead a "united nation." The scuttling of the High Seas Fleet at Scapa Flow had saved the honor of the navy and Germany. It was a "victory over the victors" that proved that the spirit of Skagerrak had not been lost. Scapa Flow represented the first turning point in the rebuilding of the nation, which awaited only the leadership of Hitler and National Socialism to lead "us and the entire German nation out of the dark into the dawn of a bright new future" and create a new *Volkstum*, a new national identity.[41] Raeder's rhetoric was matched in the speeches of other officers, official and semiofficial publications, and service manuals, demonstrating the navy's susceptibility to the "leader cult" and the "Führer Principle" and its readiness to rewrite the history of the navy within a National Socialist framework.[42]

Given these and other numerous examples encouraging accommodation with the National Socialist Party and its organizations and celebrations, it is not surprising that Raeder was hailed by Nazi propagandists for having

> sought and found a relationship with the Führer, whose fullest trust he enjoyed, even before the seizure of power by the National Socialists. He had given Adolf Hitler many opportunities to visit and inspect the fleet and through him, the entire *Kriegsmarine* greeted the takeover of power with special pleasure.[43]

Raeder had good reason to believe that his initial efforts to court favor with Hitler had achieved a measure of success. Hitler showed understanding for the usefulness of the navy as a political instrument. In a speech on the cruiser *Köln* upon its return from an overseas cruise, the führer praised captain and crew for their role as representatives of the Fatherland in spite of "today's animosity against Germany." Hitler recognized the propaganda value of such cruises, which also reinforced the peaceful mission of Germany's navy, as well as the opportunity to maintain ties with expatriate Germans. He also utilized the occasion to laud the navy for its deliberate distancing from the "men who had created the November-Germany."[44] In September 1933, Raeder proudly announced to his senior leaders: "I can state with joy and satisfaction that the *Reichskanzler* himself again and again mentions the necessity of building up of the fleet and is deeply convinced of the great political significance of the navy, especially as power and alliance factor in the politics of peace."[45]

Raeder, the Führer, and National Socialism, 1933–1939

Both during and after the war, Raeder and his supporters claimed that he was able to keep himself and the navy out of politics, far removed from the abhorrent policies and influence of the Nazi Party and its organizations such as the Gestapo and the SS/SD. Raeder took Hitler at his word when in 1933 he said he would refrain from any interference in the internal affairs of the military.[46] Moreover, Raeder believed, on the basis of Hitler's statements to him, that the excesses of party functionaries against political foes and the Jews were not ordered by him. Only over time, Raeder claimed, had he become aware that Hitler "always leaned by nature toward extreme solutions."[47] Although he contended that Hitler deliberately concealed his true plans from him, Raeder interpreted Hitler's policies through the filter of his own conservative and nationalistic views. He was willing to ignore or overlook the malevolent aspects of Hitler's domestic and foreign policy goals in order to secure his long-term goals for the navy.[48]

Hitler's decisive actions in dealing with the radicals in his own ranks also won Raeder's confidence. Although Hitler proclaimed that the Wehrmacht would be the sole bearer of arms in the Third Reich, the tension between the SA and the Wehrmacht had continued to grow.[49] On 30 June 1934, the "Night of the Long Knives," Ernst Röhm, the SA chief, and his principal followers were murdered for allegedly planning a revolutionary putsch against Hitler. Raeder had been increasingly concerned about reports of numerous clashes with the SA and units of the navy, and there is some evidence that he was aware in advance of Hitler's intention to resolve the Röhm matter by force. By May 1934, the situation had become so critical that he reported to Hitler that an SA leader, a former naval officer, was plotting to become the chief of the naval operations staff.[50]

Later, Raeder denied any knowledge or involvement with these events or their consequences. He was notably silent on the fate of General Schleicher and General Ferdinand von Bredow, who were also murdered. He admitted to having heard subsequent rumors of illegal and morally unjustifiable actions on the part of the SS troops who had "put down" the insurrection, but it was impossible "for a long time to learn any of the facts." For Raeder, it was another confirmation of the "urgent necessity" to keep as far as possible out of "internal party" and political issues and concentrate on the navy itself.[51] He, like others, turned a blind eye to the consequences of the Röhm "crisis" for the military and regarded the process as a natural course of revolutionary movements and as a welcome "reestablishment" of law and order.[52]

The military's continuing policy of ideological *Gleichschaltung* (enforced uniformity) received further impetus with the death of Hindenburg on 2 August 1934. Along with the other military commanders, Raeder took a personal oath to the person of Adolf Hitler as the "führer of the German Reich and nation." Raeder had no misgivings over this action (he had sworn personal allegiance to the kaiser) and considered Hitler as the "legal successor by universal interpretation."[53] While he downplayed any friction, he claimed that his firm leadership and the navy's outstanding reputation because of its "correct behavior and efficiency" made the party "think twice" before attacking it. Raeder did acknowledge that he had two implacable foes—Göring and Heinrich Heydrich, the head of the SD (Security Service). In 1931, Raeder had dismissed Heydrich from naval service in what he considered a breach of honor unbecoming to a naval officer, and the young officer had never forgiven him. Heydrich constantly complained to the head of the SS, Heinrich Himmler, and even Hitler, about Raeder's support for religion and his refusal to dismiss Jewish officers from the navy. Raeder was also convinced that he was under constant surveillance (e.g., telephone taps).[54]

This relationship with Heydrich further complicated the navy's relationship with the SS, whose growing power after 1934 became a new threat to the Wehrmacht in spite of Hitler's promises. The struggle between Heydrich's attempts to take over the military's intelligence arm, the *Abwehr*, led to the forced dismissal of its chief, navy captain Conrad Patzig. In order to retain this post for the navy, Raeder was reluctantly compelled to accept Captain Wilhelm Canaris. Raeder distrusted Canaris's affinity for political-military affairs and intelligence work over "purely military" matters; however, Canaris had a good working relationship with Heydrich and could work with the SS/SD.[55] Although Raeder claimed that the SS was not a major threat to the navy, competition between the SS and the military increased throughout

1935–1938. In January 1938, when Admiral Hermann Boehm returned from a long voyage, he was astonished by the strained relationship between the party and the military.[56]

Although Raeder vigorously resisted any encroachments upon the navy's independence by the SS and the Reich's other security offices and was, to some extent, successful in defending several Jewish officers, he limited his opposition to individual cases and passed all anti-Jewish decrees to his commands without comment. While he protested the excesses of *Kristallnacht* in November 1938 to Hitler on the basis of the damage it was doing to Germany's interests abroad, he was "somewhat" satisfied with Hitler's lame excuse that the attacks against Jewish businesses and the burning of synagogues were against his policy and done without his knowledge. Beyond this, Raeder felt he could do nothing further ("It would have been utopian to believe that any efforts on my part could have changed or moderated the laws that had been passed"). Any protest regarding the treatment of Jews was outside his "official" authority and might have dragged the navy into political conflict. Hitler's virulent racism, with its anti-Semitism, had been, after all, official state doctrine since 1933.[57] Raeder would later be embarrassed by Hitler's Heroes' Memorial Day speech on 12 March 1939, during which he referred to international Jewry as "race destroying" and "parasites."

Raeder's adoption of Nazi racial epithets, reflective of the assimilation of the tenets of National Socialism in the Wehrmacht, indicate his ongoing readiness to interpret and moderate Hitler's policies and ideology and assimilate them into his own Pan-German conservative worldview. By intermingling them with the ideology of the late nineteenth Bismarckian century, he could more easily accept them. At his Nuremberg trial, reflecting the traditional anti-Semitic bias of the German middle class and the naval officers of his generation, he argued that after the experiences of 1917 and 1918, "International Jewry" had "gained an excessively large and oppressive influence in German affairs," and "one could not be surprised that the National Socialist Government tried to loosen and, as far as possible remove this large and oppressive influence."[58] Although Raeder was not an anti-Semite in its virulent National Socialist form, he tolerated statements from senior officers such as Admiral Schuster (appointed by Raeder as the inspector of education and training), who told new recruits in 1937 that they must be "racially as well as morally sound."[59]

In contrast to his position on the Jews, Raeder was outspoken in his opposition to the party's attack on the Protestant and Catholic churches and the threat to the military's chaplains. He believed that anti-Christian party leaders, such as Martin Bormann, Goebbels, and Göring, were gaining influence with Hitler over religious issues and criticizing his support for the churches. In 1937, he used Hitler's reference in a speech to "positive Christianity" as evidence that his support for religion was based on the führer's own statements and declared that he intended to ignore any contradictory statements from other party members or Nazi attempts to create a "German Church."

Although he initially supported Reverend Martin Niemöller, a former U-boat commander in World War I and leader of the Protestant opposition to the NSDAP (who rejected the imposition of the party's "Aryan Paragraph" in the churches), he withdrew his support once he learned that Niemöller had offended Hitler and had been arrested for "political disloyalty." He attempted unsuccessfully to dissuade Niemöller from "politics" (i.e., Niemöller's efforts to resist the subordination of the church to Nazi ideology). He later wrote that Hitler had been willing to support Niemöller, but that the "poor relationship" between the two had resulted in a "lost opportunity" for the Lutheran Church.[60]

Hitler, for his part, tolerated Raeder's open support of religion, and Raeder continued his efforts to prevent any party (or OKW) interference in personnel matters within the naval chaplain corps. One leading chaplain regarded Raeder as the "defender of the Christian churches in Germany" and credited his intervention as having personally saved the military chaplain corps. Yet, as his attitude toward Niemöller (which Raeder admitted did not please the Reverend's supporters) demonstrated, his position in this conflict was to maintain strict neutrality. He would not allow any discussion of religion in the navy and justified the continuance of religious observations as part of military tradition in the spirit of the Imperial Navy. He would not tolerate any renunciation of the navy's religious regulations and declared "such matters are not open to question by outsiders either by the Führer or by representatives of the German Faith Movement," and he prohibited any participation in the Nazi pseudo-religion.

His instructions to a new chaplain in December 1937 reflected the traditional Lutheran respect for (and obedience to) the ruling power: "It will not be your duty to wage a church-political battle in the navy or to go expressly into an analysis of the intellectual currents that National Socialism has aroused. You are to preach Christ earnestly and without compromise."[61] His firm religious conviction may have sustained him during the increasingly obvious—even to a naive or self-deluded Raeder —nature of the *Führerstaat*. In fact, his main defense at Nuremberg would be his personal profession of Christian faith and defense of religion in the navy.[62]

In spite of the growing tensions between the military and the domestic and foreign policy measures of Hitler and the party organizations, Raeder largely glosses over them in his accounts of the period 1934–1937. It was not until 1938, he claimed, that his confidence in Hitler's honesty was shaken. The first incident involved the scandal around Blomberg's marriage to a woman of ill repute. Blomberg's resignation was followed by that of Werner von Fritisch, the commander in chief of the army, after trumped-up charges of homosexuality. Although Raeder claims that they did not directly concern the navy and minimizes his own involvement in these affairs, they were to have a profound effect on the Wehrmacht and the consolidation of Hitler's power over the military.[63] While Raeder suspected that Göring played a role in these events with hopes of becoming head of the armed forces, Himmler and Heydrich saw their opportunity to defeat the "reactionary" generals (and Raeder).

In the case of Blomberg, Raeder had been tipped off that he, along with Fritsch, would be compromised if they served as witnesses at Blomberg's wedding. Göring had suggested this as a means of mitigating any criticism from the officer corps of the general's marrying a "child of the people" with a "certain past" (as Blomberg shared with Göring). Forewarned, Raeder and Fritsch declined and suggested to Blomberg that he ask Hitler to be a witness. It is unlikely at this point that Raeder knew the full story behind the bride's past; he knew only that Heydrich was involved in some intrigue against the general. The resulting scandal, when the police file on Frau Blomberg became known after the wedding (12 January 1938), shocked the officer corps, who repudiated Blomberg and made his continuing in office impossible. Raeder, too, regarded the marriage as a disgrace to the honor of the officer corps and dispatched Blomberg's naval adjunct to Rome to inform the general of the complete story of his wife's past and, if he refused to leave her, to do the honorable thing and commit suicide.[64] A puritanical Raeder later expressed his incredulity that Blomberg believed that marrying such a woman was "acceptable in the present *System* [National Socialism]."[65]

At the end of January 1938, Raeder, hoping to derail Göring's ambitions, went to see Hitler to promote Fritsch as Blomberg's successor. Hitler, however, shocked Raeder with sordid details of Fritsch's homosexuality. At the same time, according to Raeder, Hitler offered him Blomberg's position. Raeder (unaware of Hitler's decision to assume this function himself), "declined."[66] Later, he wrote he had been right to "definitively reject" this position, given the dangers associated with dealing primarily with army issues and also because, at this point, he was considering resigning.[67] Fearing the possibility of either Göring or Himmler replacing Fritsch, Raeder proposed General Rundstedt.[68]

Given his focus on Göring and Himmler as the chief plotters in the fall of Blomberg and Fritsch, Raeder overlooked Hitler's key role in these events. As he wrote to Fritsch later, he did not believe the führer had any intention to dismiss the general in the winter of 1938 because he had heard Hitler repeatedly express his full trust in him, but he believed there were those in the party who had conspired against him.[69] Raeder continued to view Hitler as "the personification of the authority of the state" and not the "demagogue and radical party leader" (as he had first viewed him prior to 1933) and was willing to continue to believe in him in spite of these disgraceful incidents. Although in March 1938 he served on the court during Fritsch's trial (which acquitted him), Raeder had been very passive in spite of being coached on how to confront Fritsch's accusers—a fact which did not escape the notice of the general's supporters.[70] Remarkably, Raeder later even praised Göring's objective and fair handling of Fritsch's trial in his role as presiding officer.[71]

Raeder's memoirs are misleading, or at best confusing, on his efforts to rehabilitate Fritsch. Although he insisted that the day after the trial he urged Fritsch not to "resign," Fritsch could not have been restored to (let alone resign from) a position that he had been dismissed from six weeks earlier. Although he expressed support, Raeder refused to be drawn into attempts by Fritsch's supporters to join any opposition to those who had implicated the army chief, arguing that it was strictly an army issue and outside his provenance. He declined requests to appeal to Hitler on Fritsch's behalf, arguing that Göring, not he, was the senior ranking officer of the Wehrmacht. His only public support on behalf of the former army chief was to invite Fritsch in June 1938 to participate in fleet exercises, where he was received with full naval honors (although Raeder did not attend).[72]

Raeder may have suffered from a bad conscience, but he expressed himself fully satisfied with the führer's justification for his actions. He seemed oblivious to the consequences of Hitler's consolidation of power over the army (which he no doubt assessed as a weakening of the army leadership to the good of the navy) and the wholesale personnel changes that followed the creation of the Supreme Command of the Wehrmacht (OKW) on 4 February 1938. Nor was he was threatened by the ascendancy of the "office manager," Wilhelm Keitel, as OKW chief of staff—whom neither service respected.[73] Hitler was now "Führer and Supreme Commander of the Armed Forces" and with no serious opposition, especially from Raeder, who viewed this development as guaranteeing the independence of the navy and providing him with direct access to the Supreme Commander.[74] As a result of the excesses of the Nazi state and the consequences of the events of 1938 (which also saw Hitler's diplomatic successes in the *Anschluss* of Austria and in Czechoslovakia), Raeder claimed he "gradually" had begun to doubt the integrity and intentions of the führer. In spite of a growing "emotional burden" that caused him several times to request his retirement in 1938–1939 (which Hitler refused), he remained in his post, believing that as long as he could continue to enjoy the führer's confidence and maintain his independence, he could secure the necessary resources for the navy. He attributed Hitler's attitude toward him and the navy to his own unconditional obedience and loyalty and abstinence from any "political" activity. He regarded himself as the only one who could fulfill the navy's ambitions and was convinced that he had skillfully created a position from which he could counter any interference. He also believed, egotistically, that he alone had succeeded in winning the respect of the National Socialist state and Hitler. At the same time, he had not planned for any successor and, in the aftermath of the Blomberg and Fritsch dismissals, feared that his replacement might be someone "more subservient" to party influence.[75]

Up to the outbreak of war, he continued to believe that he was leading the navy in a "frictionless" coordination into the führer state without identifying himself with the criminal ideological implications of

National Socialism.[76] He expressed confidence in Hitler's support to rebuild the fleet in the tradition of Tirpitz and the direction of the führer's foreign policy—even accepting Hitler's willingness to risk war with England in pursuit of German ambitions of continental hegemony, counter to his often expressed "taboo" against any possibility of conflict with England.[77] As one former officer explained after the war, "We saw Hitler not as he was . . . but we saw him as we hoped and wished he was. We placed our ideals in him . . . [and] thus we officers became fixed on our highest military virtue—obedience."[78]

The congruence between Hitler's aims and Raeder's understanding of them did not make him a National Socialist by conviction but certainly, by implication, he was guilty by association and complicity. As uncomfortable as he was with the party leaders and the ritual observations of the movement that he was forced to attend, he found this a small price for what he believed the navy—and, by his extension, the "state" and the "nation"—was receiving in return for his loyalty.[79] While he may have declared, as reported, that he only said "Heil Hitler" to people he did not like, it would have been more a reflection of his attitude toward the party leaders he despised than of his true feeling toward his political and military superior.[80] In spite of increasing evidence that National Socialism threatened the values that Raeder espoused, he held closely to his authority, believing he was preserving the navy's "independence." His myth that the navy had been allowed to develop independently in the Third Reich was as much an illusion as were his claims of keeping the navy "apolitical." The reality is that the navy's sea power ideology had allowed it to be seduced by the appeal of Hitler and National Socialist ideology and goals, both consciously and unconsciously.

The "national-political education" embraced by the navy after 1933 notwithstanding, Raeder's preoccupation with discipline, "tradition," and character building and his steadfast determination to "build ships and keep your mouth shut" had isolated his service morally and intellectually from the world around it, even as the navy moved to accommodate itself to National Socialism.[81] His hubris and self-delusion led him to declare at Nuremberg that the "basic principles" of National Socialism and the military must agree: "But I must myself decide the extent to which these principles [National Socialism] were adopted—that is to the degree where the navy maintained its internal independence and yet occupied the appropriate position with regard to the National Socialist state."[82]

His defense of the necessity to create a "real people's community" reflected his conviction that the incorporation of National Socialism into the military would allow the commanders to educate the branches of the service—as he had done with the navy—"in such a way that they would recognize and live up to the good national and socialist ideas of the National Socialist state. . . . In this way it was possible to incorporate the Armed Forces in an orderly manner, to keep them from all exaggeration and excesses. . . ."[83]

The führer's later complaints about fighting World War II with the "Imperial Navy" or "Christian Navy" simply reflect Raeder's attempts to maintain its conservative, authoritarian orthodoxy as a means of perpetuating the exclusivity and unity of the officer corps.[84] With the rapid expansion of the navy after 1933, Raeder was concerned for the unity of the officer corps as well as the composition of the expanded navy's personnel. Not only did the navy extensively expand its social infrastructure to deal with the demands of rearmament for both naval personnel and workers (wages, housing, etc.), but it also had to accept a more diverse social representation in its ranks.[85] He placed renewed emphasis on character, ethics, and morality, especially with the increasing numbers of applicants from the Nazi Party and its ancillary organizations, who were viewed as a potential source of disruption insofar as they exhibited the worst traits of the new generation—arrogance and a lack of respect.[86]

These challenges to the internal solidarity of the navy notwithstanding, his most serious threats to resign prior to 1939 were related to his defense of his *Ressort*, his sphere of influence. For example, he threatened to resign if Hitler did not allow him to dismiss the führer's naval aide over an issue of an unsuitable marriage and also, on another occasion, over the führer's criticism of the navy's building policy, but never out of dissatisfaction with Hitler and his policies.[87] In this sense, he was a demonstrably obedient "useful idiot" (Salewski) whom, unlike so many other military leaders, Hitler never felt a need to replace until January 1943 when conflict between the two over operational issues culminated in Raeder's departure.[88]

There was a darker side to Raeder's loyalty. Although he and his wife expressed the virtues of Prussian thriftiness and self-sacrifice, he accepted the perks of his position in Hitler's Third Reich with salary tax-exempt supplements and a major bequest (*Dotation*) of 250,000 RM from Hitler on his sixty-fifth birthday (24 April 1941)—the first of Hitler's high-ranking officers to receive one.[89] At Nuremberg he lamely attempted to justify this gift as a tradition of the monarchy going back to Frederick II, but he remained silent in his memoirs on these issues, as he did regarding his cheating on the interest taxes that he was expected to pay on his *Dotation* or the scandal when he and other prominent officials were caught using the black market.[90] Until March 1945, when he personally saw the results of Hitler's torture of a friend, he continued proudly to wear his Nazi Party Golden Badge, "the highest decoration National Socialist Germany could bestow."[91]

The world power position of nations is identical with their
ranking as sea powers.

—*Raeder, 1934*

6

Between Raeder and Hitler:
Fleet Building and Strategy in the
Third Reich, 1933–1939

The Origins of the Anglo-German Naval Treaty

In March 1934, Raeder proposed a new replacement shipbuilding program that called for the construction of eight battleships, three aircraft
carriers, and seventy U-boats. This program, to be completed by 1949,
vastly exceeded the "Versailles fleet," in both ship types and total displacement, and reflected the navy's needs without regard to any international naval agreements or discussions.[1] His new plans were based on
"parity" in naval armament with France and Italy. Parity with France
meant that the size of the fleet was to be fixed at 35 percent of the
Royal Navy's strength in accordance with the 1922 Washington Naval
Agreement.[2] Undeterred by potential conflict with Hitler's desire to
negotiate with Britain and conscious of internal critics, Raeder proposed in June 1934 that the ratio with the British fleet should be increased
to 50 percent.[3] He continued to remind Hitler and the senior political and
military leaders that "the world power position of nations is identical
with their ranking as sea powers."[4]

On 27 June 1934, he secured approval for a dramatic increase (18,000
tons to 31,800 tons) in the tonnage of the Panzerschiffe "D" and "E"
(*Scharnhorst* and *Gneisenau*) and an increase in their armament, Both
changes were to be kept secret along with plans for building a U-boat
fleet.[5] More intriguing were Raeder's abbreviated notes from this

112

meeting: "Development fl[eet]. Later poss[ibly] against E[ngland]. . . . Maintain tradition. Me: from 1936 on, lge. ships with 35cm. If money yes. Alliance 1899. Situation 1914?"[6]

This contradicts Raeder's assertion he had no thought of England as a potential adversary. Challenging England's supremacy at sea was a given, even if a short-term alliance could be developed. The idea that an alliance with England in 1899 would have served Germany in the short run is wishful thinking at its best. Influenced by Hitler's diplomatic goals, Raeder had first proposed to the British naval attaché in fall 1933 that a "German fleet of a certain size" might be politically advantageous for England and Germany—"given the quantitative equilibrium between the British and American fleets." This represented a complete mis-reading of Anglo-American relations and a sharp contrast to the navy's traditional view that the United States and England represented an "Anglo-Saxon" alliance that would oppose Germany's development as a world power.[7]

Raeder did not expect British acquiescence to a major German naval rearmament in the long term. Parity with France and the building of large battleships with 35-cm guns to match the new British battleships were necessary as soon as possible. He never acknowledged the implications of the navy's existing operational plans for attacking French sea communications in the Atlantic and Mediterranean—plans that would clearly support a war against England.[8] Notwithstanding his assurances that concepts from the Tirpitz era had no place in the present day, Raeder's assumption that the British would not recognize the threat posed by his fleet appears terribly facile, if not misguided. The British had already recognized the potential of an opponent with a navy half as large as theirs and composed of ships especially suited for commerce raiding.[9] Raeder required time, but, like Tirpitz, he would never have it. For him, the buildup of the navy was to be dictated by "practical considerations," justified by terms such as "a fleet worthy of an alliance" or "parity with France," which served to disguise the long-term goal of "solving the English question." Nevertheless, as long as Hitler was committed to expanding the fleet, Raeder would continue to push "equality of status." He could incrementally secure approval for increases in tonnage and armament. The fleet could be built in stages without having to tip its hand as to the ultimate vision—or so Raeder believed at this point in his relationship with Hitler. Like Tirpitz, he was prepared to carry out his plans to "achieve the strategic purpose without calling in question its political preconditions."[10]

Disappointed that Hitler opposed Germany's participation in the upcoming multilateral naval conference, Raeder informed his British liaison on 27 November 1934 that Germany would welcome "direct negotiations" to establish a ratio between the two navies that he promised "would be surprisingly low."[11] At the same time, Hitler's support of naval expansion, though uneven from Raeder's perspective, promised freedom from the restrictions of Versailles and a second chance to pursue German global sea power. No longer restrained by issues of domestic policy and funding, as they had been during the Republic, the shape and pace of German naval rearmament were now driven by Hitler's foreign policy agenda. Hitler's involvement, at every level—from the size and armament of individual ships to the composition of the fleet itself—caused Raeder to change plans continually and make frequent compromises. At the same time, he had to convey these changes to his subordinates without jeopardizing his status as the architect of Germany's naval renaissance.

The events leading up to the signing of the Anglo-German Naval Treaty illustrate the first phase of the Raeder-Hitler relationship and their sometimes competing agendas. Following Hitler's agreement in June 1934 to increase the size and armament of the two new Panzerschiffe, Raeder issued orders to prepare plans for the *Bismarck* class battleships. In the face of Germany's increased diplomatic isolation in the wake of the Röhm affair (June 1934) and German interference in Austria, Hitler sought to undermine the united front against Germany and legitimize his violations of the disarmament clauses of Versailles. By signing a bilateral naval agreement with England, Hitler believed that he could free himself of any British interference in his continental ambitions for eastern and southern Europe.[12] For Raeder, such an agreement could only be "provisional."[13] His later arguments that the naval agreement with England offered "a basis for peace for Germany and the rest of Europe far into the future" were disingenuous. Raeder privately proposed that a treaty should be concluded for "as short a period as possible (about five years) . . . especially as we can reach 35 percent of the British tonnage in considerably less than ten years."[14] Raeder also intended to use the prenegotiation period to "accelerate important armament plans even more than has been done up to now to achieve the . . . highest possible level."[15]

In light of anticipated French and British resistance after the Saar plebiscite (January 1935), Raeder made full use of Hitler's willingness to allow the navy to move rapidly ahead. He ordered the assembling of the first U-boats and an earlier start to Germany's first aircraft carrier. Hitler also agreed to another review of the size and armament of "D" and "E" and gave permission to arm "F" with 38-cm guns. The navy also began preparations to increase its infrastructure (e.g., floating docks) to a size that far exceeded the requirements of the *Bismarck* class.[16] Raeder knew that Hitler's plans and the navy's vision of its future growth were compatible—the British naval negotiations were a benchmark in fleet building, not a brick wall to future development.

Raeder anticipated criticism of the 35 percent ratio from those who had hoped for a more rapid and extensive buildup of the navy. In a statement to the officer corps, he pointed out that by combining the tonnage allowed with that remaining under the existing limitations of the Treaty of Versailles, the navy would be able to achieve a *fourfold* increase in actual tonnage (520,000 tons).[17] "Any substantially larger figure," he declared, "could hardly be reached in the next decade." He also asserted that the treaty with the British provided the "opportunity of creating a modern fleet appropriately constituted and in accordance with our maritime needs."[18] In spite of the official line that the treaty was a political success, the disappointment over not being able to pursue its long-standing goal of achieving Weltmacht "independent of England" (depending on British neutrality) was evident; even if it was tempered by assurances that clearly left the impression of a "temporary" agreement."[19] For Raeder, in contrast to Tirpitz's "danger zone," Germany's naval buildup was to proceed under the cover of a treaty with its long-term foe.[20] During the winter of 1934–1935, the navy made decisions regarding the size of its future battleships that were in direct contradiction to the agreement reached with the British (and to international naval agreements).[21] Hitler's decision that Germany's ships were "to be second to none" suited Raeder's belief that quality would make up for numbers in the short run without precipitating another naval race.[22]

With the signing of the Anglo-German Treaty on 18 June 1935, Hitler's self-proclaimed "Happiest Day," Raeder could look back at his accomplishments over this period with justifiable pride. He had accomplished, on paper at least, what had been denied to Tirpitz. In May 1935, the Reichsmarine became the Kriegsmarine, and Raeder's new title was officially changed to *Oberbefehlshaber der Kriegsmarine* (ObdM). He had achieved the unity of command denied Tirpitz. However, his ultimate ambitions depended on two factors: Hitler's continued diplomatic successes in achieving his continental ambitions and the ability of the German shipyards to fulfill the demands placed on them. Failure to achieve either would seal the navy's fate in World War II.

The failure of the London Naval Conference (December 1935 to March 1936) and the decision by the British to expand their fleet provided more "elbow room" for expanding tonnage, allowing Raeder to build additional battleships (two to six) and two more aircraft carriers (for a total of four). By 1944, the navy would have 365 ships compared to the Imperial Navy's 324 ships in 1914.[23] The quality and balance of this fleet would have embodied Raeder's strategic design and would present a significant threat to England's worldwide maritime supremacy.

The gap between planning and reality in German naval construction, however, was steadily widening. As early as April 1935, the OKM pointed out that an acceleration of naval construction would not be possible unless the time of construction could be shortened.[24] The forced pace of rearmament was leading to major complications, ranging from the need for more personnel, to shortages of labor and steel, to compromises in design and equipment for the new fleet. Since any delays were unacceptable to Hitler and therefore to Raeder, decisions such as the one to install the high-temperature, high-pressure steam power plants instead of diesel propulsion were made on the grounds of rushing as many units as possible into the fleet, without the necessary testing. The sacrifice of the diesel's superior cruising radius in favor of the higher speed of the new steam turbine reflected the lack of time to develop a more suitable diesel for the larger battleships.[25] Raeder remained, however, committed to a still undefined "Atlantic war."[26]

Raeder's Strategic and Operational Planning, 1936–1939

The long-term taboo against any consideration of England as a future enemy remained in force for most of 1936, reinforced by "the unquestioning belief in Britain's benevolent neutrality" in the event of a European war. This restriction continued to hamper the development of the navy's strategic goals and the composition of the fleet.[27] Raeder's repeated statements that "war with England was unthinkable" were, however, increasingly inconsistent with the decisions he made.[28] The "temporary" nature of the Anglo-German treaty became more and more evident in late 1936, especially after the announcement of British naval rearmament plans made it increasingly difficult to avoid the issue.[29] Raeder's formula of "parity with France," which had sustained the navy's construction and operational strategies planning to this point, was becoming less and less relevant.

In his memoirs, Raeder suggests that it was Hitler who was responsible for creating his first "vague doubts" as to England's neutrality in the face of the führer's aggressive European policy goals at the end of May 1937.[30] Raeder's eagerness to send naval forces to Spain in July 1936 and his active support for Franco in the face of British sympathy for the Spanish Loyalists represented his early recognition that conflict with England would have to be considered.[31] In his support for Spain, he saw the possibility of acquiring bases in the Atlantic and the Mediterranean, especially the triangle formed by the Iberian Peninsula, the Azores, and the Cape Verde Islands.[32] The increasing emphasis in naval planning, focusing on the need for bases in a war of sea communications, represented his first open advocacy of *Überseepolitik*, a global policy, that he knew could resolve Germany's strategic dilemma and threaten British sea communications.[33] Reflecting Mahan's dictum, "Naval strategy may win victories even in peacetime by the acquisition of local bases on foreign shores," he called upon the "political leadership" in early January 1937 to establish long-term goals appropriate to Germany's "power political" requirements and the necessary naval strategy to support this goal. Without bases, "the outcome of the next naval war against one or more of the sea powers was in question."[34]

Determined to create a more significant role for the navy in Hitler's rearmament plans and to support the führer's expansionist ideology, Raeder presented his ideas to Hitler and other senior political and military leaders on 3 February 1937. In this carefully prepared lecture, he provided a detailed explanation of the principles of naval warfare, making the case for a long-term naval building program and advocating the navy's role as the key player in a global war.[35] Although he referred only to France and the Soviet Union as Germany's potential enemies, his

remarks reflected a clear formulation of his naval strategy and the culmination of his own strategic studies and experiences and the themes
that had dominated the debate over naval strategy since the end of
World War I.[36] The next war, Raeder predicted, would be a struggle
not just between military forces, but also of "nation versus nation" and
Volk against *Volk*. In this *Gesamtkrieg* (total war), "final success would go
to the state that [possessed] the greatest number of people, more importantly, unlimited material and food supplies." If Germany were "unable
to obtain on a continual basis the raw materials it lacks," it would suffer the same fate as it had as a result of the economic blockade of 1914–
1918. He emphasized the importance of the "possession and geographical location of naval bases," and how they related to "the degree to
which a country depended on sea imports for the national economy
and the support it could hope for from overseas allies."[37]

The object of the "battle for naval supremacy" would be the Atlantic
arteries through which all German and enemy trade must pass.[38] The
principal task of the navy was to be "the defense of our own sea communications and the interdiction of those of our enemy."[39] His concept
of *Wirtschaftskrieg* (economic warfare) under a unified leadership reflected
his efforts to develop a viable naval strategy based on the vulnerability
of Germany's maritime enemies and the dependence of both continental and maritime nations on the political and economic importance of
sea lines of communication. The value of sea power had never been more
self-evident, and it demanded the subordination of Germany's continental interests to a fundamentally maritime strategy.[40]

In his arguments for a national maritime strategy, he clearly disasso-
ciated himself from the Mahanian-Tirpitz legacy of a single "decisive
battle" in favor of a strategic offensive framework involving numerous
operations, and he acknowledged the importance of geographic position. As opposed to his earlier position that the Royal Navy would have
been forced to seek an "annihilation battle" with the High Seas Fleet if
Germany had attacked its commerce, he proposed a more fluid concept
of continuous ocean operations against the enemy's sea communications.[41] His conception of seeking operational possibilities within the total
theater of operations—his *Vielseitigkeit* ("multiplicity") factor—fit well
with his determination to seize the initiative and attack Germany's foes
on a global scale. "Despite the expanse of the oceans, they nevertheless

comprise a single interconnected theater of war" which, through a diversionary operation in one area could "in a relatively brief period of time . . . contribute to the creation of the preconditions for success in battle elsewhere, however distant the two areas may be"—a blueprint for how a numerically inferior German navy could challenge a stronger naval power.

> An energetic effort by a few of our own striking forces against vulnerable sea lines of communication or some other object of a superior enemy can—through strategic pressure alone—tie down powerful forces and thereby bring about an equalization of forces elsewhere. To bring about such an interaction will be the guiding thought of the conduct of war. . . .

Unlike its performance in 1914–1918, Raeder promised, the navy would undertake an "energetic" Atlantic offensive against enemy sea-lanes and would attack "from the first day of the war." The only way the navy could protect Germany's sea communications—its "first task" in war—was to bind the enemy to the defense of its own sea-lanes, weakening its capability for offensive action and allowing for an "indirect" defense of German trade. Hitting the enemy at its weakest points would prevent the enemy from concentrating its forces. The fact that the navy would confront a superior enemy required the "fullest commitment of the forces of the state" and the "exercise of the strongest initiative." Such a strategy would require combined operations with the army and Luftwaffe overseas, but the navy must assume the decisive role.

Convinced of the importance of sea power in the next conflict, Raeder pointed out the limitations of land warfare and the Luftwaffe for a global war. Believing that decisive land operations were questionable in an age of Maginot lines, he contended that combined land-sea operations such as the British had conducted in the 1915 Dardanelles campaign represented a classic diversion strategy (as effective as the Imperial Navy's cruiser operations at the beginning of the war in 1914). Moreover, the Dardanelles example had demonstrated how a single unified command coordinating all political and military organizations could wage a global war to provide Germany with the best opportunity to reach its status of a Weltmacht. The operation had failed because the Allies had not been able to see beyond their own "fronts"—a concept outmoded by the nature of modern war, which required the leadership to determine where the decisive center of gravity lay. Modern warfare required that all potential targets of the enemy's land, air, and sea boundaries and those of all its colonies, as well as its communications and resources, must be targeted. He observed that the introduction of the airplane, submarine, and tank in World War I had not replaced other weapon systems but had served to augment the overall strength of the military and increased operational possibilities. The "armored, well-constructed battleship" remained the *sine qua non* of sea power and naval strategy."

While Raeder referred only to continental enemies and assumed British neutrality, he pointedly observed that future naval development had to take into account not only "the probable enemies of the present, but the possible enemies of the future" and then emphasized *"political constellations can be altered more quickly than ships can be built."*[42] His strategic vision of an Atlantic war clearly encompassed the challenges of having to fight England, even if he would not allow open discussion of it.

Raeder's ideas on the importance of geographical position and fleet closely matched those of Wolfgang Wegener's (from whom parts of his speech were cribbed outright).[43] He even admitted—disassociating himself from Tirpitz's apologists—that the government in 1914 had not been totally responsible for the failure of the fleet. He argued that the Imperial Navy could not have pressured England's sea communications from its base in the Helgoland Bight (the "dead corner of the North Sea"). Only continuous German pressure on the trade routes and the use of forces from the High Seas Fleet to break through the blockade would have forced the Royal Navy to attack.[44]

To achieve Raeder's strategic vision required ships. However, the increasing difficulties in meeting the demands of Hitler's forced pace of rearmament led him in October 1937 to issue an ultimatum: either the navy received a higher priority in resources or the naval forces required for Hitler's first stage of expansion would not be ready. The navy would be unable to complete the six planned battleships ("H" Class), expand the U-boat fleet to match the British submarine fleet, or meet critical infrastructure needs (e.g., the two large building docks for the projected super battleships) in the timetable demanded by Hitler. The result, he warned, was that Germany would have a fleet of only two 35,000-ton battleships—which "would neither be the match of any of our conceivable enemies at sea nor possess sufficient alliance value." Since this would have a decisive impact on foreign policy, he demanded an immediate führer decision in an effort to accelerate his massive naval construction.[45]

Although not widely recognized, this crisis provided, in large part, the impetus for the 5 November 1937 conference with the military's senior leaders in which Hitler informed them of his foreign policy aims for the next six to eight years and Germany's need for *Lebensraum*. In this meeting, described in the "Hossbach Memorandum" (written by Hitler's adjutant, Colonel Friedrich Hossbach), Hitler announced his intention, as a temporary solution, to deal with Austria and Czechoslovakia at the earliest possible moment. By 1943–1945, at the latest, Hitler indicated he was determined to solve by force the needs of Germany's expanding population. This timetable reflected the fact that the rearmament of the air force, navy, and army would be "almost complete" and Germany would have an advantage over its foes. Germany's eastward expansion would provide the resources for self-sufficiency and also provide a buffer from the Soviets. Moreover, in the face of a strong and well-armed Germany and a declining British Empire, it was possible that Germany might reacquire its overseas colonies and, with its expanded navy, protect trade and avoid a repeat of the World War I blockade. For the first time, publicly at least, Hitler acknowledged the possibility of hostilities with the "hate inspired opponents," England and France, who would oppose any further German strengthening in Europe or overseas.[46]

Although he later acknowledged the "somewhat sharp tone" of Hitler's words and his own increased "uneasiness," he believed the führer "had no intention of changing from his policy of peaceful negotiations to one of warlike threat." It was clear to others, if not to him, that Hitler's preferred course of action was war. Raeder "accepted" Göring's assessment that the führer's remarks were simply intended to spur the army into increasing its pace of rearmament.[47] He made no mention of the second part of the meeting, which focused on the industrial and economic preparations necessary to support the rearmament required for Hitler's timeline—Raeder's real interest in this meeting.[48]

The fact that he did not express any opinion, either at the meeting or in his memoirs, regarding the army's objections to a possible conflict with England and France or Hitler's intent to use force by 1943–1945 showed his satisfaction with Hitler's plans for the navy. He felt confident that an expanded navy was integral to Hitler's first phase of continental expansion and pleased that the führer had expressed the possibility of reacquiring colonies as the linchpin of German global power. More important, the navy was to receive an increase in its steel allocation (from 45,000 tons to 74,000) and other essential materials.[49] In return, Hitler expected Raeder to keep up with him.

The Turn against England

With the führer now prepared to continue his expansion in the face of British opposition, Raeder's long-term Anglophobia came into play. Although a 1936 study of a naval war with England was thoroughly pessimistic, Raeder had already begun to explore ways to meet the anticipated British reaction to an expanded German navy and what he now recognized as a serious international situation.[50] He did not air his thoughts on this prospect outside of his narrow circle of advisors until 12 April 1938, when he acknowledged that a war with England and France was a possibility "which completely changes the foundations of [our] naval warfare." He emphasized that the navy had to prepare for the "worst case" scenario and wait for the political leadership to create "favorable" conditions for the navy.[51] Raeder did not have long to wait. On 24 May 1938, Hitler asked him how he would expand the U-boat fleet and complete battleships "F" and "G" by early 1940, as well as increase the caliber of the guns for "D" and "E."[52]

Alarmed by the implications of Hitler's requests, several of Raeder's staff urged him to raise with Hitler the threat to the "greater goals" posed by the führer's plans for war with Czechoslovakia. These officers seemed singularly ignorant of the contents of Hitler's *Mein Kampf* or simply did not believe them. Raeder knew better and raised no protest. The public view, which Raeder advanced in his defense at Nuremberg and in his memoirs, was that he still believed that Hitler had not changed his "prudent" policy of good relations with England and that he had continued to receive reassurances that the fleet would not be needed before 1944 at the earliest. Raeder was ready to turn a blind eye to what was obvious to others, and he was loath to challenge Hitler, convinced that his loyalty had benefited him and the navy; moreover, he was determined to take advantage of Hitler's new anti-British policy.[53] Any open opposition was counter to his nature as defined by his narrow Ressortegoismus and his selective definition of "politics." Raeder insisted that he had tried to impress upon Hitler that the fleet was only in the initial stages of rearmament, and even with the shipyards at full capacity, "we could not think of contesting England before 1945 or 1946."[54]

On 28 May 1938, Hitler announced that it was his "unalterable will" to smash Czechoslovakia.[55] In response, Raeder ordered his staff to explore the possibility of a naval war against the British.[56] The result was the "England Memorandum" of 1938, the navy's "most decisive and historically most important document" before the war.[57] The initial study (Hellmuth Heye), submitted in August 1938, outlined the dilemma of challenging England's maritime superiority and sea communications and established the foundation for the navy's future strategy, wherein the destruction of commerce was seen as more important than a decisive battle between fleets. In short, the concept of sea control favored by the Tirpitz traditionalists had been replaced by the concept of sea denial.[58] As World War I had demonstrated, it concluded, a war could be won or lost without a major engagement. It also assumed, for the short term, that the fleet would be insufficient to defend Germany's imports or break a blockade. Even assuming equal fleets, a victory was judged almost impossible. Waging economic warfare and cutting off the enemy's commerce in conjunction with the other services could, however, "considerably enhance" the chances of success in a global war.[59]

The ships needed for such a role, however, could not be those designed for a *Normalflotte* in accordance with international treaties and the Anglo-German Naval Treaty. Each ship had to be faster than the enemy's heavily armed units and be able to outgun the foes' fastest ships. Even this weaker fleet must be "balanced" and utilize a mix of all types (and naval airpower) to be successful. The ships to be built, under Germany's "current" treaties, were to be improved or replaced by new construction more suited to oceanic warfare. The navy rejected *"substantive successes from an offensive naval strategy with U-boats only"*—reflecting the long-standing dogma that submarines could not provide the foundation for German *Seegeltung,* as well as the bias, shared by Hitler, in favor of the battleship.

In the face of Germany's poor geographic position and the difficulty of breaking the British blockade, the fleet would need to be at sea before any onset of hostilities and be able to operate independently for at least three months. The pressure on British trade routes would force the Royal Navy to divert resources overseas, thereby creating the opportunity for future breakouts into the Atlantic. The weakness in this strategy was apparent (e.g., logistics, battle damage), and it was acknowledged that it was an *"open question"* whether such a fleet could achieve a decisive victory.[60] Faced with this dilemma, Raeder invoked Tirpitz's deterrence factor. The mere threat of such a fleet would force the British to be more compliant, even to the point of reaching an understanding with Germany—an example of the pervasive wishful thinking on the part of the navy from Tirpitz to Raeder.

As a follow-up to Heye's study, Raeder established a committee to develop a "uniform view" of the strategic principles for the navy's buildup. Its conclusions closely followed the outlines of the "England Memorandum."[61] Battleships would force the British blockade and engage detached surface units of the Royal Navy in the North Sea. However, instead of building a larger number of smaller battleships that could be constructed faster and allow the navy to absorb the losses inherent in such operations, the committee, under "the strong personal influence of the Führer," envisioned larger and more heavily armored battleships than the *Bismarck* class. The new battleships of the "H" class were to have a maximum displacement of over 56,000 tons and 40.6-cm guns.[62]

Raeder also asked Admiral Rolf Carls, the fleet commander and his close confidant, to comment on the navy's strategic options. Carls supported the basic premises of the "English Memorandum" and advanced the navy's ultimate long-held ambitions—"to conquer the road to the [Atlantic] ocean." To achieve a "world-power position," Germany would need, "in addition to sufficient colonies, secure sea routes and access to the high seas. . . . A war against Britain means a war against the Empire, against France, probably also against Russia and a number of countries overseas, in other words against one-half or two-thirds of the whole world."

In addition to a powerful home fleet, which could operate to the west of the British Isles and thus break the Atlantic lifeline, Carls proposed the construction of four task forces. Each would be comprised of a battle cruiser, a heavy cruiser, and an aircraft carrier, along with destroyers and U-boats, with each group prepared to operate independently on the high seas. These ideas, which Raeder had studied in World War I, reflected an eager acceptance of a war against the Atlantic sea lanes. Carls also called for the conquest of the French Atlantic coast, Holland, and Denmark in order to improve Germany's geographic position.[63]

The committee's final report, presented to Raeder on 31 October 1938, called for a "provisional target" of building 10 battleships; 15

pocket battleships; 5 heavy, 24 light, and 36 small cruisers; 8 aircraft carriers; and 249 U-boats, in addition to support ships. Responding to the increasing realization that the navy needed ships, not plans, the committee proposed postponing the construction of the battleships until 1945.[64]

It is important to point out that these studies evolved against a background of fleet expansion preparations based on ideas that did not always take the form of concrete plans, much less contracts.[65] The deliberations over the type of ships to build (and their role in an Atlantic war), compounded by the ongoing construction delays, demonstrate Raeder's struggle to reconcile both short-term and long-term planning with Hitler's aggressive political agenda. Facing the prospect of war sooner rather than later, Raeder was forced to develop a strategy of a commerce war limited to the ships already being built. He vigorously campaigned to increase the number of ships that could be built more quickly, including U-boats, cruisers, and new, improved Panzerschiffe at the expense of postponing some of the larger battleships.[66]

By October 1938, Raeder's attempts to balance Hitler's demands with the threat of a war involving England and the difficulty of securing the necessary resources became even more desperate. Facing criticism from those who questioned his decisions, he used the anniversary of his ten years as navy chief to describe his struggles with the government, the Reichstag, and the other services in building the fleet. Always conscious of his authority, Raeder sought to present himself as the initiator and not as the mere executor of Hitler's plans. He described the development of the fleet and the preparations under way to deal with England (the Z-Plan). The navy, he promised, would not find itself in a similar position as in 1914–1918 because the führer would create the political conditions that would allow the navy to build a fleet sufficient for a successful war. The alliance with Italy and Japan would force the British to fight on three widely dispersed fronts. Hitler, he declared, was prepared to abrogate the naval treaty with England, and he stated that Hitler had agreed to the 35 percent ratio only because Germany did not have the short-term capacity to build up its forces beyond that level.

Raeder said that the increased pace of the navy's rearmament would begin in winter (1938–1939) and that plans were being made to increase the navy's U-boat program and build two more battleships ("H" and "J"), which "corresponding to the direction of the Führer" would be armed with 40-cm guns. All ships were to be developed for "oceanic warfare," with the highest priority being the widest steaming radius possible (the "fundamental principle"). To compensate for the lack of bases, the navy would build a network of supply ships to support worldwide operations. He elaborated at length on the expansion of the navy's ports and infrastructure (including locks, building slips, and dry docks with dimensions that could accommodate 100,000-ton battleships!). Nothing, he declared, was being withheld for the navy's rebuilding—not money, not workers, not material. *"We have only the duty to build the fleet as strong and as fast as possible."*

> This means a tremendous adjustment for all of us. In this *the army and navy are in a much more disadvantageous position than the Luftwaffe* which, not burdened by memories in the ways of work of the *Systemzeit*, only know the work pace of the Third Reich. I openly acknowledge that even I have had to learn to rethink.

Raeder had quickly learned Hitler's intentions and "it was now my task to awaken the understanding for [Hitler's] work tempo in all parts of the navy. The further one is from the Führer, the less he personally feels [Hitler's] pressure to move forward and it is even more difficult for him to think in the new work methods."

He openly acknowledged major operational problems with the navy's new ships. These were the results not only of insufficient building capacity, but also of the lack of experience in building warships due to the Versailles treaty limitations and Germany's poor economic situation in the 1920s. Because of the forced pace of rearmament, time did not permit the testing of new developments in naval construction. He accepted responsibility for the decision to install the new high-temperature, high-pressure steam turbine engine in the new battleships, cruisers, and destroyers (which Hitler also had criticized). He noted the problems with these engines, especially the reduced cruising radius, but promised the navy would develop new systems that would provide both the range and speed required for the commerce war.

Raeder accepted personal responsibility for carrying out Hitler's order to expand the fleet as quickly as possible. He had assumed this immense task with "a joyful heart," because of his "rock hard trust in our Führer, who will control every political, military and economic situation" and will decide the necessity and timing of any conflict. The experiences over the last months (i.e., the Munich crisis) only reinforced his "unreserved trust in the superior statesmanship of the Führer." And "It was our duty to follow unconditionally the Führer . . . whose last goal we ourselves cannot see."[67]

The Development of the Z-Plan

Although Raeder had been promised a larger share of resources, he was becoming increasingly concerned that war was imminent in spite of Hitler's assurances. He proposed to increase U-boat construction and delay the building of battleships and aircraft carriers in favor of the ships required for cruiser warfare. He believed he could still provide "forces suited to conducting an independent war at sea." The building of a fleet capable of challenging the British battle fleet that "undoubtedly [would] carry greater weight, both politically and militarily," however, would have to be postponed.[68]

Then, in November 1938, Hitler emphatically rejected any changes in the number or types of ships, especially the battleships that he wanted ready by 1944, and criticized "everything we are building and planning."[69] He was dissatisfied with the "weak" armament of the new *Bismarck* class and lack of speed. There is also evidence that Hitler had heard grumblings from younger officers regarding Raeder's plans.[70] For Hitler, problems could always be overcome through "force of will." Insulted, Raeder immediately asked to be relieved of his command. Hitler, according to Raeder, backed off and "promised" him "complete freedom of action in any program for the fleet's expansion."[71]

On 17 January 1939, Raeder tried again, proposing the "Z" plan (following "X" and "Y") with a completion goal of 1948.[72] Hitler demanded that all six new battleships be ready by 1944. He refused to listen to objections, declaring, "If I can build the Third Reich in six years, then the navy can surely build these six ships in six years."[73] The only way to meet Hitler's timetable was to increase the navy's allotment of resources at the expense of the other two services."[74] To secure Göring's support, Raeder now renounced the independent development of a naval aviation arm—a decision he later regretted.[75] The Z-Plan, however, was a hollow achievement, lasting only nine months, and largely on paper. Over the next seven months, international developments and the substantial material and labor deficiencies would lead to the unraveling of the Z-Plan.[76]

The inadequacy of the "stop and start" construction program and the gap between the long-term nature of fleet building and the short-term nature of political decisions became even more evident.[77] This situation was further exacerbated by the inability to develop a clear strategy for the navy in both its current and projected state and the lack of consensus on the proper mix of ships for the fleet. Hitler's rejection of any changes reflected his lack of understanding of the implications of a commerce war; his attention was focused only on a fleet that could create the foundations for a future conflict with the world's maritime powers. The precondition for this global (and thus maritime) stage in Hitler's "program" would be the achievement of continental hegemony. Ultimately the opportunity to build the long-dreamed-of *Weltmachtflotte* seduced Raeder, as did the image of building powerful German battleships for Hitler.

The depth of Raeder's complicity with Hitler's program, his identification with Hitler's goals, and his personal confidence in the führer's leadership are beyond question. Following his 1 November 1938 meeting to convince Hitler of the need for a more immediate buildup of his forces, he abdicated authority for the settlement of all issues over resources to the führer. Hitler's failure to adhere to his own timetable regarding the start of hostilities and Raeder's desperate hope that the führer would "achieve another of his amazing political successes through diplomacy alone" underlie his expressed bitterness over the British declaration of war in September 1939.[78] His disappointment reflects how deeply conscious he was of the failure of his policies and of his subservience to Hitler. It presaged too, how little influence he was to have on the conduct of the war.

Operational Planning Implications, 1938–1939

With England as the primary enemy, the navy developed its "double pole" strategy—calling for attacks on the British sea-lanes and operations against the Royal Navy. If successful, this strategy could enable even limited German naval forces to win a "decisive battle" over an enemy weakened by having to divide its own forces to protect its worldwide commerce and empire. Raeder optimistically anticipated strategic success in the economic war, but only tactical success against the blockade.[79] The evaluation of the February–March 1939 war games concluded that the available forces were insufficient to achieve any real success against the British and French, even if Italy was an active ally. Only after 1943, when the navy received its new ships, would there exist "promising opportunities for battle" not only in the North Sea but also on the "high seas of the world."[80] For Raeder, if the navy were to change its overall strategic situation, it was an "absolute priority" for the army to secure bases on the French Atlantic coast and outflank the British blockade and gain access to the Atlantic.[81]

As the navy struggled with its strategic operational issues, the preparations for "Case White" against Poland necessitated updated operational directives. The May 1939 edition demonstrated the difficulties inherent in the navy's strategic situation. The directives, although still considered "provisional," assumed a world war based on a "clear grouping" of nations: the Western democracies on one side and Germany and Italy, along with Hungary, Spain, and Japan, on the other. Russia's position in this scenario was unclear. The navy was directed to remain in a high state of readiness in what was clearly recognized as a prewar situation. The navy's major task was to secure the access to the Baltic and North Sea in order to move forces quickly between the two as circumstances warranted. At the same time, U-boats would attack trade on the enemies' coasts and all available raiders would be fully committed to the Atlantic. Because the limited number of ships was insufficient to protect German trade in the North Sea, the fleet would be concentrated in the northern waters of the North Sea, where they would represent a potential breakout threat and make it easier for the raiders to leave and return to the Atlantic. Although Raeder continued to believe in the führer's infallibility, it was clear that Hitler was determined to pursue his expansionist policies—with or without British acquiescence. The navy and Luftwaffe would be readied to counter any interference during the campaign for continental hegemony. In the second half of the 1940s, Raeder expected that the Kriegsmarine would be ready to support Germany's overseas expansion.[82]

Raeder's Atlantic Strategy: An Assessment

No plan survives its first meeting with the enemy. Raeder's attempts to formulate an effective naval strategy for a war against Britain have been both praised and condemned. Salewski praised Raeder's Atlantic strategy as a "daring, first-rate plan" in spite of its failure, although he questions the aim of such a strategy if it could never realistically accomplish its objectives.[83] Ruge argues that the framing of the Z-Plan showed that the navy clearly knew how to tackle the many problems involved in a war against British sea power—a "genuine 'fleet in being' exerting pressure on a superior enemy's sea communications while itself choosing the moment to strike at his locally weaker forces."[84]

Among Raeder's critics, Edward Wegener, following in his father's footsteps, condemned Raeder as being just as "continental minded" as Hitler and objected to Salewski's description of using capital ships in commerce war as an "offensive" naval strategy. The Z-Plan, for Wegener, was "defensive"—"nothing more than cruiser warfare escalated to gigantic proportions."[85] Raeder's supporters such as Rear Admiral Fuchs defended the use of these battleships, arguing that they could operate without bases for up to a year.[86] For Dönitz, the Z-Plan strategy of battle groups with its oversized ships was "utopian."[87] Other critics charged (as did Wolfgang Wegener) that a true strategic offensive was dependent on improving Germany's geography relative to the Atlantic, but never resolved how the navy was to gain command of England's sea communications.[88]

The problem, as Herbert Rosinski expressed it in his cogent criticism of German naval thought, was that command could only be exercised by *"controlling the enemy"* and not merely by a sea-denial strategy of cruiser warfare.[89] More important, none of the navy's strategists, including Tirpitz, Raeder, Wegener, and Kurt Assmann, ever solved the question of how a weaker fleet could gain a victory in challenging the Royal Navy.[90] For Rosinski, Raeder had simply gone from one extreme (Tirpitz's "final battle") to the other (trade warfare—avoiding combat whenever possible with enemy naval forces). Raeder's "fatal error" had been to use the fleet as commerce raiders (as Rosinsky put it, to add their "mite") instead of concentrating these forces, which might have "at least disputed the Allied command of the seas with more substantive results."[91]

Raeder's concept of an Atlantic commerce war was, in fact, a daring, offensive strategy that had the potential to disrupt Britain's commerce to the point where the enemy would either acquiesce to Germany's continental expansion or sue for peace. This strategy fit well into Hitler's "English policy" during his short-term quest for continental hegemony. Significantly, the British Admiralty, who had studied Raeder's writings on Kreuzerkrieg, took the German threat seriously, recognizing that this type of commerce war could generate a strategic leverage against them far out of proportion to the size of the German fleet.[92] As recent research shows, the British Admiralty used treaty negotiations to direct Germany's naval rearmament along more traditional lines and to buy time for building the necessary forces to counter any commerce raiding strategy. Given the threat of an asymmetrical German naval force structure, the Z-Plan's battle group concept and specialized raiders might have been more viable than critics have given them credit for being.[93]

Although both Hitler and Raeder saw the battleship as the symbol of national power, the führer's support included no indication of how such a navy was to fight. In large part, in spite of his involvement in the deliberations and execution of the navy's rebuilding program, Hitler left the decisions on the navy's operational planning to Raeder—at least until the loss of the *Graf Spee* in late 1939. The navy also had no qualms about designing 100,000-ton super battleships that were compatible, whatever their military usefulness, with its dreams of a Weltmachtflotte and Hitler's vision for *Grossdeutschland* on the same scale as Albert Speer's plans for a post-war Berlin as the capital of a world power.[94] That the navy continued its push for the creation of a massive battle fleet, ignoring the concomitant strategic and economic difficulties, reflected both the strength of Tirpitz's navalist legacy and the bankruptcy of Raeder's political and strategic program.

Further complicating an understanding of Raeder's efforts to develop an effective naval strategy, the navy's construction programs, operational plans, and ultimately its strategic goals were never based on present realities but were focused on a distant future in which the appropriate ships were available and Germany's foreign policy objectives had been achieved.[95] And, in September 1939, because the fleet was incomplete, naval planning and operations became of necessity a war of improvisation, in which the navy still attempted to follow the strategic principles that Raeder had developed over the course of his career.

Raeder's claims (and those of his postwar supporters) that Hitler (a self-proclaimed "coward at sea") had never understood sea power and was a "pure continental politician" reflect his attempts to blame Hitler and other military leaders for the failure of Germany's naval warfare.[96] According to Raeder and his supporters, the navy "alone properly appreciated the threat from England, and alone took all appropriate measures to pursue the relentless fight against British sea communications."[97] Yet, as we have seen in the navy's prewar construction program, Hitler played a deciding role in Raeder's planning, and the navy understood its naval aims in the context of the führer's pursuit of *Weltmacht*. Contrary to those who argue that Hitler neglected sea power, the Z-Plan represented Hitler's appreciation of the role that an expanded fleet would play in his short-term strategy to achieve continental hegemony, with or without British acquiescence, before proceeding to his next stage of German expansion. Even so, he was willing to risk a war before the fleet was ready. For Hitler, strategy and ideology were "inextricably and dialectically linked with each other." His miscalculations regarding England were also Raeder's, who believed that his führer would take into consideration the necessary economic constraints and time required to build the fleet. Meanwhile he chose to ignore the danger signs, lest the navy be disadvantaged in its competition for resources.[98]

Until the declaration of war by the British, Raeder believed that he had successfully "educated" Hitler and had exceeded Tirpitz in gaining the support to build a sea power second to none. If, as the navy's apologists lamented, Germany's national strategy had been too "continentalized" in 1939–1945, it was largely a result of being too "compartmentalized" as a result of Hitler's preference to meet individually with his commanders in chief, which allowed Raeder to advocate his own, often competitive, strategic views against Hitler, the OKW, and the other two branches of the armed forces.[99] Raeder himself contributed to this situation by zealously guarding his prerogative of *Immediatstellen* to the führer as he did his own *Ressort* and believed, for a long time, that he was effective with Hitler, especially one-on-one. Only too late did Raeder recognize how this practice contributed to the "land-mindedness" of the higher military levels and fueled Hitler's divide-and-conquer strategy and the palace politics of the Third Reich. Not until April 1942 did Raeder petition Hitler to appoint a liaison to the Führer Headquarters in an attempt to address the unequal representation of the navy in Hitler's military planning and decision making. Except for a brief period before the war, Hitler consistently failed to give the navy the resources it needed, in part because they were insufficient to meet all the plans he did approve. Moreover, he redirected U-boats and the fleet away from operations against commerce to support other campaigns once the war began. Yet, Hitler, more than Raeder, understood that, while Germany's future might lie on the water, the failure to create the *Grossraumwirtschaft,* the autarkical large-space economy, especially after the invasion of the Soviet Union in June 1941, meant that Germany's fate would be decided on land.

A precondition for the realization of all of our plans and
hopes is the successful ending of the present war for which
for Germany there can be only one "Ceterum censeo":
"Britanniam esse delendum."

—*Kapitän zur See Frank Aschmann, 1940*

7

Once Again, World War

Preparing for War: From the Abrogation of the Anglo-German Naval Treaty to the Solution of the "Polish Question"

At the launching of the *Bismarck* on 14 February 1939, Hitler hinted at
a possible renunciation of the Anglo-German Naval Treaty if England
persisted in "further unfriendly behavior."[1] Raeder echoed Hitler's rhetoric during ceremonies for *Heldengedenktag*, Germany's Memorial Day,
on 12 March 1939. On the eve of the German march into Prague, he proclaimed the readiness of the military to defend the nation.

> Where we have an advantage, we will maintain it! Where a deficiency
> exists, we will correct it! When we need to modernize, we will do it! And
> no one should believe that our weapons will remain passive if German
> land should be violated or German blood shed. Germany is the protector
> of all Germans whether they live on this side or the other side of the
> border! The shots fired on Almeria are proof of this. Germany strikes fast
> and hard![2]

After the launching of the *Tirpitz* (1 April), Hitler warned the British
again that, if England no longer shared the desire to work for peace,
"then the practical assumptions for the treaty no longer exist." In another
sign of his support for the navy (and a warning to the British), Hitler presented Raeder with his *Grossadmiral* baton as "the first Grand Admiral
of the Third Reich." In a handwritten note, Hitler hailed Raeder's forty-
five years of service.

> You experienced the building of the powerful prewar fleet under its great
> creator. You led the engagement of this instrument of German *Seegeltung*
> in this great time at the side of an outstanding fleet commander [Hipper]

and held fast to the concept of German *Seegeltung* during the period of decline with all [your] strength. For ten and a half years you have been the leader of the German armed forces at sea which carry the stamp of your personality.

He called upon Raeder to build a fleet "worthy of [Greater Germany]" and hoped that he would remain as his "advisor and collaborator for a long time to come."[3]

Raeder claimed he was "stunned" when Hitler abrogated the Anglo-German Treaty on 28 April 1939.[4] If he was surprised, it was by the timing, but not by the action itself. He had already been struggling with how much of the Z-Plan could be initiated before it would become obvious that Germany intended to violate its treaty with the British. His refusal to begin any renegotiations with the British and the internal discussions over how long the navy could appear to adhere to the 35 percent ratio clearly indicated that a denunciation of their treaty was all but inevitable.[5] An abrogation would buy the navy time, especially given the obligation to provide details regarding its new ships, which would have revealed the anti-British intent of his naval program.[6] Rumors of a massive German naval expansion began to circulate following a speech by Raeder in Stuttgart on 9 June 1939, in which he stated that the führer had ordered a "large-scale buildup of the Kriegsmarine." When questioned by the British, Raeder responded disingenuously that "since the termination of the naval treaty no new building program had been ordered." He was factually correct, if not deliberately misleading, since the Z-Plan had been approved almost six months earlier.[7]

As Hitler intensified his pressure on Poland, Raeder continued to believe in Hitler's abilities to create another diplomatic miracle, and he never seriously addressed the possibility of any English, French, or Soviet naval intervention over Poland.[8] On 23 May 1939, Hitler "shocked" Raeder with an announcement that he intended to deal with the Polish problem. If the British interfered, then the "showdown with England is a matter of life and death."[9] Prompted by Hitler's "remarkably inconsistent remarks," he privately expressed his concern over how it was possible to "believe that war against Poland was possible on one hand, [while] arriving at a peaceful settlement on the other." However, he maintained later that he still did not believe that Hitler had deviated from his "original concept" of maintaining friendly relations with

England. Hitler's insistence that there was to be no change in the navy's construction program or the overall timetable for rearmament reassured Raeder that there was no immediate threat. Moreover, Hitler personally assured him that the British would never go to war over demands for the return of the Polish Corridor (his last "revisionist demand").[10] Others were more skeptical, including Dönitz and Admiral Boehm, the outspoken fleet commander, who criticized the lack of preparations for war, arguing that it made no sense unless one assumed that war with France and England was "highly unlikely."[11] Yet, the navy's May 1939 directives acknowledged Germany was already in a "prewar period" and that the conflict had already begun "even if no shots had actually been fired."[12] Preparations for war were becoming increasingly obvious with such measures as full-scale readiness alerts, live fire exercises, and the painting over of the identification numbers on U-boat conning towers.[13]

By mid-August, a nervous Raeder decided to take precautionary measures, recalling Dönitz from leave and deploying the *Deutschland* and *Graf Spee* and a number of U-boats to the Atlantic and North Sea. On the same day that Hitler received a warning from the British government (22 August), he briefed his senior officers on the Polish crisis. To Raeder, Hitler seemed intent on justifying his actions, given the possibility of a wider war, and the navy chief was convinced that "we stood close to the brink of war." Alarmed, he went to Hitler, but the führer convinced him that he had the situation well in hand and that negotiation, not war, would resolve this crisis.[14] What Raeder did not report—unlike others who were present—was Hitler's aggressive tone, emphasizing that the total annihilation of Poland must be "pursue[d] in new ways. . . . We must all steel ourselves against humanitarian reasoning!"[15] Although Raeder may have considered these remarks as typical of Hitler's rhetoric or interpreted them into his own framework (i.e., the call for Lebensraum represented the nineteenth-century colonial expansion of territory —"*Raumerweiterung*"), it would become increasingly obvious as the war progressed that they were an integral part of Hitler's ruthless extermination policies.[16]

Raeder's concerns were further assuaged when he learned that foreign minister Joachim von Ribbentrop was preparing to sign a non-aggression pact with the Soviets. As Raeder reported it, "We felt once more one of Hitler's clever political chess moves was coming up, and that he would win peacefully again, just as he had always done before."[17] Once again, Raeder fell back on his faith in the führer and his determination to concentrate on his own *Ressort*. Anticipating that the conflict in Poland could be localized, the navy did not completely mobilize. The navy's instructions for dealing with England and France in Hitler's first war directive, of 31 August, were only precautionary, calling upon the navy "to operate against merchant shipping with England as the focal point."[18]

From Resignation to "Total Engagement"

At 0448 hours, on 1 September 1939, the navy fired the first shots of World War II with the surprise attack of the pre-dreadnought *Schleswig-Holstein* against Polish positions on the Westerplatte.[19] The consequent British and French declarations of war hit Raeder "like a bombshell" and Hitler "embarrassedly" admitted to him that he had been unable to avoid war with England.[20] A bitter Raeder officially recorded his feelings for the navy's desperate situation: "Today the war against England-France broke out, which the Führer had previously assured us we would not have to confront until 1944 and which he believed he could avoid up to the last minute . . . even if a thorough resolution of the Polish question had to be postponed."

Justifying his prewar policies, he detailed how the Z-Plan, in concert with Italy and Japan, would have provided the best chance of success in defeating the British fleet and cutting off Britain's imports. The forces now available were obviously "in no way ready" for this great struggle— "that is, the final solution of the English question." In spite of a "well trained and well organized U-boat arm," it was still "too weak to exert a *decisive* influence on the war." Echoing Trotha's call in 1918 for the fleet to "go down with honor," Raeder acknowledged that the surface forces were "too weak in number and strength" and could only "show— through [their] full engagement—that they know how to die gallantly and thereby to create the foundation for a future rebirth."[21]

In spite of his grim analysis that the existing ships could not be expected to have any decisive effect on the war, he called for *Angriffsgeist*, an "unbridled offensive spirit." The lessons of World War I and the shame of the Imperial Navy's inactivity were deeply ingrained in Raeder.

A navy that did not commit itself to combat could not expect to survive. Nine months later, he expressed this thought more explicitly.

> The great aim that the Führer has set forth for the German *Volk* requires above all the utmost engagement of the navy. . . . A *Kriegsmarine* that undertakes bold actions against the enemy and thereby suffers losses, will be reborn on a larger scale; if it has not fought this action, then its existence after the war will be threatened.[22]

Even with this initial grim assessment, Raeder did see some advantages. The navy's inferiority freed it from the burden of defending its own commerce, and a war of attrition might create opportunities for the fleet to engage the enemy under more equal circumstances. He also regarded the British as "orthodox and conservative," ill-prepared to meet the three-dimensional threat posed by the Kriegsmarine's surface and submarine forces and the Luftwaffe.[23] Hitler, however, thwarted Raeder's determination to seize the initiative, refusing him the operational freedom he demanded. Hitler believed that inflicting losses on the British might hurt their pride and "spoil" any chances for future negotiations. Raeder fretted over the "psychological" effect on the crews if they did not go into combat as soon as possible and noted that successes would be easier at the beginning of the war. He blamed Hitler for depriving the navy of opportunities to inflict as much damage as possible before the enemy instituted defensive measures such as convoys.[24]

Raeder believed that unrestricted submarine warfare should be implemented regardless of the violation of international treaties. He was well aware of the potential effect on neutral powers, especially the United States, but he expected that quick successes would outweigh any risks. He also considered American support of the British and an eventual Anglo-American alliance as a given. Despite Hitler's reluctance, Raeder hoped to escalate the U-boat war in stages in response to British countermeasures (e.g., arming merchant vessels)—actions that Germany could then use as the pretext to lift some of the restrictions until all enemy shipping could be attacked without warning. Raeder supported the declaration of a war zone (as Germany did in 1915) and the waging of unrestricted submarine warfare as a means of "achieving the greatest damage to England with the forces at hand."[25]

Raeder argued with Hitler and the Foreign Office that the political consequences could be reduced, if the timing was right and supported by a propaganda campaign. He proposed to replace the term "U-boat war" with "commerce war" and avoid any reference to "unrestricted submarine warfare." The SKL also claimed that declaring a *Belagerung,* a "siege" of England, would provide some cover for Germany's violations of international law.[26] Unfortunately, *U-30*'s sinking of the passenger ship, *Athenia,* mistaken for a British armed merchant, on 3 September 1939, provided the British with a major propaganda victory, Germany having previously announced that it would adhere to international rules. Hitler directed that the navy deny any involvement, and Raeder publicly denounced the British charge that the *Athenia* had been torpedoed by a U-boat as an "abominable lie."[27]

The question of Raeder's support of the U-boat arm had become a contentious issue among the officer corps. In 1938, Dönitz had called for a minimum of three hundred U-boats and, once the war began, pleaded with Raeder to concentrate all resources on the U-boat arm.[28] Raeder did, in fact, press Hitler for a large-scale expansion of U-boat construction as the most effective way to produce an effective weapon in the greatest numbers in the least time. Arguing that the "entire weight" of the war against England "fell on the navy alone, that is, on the U-boats," he vigorously continued to appeal for Hitler's support to expand U-boat production at the expense of the other armed forces. Although Hitler agreed, he still refused to give the navy priority and, in spite of Raeder's efforts from September 1939 to January 1943, U-boat production never reached the levels he sought. The ongoing shortages of resources and labor and the changing scope of the war after the autumn of 1940 all contributed to the failure to meet the desired numbers. The lack of coordination in planning and the contradictions in Hitler's own directives (e.g., issuing orders to give priority to the Luftwaffe and then demanding that there be no reduction in the production of U-boats), symptoms of Hitler's prewar rearmament program, further contributed to the lack of progress during Raeder's tenure.[29]

Raeder blamed Hitler's refusal to lift restrictions or support his U-boat program on the führer's "warped land-minded outlook shared by many of his advisors," as well as Hitler's continuing hopes of negotiating a settlement with his enemies. In Raeder's view, these hopes should have ended with the Allies' rejection of Hitler's "great peace address" of 6 October. Raeder's lamentation—"It was my constant and thankless job to warn him [Hitler] that now, and in the long run, England was our most dangerous adversary"—reflected his long-term anti-British policy and his intent to wage a global war.[30] Raeder's continual pressure for an intensified war against Britain and his willingness to risk war with the United States, however, conflicted with Hitler's short-term continental goals. Raeder persistently tried to influence Hitler's every decision in favor of preparing the foundations for the next step in the navy's ambitions. Above all, he wanted to ensure that the navy would have a preeminent role in Hitler's *Weltreich* and armament priorities far beyond what it could hope to achieve in this war.

Raeder began his major campaign to convince Hitler of the importance of the navy on 23 October 1939 when he called for the creation of a unified leadership organization to counter the British economic blockade. He argued that Germany must adopt *"the same methods of brutal economic warfare"* as their enemy. As he did in February 1937, Raeder pointed out that in economic warfare, politicoeconomic considerations and land, sea, and air warfare must be considered as an *"inseparable whole."* He proclaimed the preeminence of the Kriegsmarine in the conduct of economic warfare because of the "special impact" of naval warfare. Compared to the minor role of the army in the economic war, the Luftwaffe would play a decisive role in the attacks against the enemy's land and sea commerce. If political considerations would not allow the navy to make an immediate transition to the "strongest and most ruthless form of commerce war that is necessary," then the navy would intensify the war "step by step" corresponding to the course of the war.[31] Although Hitler approved Raeder's concept of an "Office for Economic Warfare" in the OKW, his hopes for a successful collaboration between the OKW and the other services never came to fruition, and this office was later described as a "stillborn child."[32]

Even as Raeder argued for a larger share of resources, he hoped that the "full engagement" of the U-boats and surface forces would produce early successes to demonstrate the role that even the small Kriegsmarine could play. Buoyed by results of the first "wave" (thirty-nine British ships including the carrier *Courageous* were sunk), Raeder believed the navy had dealt a considerable psychological blow to the British. After the *U-47* sank the *Royal Oak* in Scapa Flow, an impressed Hitler ordered that British or French merchant ships could now be attacked without warning.[33]

In the surface war, in spite of the limited success of the Panzerschiffe in late September 1939, Raeder's initial pessimism gave way to a more positive assessment that continuous attacks on the enemy's trade routes would achieve a "maximum effect" in disrupting enemy and neutral trade.[34] Moreover, he successfully expanded resupplying opportunities for the navy's raiders by utilizing Spanish, Russian, and Japanese bases.[35] Although he never officially changed his call for "total engagement," he now introduced an element of caution to avoid unnecessary risks that affected Panzerschiff operations and later those of the battleships. This change was initially tactical, as Raeder wanted to avoid losing any ships, hoping that the Italy's entry into the war would tie down British and French forces in the Mediterranean and provide even more freedom for his raiders. The standing operational orders called for commanders to obtain all possible successes, yet ensure that they could stay at sea as long as possible to create as much of a disruptive effect as possible. As the orders to the *Deutschland* and the *Graf Spee* on 4 September made clear, enemy naval forces, "even if inferior," were only to be engaged if it would further the principal task of the war on merchant shipping.[36] At the same time, the operational directives concluded with the führer's admonition that he expected aggressiveness from his officers: "Rather death with honor than strike the flag!"[37]

Raeder blamed Hitler for the "holding back" of the fleet, citing the führer's constant worry whenever the capital ships were at sea and his preoccupation with capital ships as symbols of prestige (the *Deutschland* was ordered home and renamed *Lützow*). Raeder could not ignore the führer's caution, but neither had he resolved in his own mind the balance between full engagement and avoiding risk. At one point early in October 1939, he bragged to Hitler that *Gneisenau* and *Scharnhorst* were more than a match for the three British battle cruisers, but then noted that "all-out operations" were restricted until the two new *Bismarck* class battleships were ready.[38]

In early October, Raeder launched an operation by the *Gneisenau*, the *Köln*, and nine destroyers in the North Sea to pin British forces in home waters. Believing this had created a successful diversion, he then ordered a mining campaign by German surface forces on the British east coast (sixty-six merchant ships and three destroyers were sunk).[39] In November 1939, he committed the *Gneisenau* and *Scharnhorst* to a mission that, despite meager results, he believed (albeit wrongly) to have forced enemy forces to withdraw from the hunt for the *Graf Spee*.[40] To Raeder, it confirmed how an inferior fleet could still challenge British command of the sea in its own home waters and the potential of a breakthrough into the Atlantic. It also indicated that the British were fighting a defensive naval war.

However, criticism over the new fleet commander's (Admiral Wilhelm Marschall's) failure to continue the November attack against the British naval forces or to feint a breakthrough (the original orders) revealed the growing contradictions between Raeder's call for "full engagement" and his instructions to avoid unnecessary risks, as well as the conflicts between the SKL and the fleet command.[41] Hitler also was not pleased. Informed of the operation only after the battle, he perceived the results as disproportionate to the risks involved.[42] This was an ominous sign that there were considerable differences between Raeder and Hitler over the conduct of naval warfare and the use of capital ships in the commerce war—a situation that would become even more apparent with each subsequent engagement.

Meanwhile, Raeder's command structure led to conflicts between the newly established group commands (West and East) and the fleet commander. These problems had first emerged in the use of the fleet to cover mining operations off the English coast in early October 1939 and led to the replacement of the fleet commander, Admiral Boehm. Although Raeder supported in theory the commander's rights to make decisions independently, based on his tactical assessment, his disposition toward strict adherence to his authority in his role as both commander in chief and chief of the SKL led to instructions that the fleet commander was expected to carry out the orders of the group command as closely as possible.[43] Raeder later admitted that his new command structure had raised questions "as to where the proper authority lay, and what were the limitations as to giving orders."[44] Boehm regarded it as "superfluous" and criticized it for causing unnecessary friction between the multiple levels of command.

In early October 1939, Boehm, after being overruled by Group West (and SKL) issued an order that the battleships would not cover a mining operation, "by the order of Group West." Raeder regarded Boehm's order as a "demonstration" against him and expected Boehm to rescind it and fire his chief of staff. When Boehm threatened to resign, Raeder promptly relieved him, rebuffing his repeated pleas for a meeting.[45] Raeder found Boehm's outspoken questioning of his policies disloyal, and he was particularly sensitive to Boehm's justification for deploying the battleships—the frequent breakdowns of the destroyers.

In December the scuttling of the *Graf Spee* on 17 December 1939 off Montevideo, Uruguay, precipitated the first major conflict with Hitler over fleet operations. From Raeder's perspective, the differences between his concept of naval warfare and Hitler's were so diametrically opposed that it represented "one of the causes of our quarrel later."[46]

The story of the *Graf Spee* and the "Battle of the River Plate" is well-known. Unable to obtain enough time for repairs, the captain of the *Graf Spee*, Hans Langsdorff, asked Raeder whether he should allow his ship to be interned in Montevideo or scuttle it. In discussing this situation with Hitler, Raeder suggested that the ship should attempt to fight its way out—to which Hitler agreed—stating that internment was out of the question and, at the very least, the *Graf Spee* might sink an enemy ship before being lost. Hitler was angry with Langsdorff's decision (based on false reports that British reinforcements had arrived) to blow up the ship without a fight and expressed his dissatisfaction with a lack of fighting spirit. He was disappointed that the *Graf Spee* did not finish off the badly damaged British cruiser *Exeter*, remarking that the senior officers— as opposed to the "daring young destroyer and U-boat commanders"— were "moved too much by strategic considerations and paid little attention to the immediate job of fighting." He sharply disapproved of any orders for ships to avoid battle in favor of destroying enemy commerce. Although he agreed that the use of cruisers and Panzerschiffe for the commerce war might be justified to a limited extent, this was not true for battleships. Commanders should fight it out to the end regardless of the consequences.[47] Although Raeder publicly defended Langsdorff, he criticized him personally. "The German warship and her crew are to fight with all their strength to the last shell, until they win or go down with their flag flying." Once engaged, the battle was "to be fought to the finish."[48]

This episode presaged future conflicts over the navy's operational freedom and Raeder's failure to convince Hitler of his principles for conducting commerce war. He remained determined to demonstrate the value of the navy's surface forces to Hitler. He remained optimistic about the battle for the "gates to the Atlantic" and looked forward to achieving not only "strategic goals" (i.e., diversion), but also attacking enemy naval forces beyond the North Sea. This represented a reversal of his "double-pole" strategy by which the diversionary effect of the raiders on shipping would create opportunities for the deployment of the capital ships in the North Sea and the Atlantic.[49] With the other services concentrating on the Western campaign, Raeder saw disturbing signs of the "continental thinking" of the OKW, with a further marginalizing of the navy and a relegation of the economic war solely to the navy. The continuing lack of support from the Luftwaffe and orders from OKW to siphon off naval personnel for the army, as well as the suggestion that the capital ships be disarmed to secure the artillery for a long war, led Raeder to protest vigorously against the "demoralizing" effect such ideas were having on the navy. He complained to Hitler that the "false conception" that the navy could do without a minimum of four battleships disregarded their critical role in protecting mining operations and iron ore shipments from Narvik while tying British forces in home waters. Only battleships could enable the navy to threaten the eastern part of the Atlantic trade routes and the patrol lines in the north.[50]

The stinging loss of the *Graf Spee* and the impending attack on the west made Raeder eager for a major victory of the capital ships to demonstrate their worth and make a contribution to the war. In late February 1940, intelligence reports indicated that conditions were favorable for surface attacks on convoys The heavy demands that had been placed on the Royal Navy as it pursued the German raiders and performed escort duties meant that now many of its ships required overhaul, and the chances of encountering heavy British forces would be reduced.[51] The conflicts between the different commands and interpretation of orders, however, continued, with Raeder's angry attack against the fleet commander, Marschall, whom he accused of a lack of initiative and weak offensive spirit ("battleships are supposed to shoot, not lay smokescreens"). He believed, more than Marschall and his officers in Group West, that opportunities for tactical and strategic (diversion) successes, even against enemy warships, were within reach of the battleships, and he was prepared to restrict the freedom of the commander at sea even more to achieve the opportunities he expected. In the future, Berlin and the group command would play a more active role in operations.[52] Raeder also did not want to hear that issues of training or battle readiness would affect his efforts to deploy the fleet continuously. Raeder's hopes for a resumption of more aggressive operations were thwarted by repairs to the *Scharnhorst*, and, more significantly, by preparations for the occupation of Denmark and Norway which, as of 1 March 1939, took precedence over all other operations.

Weserübung: The Navy and the Norwegian Campaign

Raeder's anxious efforts to maximize the fleet's role became more pressing as Germany prepared to attack in the west. Although he was aware that the army hoped to seize bases in the Low Countries and northern France for use in air and naval operations against England, he suggested to Hitler on 10 October 1939 that bases on the Norwegian coast would be of more value to the U-boat war—an idea which intrigued Hitler. Even more important, maintaining Sweden's iron ore shipments was, as Raeder and Hitler recognized, "absolutely vital," and if they were threatened by the enemy Germany's entire war effort would be at risk.

Raeder's support for the occupation of Norway was a calculated risk, with implications for both the immediate and long-term future of his fleet. He was well versed in the advantages of Scandinavia as a solution to Germany's poor geographic position; however, he knew that expansion northward was not the most desirable strategic alternative, because the British would still block the doors to the Atlantic. Yet, hopes of obtaining bases on the French Atlantic coast appeared remote.[53]

His growing interest in Norway, in addition to what he regarded as a growing British threat during the period 1939–April 1940, can be related to his primary goal of ensuring that the navy's share of resources, both short-term and long-term, would not diminish.[54] By early December 1939, Raeder was fully committed to planning a Norwegian operation despite his doubts over a move that, as he later admitted, "breaks all rules of naval warfare."[55] In spite of its risks, Operation *Weserübung* (Weser Exercise) promised to demonstrate the importance and role of the navy in the Wehrmacht's future operational planning. For Raeder, the leadership of the navy in this campaign represented the first time it could have a "decisive" impact on the war.[56]

Fearing a possible British intervention following the Soviet attack on Finland (30 November 1939), he warned Hitler that it was important "to occupy Norway."[57] In December, after a meeting with Vidkun Quisling, the leader of the Norwegian nationalist party, Raeder believed a British occupation of Norway was imminent. The British influence was significant, he noted, especially with the "Jewish" president of the Norwegian Parliament, Carl Hambro. The loss of Norway would make the Baltic a battleground, "completely hindering" the conduct of a naval war in the North Sea and the Atlantic campaign. Raeder requested that Hitler direct the OKW to work with Quisling to develop plans for an occupation by force or under the pretext of a Norwegian "request."[58]

In February, the British destroyer *Cossack* attacked the *Altmark,* a supply ship of the surface raiders, carrying British prisoners, in Norwegian waters, raising questions over whether Norway was prepared to defend its neutrality. On 1 March 1940 Hitler issued his directive for Weserübung without any specific timetable. If British naval activity and intelligence reports indicated a "major operation," Germany would intervene quickly and invade before the British landed.[59] Although Raeder believed in late March that the threat of a British occupation had lessened, maintaining readiness for Weserübung was having an effect on operations overall, especially in Atlantic U-boat operations. He urged that the decision to execute Weserübung be made soon.[60]

On 1 April Hitler met with his commanders to discuss the operation. He declared that Weserübung would be hailed as one of the "rashest undertakings in the history of modern warfare."[61] The operation was, however, only part of a larger campaign against England. Germany "must finally acquire access to the open seas; it was intolerable that every successive German generation should be confronted with the problems of British pressure. The conflict with England was inevitable, sooner or later; it must be fought to a finish."[62] Several days later, upon receiving reports of British invasion preparations, Raeder's strategic defensive operation became a "preventive strike."[63] On 8 April, when the British mined the Norwegian waters and embarked troops on their transports, Raeder's ships were already at sea.

As Raeder had hoped, the element of surprise resulted in a stunning tactical success but at the cost of heavy losses for the German fleet (one heavy cruiser, two light cruisers, ten destroyers, and six U-boats). The losses were acceptable, given the scope of the operation, and Hitler expressed his appreciation for the "great achievements of the *Kriegsmarine*."[64] However, the loss of the destroyers and the damage to the *Lützow* would hamper future operations. OKW had insisted on including the *Lützow* along with the new heavy cruiser *Blücher* in the Oslo invasion forces. Raeder had been opposed, but he had reluctantly agreed to for "prestige" reasons—a decision he later recognized as an "unequivocal strategic mistake."[65]

Weserübung also ensured the flow of Swedish ore and protected the U-boat training grounds in the Baltic. More importantly, from Raeder's point of view, the "operation would remain for all time, the great feat of arms in this war."[66] Against that, it brought the new problem of defending a conquered Norway. Hitler's belief that Norway would be the "zone of destiny" of the war and Raeder's stubborn adherence to the navy's Norwegian position, without regard to any "sober strategic analysis," diverted valuable resources for the rest of the war.[67] The concentration of resources in Norway, the creation of numerous new minesweeper, patrol boat, and antisubmarine flotillas, and the navy's rapid buildup of its shore defenses reflected Raeder's obsession with Norway and its importance for the navy's future.[68] At the same time, the strategic gain proved to be slight after the army's defeat of France in June 1940 provided the navy with bases on the French Atlantic coast.

Raeder's subsequent intervention in politics outside his command sphere during the Norwegian occupation demonstrated his determination to ensure that the navy would not lose any of the gains from its costly victory. Raeder's claim for the navy's preeminence in the administration and planning for the new Norway led to his active role in trying to shape policy. He supported concluding a peace treaty with Norway and the establishment of a pro-German government.[69] Raeder disapproved of Hitler's appointment of Josef Terboven (a close associate of Göring) as the German commissioner in Norway and actively sought to get him dismissed.

Raeder's advocacy of Quisling and his pro-Nazi party represented a total misreading of the political landscape of Norway. He persisted in pursuing his political goals, insisting that Quisling was the only one who could handle things "according to our wishes"[70] Raeder's motives, however, were not much different from Hitler's. He favored the establishment of a "North German community" in the occupied northern countries in which the members (including neutral Sweden and Finland) would have a certain measure of sovereignty over their own military but would be closely tied politically and economically to Germany. His vision of Norway was not that of a conquered province but as the locus of the postwar navy; he urged the development of a new German city and base near Trondheim where the largest ships could be built "without regard" to water depth.[71] Raeder later would blame the failure to improve relations with the Norwegians as "one of my main reasons for resigning."[72]

Operational Issues: Fall 1939–Spring 1940

During the Norwegian campaign, Raeder had to confront a major controversy over technical problems with the navy's ships and torpedoes as well as continuing conflict over his command structure. The failure to respond decisively to the problems of the new magnetic firing pistols during the Norwegian campaign precipitated a crisis within the navy that had been simmering since 1935. Dönitz complained that torpedo malfunctions rendered his U-boats practically "unarmed," costing them "certain success."[73]

Raeder answered his critics with a strongly worded memorandum on 11 June 1940 that addressed not only the torpedo problems but the entire prewar shipbuilding program—in particular, whether more U-boats should have been built after 1938. Aware of the extent of the dissension, especially among the younger officers, Raeder chastised his senior officers for not doing enough to "counter objectively the all too temperamental assertions of younger officers." He would permit criticism only from those who could make "positive suggestions—that is, mainly from those who are actually using the weapon concerned."

Raeder justified the building of capital ships over U-boats as having been "governed by the political needs of its time . . . *decided by the Führer.*" Hitler had hoped *"until the last minute"* to postpone war with England until 1944–1945, when the navy would have a "huge superiority" in U-boats and a "much more favorable ratio [relative to] the enemy in all other types of ships." Raeder emphasized the "remarkable and—despite the political restrictions—extensive preparations for U-boat construction" that had been made during the years of "external control." These efforts had made possible the extraordinarily rapid buildup of the U-boat arm. If the navy had decided not to proceed with the building of capital ships and destroyers, he declared, it would have been "inexcusable," and the years lost in gaining experience in shipbuilding, weapons development and tactics "would never have been made good."

Raeder claimed that the defensive bearing of the British was "undoubtedly largely" a result of Germany's capital ships, the mining operations in the North Sea and destroyer operations off the English coast. Above all, the Norwegian campaign had "amply confirmed the *soundness*" of the navy's construction program." These successes would have been "quite impossible had the fleet not existed in its present form." To Raeder the decisive factors in the navy's "splendid performance" were the ready assumption of responsibility by the SKL, "the fine offensive spirit of the participants, the courage to take risks, and the trust reposed in the leaders." Raeder emphasized that he had full confidence in his officers, but he warned that he expected "an equal measure of confidence and not cheap, destructive criticism calculated to undermine which until now has been our finest asset: the navy's unity."[74]

Raeder's determination to maintain his authority and the navy's unity was equally evident in his attempts to spur the front commands, Fleet and Group West, to see the possibilities for and necessity of waging a proactive offensive war with the surface fleet. Raeder's impatience with his commanders increased with the expanded operational opportunities for his Atlantic strategy as a result of the occupation of Norway. He lectured his officers that they had to free themselves from the "psychological" pressure of always facing a superior enemy ("the classical task of every German navy") and attack the enemy at its key strategic points.[75] Although Weserübung had a positive impact on the navy's confidence in overcoming its "inferiority complex," the severe losses and the lack of results to date made the issue of how to engage the fleet even more compelling. The capital ships could not remain a "fleet in being," especially as the Norwegian campaign was reaching its conclusion without the battleships contributing in any significant way.[76] At the same time, with the army's advances in France, the war appeared all but won, with the navy having played a minimal role.

His exhortations to the fleet commander and Group West to deploy *Scharnhorst* and *Gneisenau* as soon as possible, however, did not receive the support he expected. As a result, Raeder issued two directives (18 May and 23 May 1940) to outline his views on future operations. Noting the possible operations areas in the North and the Atlantic, Raeder explained his intent to achieve direct or indirect successes through "frequent, active and many-sided" operations. Unlike the British, who were "enslaved by conventional modes of warfare," the navy would employ operations, like Weserübung, of a "type never seen before and virtually unknown to the established rules of warfare." For Raeder, any adherence to the technical and operational concepts of World War I was not only "invalid but false." The navy could "only fulfill its tasks . . . by showing an uncompromising offensive spirit and a resolve to inflict damage to the enemy whatever the risk."[77]

On 21 May 1940, Raeder proposed an offensive that would demonstrate the value of Norway. Beginning on 4 June 1940, Operation Juno would interdict commerce bound for England and British naval forces and transports en route to Narvik and relieve pressure on the German troops in Narvik as well as in France. Raeder made the stakes for the navy very clear: without a bold engagement of the enemy, even at the risk of losses, the future existence of the navy would be threatened. His position on the conduct of the naval war, he declared, was at one with the führer's, and he repeated that adhering to "orthodox" principles of naval warfare would not produce the results needed to damage the enemy's prestige and thereby contribute to "total victory." He called for a new offensive spirit—without regard for the enemy's superiority—and announced that he would deploy heavy units individually in order to create ongoing pressure on the enemy.[78]

Marschall received his orders for Operation Juno from Group West on 29 May and privately from Raeder on 31 May. Although Marschall's orders included attacking enemy shipping and the protection of supplies for the German relief forces linking up with the Narvik troops, Raeder failed to sufficiently impress upon his fleet commander his expectations for the ongoing deployment of the fleet. Marschall believed that Raeder had given him broad freedom of action, as compared with Group West's more rigid order to penetrate the fjords leading to Harstad. Without any up-to-date intelligence or adequate air reconnaissance, Marschall decided on 7 June to abandon his attack on Harstad in favor of engaging reported enemy ships. In spite of Hitler's primary concern to support the army,

Marschall considered attacks on the enemy of equal priority. Although he was reminded by Group West that his main objective was Harstad or Narvik, Marschall received information that the enemy was evacuating and redirected his forces to attack them. Although the battleships sank the aircraft carrier *Glorious,* a torpedo hit on the *Scharnhorst* forced its return to Trondheim. A resumption of operations on 10 June failed to produce any results.[79]

What had originally been hailed as a success for the capital ships was now derided by the SKL as a "decided stroke of luck."[80] Marschall's failure to understand Raeder's desire to operate the battleships on an ongoing basis ran counter to his own assessment of the situation, and he failed to see the motivation behind the orders from Berlin (to justify the battleships). Believing he had lost the element of surprise—a precondition for any breakout of the fleet—Marschall claimed that he did not see any clear purpose in continuing operations where the risks outweighed any anticipated results.[81] When he learned of the harsh criticism being leveled against him by Raeder, he reported sick and was replaced by Admiral Günther Lütjens. After more bad luck, the torpedoing of the *Gneisenau,* repairs to the battleships prevented further operations until December 1940.

In reaction to these events, Raeder's admonitions to his fleet commanders from Boehm to Lütjens were consistent. In spite of Hitler's concerns for losses after the *Graf Spee,* the ObdM continued to urge his commanders to undertake "daring actions." This reflected the tradition of a navy haunted by its insignificant role in previous wars and a Raeder eager to vindicate the navy in the eyes of Hitler. The war was about to be won without any significant contribution from the ships that were to be the core for his future "world fleet." As Marschall later quoted Raeder, "It doesn't matter if a battleship is lost. It is necessary that the battleship fight, even if it should be destroyed. . . . If there is no battle, it will be said that battleships are useless and superfluous."[82] The Norwegian campaign further reinforced Raeder's faith in surprise and his willingness to take risks in a series of individual actions, which he expected would contribute to achieving the overall objectives. As with Boehm, Raeder refused any meeting with Marschall. He regarded Operation Juno as a lost opportunity for the navy at a critical time that robbed the navy of any results that could have vindicated both his strategy and the battleships.[83]

The contradiction between the offensive spirit and freedom of action promised by Raeder to his commanders and the demand for strict adherence to operational orders had resulted in conflicting interpretations over how to conduct missions, as well as what the objectives were. Raeder's decision to establish Group West as the operational command center had created an additional point of conflict and confusion between the fleet commander and the SKL. Raeder, as he had done with Boehm and Marschall, would not tolerate any criticism or second-guessing of his strategic principles or his organizational structure, nor was he willing to change his position once he had made his mind up.

In spite of the capture of the French Atlantic coast and the vulnerability of Trondheim to air and submarine attacks, Raeder persisted in his belief that Norway represented the most important operational base for the surface fleet. He insisted as late as 22 June, the same day the armistice was signed in Compiègne (at which a glowing Raeder participated), on deploying all heavy units and security forces to Trondheim. He justified this decision on the grounds that it would be "intolerable" if the navy declined to take advantage of the "great military advantage that the occupation of Norway offered to the navy."[84] Raeder's behavior, at times irrational during this period of conflict with his fleet commanders and Group West, must be seen against the background of the navy's sacrifices for Norway and the imminent defeat of France, combined with his desire to demonstrate the value of his surface ships and the newly gained bases in Norway for the war against England. Raeder's apparent disregard for any sound strategic deliberations during this phase of the war reflects the interplay of "psychological" factors in his decisions and actions. (If Norway had now lost its strategic value, were all the sacrifices of the navy in vain?) [85] As one of his close colleagues, Admiral Conrad Patzig, observed, "Raeder is strongly influenced by [his] surroundings and exceptional circumstances and under stress is impulsive and unpredictable if his pride and vanity are involved."[86]

Raeder in June 1936 after his promotion to *Generaladmiral* on 20 April. The fourth stripe above the broad one was the insignia for the commander in chief of the *Kriegsmarine*. Other officers of this rank had only three. —Naval Historical Center

Raeder at his desk at the *Oberkommando der Kriegsmarine*, circa 1936.
—U.S. Naval Institute Photo Archive

Photograph of Grossadmiral Raeder on the celebration of his fifty-year anniversary of active service on 16 April 1944. He had been promoted to grand admiral on 1 April 1939 and in January 1943, at the age of sixty-seven, had been named *Admiralinspekteur der Kriegsmarine des Großdeutschen Reiches.* Note the Nazi Party badge that he received, along with Army Chief General von Fritsch, on 30 January 1937, the fourth anniversary of Hitler's assumption of power.
—*Bibliothek für Zeitgeschichte,* Stuttgart

Raeder and Hitler during the führer's visit to the fleet, 1935. —Naval Historical Center

The *Scharnhorst* was the first battleship to be built after the war, and it exceeded the displacement limits of the Versailles treaty. Its launching on 3 May 1936 was attended by Hitler, Raeder, and the defense minister, General von Blomberg (who gave the christening speech). —Naval Historical Center

Raeder converses with Fleet Chief Admiral Richard Foerster (who served in that position from 1933 to 1936). —U.S. Naval Institute Photo Archive

Raeder and the chief of the Baltic Naval Station, Admiral Conrad Albrecht, in conversation with the League of Nations' High Commissioner for the Free City of Danzig, Carl Jacob Burckhardt, during the international regatta at Kiel, 23 June 1938 (on board the starting ship, the *Undine*).
—U.S. Naval Institute Photo Archive

Raeder and Foreign Minister Joachim von Ribbentrop listen to Hitler's speech to the Reichstag on 26 April 1939, in which he justified Germany's position against the Western powers, the United States, and Poland. At the same time, Hitler's diplomatic liaison in London served notice of Germany's intent to abrogate the Anglo-German Naval Treaty. —*Bibliothek für Zeitgeschichte*, Stuttgart

Raeder and foreign naval officers on board the state yacht, the *Aviso Grille* (1934), during the international regatta (Kiel Week), 1939. —U.S. Naval Institute Photo Archive

Raeder on board the *Schleswig-Holstein* (22 September 1939) shortly after it fired the first shots of World War II in attacking the Polish defenses on the Westerplatte and after Danzig had been secured by the Wehrmacht. —*Bibliothek für Zeitgeschichte*, Stuttgart

In October 1939 Hitler accompanied Raeder and the *Führer der U-Boote*, Rear Admiral Karl Dönitz, to greet the returning crew of the *U-29* (*Kapitänleutnant* Schuhart), which had sunk the British carrier *Courageous* on 17 September 1939. —*Bibliothek für Zeitgeschichte*, Stuttgart

Raeder is seen after having completed an inspection of one of his warships in December 1939.
—Naval Historical Center

Hitler and Raeder after the defeat of the French, June 1940. —*Bibliothek für Zeitgeschichte*, Stuttgart

Raeder reviews the description of the previous night's engagement of his minesweepers with British fast patrol boats (5 November 1942). —*Bibliothek für Zeitgeschichte*, Stuttgart

Raeder arrives in France to visit the fleet at Brest 1941, which he hoped would provide the long-desired Atlantic base for waging commerce war with a powerful task force of capital ships.
—*Bibliothek für Zeitgeschichte*, Stuttgart

Top: Raeder and his officers visit
German naval forces in Narvik
(circa 1942). —Naval Historical Center

Right: Raeder on board a
minesweeper at Narvik, circa
1942. —Naval Historical Center

Raeder lays a wreath at the German military cemetery in Narvik (13 July 1942).
—*Bibliothek für Zeitgeschichte,* Stuttgart

Raeder walks with Hitler and other political and military leaders at Führer Headquarters (Wolf's Lair) in East Prussia (Rastenburg), circa 1942. —Naval Historical Center

The Nuremberg War Crime Trials, circa 1946. Raeder is second from the left in the back row of defendants. On his right is Admiral Karl Dönitz. —Naval Historical Center

Those people [Admirals] dream in continents.
—*General Franz Halder, 12 June 1942*

8

Dreaming in Continents, 1940–1942

Preparing for Weltmacht and Weltmachtflotte: Naval Planning and Fleet Building, 1940

The navy's full commitment to Exercise Weser resulted in an even more diminished role of the navy in the western campaign. As German troops reached the French Channel coast, Raeder sought to convince the führer of the importance of the navy for the next stage of the war and to shift all the Wehrmacht's resources to defeating the British. As hopes waned for a political solution, Hitler directed him to develop a long-term submarine building program and promised that after the campaign in France was over, the U-boat and *Ju 88* bomber programs would receive priority. Hitler also lifted the previous restrictions on U-boats and called for an intensification of the "siege" of England—actions that appeared to confirm that the navy would soon receive additional resources.[1]

Beginning in May and June of 1940, Raeder and his staff had begun the process of evaluating the gains brought about by the occupation of Norway and the fall of France. Along with the French Atlantic and Channel ports, they anticipated a settlement that might involve concessions of French colonies in Africa and the Middle East or even the use of the French fleet. With Italy's entry into the war on 11 June, only England stood between Germany and total victory. In the euphoria of victory, Raeder and his close advisors did not concern themselves with Hitler's continuing hopes for a rapprochement with the British. In fact, the navy feared that a "compromise peace" might allow the British to keep its "great sea power" for defense of its empire, and then, in alliance with the United States, Germany's rival for "world mastery," the Anglo-Saxon powers "will become that opponent with whom we have to reckon in the near future."[2] Some of Raeder's staff even contemplated a future German-Japanese conflict in the Far East to decide which of the two Axis partners would become the world's dominant sea power.[3] Envisioning the European continent in German hands, a colonial empire in Central Africa and German control of the North Sea, Mediterranean, Black Sea, and Baltic Sea, Raeder asked his staff to prepare studies for the rebuilding of the fleet after the war. In this propitious moment, he saw an opportunity to influence Germany's foreign policy goals in the interests of the navy's global strategy and ambitions.

While Raeder's staff was in the middle of formulating its anti-British war aims and postwar construction plans, they also proposed a wish list of demands for the armistice with France that closely paralleled those imposed on the German navy in 1918.[4] When Raeder met with Hitler on 20 June, Hitler sharply rejected them, concerned that any draconian claims on the French fleet or its colonies might result in the defection of the French navy to the British. Raeder had suffered a "lost opportunity" to gain any material advantage from the French defeat, but Hitler mollified him by giving him a free hand in making use of the newly won French Atlantic bases.[5] Reflecting his expanded "Atlantic" strategy, Raeder also lobbied for additional bases on the Atlantic, such as Dakar. His suggestion for acquiring French Madagascar to gain access to the Indian Ocean, however, was rejected by Hitler, who planned to use Madagascar for the settlement of Jews.[6]

With the Royal Navy's attack on the French fleet at Mers el-Kebir on 3 July 1940, a clear signal of the British resolve to continue fighting, Raeder urged Hitler to prepare for the next steps to defeat the British. Conscious of the strategic impasse now facing Hitler and his military advisers, none of whom knew how to bring the war to a close, he became convinced that an occupation of Gibraltar was critical for Axis naval operations.[7] Hitler, however, refused to act on Raeder's pleas to place a priority on the naval war, because neither it nor proposals for indirect attacks on the periphery of the British Empire (Suez Canal and Gibraltar) promised the immediate results he sought.[8] If the British did not yield, argued Hitler, the newly won bases on the Atlantic would

provide a significant advantage for the naval war. Once the British recognized Germany's dominant position and hostilities ceased, he promised again, he would concentrate resources on the U-boat war and
the Luftwaffe.[9]

Assuming total victory, Raeder and his staff outlined their future plans
for the next phase of Germany's expansion. Characterized by some as "the
colorful dreams of a prisoner in solitary confinement" or dismissed as "the
alternative to reality: fantasies and utopias," the scope of the navy's proposals for bases and its future construction program reflected the ultimate
aims of German naval policy since Tirpitz.[10] These plans revealed the continuing influence of the ideology of sea power and undervalued the role
that aircraft carriers, submarines, and naval airpower would play in the
further course of the war. More important, they illustrated what the
navy considered to be the goals of the National Socialist colonial and
foreign policies in the next stage of Hitler's "Program."[11]

The memorandum of the postwar requirements that Raeder presented to Hitler on 11 July 1940 represented a synthesis of studies submitted to him by his principal advisors. Each assumed that Germany
would require a large number of bases to protect a Germany-dominated
Europe and a future empire in Central Africa stretching from the Atlantic
to the Indian Ocean. Kurt Fricke emphasized that the strategic needs of
Greater Germany demanded a blockade-proof New Europe dependent "politically, economically, and militarily" on Germany, ensuring its
free access to the sea.[12] Carls detailed demands for Germany's new
strategic conditions that he acknowledged "may sound fantastic." At
stake in the "present war" was Germany's status as a world power with
open access to the high seas, the crushing of France as a major power,
and a greatly diminished British Empire. All of the enemies' colonial possessions were to be carved up between Germany, Italy, and Spain. Carls
justified his colonial aspirations as the "natural outcome of the war and
from the necessary rounding out of the colonial holdings that will secure
Germany's claims once and for all to her share of the globe."[13]

The final document maintained the strategic assumptions that the
Reich controlled the continent and a large Central African empire from
the Atlantic to the Indian Ocean. It was expected that a weakened Britain
would seek support from the United States, with the inevitable result that
the "two Anglo-Saxon powers would do everything to maintain or

enhance their great sea power, and thereby, would become the first natural enemies for Germany to consider." The need to defend Germany's
new overseas possessions and the corresponding growth in trade would
compel Germany to become "an oceanic naval power of the first rank"—
thereby bringing "with this step a definite conclusion to a centuries-
long development of German sea power, which has been hindered by
numerous errors and miscalculations in the past."[14] Raeder's presentation did not incorporate the wide, sweeping demands for bases proposed by his staff. These had already been transmitted to the Nazi Party's
Colonial Policy Office and to the Foreign Office.[15]

The primary weapon of Germany's new Weltmachtflotte would
remain the battleship. Given the "new strategic situation," only the
battleship was capable of protecting Germany's trade and attacking the
enemy's sea communications and eliminating the enemy's sea power—
a return to the primacy of the battle fleet and the decisive battle. Until
the fleet was ready to attack the enemy's trade routes, the U-boats were
to act as a deterrent and carry the fight to the enemy's sea lanes.[16]
Although he did not detail for Hitler the size of the navy he ultimately
envisioned, it was clear that the future fleet was designed for the worldwide defense of German trade and empire. The numbers provided to
Hitler in July 1940 were only the first step to the realization of these other
goals. They were to be measured according to the final outcome of the
European war and the extent to which its successful conclusion would
produce both the geographic and material conditions for waging war on
a global scale. The "final goal" included up to 80 battleships, 20 aircraft
carriers, 225 cruisers, and 500 U-boats (the "provisional final goal" was
for a fleet of 50 battleships, 12 aircraft carriers, 105 cruisers, and 500
U-boats).[17] Although Raeder was careful not to share all his plans with
Hitler or the OKW and did not always agree with his staff's ideas, it
seemed highly probable that in the heady days of summer and fall 1940
the long-held ambitions of the navy could be realized under the seemingly invincible leadership of its führer.[18]

Operation Sea Lion

Hitler's apparent affirmation of the navy's future plans and his willingness to discuss its persistent demands for bases led Raeder to believe
that he had won support for his Atlantic strategy and the navy's global

ambitions.[19] For Raeder, England's defeat remained a *sine qua non* for any future German Weltmacht.

Although his anti-British strategy had successfully influenced Hitler in the case of Operation Weser, Hitler still remained preoccupied with reaching a settlement with England. During the period following the defeat of France in June 1940 to September 1940, he simultaneously considered a number of military and political options, which together, or individually, might bring about a settlement. They included a direct assault on Britain, as well as coalition building with Italy, Spain, and even, in the short term, the Soviet Union. But Hitler was already thinking beyond England, believing like some that "Britain probably still needs one more demonstration of our military might before she gives in and leaves us a free hand in the east."[20]

Eager as he was for concentrating all forces against England, Raeder feared that Hitler's interest in an invasion of the British Isles would present the depleted navy with "impossible tasks."[21] He was concerned that the success of Weserübung might suggest to Hitler that a Channel crossing would be less dangerous than he was convinced it would be. This appeared to be the case when Hitler asked him in June 1940 to develop plans for an attack of Iceland as part of a "ring strategy" against the British Isles, with occupations of Norway, Ireland, and Iceland.[22] Although Raeder dutifully reported on the preparations for Iceland, he was able to convince Hitler that this operation (as well as that against Ireland) was too risky. Raeder acknowledged his role as the chief proponent for the attack on Norway, but he would never be an advocate for an invasion of England.[23]

Raeder's attempts to dampen Hitler's interests in an invasion became more pronounced after the fall of France, when he became "suddenly aware" that the OKW and the army had developed an "unexpected interest" in an invasion. Although dubious of success "from the first," he acquiesced to Hitler's request on 2 July to begin planning, but jealously insisted that any decisions regarding the operation would be determined by the navy.[24] Hitler agreed with Raeder that the invasion should be used only as "a last resort," assuming certain conditions, the most important being air superiority. It was apparent that Hitler was dubious not only about the military difficulties but also about the political consequences of an invasion. A defeat of Britain and the disintegration of its empire would benefit the United States and Japan. He continued to be puzzled by the continuing British unwillingness to make peace, but he and the army leaders believed that an invasion had to be seriously considered.[25] This background explained the ambivalent language in the Führer Directive for Operation Sea Lion (*Seelöwe*) issued on 16 July 1940, which called for preparations to be completed by mid-August and then, "if necessary, to carry them out."[26]

Raeder loyally (albeit without conviction) complied, diverting his scarce resources to preparations for Operation Sea Lion. At the same time, he took every opportunity to detail the difficulties—particularly the transport problems. He complained that the navy had greater responsibilities than the other services and rejected any idea that the navy should accede to the "wishes of the army." As preparations began in earnest, the army and navy clashed over the timing of the landings and in particular whether to land over a broad (army) or narrow (navy) front.[27] On 31 July, Raeder pressed Hitler to support the navy's position and advocated late May 1941 as the best time for an invasion. Hitler, however, insisted on 15 September 1940 if the Luftwaffe campaign against enemy air and naval forces and ports in Southern England proved effective; otherwise, Sea Lion would be postponed until May 1941. At the same time, Hitler indicated that he was considering several "interim actions," including an attack on Gibraltar and the sending of Panzer divisions to support the Italians in North Africa—a further sign to Raeder that Hitler's commitment to an invasion was less than wholehearted.[28]

By late August a compromise with the army was finally reached, reducing the width of the landing front by approximately 50 percent; by the beginning of September, the invasion fleet of tugs, barges, and an assortment of vessels had begun to assemble in the Channel ports. Encouraged by the Luftwaffe's exaggerated reports of success, Hitler targeted the 20 September as *S-Tag*, S-day. Although Raeder bravely proclaimed that Sea Lion was still possible, he pressed Hitler as to Germany's political and military options if Sea Lion did not take place and proposed, for the first time, the alternative of an indirect strategy in the Mediterranean, "in addition to, or instead of [an invasion]."[29]

In mid-September, Hitler announced, contrary to Raeder's expectation, that, although an invasion was not yet "practicable," he was not ready to abandon it. The continuing air attacks might still be decisive and a cancellation of the invasion would only lift British morale. In spite of the burden on the navy's resources, Hitler declared he would continue to use Sea Lion for psychological reasons—which might produce "mass panic" even before the anticipated air victory "within the next ten or twelve days."[30] Raeder notably did not criticize, as he would later, the Luftwaffe's decision to concentrate on London instead of attacking targets in support of an invasion. In fact, Raeder agreed with Göring's assessment that attacks on strategic targets would not be sufficient to affect British morale. Raeder now urged that the invasion be postponed until October and counseled that Sea Lion could be cancelled without loss of prestige "at the moment of maximum air successes, on the grounds that it is no longer necessary."[31]

When it became evident that the enemy's air losses had been overestimated, and with bad weather approaching, Hitler decided that Sea Lion should be indefinitely but inconspicuously postponed "until further notice."[32] In October, the operation was definitively deferred until the spring of 1941 "solely for the purpose of maintaining political and military pressure on England" (a deception that would continue until 1942). The navy, however, was still required to maintain, if not improve, its readiness for an invasion.[33]

In the final analysis, although it was more than a mere feint, given the extensive resources and planning devoted to its preparations, Operation Sea Lion served as a bluff, a propaganda ploy, and a diversion for other military operations (the Russian campaign). Hitler did express a momentary interest in the invasion during the period between July and September 1940, but he waited to see if the Luftwaffe could achieve results or if other diplomatic and military pressure could force England to admit defeat. After this period, he pursued other options that would make an invasion of England a *coup de grâce*, if necessary at all. Ultimately, as Raeder later reflected, the massive preparations for Sea Lion had tied up resources needed elsewhere: "wasted—and to no effect." He considered it good fortune that the invasion was never carried out, because the resulting setback would have been "disastrous."[34]

Nevertheless, Raeder had used Sea Lion as a means of acquiring as many resources as he could for the navy and keeping the navy's requirements and priorities in front of Hitler. Moreover, Göring's boast that his air force could assume many of the navy's tasks (e.g., replace U-boats), followed by his failure to win the air war, encouraged Raeder to challenge his rival more aggressively in his bid to receive more Luftwaffe support for the naval war.[35] Sea Lion was always at the bottom of Raeder's list—to be utilized only as a last means once other military objectives had been achieved and once the navy possessed the resources it required to counter the British. At the same time, if the navy's rebuilding plans were realized, a direct attack on England would no longer be needed.

The planning for Sea Lion further demonstrated Germany's continuing High Command problems, with each service protecting its departmental interests, and the lack of coordination for conducting combined operations that Raeder advocated but never supported unless they conformed to his strategic objectives. Yet, Raeder remained sensitive over the charge that the navy's reluctance and "misgivings" had cost Germany a chance of a successful invasion. Later an internal study was ordered to justify its actions.[36]

The Search for Alternatives: Raeder, the Mediterranean, and Russia

Even during the debate over Sea Lion, Hitler began to focus on resolving his long-standing ideological and strategic objective, the defeat of the Soviet Union and the creation of a blockade-proof empire. At the same time, he actively sought military and diplomatic victories, which would provide bases in French North and West Africa and the Atlantic islands for the navy and the Luftwaffe to operate against the Western Hemisphere. These efforts represented a long-term objective that supported Raeder's July 1940 building program and reflected the navy's long-held colonial aspirations.

Raeder saw Hitler's interest in acquiring new bases as an opportunity to influence the direction of the war in the favor of his maritime strategy. Faced with growing American support for England, a fall-off in the U-boat tonnage war, and the unwelcome possibility of an invasion of England, he energetically pursued his concept of a "Mediterranean strategy" as the best means of attacking England indirectly and an alternative to Hitler's invasion of the Soviet Union. This strategy would ensure control of Northwest Africa, turn the Mediterranean into an "Axis sea," and secure Germany's access to raw materials. Although at times their goals seemed to coalesce, Hitler was more focused on the long-term need for bases in North Africa, while Raeder insisted on striking the

British on the "periphery." This was particularly reflected in Hitler's interest in Gibraltar, which waxed or waned depending upon his feelings toward France or Spain, in spite of the advantages its capture offered to the Axis.[37]

Raeder's supporters have agreed with him that the Mediterranean strategy represented a realistic blueprint for victory over the British, described by some as "far-sighted" and a "brilliant war-winning campaign." Hitler's failure to support it lent credence to Raeder's condemnation of Germany's leadership as hopelessly land-minded and ignorant of the importance of sea power.[38] Hitler's decision to invade the Soviet Union over Raeder's persistent advocacy of his *Mittelmeer* strategy was a fateful mistake with catastrophic consequences. Other scholars see no evidence to suggest that the loss of the Mediterranean would have caused England to sue for peace—and neither, some have argued, did Raeder and the SKL. For Hitler's part, Germany's involvement in the Mediterranean ultimately remained a "side show."[39]

From May 1940, when France fell, to Raeder's resignation in January 1943, his efforts to influence Hitler's diplomatic deliberations with France, Italy, Japan, and Spain and his repeated attempts to push his strategy went far beyond his authority as navy chief. His actions reflected his willingness to involve himself and the navy in matters that contradicted the führer's expressed wishes and orders. For Raeder, the navy and the sea war should dictate Germany's strategy in a global war (*Gesamtkrieg = Seekrieg*). Raeder's single-minded defense of his departmental interests led him to place his them ahead of Hitler's national diplomatic and military requirements. His determination to divert Hitler's attention from planning for Operation Barbarossa has in fact been labeled by one scholar as "criminal folly."[40] The German decision to open a theater in the Mediterranean was a turning point, a critical error that created a "killing ground" ill-suited to the strengths that had brought the Wehrmacht success.[41] The same could be said of Raeder's renewed attempts in 1942 to increase Germany's thinly stretched military resources in the Mediterranean theater that were critically needed in the face of Russian advances on the eastern front.

Raeder launched his campaign for a Mediterranean strategy during his 6 September 1940 conference, which coincided with the American Destroyers for Bases Deal. Raeder sought to convince Hitler that the

American acquisition of British bases represented a "hostile" act and a prelude to a new "Anglo-Saxon empire." Raeder speculated that the United States might next occupy key Atlantic islands and possibly British or French possessions in West Africa.[42] He used America's growing involvement in the Atlantic war and General de Gaulle's August coup in central Africa to point out to Hitler the increasing threat of American landings in Casablanca or Dakar. Like Hitler, he still did not fear American intervention as "decisive," but, if a long war were to develop (which he expected), the United States had to be denied any strategic advantages for its global ambitions. Spain's entry into the war and control of Gibraltar now became even more urgent.[43]

Raeder's efforts to persuade Hitler to give more priority to the maritime aspects of a global war intensified with the changing situation in Africa. The military and political questions involved, he argued, went far beyond European issues and could not be measured in any way in terms of traditional continental land warfare. He pleaded, "More than before, the SKL . . . must be involved in the decisions of the leadership of the High Command." In late September 1940, he privately requested permission to express his views on the progress of the war, including matters "outside his provenance." Believing that Hitler had not yet finalized his plans, he argued that the Mediterranean was the "pivot" of the British Empire. If Germany intended to concentrate on defeating Britain, the "Mediterranean question" must be resolved by "all means and without delay" during the winter months of 1940–1941 "before the United States is able to intervene effectively."[44]

Best of all, Raeder believed, his Mediterranean strategy would not involve any significant commitment of the navy's limited resources and would not affect the Atlantic campaign. The primary forces necessary would be from the army, the Luftwaffe, and the Italian armed forces. His proposals, however, were ultimately predicated on successful diplomatic negotiations in October and November 1940 with Spain, France, Russia, and Italy—none of which produced satisfactory results and only hardened Hitler's determination to resolve the "Russian question." Raeder tried to dissuade Hitler from attacking Russia by proposing operations against Gibraltar and the Canary Islands (by the Luftwaffe) and attacking the Suez Canal. With German troops advancing through Palestine and Syria as far as Turkey, "the Russia problem will then appear in a different light. . . . It is doubtful whether an advance against Russia from the north will be necessary." Raeder also pointed out that if Germany controlled Gibraltar and the Dardanelles, it would be easier to supply Italy and Spain (perhaps overcoming the latter's reluctance to join the war). He reemphasized the importance of cooperating with Vichy France and gaining Dakar and bases in northwest Africa for preventing British and Gaullist forces (and American) from gaining a foothold in this region.

Hitler initially appeared generally receptive to Raeder's ideas. He had already expressed his interest in Gibraltar and bases in North Africa (Casablanca) and had ordered a study (5 September 1940) of the occupation of the Atlantic islands, but he had to decide whether cooperation with Spain or France was more profitable. If Spain were amenable, the Canary Islands and possibly the Azores and the Cape Verde Islands would be seized by the Luftwaffe. He shared Raeder's concern that England and the United States must be prevented from occupying Northwest Africa.[45]

Raeder's renewed determination to focus Hitler's attention to the Mediterranean also reflected other events that affected the navy's deliberations. On 28 October 1940, Mussolini's surprise attack on Greece forced Hitler to act. On 12 November 1940, he issued a directive to aid the Italians in Egypt and Greece and launch Operation Felix (Gibraltar) and take control of the Atlantic islands. His orders also included measures to bring France into the war as Raeder had urged.[46] Sensing Hitler's desire to utilize the Azores as a base for the Luftwaffe's new long-range bomber to attack the United States, he declared that an occupation of the Azores would be "very risky but, with luck, [it] *can* succeed." However, he then attempted to dissuade Hitler, warning that holding the Azores would be "quite unlikely" given the difficulties in repulsing a British counterattack and would adversely affect operations, especially the U-boat war in the Atlantic.

Their exchange on these issues revealed a fundamental disagreement over the role that the Atlantic islands could play in Germany's naval strategy. The relegation of the Atlantic islands to secondary importance reflected Raeder's fear that the British naval and air bases on Crete and Greece had improved the enemy's strategic position in the eastern Mediterranean. Not only was it unlikely that the British fleet could be driven from the Mediterranean, but the very outcome of the war had been tipped in the favor of the enemy. Although control of the western

Mediterranean and the elimination of Gibraltar would secure North Africa and the supply base for Spain and France, the domination of the eastern Mediterranean was "urgently necessary."[47]

In early December 1940, British successes in Libya were accompanied by Spain's refusal to join the Axis. Hitler's suspicions over France's reliability led him to order preparations for seizing unoccupied France, and he directed Raeder to prevent French naval forces from going over to the enemy.[48] To resolve "both the English and French danger simultaneously," Hitler began to consider the occupation of Morocco and reactivating Operation Felix.[49] These operations proved a chimera, though they persisted until the Allied invasion of North Africa in November 1942. By the beginning of January 1941, however, the military situation in the Mediterranean, as Raeder warned, had deteriorated to the point that the "wretched [Italian] leadership" was forced to request German assistance. General Erwin Rommel and his Africa Corps were sent to Libya in February 1941, and Germany invaded Yugoslavia and Greece. Timing was now the critical issue as forces sent to the Balkans were also scheduled for the invasion of Soviet Russia.[50]

On 8 January 1941, Hitler told his commanders, in a clear repudiation of the "periphery" strategy in the Mediterranean, that even if North Africa was lost, Germany's position in Europe was so firmly established that the "outcome cannot possibly be to our disadvantage." Although he believed that the Luftwaffe's and navy's attacks on British imports might lead to victory as early as July or August (1941), he contended that the British would continue to fight as long as they believed that the United States and Russia would sooner or later join in the war against Germany.[51] As a result of the Mediterranean operations and preparations for the Russian campaign, the navy would have to bear the brunt of the war against "the English war economy" and its shipping—England's "primary vulnerable spot."[52]

Raeder and Operation Barbarossa

Raeder's opposition to Hitler's plans to attack the Soviet Union reflected not only his advocacy for the Atlantic and Mediterranean theaters as a means of achieving a decisive victory, but also his aim to exert a leadership role (and secure resources) for the navy in Germany's overall military strategy and planning. His pleas for the intensification of the commerce war and proposals to attack British sea communications in the Middle East were in direct conflict with Hitler's resolve to settle his "Russian problem."

Raeder's subsequent efforts to disassociate himself from Hitler's decision to launch Barbarossa—a "wrong track"—began shortly after the disastrous turn of the Russian campaign in winter 1942, when he ordered a study to justify his position regarding the invasion of the Soviet Union. In a confidential 1944 transcript, he detailed his opposition and condemned Hitler's rejection of sea power in favor of a "pure continental policy." His comments were as bitter as those made by the navy's leaders against the German leadership in World War I and, in the context of Nazi Germany in 1944, defeatist. Raeder stated that he was "never convinced" of the "compelling necessity" of Barbarossa, and he praised Stalin as a "far seeing genius," a statesman, and a soldier. He did not subscribe, as others did, to the notion that Stalin had any intention of attacking Germany in 1941 (a disavowal of the "preventive" war justification). He believed that Stalin had long since given up the ideological goals of Marxism-Leninism (world communism) in favor of the long-term Russian objectives represented by the "program of Peter the Great." Stalin's dissolution of the Komintern should have been a signal to Germany that a durable Russo-German friendship was possible because both nations were threatened in the long term by the United States.[53]

In his memoirs, Raeder recounted that his first discussion of Russia with Hitler was on 9 March 1940, when Hitler rejected his proposal that the Russians occupy Tromsö as part of the Norwegian operation. It was not until mid-September 1940 that Hitler acknowledged that he had definite intentions against Russia.[54] Those intentions, however, were already on record. In defending his decision to attack England and France in a speech to his commanders on 23 November 1939, Hitler had made it clear that Germany "can only engage Russia when we are free in the West."[55] This was followed by Hitler's January 1940 directive to delay giving plans of the *Bismarck* or delivering the hull of the *Lützow* to the Russians as long as possible and the need to reinforce defenses in the Baltic.[56]

Although he claimed in his memoirs that Hitler made no reference to Russia during his 6 September 1940 meeting, the record shows that Raeder and Hitler had discussed "Problem S" (the Soviet Union) and that he had informed Hitler that it would be *"impossible"* to carry out Sea Lion and "S" at the same time.[57] Although Raeder had already left the meeting on 31 July at which Hitler announced his decision to attack Russia in spring 1941, he had received an indication of these plans at least three days before from one of the naval liaison officers at the OKW.[58] A follow-up SKL assessment on 28 July illustrated how closely the navy was aligned with the führer's plans. Although warning that the Russian campaign would drain further resources from the navy, it acknowledged that Germany's security required a broad, open territory in the east to act as a buffer and provide Lebensraum, which the "Anglo-Saxons could not . . . defeat."[59]

Raeder claimed later that he told Hitler that he was shocked that the führer would even consider launching a two-front war, especially given Hitler's assertions that he would never repeat the "dumb" decision of the imperial government in 1914. He also warned Hitler that breaking the treaty with Russia would be "immoral" and negate the "great advantages" that the treaty brought to Germany.[60] There is no doubt that Raeder saw only negative consequences for the navy in a war with Russia. Moreover, it would provide no significant role for the navy or opportunity to influence Germany's strategic direction toward his maritime goals.

Raeder's persistent efforts to present alternatives for a Mediterranean and Northwest Africa Lebensraum in the period from 6 September 1940 to 6 June 1941 reflect in part his personal views that, for the time being, cooperation with the Soviet Union was more desirable than conflict. The Russo-German pact in 1939 had brought both strategic and logistical advantages to Raeder that he had been quick to utilize. The German use of the northern sea route in 1940–1941 and the loss of the French fleet in June 1940 had forced the Royal Navy to patrol both the Atlantic and the Pacific, as well as to protect its home shores against a possible German invasion. Without Russia's substantial fuel and material support, the Kriegsmarine would have been severely hampered in carrying out the naval campaign against England in 1939–1941.[61]

On 14 November 1940, when Raeder learned that Hitler was "still inclined" toward war with Russia, he urged Hitler to at least postpone this operation until after Britain was defeated. There was no immediate threat that Russia would attack; Germany was helping to build Russia's navy, and Russia would remain dependent on this support for years to come. He also repeated his warning that war with Russia would threaten U-boat training in the eastern Baltic and could have a severe impact on the U-boat war. Although Raeder momentary believed that he had talked Hitler out of his "dangerous Russian gamble," the führer ordered Operation Barbarossa on 18 December 1940, declaring that he was "irrevocably determined" to attack in 1941.[62]

At this stage, Raeder felt that any chance of changing Hitler's mind was "exceedingly dim," but he decided to make another attempt.[63] In his 27 December 1940 conference, describing the worst fears of the SKL, he cited the deteriorating situation in the Mediterranean and the shift of the naval balance of power to the British. He argued for a speedy execution of Operation Felix to protect the western Mediterranean (and the Axis supply lines) and the use of Spanish ports for U-boat and battleship attacks against enemy convoys. Hitler agreed that the U-boats with Luftwaffe support were the "decisive weapons" against England, but he reminded Raeder that it was necessary "at all costs" to eliminate the last enemy remaining on the Continent before dealing with the British. He attempted to mollify Raeder by assuring him that, once Russia was defeated, the "blockading" of Britain would resume in full force.[64] This exchange highlighted their fundamental differences over the central strategic focus of the war. Raeder was still actively pursuing his long-term economic warfare against an enemy that Hitler considered a lesser threat than Russia. It was apparent that Hitler was never really focused on a coordinated, unified "world war" that corresponded to Raeder's conception of *Gesamtkrieg*, total war.[65]

On 6 June 1941, two weeks before Barbarossa, Raeder came prepared with extensive documents to make his case for the importance of the Mediterranean and an immediate attack on Egypt. The notes from this meeting, however, raise the question of why he did not press his case more forcefully. Asked in 1944 why he appeared to have "held back," Raeder sharply denied that he had in any way abbreviated his presentation or deviated from support of his Mediterranean strategy. Because of Hitler's preoccupation with the upcoming Russian campaign, he had decided to concentrate only on those issues related to increasing the contributions of the Italians in the Mediterranean, thereby allowing Germany to shift more resources to Barbarossa. When asked why, if he was so opposed to the invasion of Russia, did he not resign rather than be a party to such a disastrous policy, Raeder argued that further warnings would have been for naught, and, as head of the navy, he was compelled to bow to necessity.[66]

As many of their postwar accounts allege, other military leaders opposed or at least wanted to delay the Russian campaign.[67] Still, they accepted the "ideological foundations" that made the decision to invade Russia unavoidable.[68] Raeder understood this and finally accepted the fact that Barbarossa was an "unalterable fact." He still cautioned against any reduction of efforts in the Mediterranean theater.[69] In a remarkable demonstration of the navy's attitude toward Russian operations, the SKL directed its front commanders to avoid heavy losses since naval forces were not necessary for the outcome of the operation and would be needed for the further struggle against the British.[70]

Creating the Foundations for a New Maritime Strategy: The SKL and the Mediterranean, June 1941–December 1941

Although Barbarossa now took precedence over all other operations, Raeder persisted in lobbying for his maritime strategy. The failure of a quick victory in the east, combined with developments in both the Mediterranean and the U-boat war, and finally the entry of Japan and the United States into the war in December 1941, provided Raeder with his last opportunity to influence Germany's strategic direction and pursue his global diversionary strategy.

In July 1941, Raeder presented what one scholar refers to as "perhaps the most comprehensive and clear formulation" of his strategy. Declaring that the defeat of Britain was "the law of this war," he concluded that the Battle of the Atlantic ("the most powerful and comprehensive battle of this war") was "decisive for the outcome of the war." A collapse of Russia would not break Britain's will or affect American support. The fate of the Atlantic was closely intertwined with the fate of the Mediterranean. If French North and West Africa were lost, it would no longer be possible to defeat the British and the southern flank of Europe would be threatened. As Raeder had consistently urged, collaboration with France represented the key to providing the strategic bases (and potentially its naval forces) from which to successfully wage the battle against the Anglo-American sea-lanes. At the same time, Italy and Japan could contribute to relieving the pressure on the Atlantic and prevent the Americans and British from withdrawing their naval forces in the

Pacific.[71] Although the "July memorandum" was received very positively by the OKW, its efforts to promote the Atlantic as the zone of destiny ("the main battleground of the greatest economic war of all times") foundered on Germany's lack of military and economic resources to deal with a global war.[72]

In late July 1941, Raeder confronted Hitler with his concern that the naval war was receiving short shrift. He was disturbed by Hitler's suggestion that the U-boat war in the Atlantic should be curtailed to avoid provoking the United States. Moreover, Hitler's reaction to the loss of the *Bismarck* in May 1941 and his comments on the capital ships as useless also reflected directly on Raeder's leadership. Although Hitler stated that he had not changed his mind on the importance of the naval war, he repeated his desire to avoid confrontation with the United States until after the Russian campaign.[73]

There were other signs of a growing trend that minimized the importance of the Atlantic war and reflected the increasing loss of Raeder's independence in the conduct of the navy's war. Ignoring Raeder's opposition, Hitler insisted on sending U-boats to the Mediterranean to help relieve Rommel.[74] More significantly, in September 1941, Hitler suggested that the battleships should be sent to defend Norway.[75] It was clear that Hitler's highest priority for the navy was its role in supporting the Eastern and Mediterranean campaigns. Nevertheless, Raeder continued to assert his fundamental principle—that this war is "a struggle against the strongest sea power but, at the same time, a nation that is the most dependent upon its overseas imports." Although proceeding from the assumption of victory in Russia (but no longer in 1941), the SKL's October 1941 situation report focused on how the navy and the Luftwaffe should be expanded as quickly as possible in order to concentrate on the destruction of British imports (including a totally unrealistic proposal to resume building battleships). The report decried the lack of an experienced, senior naval officer in the highest military command "in a war with the greatest sea power of the world . . . as a deficiency of the leadership organization" and called for closer collaboration between the OKW and the Luftwaffe.[76]

By mid-September 1941, as Raeder had predicted, the Mediterranean situation had dramatically worsened, with significant losses of Axis shipping. He called upon the OKW to transfer Luftwaffe forces from Russia—an idea emphatically rejected as one that "contradicted all the principles of warfare."[77] A month later, a worried Hitler now declared that an Axis defeat in the Mediterranean "threatened the security of the Continent." He demanded a commitment of all available naval forces, including a withdrawal of more U-boats from the Atlantic. He rejected objections that the Atlantic war was more important or that Mediterranean waters were unsuitable for U-boats.[78] Raeder had no other choice other than to adjust his strategy in line with Hitler's. With the beginning of the British North Africa offensive in mid-November and reports of possible Anglo-French landings in North Africa, he was compelled to send every available U-boat to the Mediterranean. By the end of November, Atlantic operations had come almost to a standstill.[79] From Raeder's perspective, in spite of his conviction that he was as responsible for the naval war as Göring was for the Luftwaffe and Hitler was for the land war, he felt a further eroding of his independence and the compromising of his strategic principles.[80]

Raeder's "Great Plan"

On 7 December 1941 the unexpected Japanese attack on Pearl Harbor gave Raeder new hope for waging a global naval war with Japan, France, and Italy. As was the outbreak of war in September 1939, Pearl Harbor was a painful reminder of the weakness of the Kriegsmarine. Because the war "came five years too soon," the navy would not be able to capitalize on the "decisive advantage in the Atlantic and in the Mediterranean of the significant easing of the burden that the Pacific brings with it." At least, the "extension of the struggle to the distant oceans . . . will make the recognition of the decisive meaning of the terms *maritime trade* and *maritime power* part of the general knowledge of the last European."[81]

From Raeder's perspective, the opportunities for strategic and operational coordination with the Japanese, and the potential for his strategic interaction between the Atlantic-Mediterranean and Pacific–Indian Ocean theaters, provided an even stronger case for influencing the direction of the war in the navy's favor. With the Allies forced to fight a two-ocean war and the demand on Allied merchant shipping, he believed the navy's overall importance had significantly increased ("the entire war [is] put on a new basis").[82] The Japanese amphibious operations in the Pacific also suggested that the Kriegsmarine could play a larger role in the Mediterranean. The SKL briefly entertained the idea of sending landing craft and even its capital ships to the Mediterranean. Once again, the flights of fantasy, characteristic of earlier optimistic evaluations of Germany's military situation (1940, 1941), for worldwide operations and the fulfilling of long-held ambitions (e.g., acquiring African colonies and incorporating the Mediterranean into the Reich's sphere of influence) came to the fore.[83]

By February 1942, the British were once again on the defensive, and the possibility of gaining control of Gibraltar, Malta, and Suez appeared to be in the grasp of the Axis.[84] For Raeder, the potential to influence the war's strategic direction now appeared to be in the Near East, where an Axis victory could possibly bring about a quicker defeat of the British than could the U-boat war.[85] Raeder's "Great Plan," which he unveiled to Hitler in mid-February 1942, was designed to collapse the British Empire and assign half the world to the Axis. Asserting that the Axis ruled both the sea and the air in the Central Mediterranean, he proclaimed that the situation was "definitely favorable" for a decisive victory and urged an immediate attack on Egypt and the Suez Canal in conjunction with Japanese initiatives in East Asia and the Indian Ocean.[86]

With the success of the Japanese in the Far East, Hitler seemed momentarily ready to embrace Raeder's strategy of coalition warfare. Seizing the moment, the SKL produced another detailed memorandum in February outlining the strategic options that had created a critical congruence between "their" maritime war and the overall war. An operation against Suez and the subsequent elimination of Malta and the securing of North Africa would lead to a "full settlement" of the Mediterranean situation and establish a sea link between the Italians and Germans and the Japanese in the Indian Ocean—a key component of the world war against the United States.[87] In this concept of the SKL's self-promotion of its strategic vision, Rommel's *Panzerarmee* was in effect "an organ of the Seekriegsleitung." This "historic opportunity" to attack Britain's "Achilles heel" in the Near East would require "relatively few forces" and potentially could lead to a collapse of the British position. An Axis drive on Suez, in coordination with an offensive to occupy the Caucasus oil fields, would encourage the Japanese to commit its forces in support of the Near East and cut off the Allied supply lines to Russia. Raeder's plan also assumed that France would be allowed to have the necessary resources to defend its African colonies against an Allied attack.[88]

Although an annoyed OKW sharply rebuked the SKL for exceeding its authority and intruding into its prerogatives to formulate strategy,

Hitler agreed in principle, but he doubted whether the necessary forces and transport for an operation against Suez were available.[89] Although the offensive against Egypt ("Aida") began on 26 May 1941, problems on the Eastern Front forced Hitler to focus on Russia.[90] In spite of Raeder's insistence that the elimination of Malta was the prerequisite for the success of his "Great Plan," Malta recovered, leading to the loss of almost 40 percent of valuable Axis shipping. The Great Plan and, with it, Raeder's last attempts to influence the strategic direction of the war, were finished.

Raeder's Great Plan had asserted the role of naval warfare in Germany's total war but it was dependent upon the closest possible cooperation between its land, sea, and air forces and those of Italy, which never really materialized in any sustained way. It was also based on cooperation with the Japanese, which also never occurred. The SKL blamed the lack of collaboration on the OKW, who, in the SKL's opinion, lacked the "correct" strategic perspective on the navy. The SKL, however, continued to misread the objectives of the OKW/OKH, who only thought of Japanese support in terms of its contribution to victory in the East.[91] In spite of collective wishful thinking on the part of the Germans, Japan's policy was to avoid any conflict with Russia in favor of its interests in Southeast Asia. Moreover, after the Battle of Midway in June 1942, the Japanese had lost the offensive in the Pacific war and were unable to undertake any initiatives that would support Raeder's grandiose plans. The promise of Raeder's global coalition war—which, at its best, was utopian—had evaporated.

The complicated tangle of military and political interests that Raeder was trying to influence went far beyond his ability to control. Nevertheless, it, did not keep Raeder from promoting plans that were dependent on forces from the other services and Germany's allies.

The SKL's subsequent situation reports continued to reflect a weakening grasp of reality and misplaced optimism.[92] Although Raeder had been urged to have a more personal presence at Führer Headquarters to gain a larger role in the conduct of the war, he had confined himself to attending only when he had specific items to present. However, as his staff bitterly recognized, Barbarossa had relegated the naval war and the navy to a background role and, if the navy was to have any influence in Hitler's decision making, it needed to be represented at all conferences dealing with the conduct of the war. Raeder did not act upon this advice until April 1942, when he appointed Admiral Theodor Krancke as the permanent representative of the ObdM at Führer Headquarters.[93]

In spite of all the efforts to increase its influence in strategic matters, the navy's plans were greeted with disdain or ignored by the army. After a briefing with the navy's operations staff on 12 June 1942, General Halder characterized the admirals' assessment of the situation as:

> . . . dreaming in terms of continents. Having watched the army's perform-
> ance to date, they assume without another thought that it all depends on
> what we like to do and when, to push through on the land routes to the
> Persian Gulf over the Caucasus, or from Cyrenaica to the Suez Canal via
> Egypt. They are glibly talking about land operations through Italian Africa
> to the East African coast and South Africa. The problems of the Atlantic are
> treated with offhanded superiority and those of the Black Sea with crimi-
> nal unconcern.[94]

Raeder's Finale: The Allied Invasion of North Africa, November 1942

The surprise Allied landings (Operation Torch) in Algeria and Morocco on 8 November and the subsequent German occupation of Southern France on 11 November changed Germany's strategic situation dramat-ically. Although Raeder, like Hitler, regarded the new phase of the war that put the Axis on the defensive as temporary, there is strong evidence that Raeder's self-confidence had been shaken by the total collapse of his two-year effort to bring about a German-Italian-French coalition against England. At the end of November, he confided to a "small circle" of his staff his growing concern over the outcome of Axis strategy in the Med-iterranean. "Without being pessimistic," as he told his staff, he was com-pelled to consider the possible unfavorable situation in order to take the "necessary precautions."[95]

Disillusionment and the gap between vague expectations of "improve-ment" and objective assessments of the political and military forces available for and against the navy continued to plague planning in the remaining months of 1942. On the other hand, the overestima-tion of enemy losses also contributed to Raeder's optimistic assess-ment that enemy shipping could not support another offensive, even when it became apparent that the "race" between sinkings and new Allied construction could not be won. In spite of his repeated empha-sis on the U-boat war as "decisive," more sober internal analyses recognized a "serious danger" in the increasingly effective Allied antisub-marine defenses.[96]

Raeder now regarded the role of the naval war as contributing to the defense of Europe by preventing an Allied offensive as long as possible. As long as the precondition for concentrating all resources on the naval war—the defeat of the Soviet Union—remained elusive, the question of how the war could be won militarily could not be openly discussed.[97] In his meetings with Hitler in November and December 1942, Raeder vac-illated between reassurance and reality. He still believed that Germany had options to counter the Allied threat and tried to portray the Allied landings as an opportunity. If the Mediterranean was now the "major focus of Anglo-Saxon warfare," a defeat of the Allied forces would have the "greatest effect on the entire war and the political situation." Regard-less of his earlier statements, he was forced to admit that the Allies would be capable of launching another operation of even greater scope by mid-December.

Meanwhile Hitler continued his preoccupation with a possible Allied invasion of Norway and once again raised the unrealistic prospect of invading U.S.-occupied Iceland to establish an air base with the aid of new U-boat transports.[98] Raeder became more and more critical of Hitler's assessment of the military situation. Hitler's comment that the situation in Tunis could be "fateful" struck him as "banal," and he recorded in the War Diary, "the ObdM is of the opinion that the Führer is not totally con-vinced of the seriousness of the present situation."[99]

Flights of fantasy on both their parts persisted in Raeder's final con-ference with Hitler in 1942 (22 December), when a stubborn Raeder con-tinued to argue for operations for which Germany did not have the resources. He advocated an occupation of Spain and Portugal to counter the Allied moves in North Africa, which would allow the navy to inten-sify the U-boat war. In this, their last conference before their final confrontation in January 1943, Raeder continued to demonstrate his single-minded focus on promoting his interests, whether for his version of grand strategy or competing with the other services, some of them trivial—but to Raeder, matters of principle. His arguments appeared devoid of any realistic consideration of the resources available to Ger-many, either economically, politically or diplomatically, or the priorities of facing war on multiple fronts, including the air battle over Germany.[100]

9

Raeder and German Surface Operations: Fall 1940–December 1942

The High Point of Commerce War with the Surface Fleet, October 1940–April 1941

The acquisition of the French Atlantic ports appeared to fulfill the ultimate goal of the navy to improve Germany's poor geostrategic position. For the first time, the navy enjoyed direct access to the Atlantic, outflanking the British Isles and providing a new foundation for Raeder's economic warfare. With the easing of operational readiness for Operation Sea Lion (October 1940), Raeder ordered the full deployment of the fleet, exploiting "operational surprise and other favorable circumstances" to overcome the superiority of British forces and disrupt *"the enemy's supply and convoy system."*[1] Initially, Trondheim would serve as the base for operations in the Arctic Ocean and Atlantic. From there the capital ships would attack the British forces between the Faeroes and Greenland. Once the French Atlantic ports were available, he expected to launch continuous operations against the Atlantic sea-lanes.[2]

The heavy cruiser *Admiral Hipper* began this new phase of operations in late September 1940, followed a month later by the *Admiral Scheer,* the most successful warship of the war (seventeen enemy ships captured or sunk). In October 1940, Raeder announced his plans to begin Atlantic operations with the battleships and cruisers operating out of Brest.[3] On 27 December 1940, *Hipper* arrived at Brest, where it was greeted with intense British air attacks (despite Raeder's assurances to Hitler that the antiaircraft defenses were sufficient)—a sign of what was to come.

Raeder believed that the operations of the *Scheer* and the *Hipper* represented the first fruits of his "tip and run" strategy. In late December 1940, Raeder informed Hitler he was deploying *Gneisenau* and *Scharnhorst* to the Atlantic. With the fate of the *Graf Spee* still on his mind, Hitler questioned Raeder as to the purpose of the mission. Sensitive to Hitler's concern over losses and his demands for ongoing reports once operations were under way, Raeder declared that the "one and only [object] is the battle against enemy commerce. The main target is, as always, only the convoys and *not* the escort forces, which are always to be avoided unless very inferior in strength."[4] The führer raised no further objections— he had praised both Raeder and the fleet's fighting spirit in the Norwegian campaign.[5]

The success of Operation Berlin (22 January–22 March 1941) appeared to validate Raeder's Atlantic strategy as well as the concepts underlying the Z-Plan. For the first time in history, German battleships were prowling the Atlantic. During Operation Berlin the battleships stayed at sea for over two months and sank twenty-two merchant ships. As events were to prove, however, Operation Berlin was both the high point and the climax of the surface war. As expected, the British escorted their convoys with battleships, and schedules were disrupted. Combined with the successes of the U-boats and auxiliary cruisers, Raeder, flushed with victory, believed that the Kriegsmarine had seized the initiative and demonstrated the viability of deploying battleships in the Atlantic without bases, claiming they had achieved "considerable tactical successes [with] . . . far-reaching strategic effects."[6] These effects, he argued, were not restricted to the selected operational areas but "extended in widely diverging directions to other theaters of war," specifically to the Mediterranean and the South Atlantic. To intensify the impact of these operations, he intended to repeat them as frequently as possible.[7] Anticipating the eventual entry of the United States, he needed immediate successes to cut off the British supply lines while both the British and the Americans were relatively weak.

Raeder well understood that the new British and American warships nearing completion would restrict the fleet's already limited freedom of action. With the approval of the Lend Lease program (11 March 1941) and with American ships escorting convoys as far as Iceland, Raeder also believed that the United States had already abandoned its neutrality.[8] His repeated attempts to expand the war zone and lift restrictions against American warships and merchant ships, however, were continually frustrated by Hitler's policy of avoiding any incidents until after the Russian campaign.[9]

Raeder's hopes for this new phase of the Atlantic war notwithstanding, the problems of the navy's long drought in building warships and its rapid rearmament after 1933 had begun to take a toll. The engines of the battleships had demonstrated their unreliability and required lengthy overhauls in port.[10] Although the new base at Brest had promised much, the RAF's heavy bombings forced Raeder to order in April 1941 that warships would put into Brest "only in exceptional circumstances."[11] The demands of continuous deployment also affected operations. The need to rotate crews and the periods of inactivity while the ships were repaired increased the need for training and led to further delays. These problems caused friction between the front commanders and Raeder, who wanted the ships to be ready for action as soon as possible.[12]

Operation Rhine Exercise, May 1941

With the battleships *Bismarck* and *Tirpitz* and the heavy cruiser *Prinz Eugen* nearing completion, Raeder eagerly looked forward to implementing his "battle group strategy." The task force would attack convoys protected by older battleships inferior to the new German battleships.[13] Reflecting Raeder's confidence, his orders on 2 April 1941 would permit *Bismarck* class battleships to engage an enemy of equal strength while the other ships of the task force attacked the convoy. Although the commander was still charged with maintaining the utmost regard for protecting his own fighting strength in these engagements, the new orders would supersede those following on the loss of the *Graf Spee*. Raeder was eager to challenge the British for command of the sea in the North Atlantic, but he knew it was not practical "at this moment," given his numerically inferior forces and the constraint to preserve them. Yet, he expected to seek "local and temporary command of the sea in this area and gradually, methodically, and systematically extend it."[14]

Bismarck's availability in spring 1941 was expected to provide the first test of the task force strategy, but repairs to the *Gneisenau* and

Scharnhorst imposed unacceptable delays. Raeder's impatience culminated in Operation *Rheinübung* (Rhine Exercise), the first and last voyage of the *Bismarck* in May 1941. He believed that the deployment of the *Bismarck*, the showpiece of German capital-ship technology, was essential to maintain the momentum in the surface war and to support the other commerce raiders and U-boats.[15] This operation was to also be coordinated with the German occupation of Crete as part of Raeder's strategic interaction between the Atlantic and Mediterranean theaters. He anticipated that the threat of the *Bismarck* to the Atlantic convoys would force the British to withdraw their heavy forces from the Mediterranean.[16] The momentum in the Atlantic war (including the U-boat successes) seemed to be in Germany's favor, and Raeder was eager to gain credit for the navy, because resources were being rapidly diverted to the other services in preparation for Operation Barbarossa.

A critical factor in Raeder's decision to force Rheinübung was his desire to produce immediate success for the navy's new battleships in order to regain the führer's favor for the capital ships. He was increasingly conscious of Hitler's recognition of the growing importance of air power (as evidenced in the success of the British at Taranto in June 1940).[17] Raeder also knew that the British had anticipated his task force threat and were moving vigorously to counter it.[18] The dependence of surface operations on tankers and the limited availability of fuel would increasingly affect operations—possibly precluding future opportunities to demonstrate the worth of the surface navy. His concern over the impact the Americans might have on future operations intensified in mid-May when he was informed of a U-boat sighting of an American battleship and three destroyers patrolling in waters where the *Bismarck* group was to operate. Against Hitler's directives, Raeder ordered that U-boats could attack any darkened warships they encountered, even American.[19] Lütjens, the fleet commander, also informed his commanders that they did not have to "respect the American neutrality zone any longer" during Rheinübung.[20]

The debate over whether Rheinübung should have been postponed until a stronger battle group was available began in the early spring of 1941. For Raeder, he considered this one of the most difficult decisions he had to make during the war.[21] As a single operation, instead of the originally envisioned task force with the other two battleships, Operation

Rhine Exercise carried a much greater risk, because the enemy could concentrate on the *Bismarck* and the *Prinz Eugen*. Lütjens protested personally to Raeder about this "piecemeal" approach. He advocated delaying the operation until at least the *Scharnhorst* was available or until *Tirpitz* was ready to join the fleet.[22] Although Raeder believed he was unsuccessful in convincing Lütjens of the necessity of Rheinübung, he had full confidence in him—which he cited as a strong "psychological factor" in making his decision.[23]

Lütjens was not the only one who questioned the mission. When Raeder informed Hitler of his plans, the führer had reservations, but he deferred to Raeder.[24] On 5 May, Raeder asked Lütjens to brief Hitler on his experiences in the Atlantic and explain the details of the operation, including the risk of encountering British carriers.[25] What neither Raeder nor Lütjens told Hitler was that the *Bismarck* had been made ready for sea only through a cannibalization of weapons and equipment from other ships and lacked a complete suite of antiaircraft fire-control equipment—factors that in all likelihood contributed to the subsequent success of the British carrier forces.[26]

On 22 May, when Raeder personally reported the *Bismarck*'s departure, Hitler expressed considerable anxiety. In particular he was concerned about the threat of the U.S. Navy and British carriers. According to Hitler's naval aide, he even asked whether it was possible to abort the mission. Raeder, however, described the extensive preparations that had been made and the favorable results he expected.[27] He did not share with Hitler the fact that the *Bismarck*'s "breakout" into the Atlantic had already been detected.[28]

Given that the other battleships were not available, Lütjens regarded his mission as a repeat of Operation Berlin, with the same restrictive rules of engagement, that is, to avoid any battle with enemy warships. The "inner contradictions" of Raeder's orders and the issue of the independence of the "front commander" and the shore commands remained unresolved. Although Raeder had emphasized that the "current tactical situation" demanded that the battleships be deployed in the Atlantic, Group West issued orders that, if the breakout was detected, the mission was to be shortened or broken off at Lütjens's discretion.[29] At his 26 April meeting with Lütjens, Raeder stressed the need for bold action and then warned him that it was "imperative" to operate "cautiously and deliberately. One should not risk a major engagement for limited, and perhaps, uncertain goals." If action was unavoidable, it should be fought to the finish—but a battle was "only a means to the end, to sink tonnage." The objective was to keep the battleship available for ongoing operations.[30]

When Admiral Marschall advised Lütjens not to feel strictly "bound" to the operational orders, Lütjens replied, "I will not be the third [fleet commander to be sacked]. I know what the Seekriegsleitung expects and will carry out its orders."[31] Personally, he was not optimistic about his or the *Bismarck*'s chances for survival, confiding presciently to friends that his return was "improbable."[32]

The outcome of Operation Rhine Exercise is well known. Lütjens rigidly followed his orders to avoid any unnecessary risks and failed to exploit his victory over the *Hood* and finish off the *Prince of Wales*. His half-hearted leadership and pessimism over each setback hindered his ability to analyze objectively either his options or opportunities. Shadowed by the Royal Navy from the beginning, he lost the element of surprise which, according to doctrine, represented a prerequisite for success.[33] He knew, however, that Raeder still expected him to continue in order to achieve some measure of success against enemy shipping. Overly influenced by what he regarded as superior British radar and failing to realize at one point that he had actually eluded his pursuers, he revealed his position by repeatedly radioing for instructions from Berlin.[34] With the *Bismarck*'s rudders disabled by the *Ark Royal*'s torpedo planes, Lütjens resigned himself to carrying out Raeder's orders to fight to the last shell—as in fact he did.

Although there is some question whether Raeder had considered the consequences of the sinking of the *Bismarck,* he denied that he expected that such a loss would be either "unexpected" or a "fatal blow." If it was sunk, it would have been consistent with his desire for "full engagement" until all the capital ships were sunk or no longer operational. When the ship *was* sunk, however, Hitler regarded it not as a heroic end but as the severe practical and prestige loss it really was. On 6 June 1941, an angry Hitler expressed his frustration as to Lütjens's decisions.[35] He questioned Raeder sharply as to why Lütjens did not return after sinking the *Hood* or why the *Bismarck* had not engaged the

Prince of Wales, which would at least have resulted in two British losses against one German loss.

Raeder attempted to justify the fleet commander's actions as consistent with his primary objective of "damaging enemy merchant shipping" and argued that, even if the *Bismarck* had attacked the *Prince of Wales,* Lütjens would have known that any damage the *Bismarck* incurred could have prevented further operations. Only if the enemy had tried to prevent Lütjens from attacking merchant shipping was an attack on warships justified, he told Hitler—a statement that would return to haunt Raeder during Operation *Regenbogen* (Rainbow) in December 1942. Although Raeder refrained from second-guessing Lütjens's decision to return directly to St. Nazaire, it was clear that a withdrawal to a more remote area or even to the east toward Norway would have been preferable. Even a "temporary withdrawal" might have stopped the enemy's convoys or compelled them to reinforce their convoys.[36]

In his post-battle report to Hitler, Raeder reviewed the rules of engagement for the surface forces and the guidelines for future operations. He insisted that the "decisive significance" of the Atlantic commerce war required that the objectives of naval warfare could be "most effectively" achieved only "in the *North Atlantic.*" Emphasizing that the primary operational orders called for the destruction of enemy shipping, the task force must "shun risks that would jeopardize the operation." Therefore they were to avoid encounters with ships of equal strength. If a battle was unavoidable, Raeder declared that it should be an *"all-out engagement."* While he acknowledged that the "breakout" into the Atlantic was the most risky part of an operation, it was an acceptable risk if the navy was "not to give up entirely the idea of disrupting British supply lines by means of surface forces." He concluded that the *Bismarck* had fought a heroic battle in the best tradition of the navy.

Raeder reminded Hitler once again of the difficulty the navy faced in confronting a superior opponent that could only be countered "by the boldness of operations and the determination to carry them out." He pointedly noted that the *Bismarck* operation had demonstrated the need for effective air reconnaissance, with pilots specifically trained for the demands of naval warfare. He continued to impress upon Hitler the fundamental principles of "true cruiser warfare," which, even if waged by battleships, utilized the element of surprise and the frequent changing of operational areas. However, a battle with an opponent of equal strength was always only a means to an end. In the absence of bases and resources to repair any battle damage, however slight, even initial successes in engaging enemy warships could lead to the disadvantage of the German warship over the course of an operation and should be avoided.

Raeder defended his strategy of deploying single battleships or cruisers, arguing that the mobility of single units or small battle groups made such operations an essential part of cruiser warfare. They also forced the enemy to concentrate forces and divert ships from other theaters and missions (e.g., convoy escort). In Rheinübung, eight British battleships/battle cruisers, two aircraft carriers, and fourteen cruisers hunted the *Bismarck*. It was more critical at this stage of the war that the navy obtain quick successes in order to make the British sue for peace—a claim that he asserted could be achieved as early as the coming summer (1941). Although it was possible that several ships might achieve more than one ship could in an engagement with the enemy's forces, he reminded Hitler once again that the primary goal was not to engage the enemy's warships but to attack the enemy's sea communications *"undetected"* and on an *"ongoing"* basis.

Meanwhile, he explained, he intended to create the larger homogeneous task force groupings with the battleships and heavy cruisers. He cautioned that further breakouts would be dependent upon the time of year during which the enemy's air operations would be most affected. He added that the most decisive factor for the surface war was the maintenance of the network of supply ships (a conclusion that the Royal Navy had also reached). Raeder admitted the success of the British carrier air forces and the unexpectedly improved British radar, but he assured Hitler that the navy had begun to improve its radar detection ability.

Raeder saw no reason to curtail operations following Rheinübung and declared his plans to send *Lützow* and *Scheer* to the Atlantic. The deployment of the other capital ships would await an evaluation of the situation in the Atlantic. Hitler was not convinced. He felt it would be "inexpedient" to undertake risks until, at the latest, mid-July, when he could assess the success of Barbarossa and the *"entire situation"* of the war. If the British were to collapse—as he still believed—Hitler was open to a *blitzartig* ("lightning") seizure of a naval base (e.g., the Azores) that could provide the fleet "with an opportunity to play an important role." He approved Raeder's decision to keep *Tirpitz* in Kiel at the start of Barbarossa and the sending of *Lützow* to Trondheim, but he served notice that he was to be briefed on any further deployment of the fleet.[37]

Increasingly preoccupied by the Russian campaign, Hitler was no longer receptive to Raeder's entreaties. He had heard all this before, and he was determined to listen to his own intuition and not that of his naval "specialist." He was not prepared to suffer any further losses and clearly indicated his intention to approve all future operations proposed by Raeder.[38] Contrary to Raeder's belief that he had "educated" Hitler, the führer never believed in the role of capital ships in the commerce war. Battleships were supposed to fight it out with their counterparts and represented the power and prestige of the Reich. If Raeder had hoped that major naval victories might have assisted him in his efforts to divert Hitler from his decision to invade the Soviet Union and to keep the focus on the naval war against England, he was soon to discover that he and his surface fleet were becoming increasingly irrelevant. Instead, Hitler's subsequent control over deployment of the capital ships from May 1941 to February 1942 reflected Raeder's declining influence. As Raeder expressed it, the sinking of the *Bismarck* had "lasting effects" for the rest of the war.

> Hitler's attitude toward any proposals by me for the naval war was now completely different. Where before this he had given me a relatively free hand as long as government policies or the other armed forces were not involved, he now became extremely critical and very apt to insist on agreement with his own views. . . . Now his instructions to me considerably circumscribed my use of such heavy units. The first thing he forbade was the sending of any further surface ships into the Atlantic; with this, the war at sea—which up till now we had waged with daring and initiative, gaining successes which could hardly have been expected from our weak naval forces—was to change its character.[39]

Raeder's efforts to continue the Atlantic surface war were doomed by other factors as well. The first was the systematic elimination of the German supply system, made possible by the British success in code breaking.[40] The second was the RAF's hammering of the ports, which put the fleet out of action until February 1942. As the hunt for the *Bismarck* had demonstrated, the RAF and the British carriers had become a major factor in Atlantic operations. Raeder's renewed interest in completing the carrier *Graf Zeppelin* (which he argued might have changed the results of Rheinübung had it been available) was too little and too late, even with Hitler's support.[41] Finally, the growing lack of oil and the demands of supporting the Italians became increasingly important factors in the planning of fleet operations.[42] Clearly, a turning point had occurred in the war at sea, even if Raeder would not admit it. Whereas Raeder's acceptance of risk had once been bolder than that of the commanders at sea, now a degree of caution began to rule operational deliberations in Berlin to a degree unacceptable to the "Front." The SKL had come to the conclusion that only limited operations ("waiting for favorable conditions") to engage the enemy forces were possible.[43]

On 25 July 1941, Raeder declared that his surface operations, in spite of limited numbers and the lack of a naval air arm, were an integral part of the commerce war that *"alone"* could conquer England. In the face of growing British naval superiority and the likelihood that the fleet would gradually be destroyed, the capital ships must continue to operate against merchant shipping. The vigorous British efforts to keep German battleships from leaving port were proof of how much they feared the threat of these ships.[44] Moreover, recalling World War I, he claimed that the fleet's existence supported the U-boat war. Raeder also renewed his criticism of Göring and the Luftwaffe for their continuing failure to attack British naval forces under construction or in Scapa Flow. Bitterly, Raeder stated that the "incorrect use" of the Luftwaffe "is now having its effect."[45] For all of Raeder's plans, however, the fleet remained out of commission, undergoing repairs and overhauls; no further operations would be possible before the beginning of 1942.

The End of Raeder's Atlantic Strategy and the Retreat North, June 1941–February 1942

In mid-September 1941, Hitler shocked Raeder by asking if the battleships should be sent to Norway. A March 1941 British raid in the Lofotens area had fueled his concern that a British invasion of Norway was imminent. Raeder adamantly opposed the idea; in his mind the operational area for the fleet remained the Atlantic. He agreed that the air attacks on Brest had made that base untenable, but he reminded Hitler that the original plan called for the battleships to be deployed to Spanish bases, from which the Atlantic battle could be fought "very advantageously."[46]

Raeder's reference to the use of Spanish ports reflected his continual advocacy of policies that were outside of his own sphere—and were also unlikely to be accepted. He argued that Atlantic operations with the Brest battleships were still practicable, with good chances for success and "for strategic effect," especially with regard to the Gibraltar convoys. If there was no possibility of utilizing Spanish ports and Brest was too vulnerable, Raeder proposed to conduct limited engagements off the French Atlantic coast against the British north-south convoys until a final decision was made regarding the transfer of the battleships to Norway. In an effort to buy time, he urged Hitler to defer any final decision until January 1942 to see if Japan would enter the war or Spain would finally decide to join the Axis.

Hitler continued, however, to obsess that the "vital point" for the surface war was in Norway, expressing interest in the possibilities of a surprise breakout through the Channel that Raeder immediately dismissed as too risky.[47] Raeder hoped that the Japanese attack on Pearl Harbor on 7 December 1941 would strengthen his argument for keeping the battleships in the Atlantic. The withdrawal of American forces to the Pacific, he argued, would create "improved conditions" for the commerce war.[48] Hitler, however, vetoed Raeder's request to allow the *Scheer* to break out into the Atlantic, dashing the last hopes for a resumption of the Atlantic surface war.[49]

Although Raeder considered a "Channel dash" impossible, Hitler proposed that the battleships take advantage of surprise and bad weather. Hitler was thoroughly convinced that the British were going to occupy northern Norway and exert pressure on Sweden and Finland. For Hitler, the defense of Norway was of decisive importance for the outcome of the war, justifying the engagement of all available forces. If a breakthrough by the battleships was not feasible, Hitler threatened to decommission the ships and use their guns and crews to reinforce Norway. He criticized the battleships as outmoded and vulnerable to torpedo aircraft. Raeder countered that the battleships in Brest, even under repair, forced the British to protect their convoys with strong forces that then could not be used elsewhere. For the grand admiral and his plans for the future, a "fleet-in-being," even if incapable of fighting, was preferable to the alternative of having no fleet. Moreover, if there were any changes in the overall military situation, such as France joining the Axis, the battleships would play a decisive role in the Atlantic battle.[50]

Although Raeder had been opposed from the beginning to the Channel route ("absolutely at variance with his views"), he nevertheless dutifully presented the navy's plan on 12 January 1942. Refusing to take the initiative, he declared that the Channel passage had been thoroughly examined "under the strong imprint of the Führer's view" and requested, since Hitler had insisted upon the transfer of the heavy units, that Hitler make the final decision. Hitler remained undeterred. He was adamant that a strong task force—"practically the entire German fleet"—in conjunction with the Luftwaffe could make a decisive contribution to Norway's defense against a large-scale British-Russian offensive.[51]

Following his decision to launch Operation Cerberus, Hitler became even more convinced that Norway was the "zone of destiny" and demanded "unconditional obedience" to all his directives concerning its defense. Since the Luftwaffe was encountering major difficulties in Norway, Hitler expected the navy to do everything in its power to head off an enemy offensive at the very start. The navy, he demanded, must be ready with every available ship to provide reconnaissance in bad weather and to repulse any landing forces "entirely forgoing all other warfare except for the Mediterranean operations."[52] It was clear at this point, much to Raeder's chagrin, that the Atlantic U-boat war had become a secondary theater for Hitler. The success of Cerberus on 11–12 February 1942 was a stunning tactical victory. For Raeder, though, it was an "outright strategic retreat" that ended the surface portion of the Battle of the Atlantic.[53] After this, Hitler would not entertain any further operations by the surface fleet outside of northern waters.

Hitler's attitude toward the navy was increasingly linked to the failure of the Russian campaign to achieve the quick results that he had expected. His preoccupation with the war in the East grew, to the detriment of support for the Atlantic battle—where success was considered more long-term than the immediate demands of the land war. Moreover, beginning in March 1942, the larger Arctic convoys supplying Russia offered an even more compelling reason for a concentration of German naval forces in the North. (In 1942, the Germans estimated that more than half of the Allied support to the Russians arrived via this route.)[54] Bowing to the inevitable, Raeder and his staff adapted to the situation and began to plan new operational opportunities for the surface fleet in Norway.[55] The British attack on St. Nazaire on 28 March 1942, which shook Hitler's confidence by demonstrating the vulnerability of Germany's Atlantic coasts, represented a bitter vindication of Raeder. The major target of the raid was the destruction of the only dock on the Atlantic coast that could accommodate the *Tirpitz*.[56] If Germany's leadership did not see the threat posed by the battleships in the Atlantic, its enemies did.

Justifying the Capital Ships: Operations against Convoys in the Northern Seas, March 1942–December 1942

Faced with increased pressure to stop the flow of supplies to the Soviets, Raeder struggled with competing priorities—keeping the fleet intact for defending against an invasion versus attacking enemy convoys and thereby risking the few capital ships remaining.[57] This conflict became apparent in the first major surface offensive in the north when the *Tirpitz* pursued a convoy without success in the Arctic Ocean in early March 1942 and only narrowly missed being torpedoed by British carrier aircraft. It was obvious that the British were now free to concentrate on Germany's northern naval forces and that there were greater risks in attacking the Russian convoys. Moreover, in addition to the difficulties of weather and limited air reconnaissance in northern waters, the planning of all naval operations by 1942 was dictated by the availability of fuel.[58]

In the aftermath of *Tirpitz's* abortive mission, Raeder downplayed the fleet's chances of success. He highlighted the enemy's ability to send out strong forces with carriers. Accordingly, he proposed to hold back his ships to protect against any invasion and only to attack convoys after the enemy's exact position and strength were known and when sufficient air support was available. Hitler agreed that the Luftwaffe should target the enemy's carriers and concurred with Raeder's plans to operate a task force consisting of the *Tirpitz*, the *Scharnhorst*, one aircraft carrier, and two heavy cruisers as soon as possible, agreeing that it would constitute a "serious threat" to the enemy.[59] This sounded grand, but Raeder knew that the completion of the *Graf Zeppelin* was months (if not years) in the future; the task force plans were yet another reflection of the navy's "flight from reality."[60]

Raeder's preparations for a major operation in June against the next Murmansk convoy, PQ 17, envisioned a combined surface, air, and U-boat operation. Code-named *Roesselsprung* (Knight's Move), the plan involved two task forces (*Tirpitz* and *Hipper, Lützow* and *Scheer*). Once the Luftwaffe determined that there was no risk of encountering superior enemy forces, the task forces would attack. The *Tirpitz* and the *Hipper* would fight escort forces only if there was no other way to attack the convoy. Although Raeder was authorized to deploy the task forces to their operational stations, only the führer could give final approval. The failure to receive adequate information about enemy forces, however, doomed the fleet to inaction. Feeling constrained by Hitler's orders not to risk any confrontation with heavy British forces, Raeder ordered the fleet to withdraw. He made this decision against the advice of his own staff, not even attempting to challenge Hitler's orders because of the "sense of responsibility" that he said he owed to the führer to avoid any risks with the "few valuable units" left to the navy.[61]

Raeder's decision to withdraw, however, was not just Hitler's influence; it was Raeder himself who was hesitating out of the need to preserve the fleet as a "fleet in being," as well as to avoid the führer's anger for any losses. "A defeat at sea," he declared, "would in the present situation . . . be very burdensome."[62] Raeder also hoped that the anticipated Axis victories in Asia and North Africa would create the conditions for an "equalization of forces." The core of the remaining fleet, now referred to as the *Kernflotte*, might then play a significant role in Germany's negotiations with its allies and enemies.[63]

After all the preparation for the success of the capital ships against PQ 17, the ships returned with their "tails between their legs," as one disappointed officer wrote.[64] Ironically, it was the failure of the British to locate the German fleet that resulted in the convoy's orders to disperse, leaving it vulnerable to the U-boats and Luftwaffe.[65] The feeling of a lost opportunity was intensified even more by the success of the Luftwaffe and the U-boats in decimating PQ 17. Raeder tried to defend his decision, arguing that the risk of loss or damage to the fleet outweighed any gains that might have been achieved.[66] The increasing gulf between Berlin and the Front was becoming more evident—a direct result of Raeder's conversion from "full engagement" to a "fleet in being" and his acquiescence to Hitler's restrictions on the use of the capital ships.[67]

For reasons of prestige, and in apparent disregard of his usual concern that the battleships have opportunities to justify their existence, Raeder ignored the command issues and psychological consequences of his actions. In his memoirs, he remained silent on these conflicts, noting only the importance of his capital ships in tying up Allied forces and their role in the British decision to scatter the ships of PQ 17. Yet, as he certainly knew, the surface operations against the Russian convoys had been ineffectual. Although he was unwilling to admit it, Hitler's orders were not totally to blame; Raeder and Group North had placed additional restrictions on the fleet commander regardless of existing ideal conditions under which action was in fact permitted.[68]

After the battle, Raeder attempted to paint a positive picture. The destruction of PQ 17 had forced the enemy to temporarily give up the Murmansk route. Acknowledging the importance of combined U-boat–Luftwaffe operations, Raeder contended that the flow of Allied supplies to Russia would "remain decisive for the whole conduct of the war." The German "fleet in being" now played an important role for Axis strategy as a whole, tying down the already stretched Allied forces, especially after the heavy Anglo-American losses in the Mediterranean and the Pacific.[69] He made no attempt to seek clarification as to what role Hitler thought was more important—using the fleet "offensively" against the convoys or serving as a fleet in being. Hitler, for his part, continued to insist that he wanted only "risk-free" operations.

In July 1942, Admiral Krancke, Raeder's representative at Führer Headquarters, reported that, after the success of the Luftwaffe and U-boats against PQ 17, the führer "would balk even more than before" at the use of the capital ships.[70] After Hitler told Raeder in September 1942 that he wanted to avoid losses as much as possible "without corresponding successes," he rejected a proposal for an operation by the *Hipper* and four destroyers.[71] His hesitation was made even more evident in his December 1942 directive that no operation would be approved unless "as far as one can foresee" none of the heavy ships would be lost. For Hitler, the two priorities for the navy were the U-boat war and the defense of Norway.[72]

In addition to the difficulties of combat in the polar winter, Raeder's equivocation forced SKL, Group North, and the fleet commander to struggle to find opportunities for risk-free operations. As Admiral Otto

Schniewind complained, "Without some offensive spirit . . . operations cannot be carried out with hope of success." The successes of the Luftwaffe and U-boats against the convoys contrasted sharply with the corresponding failure of the heavy ships. The lack of any clear direction as to the deployment of the capital ships, combined with the lack of oil and the weather, represented a threat to discipline reminiscent of the resentment against the High Seas Fleet's "rusting in port."[73] At SKL, the responsibility for the inactivity of the Kernflotte was blamed entirely on Hitler.[74]

When the Allies began to send only individual ships to Murmansk, the navy saw an opportunity to attack with little risk. Several attempts failed to achieve any significant results, but the navy was still determined to find suitable opportunities and began planning for a new operation, *Regenbogen* (Rainbow).[75] On 19 November, Raeder assured Hitler that Regenbogen would begin "only when we have actual proof that the objectives will be worthwhile." He likewise noted that the anticipated resumption of PQ convoys would provide good targets, because it was unlikely that they would be heavily escorted.[76]

On 30 December 1942, a U-boat reported a lightly escorted convoy. The conditions appeared ideal, and expectations were raised at all levels, including Führer Headquarters.[77] On 30 December 1942, Hitler received a notice of Raeder's intent to intercept a convoy "subject to confirmation . . . that no superior force accompanying convoy."[78] Raeder's willingness to execute Operation Rainbow showed his increasing sensitivity to the fleet's morale and the growing criticism both within and outside of the navy as to the value of the capital ships. After the early report that only light forces were escorting the convoy, an excited Hitler asked to be kept constantly updated, thereby giving his tacit approval for the attack. Hitler's support was due in no small part to his growing concern over the fate of the 6th Army at Stalingrad and the amount of supplies reaching Russia through Murmansk.

News of the sighting had interrupted a meeting to discuss the deteriorating shipping situation in the Mediterranean and a Göring–Raeder jurisdictional feud over the Reichsmarschall's creation of a new office, the German Sea Transportation Division, in the Mediterranean. During this meeting, which included both Göring and Krancke, an increasingly irritable führer vented his frustration over the Royal Navy, which sailed through the Mediterranean with impunity, and he criticized the German navy as a "miserable copy" of the British fleet lying idle in the fjords and not even in "operational readiness." The possibility of a successful engagement at hand enabled Admiral Krancke to change the subject and respond to Hitler's eager questions as to whether the German ships could locate and intercept the convoy in time.[79]

When Krancke informed Raeder of Hitler's great interest in this operation and his requirement to be informed "immediately" of any developments, the stakes for Raeder increased dramatically.[80] The SKL had already signaled to Group North to remind them, in line with the general directives, "not to take too great a risk." Group North then forwarded this concern to the Admiral, Arctic Ocean, Rear Admiral Otto Klüber, with the warning to break off any engagement if any "opponent of equal strength" was encountered. Accordingly, Admiral *Nordmeer* obediently signaled the commander of the attacking forces, Oskar Kummetz, to "exercise restraint even with equally strong opponent, as taking major risks not desired by Führer."[81]

For Kummetz, the cautions expressed at all three command levels implied additional restrictions on his operational freedom. The poor visibility and limited daylight, combined with Kummetz's questionable decision to divide his forces (with the *Hipper* in one group and the *Lützow* in the other), further hampered efforts to gain a clear picture of the tactical situation. The result was a complete fiasco. The convoy's destroyer escorts repulsed the initial attack and, with the appearance of British cruisers and damage to the *Hipper*, Kummetz withdrew in accordance with his understanding of his orders.[82]

Kummetz's initial communications, which were eagerly read by Raeder and Hitler, however, gave no hint of the failure to close on the convoy. The messages stated only that Kummetz had attacked, reporting no enemy cruisers. After a U-boat signaled a red glow in the sky, suggesting that the battle had reached its climax, Kummetz reported that he had broken off the engagement.[83] Hitler believed a great victory had occurred and announced it to his New Year's guests. Although the führer was demanding more details, Kummetz, observing radio silence, made no further contact. Krancke, feeling Hitler's criticism of the day before and anxious to report success, passed the reports on to the führer with the same optimism with which Hitler received them. Raeder later criticized Krancke for handling Hitler in a "clumsy way" that made things worse.[84]

Although Raeder attributed the lack of timely information to normal security measures and the unfortunate breakdown of land communications in northern Norway, the lack of success alone was more than enough to cause Hitler to explode in pent-up anger. When he learned from a British broadcast that the entire convoy had escaped and that a German destroyer had been sunk and a cruiser damaged, Hitler raged that the navy was deliberately withholding information from him or giving him inaccurate details. He criticized the lack of ability and daring of the "older naval officers" and the "utterly" useless heavy ships. When the battle report confirmed the British news communiqué, Hitler's fury knew no bounds, and he announced his "unalterable resolve" to pay off the heavy ships. They would be scrapped and their guns mounted on land for coastal defense. He demanded that Raeder report to him immediately.[85]

Hitler's threats were not new, but his criticism became more and more caustic, comparing the inactivity of the ships and lack of fighting spirit to the imperial "High Seas Fleet" that became a "stronghold of revolution." Raeder was fully informed (by Krancke, whom Hitler expressly told to repeat everything he said) of his wrath and knew that the tradition and honor of the navy, even more his own standing, were at stake. Hoping Hitler would calm down, Raeder managed to postpone their meeting until 6 January 1943, ostensibly to gather more information. He contacted Karl-Jesko von Puttkamer, Hitler's naval adjutant, as to whether Hitler intended to ask him for his resignation. If that was the case, he thought it might make his presentation easier, but it was not clear what Hitler wanted.[86]

When the battle report was received, each level of command sought to justify its own actions. Neither Raeder nor his staff was willing to accept any responsibility for the failure of Rainbow. Raeder attributed the development of his "no risk" policy and the heavy ships' lack of action totally to Hitler. In the aftermath of Hitler's denunciation of the navy's leadership and the capital ships, the struggle to maintain the heavy ships, if not the future of the postwar fleet, forced Raeder and the SKL to evaluate and revise their battle instructions. As his staff began to look closer at the origins, consequences, and contradictions of the "no risk" restrictions, they began to question definitions such as "equal strength," "inferiority," or "superiority" as applied to the enemy's opposing forces.

The divergence of opinion over Raeder's definition of "no risk" lay in his extension of his orders from the strategic level to the tactical level.[87] After the loss of the *Graf Spee*, Raeder had issued orders that, once engaged, all ships were to fight to the end. Following Cerberus and Japan's joining the war, Raeder sought to utilize the navy as a fleet-in-being and held back his capital ships to await military and political developments in which the fleet could yet play a major role. Maintaining the nucleus of a postwar fleet was more important at this point in the war than dying gallantly, at least for the heavy ships. Although his commanders wanted to be more aggressive, the grand admiral had repeatedly emphasized that he was only following the führer's directives.[88]

Faced with the possible demise of his fleet, Raeder addressed the dilemma that he had caused. One of his last acts as commander in chief was to issue a directive (28 January 1943) stating that, once engaged, commanders were freed of any restrictions and should utilize "proven tactical guidelines" to destroy the enemy. The previous consideration, to avoid losses on strategic grounds and for related reasons of prestige—which "had appeared to be appropriate"—had resulted in situations in which the commanders at sea had felt that they were to avoid any risks. "The Führer has now expressed himself that such restrictions of this type can never lead to any effective success in the deployment of naval forces." It was now the responsibility of the senior commands to determine whether an operation was worthwhile and that conditions were appropriate. Once permission had been given, the commander at sea was to put aside any thoughts of damage or losses and focus only on "the will to strike at the enemy with all of his power." Raeder expressed his confidence that the navy's fighting spirit "had not waned."[89] Once again, however, he abdicated to Hitler the impetus for this change. For the honor of the navy and as a last defense for the fleet, and more important for its future, Raeder returned to his original call for the navy to die gallantly.

In February 1943, the SKL undertook a study to determine whether they or Hitler had been to blame for these restrictions. Their conclusions did not totally absolve the navy but clearly criticized Raeder, who had repeatedly stated that the führer had expressed his "view" as to any restrictions only verbally. "When the naval command raised numerous objections against the . . . restrictions whose legitimacy was recognized by *Grossadmiral* Raeder, he, however, did not believe that he would be able to make any change in the Führer's view."[90] When Raeder's successor, Dönitz, sought Hitler's permission to attack the Russia-bound convoys in February 1943, Hitler objected because "beginning with the *Graf Spee*, one defeat has followed the other." When Dönitz observed that the restrictions on avoiding losses had "severely limited" the heavy ships, Hitler emphatically denied that he had ever issued an order restricting commanding officers in this manner. If in contact with the enemy, "ships must go into action."[91]

History some day will pass verdict on this matter.

—*Raeder on Hitler's decision to decommission the remaining*
capital ships, January 1943

10

The End of the Raeder Era

The Turning of the Tide: Raeder's Isolation and Conflict

By 1942, Raeder felt himself increasingly isolated. He had attempted to remove himself as much as possible from the intrigues in the Führer Headquarters and met with Hitler only when he had a "definite agenda on which I could demand a definite decision."[1] Until late 1941, he had ignored advice that it was critical that he have more frequent contact with Hitler to represent the navy's interests.[2] Raeder had resisted the influence of Hitler's personality, learning "over the course of time to shun it with firm resolution. For my spiritual independence was important to me; without it I could not do my duty." Until January 6, 1943, he claimed that his issues with Hitler had always been handled objectively.[3]

Now it was becoming evident that, more and more, he was being shut out of any strategic deliberations as to how the war should be fought.[4] He chafed under Hitler's interference in naval operations; yet, he had abdicated to him the decision to move the battleships to Norway in February 1942 and had accepted without protest the führer's continuing restrictions on the navy's remaining capital ships. Although he believed that he had "once exercised considerable influence" on Hitler's decisions, his power to do so had gradually diminished.[5] Raeder was also acutely aware of Hitler's increasingly vitriolic criticism of the military leadership and his firing of a number of generals as the situation in Russia worsened.[6]

As Raeder prepared for his meeting with Hitler on 6 January 1943, he was prepared for the worst. He was aware of Hitler's diatribes against the High Seas Fleet and his "irrevocable decision" to scrap the navy's "useless" ships. At sixty-seven years of age and after fourteen years as head of the navy, Raeder was weary of the struggle to protect the navy's interests and his own eroding autonomy. He was ill-suited to the demands of total war and Hitler's increasing emphasis on "will" as a panacea for overcoming Germany's lack of resources. In addition to losing ground with Hitler, Raeder had poor, if not deteriorating, relationships with other military and political leaders, including Goebbels, Göring, Keitel, and Albert Speer, the minister of armaments, as well as Dönitz.

Although Raeder believed his support of religion was the cause of Goebbels's enmity toward him, it was the navy's independent handling of its news reporting that also caused friction with the minister of propaganda. Following the 28 March 1942 British raid on St. Nazaire, for example, he noted, "Only Raeder knows everything that is happening within the navy. The Führer gets to know part of it and then only a small part." In April 1942, after a bombing raid on Kiel, Goebbels criticized the navy's "unconvincing denial" of reports that the air defenses had not functioned properly. "The leadership of the navy . . . isn't what it ought to be. There is too much praying there and too little work."[7] Goebbels also wanted to make an example of Raeder's involvement in the black market, but Hitler intervened.[8]

Raeder's chief quarrel with Keitel, the OKW chief, was not only that he was Hitler's lackey and had allowed the Nazi Party to exert its authority over the army, but that Keitel was a willing stooge for Göring.[9] Göring was Raeder's principal rival. He had clashed with the Reichsmarschall over the allocation of resources before the war, and their bitter interservice rivalry at times appeared to be more important than the war at hand. He unsuccessfully opposed the appointment of a Nazi Party leader, Karl Kaufmann, as commissioner of maritime shipping (in Göring's Transportation Ministry) in May 1942 and rallied against the appointment of a deputy in charge of sea transportation in the Mediterranean in December 1942. Raeder considered these offices as an infringement of the navy's authority over merchant shipping. He was forced to rescind his orders to ignore the authority of the new Mediterranean office when the theater commander, General Field Marshal Albert Kesselring, threatened to arrest any naval officer who obeyed them.[10] Issues of principle dominated a number of their squabbles. For example, during their months-long struggle in 1940–1941 over who would control the *Lufttorpedo* (air-launched torpedoes), Germany possessed only five torpedoes.[11]

Their most serious long-standing issue, however, was Raeder's ongoing efforts to establish an independent naval air arm, which he had renounced in January 1939 in return for the resources to build the Z-Fleet. Once the war began, the Luftwaffe's lack of support seriously hampered the naval war. Göring continually opposed Raeder's efforts, claiming "everything that flies belongs to me." Raeder complained that it was impossible to counter Göring even if the facts were on his side. Göring used every occasion to tout the superiority of the Luftwaffe over the navy and criticized the diversion of scarce Luftwaffe resources to protect the "useless" surface fleet. In Raeder's opinion, the Reichsmarschall tried to divert attention from his own failings and took too much credit for the destruction of PQ 17 in July 1942. He also accused Göring of using the Luftwaffe's news service to telephone the führer with the first reports of any naval action and report information that was "mostly distorted and incorrect," causing him "great difficulty" in correcting Göring's misinformation. Göring's presence during Operation Rainbow certainly inflamed Hitler's rhetoric. Whenever Raeder encountered friction with the führer, he claimed it was "without question that Göring was the cause." His last words to Hitler as he laid down his command were, "Please protect the navy and my successor from Göring!"—and he knew Hitler "understood very well" what he meant.[12]

For his part, Raeder stubbornly rejected any "combined policy" for the navy and the Luftwaffe in favor of a *"single undivided* operational offensive . . . under one direction and command."[13] After the stunning success of Japanese carrier forces at Pearl Harbor, the navy's bitterness against the Luftwaffe and Raeder's efforts to create an independent naval arm became even more pronounced. He blamed Göring's incompetence for the Luftwaffe's failure to develop a long-range four-engine bomber that would have greatly enhanced the naval war.[14] Early in the war the Luftwaffe's premature dropping of the new magnetic mines where they were soon disarmed by the British cut short the anticipated success of these weapons; the enemy quickly developed counter-measures.[15]

Communication failures in February 1940 between the two services also led to the loss of two invaluable destroyers.[16] More significantly, limited Luftwaffe reconnaissance further enhanced the effectiveness of British Special Intelligence in steering Allied convoys away from U-boats during those periods when the German naval code was being read in close to real time (e.g., mid-1941 to early 1942).[17] Given their mutual animosity and their determination to pursue their own strategy, cooperation, where it existed, was between local naval and Luftwaffe commands.[18] Attempts to arbitrate between the two services failed to reconcile differences because, as Raeder's senior officers acknowledged, his own isolationist policies had helped to preclude the specialized knowledge of naval air warfare that was necessary to instruct the Luftwaffe.[19]

Although it is not surprising that he blamed Göring for "a great part" of the failure of the naval war, it was Raeder who had continually pushed for battleships over aircraft carriers and had delayed construction of the *Graf Zeppelin* until declining resources and the military situation precluded any further work. The failure to develop carrier aircraft was due as much to this as it was to the secondary role that Raeder envisioned for aircraft carriers. It was also reflective of the overall technological shortcomings of the navy in all areas of naval warfare. Even a prototype carrier for experimental purposes might have spurred the Luftwaffe and Hitler to develop carrier aircraft earlier than 1942.[20] Only belatedly, as it became obvious that the fleet could no longer operate without air cover, did Raeder recognize the need to accelerate the construction of aircraft carriers.

Raeder complained of Göring's use of his influence with Hitler, but he likewise utilized his own meetings with the führer to drive his agenda. In January 1941, for example, in Göring's absence, Raeder made his case with Hitler to have the Luftwaffe's long-range reconnaissance squadron I/KG 40 support the U-boat war. When he returned from leave, an enraged Göring prevailed upon Hitler to establish the *Fliegerführer Atlantik*, a new Luftwaffe command that would control all naval air support in the Atlantic commerce war. This proved to be a hollow promise, as British air superiority and the lack of aircraft made it impossible for this group to fulfill any of its objectives in the war against enemy shipping.[21]

The ongoing problems with Göring intensified during 1942, culminating in the Luftwaffe's failures on all fronts. With Germany being heavily bombed, Göring's stock with Hitler was eroding and Raeder anticipated that he might be able to win some concessions from Hitler.

In May 1942, Raeder requested that the führer put pressure on Göring to develop carrier planes, but Hitler doubted that it would be possible to build up a naval air force "during this war."[22] In June 1942, Raeder succeeded in using Hitler's concern over enemy carriers to force a reluctant Luftwaffe to commit more aircraft to support surface operations against convoy PQ 17.[23] In spite of good Luftwaffe reconnaissance efforts, however, doubts over whether an enemy carrier was present forced a jittery Raeder to recall his ships—a decision that Göring quickly used to criticize the grand admiral's overprotection of his large ships.[24]

The creation of a unified armaments organization under Albert Speer as the minister of armaments in February 1942 represented another threat to Raeder's authority. Up to this point, Raeder had zealously guarded the navy's independent armaments program, and only under protest did he agree to recognize Speer's authority. Speer's charisma and "progressive" leadership made him a favorite with Hitler and contrasted sharply with Raeder's "old style" authoritarian leadership. The younger officers, particularly Dönitz, found an affinity with Speer. Speer was fully aware of the resistance of Raeder to his ministry.[25] The close cooperation between Speer and Dönitz in expanding U-boat bunkers in France, as well as Dönitz's receptivity to the resources and technical support afforded by Speer for the U-boat war, led an annoyed Raeder to forbid Dönitz to discuss any technical questions directly with Speer. Speer became aware of serious dissension between the two naval leaders at the end of 1942, when he heard rumors that Dönitz was going to be "relieved of duty in the near future." In early January 1943, Speer told Hitler of the problems he was having with Raeder over U-boat construction and suggested that replacing Raeder would help the U-boat war.[26]

The issues between Dönitz and Raeder dated back to the U-boat chief's prewar criticism that more U-boats should have been built.[27] As the war progressed, Dönitz became increasingly frustrated with what he saw as the lack of support for increasing the number of U-boats, the need for the development of new weapons (e.g., rockets for antiaircraft defense), and expanded Luftwaffe support.[28] The early torpedo failures only fueled what he considered to be a continuing failure of OKM to support the only effective weapon the navy possessed. Dönitz opposed Raeder's Mediterranean strategy on the grounds that it diverted resources from the main theater of operations—the Atlantic commerce war. He also opposed the diversion of U-boats for other duties, such as weather reporting, support of surface operations, and anti-invasion operations.[29] Above all, he did not feel that Raeder was committed to his tonnage strategy (Raeder allowed only six U-boats for Operation Drumbeat against the United States in December 1941).[30]

In fact, Raeder and Dönitz never resolved the issue of whether the U-boat war was a "tonnage war," to sink whatever targets were available with the least risk, or a commerce war (cargo and imports war), in which the U-boats were directed to those targets that had the greatest potential for a "decisive impact (i.e., interrupting supplies to the Soviet Union in support of Germany's strategic objectives). This strategic conflict was, according to Dönitz, the primary source of the differences between them.[31] Raeder never definitively dealt with this problem, which in many cases was dictated by Hitler over his objections. Dönitz also did not share the "old navy's" obsession with building plans for a postwar navy or its preoccupation with its "dinosaurs," the battleships, nor did he support Raeder's machinations with Hitler to increase the navy's role in the war, except for what they did to increase U-boat production or secure more Luftwaffe support. These conflicting views of the navy's role, combined with Raeder's sensitivity to criticism and concern over his authority, created a situation that neither ever forgot or forgave.

In spite of his "growing" impatience with Dönitz's ego and aggressive advocacy for "his" U-boat war, Raeder did in fact argue vigorously for the necessary resources and Luftwaffe support for submarine warfare. He included Dönitz in several conferences with Hitler to showcase the "offensive" U-boat weapon and impress Hitler with Dönitz's zealousness and confidence.[32] Given the limited surface forces and Raeder's efforts to convince Hitler of the importance of the war against England, the U-boat war was the navy's opportunity to play a "decisive" role. Raeder recognized this reality in June 1942 when he formally placed the BdU directly under the naval command, parallel to the fleet commander and the group commanders (a reorganization that he hoped would curb Dönitz's independence). Increasingly, the navy recognized it had two leaders, Raeder and Dönitz.[33]

The entry of the United States into the war and the increasing Allied shipping losses, especially in the autumn of 1942, further reinforced

Dönitz's position. As the Speer-Dönitz relationship strengthened, Raeder found himself outmaneuvered in a situation as much his own doing as it was the result of other circumstances. His only course of action by the fall of 1942 was to limit Dönitz's authority and restrict him to U-boat operations in the Atlantic—especially as the situation in the Mediterranean worsened.[34] Raeder was aware of the BdU's influence over "his" U-boat crews and the threat to his own authority.[35] He was also sensitive to the impatience of the younger officers with the navy's leadership and the tension between the U-boat fleet and the surface fleet. References to "*Freikorps* Dönitz" reflected his concern over the navy's unity.[36]

To further limit the BdU's sphere of operations, Raeder considered relieving Dönitz of the responsibility for U-boat training, which would have removed him from a major source of influence.[37] Even Dönitz was aware that he was challenging Raeder. After Raeder's written orders to confine him to operational issues, Dönitz reportedly told his aide to inform Raeder that he could not obey and then said, "If I were in Raeder's place, I would probably sack the BdU for this; but we'll see what happens."[38] In spite of their differences, Raeder wrote a glowing tribute to Dönitz that became part of his annual fitness report, stating, "If the U-boat war proves able to bring about in essentials—as I am satisfied it will—the decision of this war, this will be primarily to the credit of Admiral Dönitz."[39] Although he struggled with Dönitz's "vanity," he recognized that the navy needed Dönitz's and his crews' fanatical commitment to fight to ensure that the navy would have a future.

Raeder was also increasingly uncomfortable with the demands of "total war" in directives such as Dönitz's "*Laconia* Order" of 17 July 1942, forbidding any attempts to rescue survivors of torpedoed enemy ships, and Hitler's 18 October 1942 "Commando Order" (ordering the execution of captured Allied commandos). When a naval firing squad executed two British marines in December 1942, Raeder noted in the war diary that this represented "something new in international law since the soldiers were wearing uniforms."[40] The development of a new torpedo that could cause the loss of more Allied merchant crews reflected Hitler's growing ruthlessness in conducting the war. When Hitler made it clear on 28 September 1942 that "it was very much to our disadvantage" if a large percentage of the crews survived, Raeder responded that the new torpedo was making good progress and its "tremendous destructive power" would "increase the loss in human life considerably."[41]

Raeder increasingly felt the pressure to instill troops with the necessary "spiritual leadership" and the further incorporation of National Socialist ideology into the navy to ensure the solidarity of the navy with the German *Volk*. As the tide of war turned against Germany, Raeder emphasized the importance of ideological leadership in achieving the führer's great aims. "We cannot win the war against a fanatical enemy with the old principle of 'live and let live.'" In a war of ideologies, the officers needed to draw upon the strength of a people imbued with National Socialism and use it as a source of "tremendous moral strength." The "most important axiom" of the führer was that "it is . . . the *Volk* and the *Volk* alone [that] incorporates our highest goals."[42] These words, spoken in January 1943 to a meeting of Raeder's commanders, less than two weeks after he had resigned, reflect his determination to demonstrate the navy's loyalty and obedience to Hitler and his ideology.

Raeder and Hitler's Final Confrontation

As Raeder quickly learned on 6 January 1943, Rainbow was only a catalyst for the führer's anger. In a monologue lasting an hour and a half, Hitler attacked the spirit and tradition of the navy. It had been totally insignificant in the wars of unification, and the High Seas Fleet had played "no important role during the World War" (except for its development of torpedo boats and the U-boat—"the most important branch" of the navy in two world wars). Smarting from the accusation that he was responsible for holding the fleet back, Hitler noted that the navy had also blamed Kaiser Wilhelm II for the inactivity of the fleet in World War I. "The real reason was that the navy lacked men of action who were determined to fight with or without the support of the kaiser." Neither the revolution nor the scuttling of the fleet at Scapa Flow represented a "glorious chapter" in the history of the navy ("one could not build a new navy on such a foundation"). As shattering as these words were to Raeder, who had played such a key role in promoting the navy's traditions and history, Hitler's attack on the navy's honor was even more devastating.

> The number of one's forces in relationship to the enemy's has always played a great role with the navy as opposed to the army. As a soldier, the Führer

demands that once forces have been committed to action, the battle be fought to a decision. Due to the present critical situation, where all fighting power, all personnel, and all material must be brought into action, we cannot permit our large ships to ride idly at anchor for months.

The Luftwaffe would be more useful in defending against an invasion in Norway instead of having to protect the fleet. It was obvious that the capital ships should be scrapped and their guns used for coastal defense. The navy, Hitler pointed out, should not regard this as a degradation, because such "would only be the case if he were removing an *effective* fighting arm," similar to the army's replacing its cavalry divisions with tanks. Although he had made his decision, Hitler asked Raeder to prepare a memorandum outlining his position on the capital ships, which he promised to review carefully. The führer's willingness to at least accept a counterproposal suggested to Raeder that, even though he had barely been afforded an opportunity to respond to Hitler's monologue, the führer might *yet* reconsider if he could present sound arguments.[43]

Raeder believed Hitler's "vicious and impertinent" dressing-down was intended to insult him personally. The criticism of the spirit and morale of the navy was particularly painful, especially Hitler's derogatory reference to the crew of the *Bismarck*. Under the barrage of criticism, Raeder had struggled to keep his composure and remain silent. "I felt it beneath the dignity of the senior officer of the navy to attempt to contradict in detail such utterly prejudiced statements." Hitler's "biting words" and "loss of control" had convinced Raeder that this situation was more than an objective difference of opinion and would enable him to resign *"without creating any outward sensation which might be detrimental to the navy."* Requesting a private meeting, he informed Hitler that he did not feel capable of fulfilling the navy's "new tasks" and asked to be relieved of duty as of 30 January 1943.[44] As he wrote later, without Hitler's confidence, he found it impossible to continue in office. In order to demonstrate his loyalty and the navy's, he proposed that his "retirement ceremony" take place on 30 January—the tenth anniversary of the Third Reich and Raeder's ten years of service.[45]

Hitler accepted Raeder's offer and requested him (according to Raeder) to name two possible successors. Although he proffered the names of Carls and Dönitz, Raeder clearly favored Carls, whose military and strategic concepts paralleled his. He presented both as equals to Hitler, but praised Carls as "especially suitable" because of his "personality and comprehensive experiences in the conduct of operations and many other areas (types of ships, organization)." Since Carls was the senior ranking officer, his appointment, argued Raeder, would cause no friction among officers who otherwise might have been passed over (as would be the case if Hitler chose Dönitz). Although Dönitz was "similarly suitable" and would stress "the importance of the U-boat campaign as war-decisive," Raeder was "concerned" over whether Dönitz would be able "to dedicate himself to the immediate conduct of the U-boat war to the same extent as before."[46] Dönitz was clearly not his choice, and he later criticized the BdU's "one-sided" focus on the U-boat war and his lack of the "necessary perspective over all aspects of the war."[47]

Raeder's harsh judgment of Dönitz in his postwar Moscow writings and their differences raise the question of why he submitted Dönitz as an alternative. The fact is that he had no choice. He had promoted Dönitz as the dynamic leader of the U-boat arm, and the U-boat successes in the fall of 1942 were virtually the only good news Hitler received. Since Carls represented an extension of Raeder's leadership and policies, Dönitz would undoubtedly be Hitler's choice, and Raeder knew it. If he did not name him as a possible successor, he may have feared that Hitler would make a unilateral decision as he had done with the army. By presenting two candidates, Raeder was preserving the appearance of his authority and avoiding any further conflict with the führer.[48]

On 14 January 1943, Raeder forwarded his plea for preserving his fleet. For days, he anxiously awaited word of the führer's reaction, hoping that Hitler would reconsider. Failing that, this carefully crafted memorandum would be his legacy, written for history's verdict and to defend the honor of the navy. He was determined to counter each of Hitler's jibes about the navy's past and present history. More importantly, he wanted to warn future leaders of the consequences of failing to understand the requirements of modern naval warfare in a global war. In an accompanying letter, Raeder emphasized that the decommissioning of the fleet would represent a significant defeat and sign of weakness, causing joy among Germany's enemies and a deep disappointment among the Axis powers. Above all, it would, "reveal a lack of understanding for the paramount importance of naval warfare, above all in the approaching final stage of the war."[49]

Much of Raeder's memorandum was a repetition of his strategic concepts. The navy had recognized the vulnerability of the enemies' sea communications and had planned a fleet capable of attacking the enemy's sea-lanes in the Atlantic. The premature outbreak of war in 1939 forced an unprepared navy to emphasize the construction of U-boats. Yet, the navy fought with *all* the resources available, committing the surface fleet in offensive operations against a far superior enemy. The capital ships had fought with the "utmost offensive spirit," achieving an "extraordinary far-reaching effect." The entire world, boasted Raeder, "acknowledged the boldness of German naval leadership."

Raeder continued his criticism of Göring and lamented the Luftwaffe's lack of air support. If Germany had had a task force "with support air cover" operating off the western French coast, it would have been an effective deterrent to an Allied invasion of North Africa. At the same time, even in the absence of air support, he still expected opportunities for the remaining surface forces in the north to exploit favorable weather conditions and the element of surprise.

Raeder praised the Axis coalition's contribution to the overall conduct of the war, arguing that when the Italians entered the war, the British had to reinforce their forces in the Mediterranean and to further split their forces. Even though the Italian battleships had been unsuccessful in destroying British sea power in the Mediterranean, their very existence and strategic effect remained a factor. Moreover, claimed Raeder, the Axis naval strategy had exercised so much pressure on the British that, by spring 1941, the Royal Navy had been forced to ask for assistance from the United States.

The entry of Japan brought a strong naval power on the side of the Axis and opened a new theater of war in the Pacific that required the undivided attention of the U.S. Navy. As a result, the British had deployed all of its remaining older battleships to escort convoys and shore up its forces in the Indian Ocean. Scrapping the Kernflotte, declared Raeder, would fundamentally change the overall strategic situation. Without the fleet, the enemy would be able to operate at will in German coastal waters and the Luftwaffe would be unable to provide sufficient forces for defense, especially in northern waters and under poor weather conditions.

The final part of Raeder's memorandum concluded that the time, personnel, and facilities required for demobilizing the fleet and the building of the shore batteries (which would take twelve to twenty-seven months) was out of all proportion to any advantages to be gained. Given the length of the coast to be defended, he ridiculed the idea of replacing the mobility of shipboard artillery with stationary shore batteries and noted that only thirteen batteries could be salvaged from the remaining battleships and cruisers. Above all, these measures would bring only a slight gain to the U-boat war (approximately fifty additional officers and a short-term increase in U-boat construction—if the required workers were available). The decision to scrap the capital ships would constitute a "final and irrevocable act, it would take *years* to rebuild them." The disappearance of the fleet would not only be felt during the course of the war "but will be continued into the [following] years of peace." In the first years after the end of the war, "the navy will not be able to carry the flag of the Reich to foreign shores." The political and psychological impact, warned Raeder, would have the most serious repercussions on the German people as well as Germany's allies. The people would recognize the historical parallel between this event and the fate of the Imperial Navy in World War I and the "abandoning of any hope of winning this war through a decisive naval war." To the enemy, "the disappearance of the German warships would represent a *political and propaganda triumph*"—magnified by the fact that Germany's propaganda had repeatedly stressed the importance of the battle fleet.[50]

The first indication of Hitler's views came from a meeting on 17 January 1943 with Krancke, who reported to Raeder that the führer had not changed his mind regarding the heavy ships and now intended to cancel the construction of aircraft carriers. The situation in the East had become so critical that all forces were to be redirected to increase the production of tanks. Only the construction necessary for the U-boat war or coastal defense would continue. Once again, Hitler had disparaged the weak armament of Raeder's ships and the failure to keep up with technological improvements (e.g., the Japanese triple-barreled turrets). He disagreed with the concept of a "fleet in being" that could exert a strategic effect and achieve a victory without a battle. Although Hitler agreed that the struggle against the "great sea powers" was just as decisive for the outcome of the war as the war in the East, he supported the maintenance and reinforcement, if possible, of the U-boat war—but "all this will be of no use unless we can defeat the Russians in the East."[51]

The fate of the fleet seemed obvious from Hitler's comments, but there was still no clear indication that Hitler had even bothered to read Raeder's memorandum. Krancke himself had already concluded from several sarcastic comments by Hitler that Hitler was unimpressed, but he learned after Hitler's meeting with Dönitz on 25 January that the führer was unmoved by Raeder's arguments.[52] On 26 January, Dönitz ordered the decommissioning of all heavy ships except for training purposes. The official order noted that, because of the "political and psychological effects," it should be communicated "to as few officers as possible."[53]

The Raeder Era was over. A führer who understood that Germany's fate lay on the battlefields of Eastern Europe had rejected Raeder's last appeal. Raeder's stubborn adherence to the Tirpitz legacy and the dream of *Weltmacht*—and his attachment to the battleship as the classical expression of a nation's sea power—now served as his epitaph. His conception of the navy and its strategy, shared by his closest staff, contrasted sharply with Dönitz's ruthless practicality in addressing the immediate needs of the war. As Keitel later noted, "two military dogmas stood face-to-face against each other inside the navy."[54] It is not surprising that Dönitz subsequently purged almost all of Raeder's senior officers and drew a sharp distinction between his methods and his predecessor's, stating bluntly, "It is a question of winning the war. Considerations of how the navy should appear after the war have no value. The naval war is the U-boat war."[55]

The formal end of Raeder's administration took place on 30 January 1943. Praising Raeder for "the extent and greatness of his life's work," Hitler announced he had decided to relieve Raeder from the daily burden of leadership. He would continue to rely on him, however, as his "first advisor" in questions of naval policy.[56] In his last decree, Raeder cited his poor health as his primary reason for leaving and urged the navy to give the same toughness and resolution to his successor and the same "unshakeable will to win" and devotion to the führer as before.[57]

On 1 February 1943, Raeder said farewell to his closest colleagues. He justified his leaving with a review of his previous attempts to resign, beginning in 1933. Hitler had declined to release him then because the rebuilding of the navy had just begun. In the spring of 1939 (actually November 1938), he said, he asked Hitler to allow him to leave, but the threat of war made this impossible. In 1941–1942, on his doctor's advice, he tried twice more to resign, but both times, Hitler refused. Nevertheless, he had felt that sooner or later, an occasion would arise in which he would be obliged to step down. Given the achievements of the navy and considering the potential impact on public opinion at home and abroad, he had come to the conclusion that any change in command would have to be made "so smoothly that enemy propaganda could not make any capital out of it." When an opportunity presented itself in early January to broach the matter of his leaving, Hitler did not object, but stated that he too thought the change in command should occur smoothly and wished for him to remain actively connected with the navy.

In reviewing his command, Raeder bitterly characterized it as "a time of never ceasing tough struggles."

> Only the battlefield changed over the course of time. In the beginning, struggles against the [Defense] Ministers such as Groener and von Schleicher. Struggles at first against the army, which at that time showed a tendency to swallow up the navy. Later on for a decade a struggle against the Luftwaffe, as you know only too well. Then there was the struggle on all sides against personalities such as Todt, Speer and Kaufmann, who were supposed to support the navy but in reality never failed to put difficulties in our way.[58]

Convinced that the war would continue with full intensity for a long time, he expected that the struggle for resources would continue with the same intensity. The navy, he declared, has the hardest struggle during this war. That it was fundamentally a naval war would, he predicted, become more and more apparent as the war approached its climax, contrary to those who viewed it as foremost a war for and on land.

Raeder also addressed criticism that he had not done enough in the development of new technology and weapons development. He pointed out that the contributions of the U-boat war had been built upon initiatives begun before 1933. "Vast improvements" were currently being made to increase U-boat production as well as new weapons, and he promised that every possible sacrifice would be made to continue the U-boat war. He acknowledged that the scientists and technicians of the world, in particular the United States (which had a considerable lead in radar), were trying to gain an advantage over Germany, but any new developments "generally cancel each out quickly, as has repeatedly been demonstrated."

In his final plea, he called upon the navy to preserve its unity and solidarity. Raeder acknowledged his loyalty and the navy's in the clearest expression of his acquiescence to the National Socialist state and "our beloved Führer." Having claimed that the navy's "inner attitude" was indeed the equivalent of "a truly National Socialistic attitude," he went on to declare:

> Hence there was no need for us to change; right from the beginning we could become loyal supporters of the Führer with all our hearts. It has become a particular source of satisfaction to me that the Führer has always valued this highly and I wish to ask you to do all you can do to see that the Führer can always count on the navy in this respect as well.[59]

Ich war Seemann und Soldat, aber nicht Politiker.
—*Raeder, 1956*

11

Defending the Navy, 1943–1960

Retirement and Prisoner of War, 1943–1945

Although Raeder complained that the führer "never once" called upon him for advice after he retired, he claimed that Hitler sought to maintain the appearance "that we were still on the best of terms"—even sending him a birthday gift of an oil painting depicting a French victory over the Anglo-Dutch fleet in 1690.[1] He continued to receive regular briefings on the war at his home in Babelsberg and received two minor assignments in the role of admiral inspector. Until 20 July 1944, Raeder's retirement was quiet, broken only by visits to the naval archives and several social meetings with Dönitz.[2]

On 21 July 1944, he learned of the assassination attempt on Hitler and became alarmed that his enemies in the Göring and Himmler camps would try to link him with the conspiracy. He went to see Hitler the next day to offer his support and counter any attempts to implicate him. He was shocked to hear about Germany's "totally hopeless" military situation and assured Hitler that he "was ready at any time, to risk his life for Germany." Throughout the visit, Raeder claimed he had been carrying a loaded pistol ("for my own security") and, upon his departure, made a point of berating Hitler's SS guards for allowing this lapse of security.

Raeder's profession of loyalty was not only out of personal concern, but, as he would argue, consistent with his conviction that a military coup was completely contrary to his duty as a soldier. It reflected

210

the heavy burden he felt following the navy's desertion of the kaiser, the 1918 naval mutinies, and the Admiralty's ready acceptance of the Kapp Putsch in 1920. As he declared later, he would never have tolerated any threat to the discipline of the navy or anything that would have

> undermined the firm attitude of loyalty to the state that the navy had built up since 1921. It had neither the internal prerequisites nor the possibility to undertake any political venture such as a coup d'etat. For me, and for the navy under me, the only possible attitude was the one that we had adopted under the Weimar Republic and its two Presidents—first Ebert and then Hindenburg—an absolutely soldierly attitude.[3]

Responding later to accusations that his views on the plotters reflected his acceptance of the Nazi state, Raeder declared that he had never demanded that anyone should "unconditionally accept National Socialist views," only to uphold the time-honored traditions of the navy.[4]

Raeder's declaration of unconditional support in the wake of the assassination attempt did not go unnoticed by Hitler. In sharp contrast to the army, the navy reacted vigorously against the conspiracy. As Hitler declared, "not a single one of these criminals belongs to the navy. Today it has no Reichpietsch [Max Reichpietsch, executed as a ringleader of the 1917 naval mutinies] in it."[5] Goebbels, too, noted the great praise Hitler had for Raeder—a man of "great stature" who had shown "unwavering loyalty" and had instilled a spirit that had enabled the navy to erase the stain left on it by World War I.[6]

The subsequent mock trials of the conspirators repulsed Raeder. In particular, he was horrified to hear about the torture of the former defense minister, Otto Gessler. Raeder had initially interceded with Hitler on Gessler's behalf after his arrest, but when he learned that Gessler had been implicated in the plot, he had withdrawn his support. In March 1945, when he visited Gessler in the hospital after his release, Raeder saw the results of his treatment in prison. When he told Gessler that he intended to inform Hitler, Gessler begged him not to—his torture had been ordered by the führer. "Ashamed," Raeder took off his Golden Party Badge, which he had worn since 1937, and destroyed it.[7] Even after this incident, however, Raeder continued to profess his loyalty, but his repeated calls to Hitler were not returned. In late March 1945, hearing that Hitler intended to remain in Berlin, Raeder sent a message to Hitler that he also planned to stay. Erika Raeder later claimed that his remaining set "an example to others" and fleeing was "out of the question."[8]

As the war ended, Raeder was hospitalized, suffering from a recurrence of his heart problems. On May 16, 1945, he reported to the Soviet military authorities in Potsdam and was placed under house arrest. Although he was later sent to Moscow, he continued to receive deferential treatment and good food and medical services. When Soviet officers inquired as to his future plans, Raeder informed them that he would describe his experiences and "lessons learned" from World War II, apparently believing that they would be useful for both the German and Russian navies.[9] As he later told his Nuremberg psychologist, he expected that the Russians would want to achieve hegemony in Europe, which meant that they would have to control the Mediterranean, "and they do not know enough about seamanship for that." Raeder obviously felt that the Russians would have to be trained by someone who understood sea power.[10]

He planned to write first about the German attack on the Soviet Union—a topic that he felt would make for a more "propitious atmosphere" with his hosts. His other subjects included the Norwegian campaign, the 1942 Channel "breakthrough," the navy's relationship with National Socialism, and the "future development of naval forces."[11] His observations on future naval developments, however, were not particularly foresighted or informed. As he related later, the Soviets had tried to extract information from him on radar, but he could not provide any information because he personally had no technical knowledge.[12]

With the signing of the International Military Tribunal (IMT) charter on 8 August 1945, Raeder now became more important to the Soviets as a major war criminal.[13] When a shocked Raeder learned in mid-October 1945 that he was to be tried as a war criminal, he reportedly considered suicide.[14] In March 1946, Admiral Patzig reported that Raeder was so embittered by being brought to trial by the Western powers as a war criminal that he might accept Soviet offers to collaborate.[15] U.S. Navy officers who later met with Raeder suspected that his wife was being held in "bondage" by the Soviets to ensure that he would return to Russia in the event he was released from prison.[16] Given later controversies over alleged acts of "collaboration" by several captured naval officers, his indictment and imprisonment as a war criminal may have saved the navy from an embarrassing denouement. His conviction (and Dönitz's) at Nuremberg allowed their supporters to unite in defense of their former commanders and focus their energies on a future German navy.[17]

Raeder heard nothing further of his Moscow writings until May 20, 1946, when the Soviet prosecutor introduced excerpts during his cross-examination. An embarrassed Raeder attempted to disavow them, noting his "deep emotional depression" at the time and argued that his notes were "rough, based on memory, without references and intended only for his private use" and "representing neither final judgments nor definitive evaluations."[18] In particular, it was his comments on Dönitz and not other leaders that caused him the most discomfort. In a bitter denunciation, Raeder had characterized him as "Hitler-Youth Dönitz" because of his many public statements on behalf of the Nazi Party. He blamed Speer's ability to exploit Dönitz's "vanity" as one of the reasons for the navy's loss of control over all its construction and technical support (and "the collapse of the navy's logistics"). He condemned Dönitz's agreeing to head the remnants of the government in March 1945—a decision that violated the military's responsibility to remain "non-political"— and doubted his ability to do so.[19] Even though Raeder immediately apologized to him, Dönitz regarded the apology as merely an expedient in order to present a united front, and the relationship between them remained cool.[20]

Raeder at Nuremberg

Representatives from the U.S. Navy and the Royal Navy had urged against prosecuting Raeder and Dönitz, but the American prosecution team, along with the French and the Soviets, overrode their objections.[21] It was clear to both admirals that their trial represented an indictment of the entire service and its conduct during the war. With German "naval honor" on the line, the members of the former Kriegsmarine closed ranks, more unified than the Imperial Navy after World War I.[22]

The case against Raeder rested almost completely on documentary evidence, with the prosecution calling only a few minor witnesses. Raeder's lawyers protested that they did not have the same access to the documents captured by the Allies as the prosecution and complained about the frequent introduction of new evidence and translation issues.

They claimed, for example, that the navy's office in Holland was a "design" bureau and not a "construction" office (the Versailles treaty did not prohibit "designing" U-boats). Their greatest frustration was the fact that the tribunal would not allow any evidence regarding the actions of the Allies.[23] This was particularly galling to Raeder in the case of Norway, where there was ample evidence of British invasion plans. He believed that the sole intent of the tribunal was to convict both him and the German military organizations as "criminal"—thereby condemning the German people as a whole (and avoiding any comparison with the war guilt clause of the Versailles treaty).[24] He was particularly appalled by the prosecution's characterization of him as a "mendacious politician" who was aware of Hitler's aggressive demands and assisted in their realization as a member of the Third Reich's "main political bodies" and its "inner councils."[25]

Raeder's attorney, Walter Siemers, concentrated primarily on the charges that Raeder had participated in the political planning and preparations of the Nazi conspirators for wars of aggression. Fleet Judge Otto Kranzbühler (who was Dönitz's chief counsel) concentrated on the third indictment, that Raeder had "authorized, directed, and participated in war crimes, particularly war crimes arising out of sea warfare." His trial began on Wednesday, 15 May 1946, and ended on 21 May 1946.[26] In his opening statement, Raeder accepted full responsibility for his fifteen years as head of the navy, "which he considered his 'life work'" and admitted, "perhaps, I became rather one-sided since this fight for the reconstruction of the navy filled my time and prevented me from taking part in any matters not directly concerned with it." In response to the charges that he had conspired against peace and had built the navy in violation of the Versailles treaty behind the back of the government and Reichstag, he declared that the rebuilding of the navy was not "in any way" built "for the purposes of aggressive war." He acknowledged that "some evasion" of the Versailles treaty had occurred but, in the final analysis, Germany had not taken full advantage of the naval provisions permitted under the treaty. He testified that, in fact, so little had been done that he was "reproached for this later when the National Socialists came to power."[27]

The fact that the prosecution had a wealth of evidence regarding violations of the Versailles treaty was, for the most part, a result of Raeder's sensitivity to criticism. A 1937 study, for example, described specific measures the navy had taken to rearm the navy from 1919 to 1935.[28] Raeder rationalized these violations as "minor matters," meant only to build up a "pitiable defense of the coast in the event of extreme emergency." As to his involvement in the political decisions of the Third Reich, Raeder argued that Hitler had only expressed plans to build a strong military capable of defending Germany and a naval policy that required expansion "only to the extent demanded by a continental European policy." Hitler's announced intent to seek an agreement with the British to fix the size of the German fleet afforded "extreme satisfaction" to Raeder and the navy. Likewise, he praised the Russian-German treaty of August 1939 that promised "a guarantee of 'wonderful development' for the navy." When asked why he served a criminal regime and did not resign, Raeder praised Hitler as a "vigorous personality" who, in the beginning, was "a great and very skillful politician." Hitler's national and social aims were well-known and accepted in their entirety by the armed forces and the people. In the wake of Hitler's first victories in both domestic and foreign policy—"without bloodshed or political complications"—it was expected that he would resolve any future problems in the same way.[29]

Raeder's attempts to justify the violations of the Anglo-German Naval Treaty of 1935 and the supplemental agreement of 17 July 1937 were more difficult. In the case of falsifying or not reporting technical details about the size of the German ships under construction after June 1935, he attributed the nondisclosure to the desire to avoid any responsibility for initiating an arms race.[30] He also tried to explain that the violations were technical and not criminal in the sense of the Nuremberg Charter. The increased displacements of the battleships were defensive, made necessary by increasing compartmentalization to maximize the survivability of Germany's few battleships. The 20 percent increase in the displacement of the battleships resulted from the inexperience of German shipyards and the original intent to build the ships with broad beams to navigate the shallow waters of the naval ports and Kiel Canal. In light of evidence available today, these statements were misleading at best. Nevertheless, he argued that the navy never exceeded the amount of total tonnage allowed to the Germans under the Versailles treaty.[31]

The prosecution's proof for Raeder's participation in the planning to wage wars of aggression relied on the records of a series of meetings with Hitler from 1937 to 1939. Raeder challenged both the accuracy and interpretation of each of the documents, noting that he had never seen any official records from any of these meetings. He also pointed out that Hitler never solicited counsel but only gave undisputed orders. The navy was never ready for war, as was implied in the 5 November 1937 "Hossbach Memorandum," and war with England, as he had repeatedly told Hitler, was "sheer madness." Moreover, he declared that he did not discern any change in the führer's plans for the navy in the 23 May 1939 meeting with Hitler's senior military leaders. The navy was "fully incapable" of waging war until 1943–1944. If war was imminent, as the prosecution implied, the navy would have accelerated rearmament, particularly in U-boats. Raeder acknowledged the seriousness of Hitler's speech of 22 August 1939, but he had been convinced by assurances that France and England would not intervene, especially after the last-minute pact with the Soviets.[32]

The tone of his trial turned dramatically when Sir David Maxwell-Fyfe began his cross-examination. Under Maxwell-Fyfe's rapid firing of questions and constant interruptions, the defendant began to lose his patience and composure. Without any of the deference shown by others, Maxwell-Fyfe sought to demonstrate Raeder's pro-Nazi support and force him to admit that the navy had committed more than minor treaty infractions. He surprised him with new documents that appeared to contradict Raeder's earlier statements. Raeder insisted that the armed forces had to have a relationship with the political form of the state and declared that, while the navy had adopted these principles, he alone had determined its appropriate position to the National Socialist State and maintained the navy's independence.

In his cross-examination, Maxwell-Fyfe charged that the navy's conduct of the war at sea violated international law, citing Raeder's repeated calls for an intensification of the U-boat war. Accusing him of trying to throw international law overboard for military necessity, he cited Raeder's attempt (October 1939) to justify operations that promised decisive success "even if they are not covered by existing international law" and necessitated a "new code of naval warfare." Raeder defiantly defended his gradual lifting of restrictions on submarine warfare as self-defense and, in response to the enemy's actions, "perfectly justified and legally proved."

Since the U-boat war had been extensively examined earlier in Dönitz's trial, Maxwell-Fyfe moved to confront Raeder with his complicity in war crimes, beginning with whether he had any knowledge of the extermination of the Jews. He introduced a deposition from a naval administrator at Libau who had officially reported the shootings and "evacuations" of Jews, including those working for the navy. Raeder responded that he had not been aware of these events, but if he had been, he would have intervened. The questioning became testier when Maxwell-Fyfe pressed him on whether he had approved Hitler's Commando Order of 18 October 1942. Raeder responded that he had only passed it on as an order from his commander in chief, but he also defended it as a reprisal against the commandos for their actions at Dieppe that justified a "deviation" from international law. He acknowledged that the navy had been involved directly in the shooting of two British commandos in December 1942— a mistake that he had duly noted in the official record (they should have been turned over to the Security Service).[33]

Maxwell-Fyfe's final questioning focused on Raeder's failure to raise any protest against the political actions of the Nazi state. He accused him of ordering a cover-up of the sinking of the *Athenia*. Although Raeder claimed he was "very indignant" about the false charges, Maxwell-Fyfe pointed out that he had done nothing about it—just as he had remained silent over the plots against Blomberg and Fritsch in 1938. His only protest against Hitler and the Nazi state had been in March 1945 when he stopped wearing the Golden Party Badge after learning of Gessler's torture. Raeder angrily retorted that he had frequently made "serious protests," albeit in private meetings with Hitler, which he had been told was a more effective means of persuading him.

Raeder's attorney called only three witnesses. Karl Severing, former Social Democratic minister of the interior, corroborated Raeder's argument that violations of the Treaty of Versailles before 1933 had been carried out with the support of the government. Ernst von Weizäcker, former state secretary in the Foreign Office, testified that Raeder had not been involved in any way with the propaganda article blaming Churchill for the sinking of the *Athenia*. The third witness, Vice Admiral Erich Schulte-Mönting, Raeder's adjutant from 1933–1939 and his chief of staff from 1939–1943, noted he had reviewed every major document and had been briefed by Raeder following any meetings with Hitler.

Schulte-Mönting denied that any preparations were made for war against England and declared that the navy had fought a "clean war." He defended Raeder's actions in supporting some of Hitler's "dishonorable" decisions, because, as the head of the navy, he was compelled to accede to the higher interests of the state. Raeder had remained at his post, in spite of his differences with the führer, because Hitler had asked him to stay and had given him assurances for the integrity of the navy. Schulte-Mönting related Raeder's concern that the party might merge the navy and the merchant marine into one ministry run by Nazi officials. Still, he "frequently and very seriously" had to convince Raeder to stay and, after one major disagreement in 1939 (actually 1938), Hitler had asked Schulte-Mönting to mediate between him and Raeder. In the end, Raeder's sense of duty and patriotism compelled him to continue in office and he had "acted consistently as a good patriot would act."[34]

Siemers concluded Raeder's defense with a number of exhibits and affidavits attesting to his character and strong religious beliefs. Among the materials he presented were letters from individuals who had benefited from Raeder's personal intervention on their behalf, including the release of Jews from concentration camps as well as his efforts to thwart Nazi anti-Church policies.[35]

Raeder's final words to the tribunal on 31 August 1946 before his sentencing were defiant. The prosecution, Raeder claimed, had failed to prove the conspiracy charges against him and the organizations of the Third Reich, including the "General Staff and High Command of the Armed Forces," as well as the counts of waging aggressive war. Although he was forced to acknowledge the "indisputable evidence" of horrible crimes and genocide committed by Hitler and his henchman, he insisted that no one, outside of the perpetrators, had the "slightest" idea of them. "To most of Germany, Hitler's true face came to light for the first time at the Nuremberg trials."[36] As he told Admiral Boehm during the trial, he had never known of the atrocities against the Jews and had a "clear conscience."[37]

Moreover, he maintained, the proceedings had "fundamentally confirmed" that the navy had fought a clean and decent war. "The German navy stands before the Court and the world with a clean shield and an unstained flag." With a "clear conscience" the navy had "emphatically refuted" attempts to place the submarine warfare on the same level with Nazi atrocities. The navy had never shown "contempt for international law" but had made an "honest effort . . . to bring the conduct of modern naval warfare into harmony with the requirements of international law and humanity on the same basis as our opponents." The repeated attempts by the prosecution, who were unqualified to judge soldierly honor, to discredit him and the navy had failed. "I am convinced that the admiralties of the Allied powers understand me and that they know they have not fought against a criminal." If he was in any way guilty, it was that

> in spite of my purely military position I should perhaps have been not only a soldier, but also up to a certain point a politician, which, however, was in contradiction to my entire career and the tradition of the German armed forces. But then this would have been a guilt, a moral guilt, towards the German people, and could never at any time brand me as a war criminal. It would have not been guilt before a human criminal court, but rather guilt before God.[38]

On 1 October 1946, the tribunal found Raeder guilty of conspiracy, aggressive war, and war crimes. Raeder escaped the most serious of the original war crimes charges—the conduct of "unrestricted submarine warfare"—as a result of the ingenuity of Dönitz's attorney, Kranzbühler, in obtaining an affidavit from Admiral Chester Nimitz, commander of the U.S. Pacific Fleet, which acknowledged the U.S. Navy's initiation of unrestricted submarine warfare at the beginning of the war. Kranzbühler thus cleverly skirted the disallowed tu quoque defense ("we did wrong, but so did you") in arguing that the Americans (and the British, too) had acted in accordance with international law, as had Germany.[39]

Raeder's sentence was life imprisonment.[40] He had always assumed that he would be executed and appeared shaken by the verdict. He was appalled when he heard of the sentences—death by hanging—of Jodl and Keitel, a dishonorable form of execution for a soldier.[41] Concerned that he would be a burden to his family and having "no desire to serve a prison sentence at my age," Raeder appealed to the Allied Control Council requesting his execution by a firing squad, which was refused on the grounds the council had no authority to increase his sentence.[42]

The conviction of the two admirals shocked their supporters as well as many of their former adversaries. In spite of what even today is debated as a flawed process ("victors' justice") and sentences that were

regarded as "harsh," the trial allowed both admirals and their supporters to claim that they and the navy had been vindicated and had fought
an honorable war. The violations against the Versailles treaty and the
Anglo-Germany naval agreements seemed petty, given the size of the
navy that went to war in 1939, hardly a fleet prepared for a war of aggression. Moreover, the conduct of the war at sea seemed no different from
the war fought by the Allies. By successfully introducing the evidence of
Allied unrestricted submarine warfare, the two commanders were able
to portray themselves as martyrs.

The Nuremberg records, along with the memoirs of Raeder and
Dönitz, were to shape the navy's "official" history for years, making it
more difficult for the service to confront its history critically. By framing the arguments, the Nuremberg process allowed Raeder to distance
himself from his political role as navy chief and to minimize his complicity with the criminal nature of Hitler and the National Socialist state.
The crimes against humanity and the "final solution" appeared not to
touch the navy or its leaders. With the documentary record more acces-
sible in the late 1960s, scholars cast a new light on the continuity of the
motives of the navy's leaders and challenged Raeder's defense that he had
"distanced" the navy from the Nazi regime. In fact, his indoctrination of
the navy precluded, in his own words, any need to "re-educate" the officer corps after 1933.

A broad public debate in Germany in the late 1990s over the responsibility and complicity of the Wehrmacht in supporting the criminal
policies of the Third Reich raised new issues (and evidence) that the
Nuremberg prosecution had failed to pursue vigorously in its case against
the criminal nature of the armed forces.[43] Hitler's awarding of the
Golden Party Badge in 1937 to the two service chiefs, Raeder and Fritsch,
for example, was not just an individual honor; it represented the armed
forces' symbolic membership in the Nazi Party.[44] Moreover, Raeder's
appointment as a member of the Reich Cabinet bound him to the Nazi
regime even if it never met to formulate and coordinate governmental
policy, because, as head of the navy, he directly reported to Hitler as
the head of state and Supreme Commander.[45] Although the navy was
not the formidable "instrument of aggression" portrayed at Nuremberg,
its role as a "Blitzkrieg fleet" was designed to support an all-out naval
offensive for Hitler's first phase of continental hegemony and lay the

foundation for the navy's long-term plans for Weltmacht and Welt-machtflotte.[46] It was this coalescence of political and military aims between the navy and Hitler that created the bond between the two and put Raeder and the navy on their "Golgotha path."[47]

Imprisonment at Spandau

While Raeder awaited transfer to Spandau from Nuremberg, he met with U.S. Navy officers, who asked him to write a study of the naval war with "special emphasis on the command question." Continuing to pro-claim his innocence, he declared that he had always been "oriented toward the West" as Germany's "only chance of salvation" and held the U.S. Navy in high esteem. He believed that the British were "peeved" at him because he had beaten them to Norway, urged the Japanese to take Singapore, and had successfully carried out the "Channel dash."[48] Shortly after this meeting, however, early on 18 July 1946, the prisoners were flown to Berlin.

In his memoirs, Raeder chose not to reflect upon his Spandau impris-onment. From his and family letters, newspaper articles about the pris-oners and Spandau, and in particular Speer's memoirs, we see glimpses of his state of mind during 1946–1956. Both his wife, who was finally released by the Soviets on 1 September 1949, and his son were inexpli-cably prohibited from visiting him before March 1950. Raeder chafed over the changing and seemingly senseless rules and regulations that he attributed to the growing split between the Soviets and the Western powers and complained that some letters he received or wrote were either not delivered or had large sections deleted. Conditions were par-ticularly bad when the Russians were in charge. On 17 January 1953, after a short illness, Raeder's son, Hans, died. Raeder's requests to see him before he died or attend his funeral were denied. At the same time, his health began to deteriorate and he suffered from a painful inflammation of the urethra, requiring an operation that the Russians insisted be per-formed in his own cell.[49]

Although Raeder described the "strong bond" that developed between him and Dönitz in prison, Speer recounts a quite different story that is more consistent with Dönitz's later comments. Dönitz still blamed Raeder for his "policy of bloated surface vessels" and the failure to build enough U-boats. For his part, noted Speer, Raeder treated Dönitz as an overly ambitious officer and treated him with the condescension of a supe-rior officer.[50] However, a little over a year later, when Dönitz completed his sentence and was released (1 October 1956), their supporters made sure that any differences were muted in the interests of the navy. As Raeder expressed it in his memoirs, "Our reunion in freedom was deeply moving for us both." Their public display of solidarity would continue throughout the remainder of Raeder's life, as evidenced by the careful crafting of his memoirs praising his former U-boat commander and his request that his successor speak at his funeral.[51] Their *Bürgerfrieden*, their "public truce," as Dönitz termed it, would be maintained in the inter-est of unity and the need to restore the honor of the navy.[52]

Homecoming in the Federal Republic, 1955–1960

On 17 September 1955, without any notice, Raeder was released and immediately flown to his "temporary" home in Lippstadt, where he was met by friends and well-wishers and a deluge of flowers, telegrams, and media coverage.[53] Although elated over his release, his supporters quickly cautioned the Raeders to refrain from making any public state-ments that might hurt Dönitz or the navy.[54] Defying poor health, Raeder spent all of his remaining energies on the compilation of his memoirs. He chose Admiral Erich Förste to help him assign topics and ensure that the memoirs were given a uniform style. Differences between Raeder and others were to be glossed over in the interest of unity. Given Boehm's disagreements with Raeder, for example, his contribution was limited to his involvement in Norway.[55] The publication of his two-volume *Mein Leben* in 1956–1957 served to establish the official orthodoxy and largely achieved its goal of rehabilitating the image of the navy and painting a sympathetic assessment of Raeder.

Raeder was particularly affected by Germany's division into two states—a burden heavier than all those imposed by the Treaty of Ver-sailles. Yet he expressed his confidence in an eventual reunification. He noted in particular the consolidation of the Federal Republic and its commitment to democratic goals and especially the attitude of Ger-many's former Western enemies, who had granted the new state, in marked contrast to the treatment of the Weimar Republic, international equality—both internally and externally. "Naturally," he felt "closest of all to the German *Bundesmarine*."[56]

Raeder's role in the development of the new West German navy was direct and indirect. The founders of the Bundesmarine considered Raeder's support for former officers to join the new service "of great importance for the unbroken tradition and unity of the navy." The release of their former commanders was regarded as critical for the former officers' position toward the new state, creating a "chasm" between those who would serve the new republic and those who considered themselves loyal to their former leaders.[57] When Günter Hessler, Dönitz's son-in-law, visited Raeder in late 1955, he was taken aback by the admiral's negative attitude toward former officers joining the navy ("How is it possible for officers to join when we and others are considered criminals?").[58] This issue was finally resolved with Dönitz's release on October 1, 1956, which eliminated any further barriers to former officers' serving in the West German navy.

The former naval officers involved in building the Bundesmarine saw in Raeder (and Dönitz) the value of tradition ("the new navy cannot succeed without the respect for your past").[59] Their attempts to promote the admirals, however, resulted in a tension not dissimilar to what had occurred between the right- and left-wing parties and the navy during the Weimar period. As a result, Raeder quickly found himself embroiled in public controversy. Contact with active naval officers or official Bundesmarine functions was regarded as sensitive, and a vigilant press, including Raeder's old nemesis, the *Schleswig-Holsteinische Volkszeitung*, attacked any references to Raeder or Dönitz as signs of the "reactionary" nature of the new navy.[60]

The first major incident involving Raeder was the result of a speech on 16 January 1956 by Captain Hans-Adolf Zenker, leader of the Naval Department in the new Federal Defense Ministry, to the navy's first class of volunteers. Zenker praised both commanders, who had provided the navy with honorable traditions, and declared that there should be no stigma attached to them, in spite of their conviction as "war criminals." Although their honorable conduct of the war had been proven, they had been sentenced and imprisoned for political reasons as a result of the confusion and prejudice following the end of the war.[61] Zenker's comments caused a storm among the Social Democrats who rejected the idea that Raeder and Dönitz could serve as models for the new Bundesmarine. Indeed, there were "good traditions and terrible traditions."

How could it be said "he was an outstanding soldier and therefore is a great model!—and be able to forget that at the same time, he was also a helper of Hitler"?[62]

In spring 1956, Raeder found himself at the center of another public outcry involving his reinstatement as an *Ehrenbürger* (free citizen) of Kiel—an honor that had originally been granted to him on 16 April 1934 in recognition of his building of the fleet. This issue quickly became a contentious battle between the major political parties in Kiel and in Bonn. The Social Democratic Party sought to use this controversy to challenge the ruling right-wing Christian Democratic Union and to oppose what they regarded as the authoritarian, antidemocratic, and traditionalist tendencies of the new armed forces. For Raeder, the attacks were painfully reminiscent of the antimilitary rhetoric of the 1920s. His supporters urged him against making any public appearance, noting the strong demagoguery and polemic in the press.[63]

When the attacks on Raeder persisted, the *Bundespräsident,* Theodor Heuss, and the Defense Ministry became concerned that this issue could affect the upcoming national elections, as well as the fledgling Bundesmarine. On 12 April 1956, Admiral Ruge personally wrote to Raeder informing him of the difficulties that the Zenker "question" and his "free citizen" status was causing the government. Ruge saw no alternative, in the hardening battle lines around the Ehrenbürger question, and advised his former commander that once again the situation "could only be saved through a further sacrifice on your part." He presented Heuss's wishes that Raeder declare that he no longer had any interest in the "free citizen" honor.[64] On 14 April, Raeder decided to decline his reinstatement as a "free citizen," given the recent attacks on his honor and that of the service. He hoped that the defamation of him, and thereby the old navy, would not affect the relationship between the city and his former naval comrades, and he promised to do what he could to maintain the close ties between the navy and Kiel.[65]

After this episode, Raeder tried to stay out of the public limelight but still attended major events, such as the dedication of the naval memorial in Wilhelmshaven in June 1957, and participated in meetings of veterans' organizations and the *Marinebund.* In July 1957, the Social Democrat Press Service complained that Raeder was appearing in the foreground "more and more." The SPD regarded the announcement of his honorary membership in the Marinebund—on the thirteenth anniversary of the attempted assassination of Hitler—as a sign of the growing right-wing extremist development of the Marinebund.[66]

In failing health, Raeder withdrew to attend to his wife, who died on 2 August 1959. On 6 November 1960, he succumbed to the effects of old age and disappointment. His funeral would stage one final act in a career plagued by political controversy. Determined to avoid any incidents, the Defense Ministry decided that no official representative would be allowed to attend his funeral service. However, Ruge, the first *Inspekteur* of the Bundesmarine, would be permitted to speak as the senior active officer and one of Raeder's former subordinates. Raeder had asked Dönitz to deliver his eulogy, reinforcing the solidarity between the two. Dönitz praised his predecessor as the molder of "this splendid navy" that had achieved in a years-long struggle "more than could have been expected against a world of enemies."[67] Ruge highlighted Raeder's humane treatment of his subordinates and his harsh action against anyone who violated an individual's dignity or lacked the appropriate propriety and good morals. He credited him with keeping the navy unified and "clean" and, in large part, protecting it against the amoral influence of despotism. Raeder's faith, his defense of the military chaplaincy, and his opposition to the 1935 anti-Semitic Nuremberg Race Laws, declared Ruge, were all signs of his courage. He described the admiral's success in improving ties between the navy and the leaders from all occupations and parties, his respect for democracy, and his readiness to defend the Weimar Republic. "His lifework was the building of a navy. We know its achievements and its end." In the building of the new German navy, Ruge declared, he knew that "we are doing this in the way in which the departed would have wished."[68]

The media's response to Raeder's passing reflected the political tensions in the evolving civil-military relations of the Federal Republic. The presence of Ruge in uniform, along with officials from the Schleswig-Holstein government, gave the appearance of a "state funeral" for a convicted "war criminal.[69] Ruge's praise of Raeder contradicted the official denial in the aftermath of the Zenker affair that the former commanders could be in any way models for the new navy. One editorial sarcastically accused Ruge of painting the grand admiral as a "democrat with principles—ready to defend the Weimar Republic with gun in hand." [70]

In the North Cemetery in Kiel, Raeder's headstone bears the pennant of a grand admiral and carries the epitaph, Amara Mors Amorem Non Separat (a bitter death cannot separate the love). His last statement of how he wished to be judged as an individual—and as a soldier—was written in the final pages of *Mein Leben*.

> Human greatness is not measured by whether it reveals itself through victory or defeat, or whether the political direction of a war is approved or disapproved. It can be measured only in terms of the principle of character from which conduct stems. When the stresses and shadows of the immediate present are lifted from the German people, it is my firm belief that the human greatness exhibited by the many individuals in their different roles during the war will shine through the darker shadows of that period and take its rightful place in the nation's traditions and history.

Unlike Tirpitz, who bitterly reproached Germans for having never understood the sea, Raeder lived long enough to see a German navy join the great sea powers of the Atlantic. The navy's *Bündnisfähigkeit* had finally become a reality—and he fervently believed that Germany had learned the lessons of sea power from its two world wars and had begun to look beyond its historic continental perspective.[71]

POSTSCRIPT

Today, forty-five years after the *Grossadmiral's* death, *Die Deutsche Marine*, renamed in 1990 after the reunification of the German state, deploys its naval forces beyond the boundaries of the NATO alliance as an instrument of international security in partnership and cooperation with NATO and the United Nations. In addition to fighting terrorism, averting conflicts, intervening in military crises, and performing humanitarian work, its air and naval units operate on a global basis as an expression of political will to keep Germany's foreign policy options open. The service no longer exists for itself but to fulfill and secure Germany's maritime mission: to safeguard the 70 percent of its import and export trade that is exclusively transported by sea.

NOTES

ABBREVIATIONS

Archives and Collections

BAMA	Bundesarchiv-Militärarchiv, Freiburg im Breisgau
DNB	Deutsches Nachrichtenbüro (German news service)
IfZ	Institut für Zeitgeschichte, Munich
KTB	Kriegstagebuch (war diary)
MGFA	Militärgeschichtliches Forschungsamt (Military History Research Office), Potsdam
MOH	Marine-Offizier-Hilfe (Naval Officer Assistance Organization)
N	Nachlässe (personal papers)
NARA	National Archives and Records Administration
NHC	Naval Historical Center, Washington Navy Yard
NID	Naval Intelligence Division, British Admiralty
ONI	Office of Naval Intelligence (USN)

Publications

DGFP	Documents on German Foreign Policy (*Akten zur deutschen auswärtigen Politik*, German edition)
DRZW	*Das Deutsche Reich und die Zweite Weltkrieg* (official history of WWII published by the MGFA)
HZ	*Historische Zeitschrift*
IMT	*The Trial of the Major War Criminals before the International Military Tribunal, Nuremberg*
JMH	*The Journal of Military History*
MGM	*Militärgeschichtliche Mitteilungen*
ML	*Mein Leben (Raeder's autobiography)*
NCA	*Nazi Conspiracy and Aggression*
USNIP	United States Naval Institute *Proceedings*
VfZG	*Vierteljahrshefte für Zeitgeschichte*

GERMAN DOCUMENT TERMS

Aufzeichnung	record, note
Befehl	order, command
Beitrag	contribution
Besprechung	conference, discussion
Betrachtung	consideration, reflection
Denkschriften	memoranda
Erinnerungen	recollections

Erlass	edict, decree
Lagevorträge	situation report; esp. *Lagevorträge des Oberbehlshabers der Kriegsmarine vor Hitler 1939–1945* (Fuehrer Conferences on Naval Affairs, English edition)
Niederschrift	minutes, record
Schlussansprache	closing remarks
Sitzung	minutes
Stellungnahme	opinion (on), comment (on)
Unternehmung	operation
Verhandlungen	proceedings
Vermerk	note, entry
Weisung	directive

Introduction

1. "We have before us the example of how a vital fleet became a coastal navy by means of ideas. Therefore, we hope the opposite may be true—that today, when our navy is materially so weak, it may again be ideas that in spite of every weakness save the navy from the intellectual emptiness of a coastal navy and give it the high value of a *Traditionsmarine* for the future." Carl-Axel Gemzell, *Organization, Conflict, and Innovation: A Study of German Naval Strategic Planning, 1888–1940*, 296.
2. *IMT*, V, 279–80.
3. Raeder, *Mein Leben* (hereafter *ML*), I, 11.
4. Raeder, *My Life*, foreword by Admiral (Ret.) H. Kent Hewitt, vii.
5. The quote is from an anonymous reviewer of my 1971 dissertation. A number of Germany's former foes wrote letters supporting Raeder, notably Captain Russell Grenfall, RN, who argued that Raeder did nothing that any active naval officer did not do. Raeder N 391/6, 25.
6. See Gotthard Breit, *Das Staats- und Gesellschaftsbild deutscher Generale beider Weltkriege im Spiegel ihrer Memoiren*.
7. See Douglas Peifer, *The Three German Navies: Dissolution, Transition, and New Beginnings, 1945–1960*, and Wagner N 357.
8. See the Wagner and Ruge papers, N 357 and N 359.
9. Peifer, *Three Navies*, 188.
10. See Keith Bird's 1985 *German Naval History: A Guide to the Literature*, for the role of the scholars cited here, in particular, 3–18, 499–506, 537–47, 571–95.
11. Bird, *Weimar, the German Naval Officer Corps and the Rise of National Socialism*, 294–96. For the Schreiber controversy, see Bird, *German Sea Power*, 500–504.
12. Rolf Hobson, *Imperialism at Sea: Naval Strategic Thought, the Ideology of Sea Power, and the Tirpitz Plan, 1875–1914*, 328.
13. Hobson, *The German School of Naval Thought and the Origins of the Tirpitz Plan, 1975–1900*, 73.
14. Bird, *German Naval History*, 6–7. England was always the benchmark for the German navy. See Salewski's praise of Hobson's interpretation of Tirpitz's sea power ideology, *Buchpräsentation*, MGFA, Potsdam, 7 June 2004. Unpublished presentation sent to the author by Dr. Salewski.
15. Jörg Hillmann, "Thesenpapier zum Expertengespräch: Weltmachthorizonte von kaiserlichen Seeoffizieren: Tirpitz, Hopmann, Hintze, Raeder" and "Revisionismus oder

Weltmachtstreben." Unpublished essays sent to the author by Dr. Hillmann. See Werner Rahn's "Germany," in *Ubi Sumus: The State of Naval and Maritime History*, 137–57. Rahn points out how the German navy has a "special relationship" to its history since naval history is part of the cadet and officer training programs but is not an independent subject (or course) offered in German universities.

16. Volker Berghahn, *Germany and the Approach of War in 1914*, 214.
17. Michael Salewski in "Naval Leadership and the Ideology of National Socialism" (unpublished manuscript) argues that "obedience" is the key to understanding Raeder. I contend that Raeder was selective in his obedience, depending on his superior and circumstances. He would do anything to get his ships built.
18. Gerhard Weinberg, "Rollen- und Selbstverständnis des Offizierkorps der Wehrmacht im NS-Staat," *Die Wehrmacht: Mythos und Realität*, 67–68.
19. Much of the Raeder-Wegener "rivalry" was perpetuated by Wegener's son, Vice Admiral Edward Wegener, who argued that Raeder could have done more to promote Germany's needs for a maritime strategy. Wegener N 607.
20. See Salewski, "Naval Leadership and the Ideology of National Socialism."
21. Holger Herwig, *Politics of Frustration*, 216.
22. Gerd Ueberschär and Winfried Vogel, *Dienen und Verdienen*.
23. Daniel Goldhagen, *Hitler's Willing Executioners* (1996); Hannes Heer and Klaus Naumann, eds., *Vernichtungskrieg* (1998) and Jürgen Förster, "Wehrmacht, Krieg und Holocaust," *Die Wehrmacht: Mythos und Realität*, 948–63.
24. Strauss to Dönitz, 13 May 1960; Wagner N 539/67.
25. Friedrich Ruge, *In Vier Marinen*, 240–41; Document UK-81 (Bürkner), *NCA*, VIII, 647–53.
26. Terrell Gottschall, *By Order of the Kaiser: Otto von Diederichs and the Rise of the Imperial German Navy, 1865–1902*; Jörg-Uwe Fischer, *Admiral des Kaisers: Georg Alexander von Müller als Chef des Marinekabinetts Wilhelm II*; Hopman's *Das ereignisreiche Leben eines "Wilhelminers": Tagebücher, Briefe, Aufzeichnungen 1901 bis 1920*.
27. Raeder, *ML*, I, 12.

Chapter 1

1. Raeder, *ML*, I, 15.
2. Ibid., 16. At Nuremberg, Raeder's IQ score was 134 ("Very Superior").
3. Eckart Kehr, *Schlachtflottenbau und Parteipolitik, 1894–1901*.
4. Raeder, *ML*, I, 15–17; Otto Ciliax's assessment of Raeder's career, "Einfluss des Werdegangs eines Offiziers auf seine späteren Entscheidungen in führenden Positionen untersucht am Beispiel des Grossadmirals Raeder," *Führungsakademie der Bundeswehr*, 83–86.
5. Tirpitz, *Erinnerungen*, 16.
6. See Gerhard Schreiber's definition of *Seemachtideologie* in "Zur Kontinuität des Gross- und Weltmachtstrebens der deutschen Marineführung," *MGM* 26, no. 2 (1979): 101–71. Rolf Hobson's *The German School of Naval Thought and the Origins of the Tirpitz Plan 1985–1900* provides a comprehensive study of the evolution of this German ideology of sea power.
7. Admiral Wilhelm Meisel, *Zeugenschrifttum* No. 1739, IfZ, Munich.
8. Raeder, *ML*, I, 18–19.
9. Ibid., 18.
10. Hugo Waldeyer-Hartz, *Admiral von Hipper*, 7–9; Albert Hopman, *Das ereignisreiche Leben eines "Wilhelminers,"* 21.
11. Holger Herwig, *German Naval Officer Corps*, 39–45.
12. Hopman, "Wilhelminers," 15–19.

13. Tirpitz, *Erinnerungen*, 3.

14. Herwig, *German Naval Officer Corps*, 39–40.

15. Raeder, *ML*, I, 42–43.

16. Ibid., 21. For the "feudalization" of the executive (line) officers and the middle class during 1890–1914, see Herwig's *German Naval Officer Corps*.

17. For the evolution of German warships, see Erich Gröner, *Die deutschen Kriegsschiffe 1815–1945*.

18. Raeder, *ML*, I, 21–23, 31; Ciliax, *Einfluss des Werdegangs*, 87.

19. Raeder, *ML*, I, 31.

20. Rolf Güth, *Erich Raeder und die Englische Frage*, 17.

21. Raeder, *ML*, I, 26–28.

22. Ibid., 35; Lawrence Sondhaus, *Preparing for Weltpolitik: German Seapower before the Tirpitz Era*, 184–207.

23. Raeder, *ML*, I, 43.

24. Ibid., 37–38.

25. Ibid., 42–43.

26. Paul Kennedy, *The Samoan Triangle: A Study in Anglo-German-American Relations 1878–1900*, 304.

27. Volker Berghahn, "Zu den Zielen des deutschen Flottenbaus," *HZ* (1970): 68.

28. Raeder, *ML*, I, 44.

29. Ibid., 44–46.

30. Ibid., 46–49. The duties of a watch officer required the "sharpest vigilance." Scheer, *Vom Segelschiffe zum U-Boot*, 107, 227.

31. *Allgemeine Gesichtspunkte ber der Festellung unserer Flotte nach Schiffsklassen und Schiffstypen*, Steinberg, *Yesterday's Deterrent*, 209.

32. Jost Dülffer, "The German Reich and the Jeune Ecole," *Marine et technique au XIX siècle*, 507.

33. Hobson's *German School*, 71.

34. Wilhelm Deist, *Flottenpolitik und Flottenpropaganda: Das Nachrichtenbureau des Reichsmarineamtes 1897–1914*, 35; Michael Salewski, *Seekriegsleitung*, I, 8.

35. Raeder, *ML*, I, 54. Cf. Theodore Ropp, *The Development of a Modern Navy: French Naval Policy, 1971–1904*, 334.

36. Klaus Schröder, "Zur Entstehung der strategischen Konzeption Grossadmiral Raeders," *MOH-Nachrichten* (1971): 14–18.

37. Patrick Kelly, e-mail to the author, 7 December 2001.

38. Rosinski, *The Development of Naval Thought*, 77.

39. Berghahn, "Zu den Zielen des deutschen Flottenbaus," 70.

40. Hobson, *German School*, 62.

41. Berghahn, "Zu den Zielen des deutschen Flottenbaus," 68; Kennedy, "Tirpitz, England and the Second Navy Law," 38.

42. Hobson, *German School*, 62.

43. Ibid., 51. Emphasis in the original.

44. Ibid.

45. Hewig, "The Failure of German Sea Power, 1914–1945: Mahan, Tirpitz, and Raeder Reconsidered," *International History Review* 10 (1988): 82.

46. Hew Strachan, *The First World War*, I, 405–13.

47. Herbert Rosinski, *The Development of Naval Thought*, 55.

48. Herwig, "Wolfgang Wegener and German Naval Strategy from Tirpitz to Raeder," *The Naval Strategy of the World War*, xviii.

49. Hobson, *Imperialism at Sea*, 282.

50. Ibid., 280–84; Dülffer, "Limitations on Naval Warfare and Germany's Future as a World Power: A German Debate, 1904–1906," *War and Society* 3 (1985): 35.

51. Cf. Trotha's reports on his overseas assignments, *Niedersächsisches Staatsarchiv, Bückeburg (Depos. 18)*.

52. Güth, *Erich Raeder*, 60, also cites these observations as a source for Raeder's Atlantic ambitions and the influence of Tirpitz and Trotha.

53. Hobson, *German School*, 41. For Tirpitz's relationship with the officer corps, see *Adolf v. Trotha: Ein Gespräch mit Tirpitz*, 1 February 1938 (copy sent to Raeder), *Depos. 18-C Nr. 13, Staatsarchiv* Bückeburg.

54. Hobson, *German School*, 65, 69.

55. Ibid., 42.

56. Raeder, *ML*, I, 50–54. Officers were required to obtain imperial consent to marry (demonstrating sufficient financial resources and a background report of the bride's family).

57. Raeder, *ML*, I, 44–49, 53–54. For Raeder's writings, see Schröder, "Entstehung," 14–18.

58. Raeder, *ML*, I, 63.

59. Berghahn's *Der Tirpitz Plan*, 419–504.

60. Güth refers to Raeder as Tirpitz's "ear" in the Reichstag and press. Raeder also worked closely with Adolf von Trotha, who was serving as personal staff to Tirpitz. Rolf Güth, *Erich Raeder*, 7–8, 17–18. Cf. Herwig, *"Luxury" Fleet*, 37, and Raeder, *ML*, I, 58.

61. Raeder, *ML*, I, 58–59.

62. See Kelly's "'The Naval Policy of Imperial Germany" for Tirpitz's *Ressorteifer*.

63. Tirpitz, *Erinnerungen*, 52. See Bird, *German Sea Power*, 297–311, for the role of a "System-stabilizing fleet."

64. Raeder, *ML*, I, 37.

65. Ibid., I, 160–61, 220; Admirals Assmann and Gladisch, "Aspects of the Naval War," NID 24/T. 237/46; and Albrecht, *Erinnerungen*, III M554/4, BAMA.

66. Raeder, *ML*, I, 60.

67. The chief of the Naval Cabinet (1908–1918) was Admiral Georg Alexander von Müller, Raeder's "fatherly friend."

68. Raeder, *ML*, I, 62–65.

69. Ibid., 61, 64. See the Raeder-Levetzow correspondence regarding the kaiser in the Levetzow *Nachlass* 1918–1940.

70. Raeder, *ML*, I, 64–65, 73.

71. Raeder, *ML*, I, 67–69. Cf. Strachan, *First World War*, I, 410.

72. Raeder, *ML*, I, 74.

73. Ibid., 70–77.

74. Waldeyer-Hartz, *Admiral von Hipper*, 58–62; ibid., 31–33, 123.

75. Raeder, *ML*, I, 65–67; Ciliax, "Werdegangs," 93–95. See also Kurt Assmann's "Gross-admiral Dr. h.c. Raeder and der Zweite Weltkrieg," *Marine Rundschau* 58 (February 1961): 6.

76. Raeder, *ML*, I, 76.

77. Tobias Philbin, *Admiral von Hipper: The Inconvenient Hero*, 44–51.

78. Raeder, *ML*, I, 81. See Berghahn and Deist's documentary study, "Kaiserliche Marine und Kriegsausbruch 1914," *MGM* 4, no. 1 (1970): 37–58. Tirpitz feared an agreement with "perfidious Albion" and pleaded for an alliance with Russia if war with England became inevitable. Herwig, *Politics of Frustration*, 114–15.

79. Guidelines for a war against England distributed on 18 February 1913 still assumed a close blockade. Even though a wide blockade was seriously considered in the fall of 1913, the navy refused to drop its idea of a large-scale offensive in order to maintain its "offensive

spirit." The final operations order approved on 30 July assumed a defensive stance against a close blockade and to look for "favorable circumstances" to launch an offensive. Lambi, *German Power Politics*, 399–405, 422–23. Tirpitz, assuming a short war as many others did, supported a limited engagement to maintain his credibility and ensure the navy's place in postwar budgets. Strachan, *The First World War*, I, 412.

80. Strachan, *The First World War*, I, 412; Werner Rahn, "Kriegführung, Politik und Krisen. Die Marine des Deutschen Reiches 1914–1933," *Die deutsche Flotte im Spannungsfeld der Politik 1848–1985*, 81.

81. Raeder, *ML*, I, 101. Raeder and Levetzow both agreed that they would wait until a more worthy occasion presented itself; see Raeder to Levetzow, 9 November 1914, in Gerhard Granier's *Magnus von Levetzow*, 11.

82. Raeder, *ML*, I, 94–95. Letter to Levetzow, 2 May 1921, in Granier, *Levetzow*, 12–13.

83. Levetzow to Admiral von Holtzendorff, 15 January 1915, Levetzow N 239/90.

84. Walther Hubatsch, *Die Ära Tirpitz*, 121.

85. Philbin, *Hipper*, 101.

86. Raeder, *ML*, I, 95–103.

87. Ibid., 100–101.

88. Ibid., 97. Raeder later acknowledged the capture of the *Magdeburg's* codebook by the Russians in the fall of 1914.

89. Raeder, *ML*, I, 103–4. Cf. Philbin, *Hipper*, 115–16.

90. Raeder, *ML*, I, 105–6.

91. Bird, *German Naval History*, 461–75; Werner Rahn, "Kriegführung, Politik und Krisen. Die Marine des Deutschen Reiches 1914–1933," *Die deutsche Flotte im Spannungsfeld*, 81.

92. Philbin, *Hipper*, 113–17.

93. Raeder, *ML*, I, 104–8; Philbin, *Hipper*, 113–17.

94. 19 July 1915, Müller, *The Kaiser and His Court*, 93–94; Raeder, *ML* I, 103–4.

95. Scheer, *Germany's High Seas Fleet*, 96–98.

96. Raeder, *ML*, I, 104–5.

97. Philbin, *Hipper*, 123–24.

98. Raeder, *ML*, I, 110–11.

99. Ibid. British intelligence had warned that the Germans were preparing to sail. Halperin, *Naval History*, 315.

100. Raeder, *ML*, I, 111–12, 122–23.

101. Ibid., 117–22.

102. Ibid., 119–20. Cf. Waldeyer-Hartz, *Admiral von Hipper*, 213–14 (Raeder's approval would have been required to publish this book).

103. Raeder, *ML*, I, 120, 313.

104. Letter of 31 May 1919, reprinted in Raeder, *ML*, I, 314.

105. Letter of 30 May 1926, reprinted in *ML*, I, 314–15.

106. Raeder, *ML*, I, 118–19, 124–25. See Halpern, *Naval History*, 325–26, for the losses on both sides.

107. Philbin, *Hipper*; Scheer, *Germany's High Seas Fleet*, 168–69. Only the "crushing of English economic life through U-boat action against English commerce" could bring a "victorious end."

108. Herwig, *Politics of Frustration*, 116–33.

109. Raeder, *ML*, I, 129.

110. Scheer, *Germany's High Seas Fleet*, 191–94.

111. Raeder, *ML*, I, 132–34.

112. Herwig, *"Luxury" Fleet*, 223–25.

113. Raeder, *ML*, I. 132–34.

114. Raeder, *ML*, I, 136. Cf. Philbin, *Hipper*, 139.

115. Raeder, *ML*, I, 136–40.

116. Bird, *German Naval History*, 19–56.

117. See Raffael Scheck's important contribution on the largely overlooked political role of Tirpitz during the war and the Weimar Republic, *Alfred von Tirpitz*.

118. Hahn's memorandum, *Kommandant des Schlachtkreuzers "Von der Tann" an Befehlshaber der I. Aufklärungsgruppe, Seekriegsleitung*, II, 329–30. This report and Hipper's observations were referred to Ingenohl on 12 November 1914.

119. Herwig, "Wolfgang Wegener," xxxviii–lv.

120. Philbin, *Hipper*, 92–93.

121. Ibid., 93.

122. Raeder, *Kreuzerkrieg*, I, 253–54.

123. Philbin, *Hipper*, 134.

124. Ibid., 65–70.

125. Herwig, "Wolfgang Wegener," xxix–xxx. Wegener noted how an offensive would have provided relief for Spee's Far Eastern squadron—a point made by Raeder as well. Wegener, *Naval Strategy*, 67–68; Raeder, *Kreuzerkrieg*, I, 197–224, 269–336. Hahn viewed Wegener's work positively. Levetzow claimed that he and Scheer had visited Wegener early in 1916 and persuaded him to cease his writing for the remainder of the war.

126. Gemzell, *Organization*, 222–25.

127. See Herwig's editing of Wegener's *Naval Strategy*. Wegener's son, Edward, wrote an extensive analysis of his father's "intellectual heritage," *Das geistige Erbe Wolfgang Wegeners*. Vol. 10. Wegener, N 607, BAMA.

128. Wegener, *Naval Strategy*, 72–78.

129. Ibid., 78.

Chapter 2

1. Raeder, *ML*, I, 138, 142–47. Raeder had personally revised his crew's "patriotic instruction" and conducted religious ceremonies.

2. Herwig, *Naval Officer Corps*, 234.

3. Gary Weir, *Building the Kaiser's Navy*, 172–78.

4. Herwig, *Naval Officer Corps*, 240–41.

5. Scheer, *High Seas Fleet*, 353.

6. Raeder, *ML*, I, 147–48.

7. 10 October 1918, Hipper N 162/9.

8. Raeder, *ML*, I, 160.

9. See 22 October 1918, *Weizsäcker Papiere*, 306 and Granier, *Levetzow*, 49–50.

10. Philbin, *Hipper*, 157–63.

11. Bird, *German Naval History*, 477–80. Ernst von Weizsäcker warned Scheer and Levetzow against forming a "military *fronde*" and questioned the state of mind within the SKL that could conceive of this last battle. 2 November 1918, *Weizsäcker Papiere*, 313.

12. Granier, *Levetzow*, 55. The final plan was issued 24 October 1918, *Operationsbefehl des Kommandos der Hochseestreitkräfte, Seekriegsleitung*, II, 193–95.

13. Bernd Stegemann, *Marinepolitik*, 155.

14. Herwig, *Naval Officers Corps*, 243–44.

15. Deist, "Seekriegsleitung," 364.

16. Gerhard Gross, "Eine Frage der Ehre? Die Marineführung und der letzte Flottenvorstoss 1918," *Kriegsende 1918*, 349–65.

17. Philbin, *Hipper*, 155.

18. Herwig, *"Luxury" Fleet*, 248; Hans Wilderrotte, "Unsere Zukunft liegt auf dem Wasser," *Der letzte Kaiser*, 74.

19. 31 October 1918–11 November 1918, Hipper N 162/9; *Aufzeichnung des Kommandos der Hochseestreitkräfte, 3. 11. 1918, Seekriegsleitung*, II, 196–98.

20. Raeder, *ML*, I, 149–50.

21. Herwig, *Naval Officer Corps*, 261–64.

22. Scheer, *Hochseeflotte*, 499.

23. Bird, *Weimar*, 10.

24. Raeder, *ML*, I, 151; Granier, *Levetzow*, 62.

25. Raeder, *ML*, I, 132–34, 151–53, 155–56, and *"6er Rat im RMA"* (ca. 1919), Fasz. 4077, Bd. 7, BAMA.

26. 15.1.1919 nachm[ittags]: "Sitzung des Zentralrats mit dem Rat der Volksbeauftragten," *Zentralrat der Republik*, I, 419.

27. Raeder, *ML*, I, 148–49, 152–55. Levetzow shared Raeder's assessment of Noske, Granier, *Levetzow*, 64.

28. Gerhard Papke, "Offizierkorps und Anciennität," *Untersuchungsgen zur Geschichte des Offizierkorps*, IV, 198.

29. Raeder, *ML*, I, 157–59, 161. See Rahn, *Reichsmarine und Landesvertiedigung 1918– 1928: Konzeption und Führung der Maine in der Weimarer Republik*, 32–33, for the navy's organization.

30. Tirpitz to Trotha, 20 March 1919, Tirpitz N 253/64-K106.

31. "Sitzung des Zentralrats," 15 January 1919, *Zentralrat der Republik*, I, 419.

32. Trotha, *Volkstum und Staatsführung*, 191–92.

33. Raeder to Levetzow, 22 October 1919 and 2 November 1919, Levetzow N 239/10.

34. Carl Claussen, *Welche Vorschläge konnen gemacht werden um grossere Teile des Offizierkorps zu Führern zu erziehen? Vortrag Nr. 33*, II M 57/33, BAMA.

35. Raeder, *ML*, I, 166.

36. Trotha, *Volkstum und Staatsführung*, 197–98.

37. Bird, *Weimar*, 16–17, 43–44.

38. *Auszug aus Denkschrift Kpt. z. See a. D. Frhr. von Meerscheidt-Hüllessen von Admiral Schuster*, III M 503/4, BAMA; Tirpitz N 253/64-K106, BAMA.

39. Bird, *Weimar*, 261–68.

40. Raeder, *ML*, I, 166; Bird, *Weimar*, 141–44.

41. Bird, *Weimar*, 60–64.

42. Friedrich Ruge, *Scapa Flow*, 187–90.

43. Raeder, *ML*, I, 167.

44. Alexander Meuer, "Die deutsche Marine zu Beginn der 80er Jahre und Heute. Ein Vergleich," *Marine Rundschau* 31 (February 1926): 58–66.

45. Raeder, *ML*, I, 173.

46. Trotha to Noske, 17 May 1919, Walter Schwengler, *Völkerrecht, Versailler Vertrag und Auslieferungsfrage*, 205.

47. Rolf Güth, *Gouvernements- und Stations-Tagesbefehl vom 20.5. 1919, Die Marine des Deutschen Reiches 1919–1939*, 30–33.

48. *Aufzeichnungen*, Trotha, *Volkstum und Staatsführung*, 164–65.

49. Admiral Reuter's report to Trotha, 15 July 1919, was delivered orally by courier. Ruge, *Scapa Flow*, 213–14.

50. Raeder, *ML*, I, 167–68; Ruge, *Scapa Flow*, 191.
51. Scheer, London *Times*, 1 July 1919, 12. Cf. Trotha's 3 July 1919 statement to the navy, *Volkstum und Staatsführung*, 184–86.
52. Bird, *Weimar*, 63–65; Trotha, *Volkstum und Staatsführung*, 169–70.
53. *An die Marine*, 25 [sic] June 1919, *Volkstum und Staatsführung*, 169–70.
54. *Aufzeichnungen, Volkstum und Staatsführung*, 167–68. Schwengler cites a draft press release (along with Raeder's handwritten note) that omits Trotha's opposition to the government as compared with his 23 June 1919 decree to the navy. *Völkerrecht, Versailler Vertrag*, 240–42.
55. *Schreiben des Präsidenten der Friedenskonferenze, Millerand, an Reichskanzler Bauer vom 7. Februar*, in Michaelis and Schraepler, eds., *Ursachen und Folgen*, IV, 25–26. See Raeder, *ML*, I, 178–79.
56. Levetzow to Raeder, 1 January 1920, Levetzow N 239/26.
57. Raeder to Levetzow, 30 December 1919, Levetzow N 239/26.
58. Raeder to Levetzow, 5 February 1920, Levetzow N 239/26.
59. Raeder, *ML*, I, 180.
60. Ibid., 155.
61. Bird, *Weimar*, 44.
62. Raeder, *ML*, I, 155.
63. *Bericht Loewenfeld*, Fasz. 4077, Bd. 7, BAMA; Keyserlingk, 24 March 1919, Keyserlingk N 161/3.
64. Karl Dönitz, *Mein wechselvolles Leben*, 132; Siegfried Sorge, *Zeugenschriftum* No. 1785, IfZ; *Bericht Reinhardt*, Fasz. 4083, BAMA.
65. Noske, *Von Kiel bis Kapp*, 203; Raeder, *ML*, I, 180–81; Johannes Erger, *Kapp-Lüttwitz Putsch*, 110–11.
66. *Nachlass* Reinhardt, 59.
67. Raeder, *ML*, I, 181.
68. Erger, *Kapp-Lüttwitz Putsch*, 136.
69. Raeder, *ML*, I, 181.
70. F. L. Carsten, *Reichswehr and Politics*, 83; Harold Gordon, *Reichswehr and Republic*, 117.
71. Raeder, *ML*, I, 181.
72. *Stellung des Chefs der Admiralität, Vizeadmirals von Trotha, zu den März Ereignissen, 27 March 1920*; Fasz. 4077, Bd. 7, BAMA; Raeder, *ML*, I, 181–82.
73. *Stellung des Chefs der Admiralität*, Fasz. 4077, Bd. 7, BAMA.
74. *Stellung des Chefs der Admiralität*, Fasz. 4077, Bd. 7, BAMA.
75. Michaelis N 164/5, 31.
76. Heinz Höhne, *Canaris*, 81–83.
77. Raeder, *ML*, I, 154; Bird, *Weimar*, 44–45; *Marine-Archiv* Nr. 3203, XVII-I. 4.-6, Bd. 3, BAMA.
78. Konrad Albrecht, *Erinnerungen*, III M 554/3, BAMA.
79. *Fernschreiben an den Chef der Admiralität*, copy in Levetzow N 239/1.
80. *Ferngespräch mit Kapitän z. S. Raeder am 17 [sic] März 1920 abends*, Levetzow N 239/1.
81. Albrecht *Erinnerungen*, III M 554/3, BAMA; *Bericht Loewenfeld*, Fasz. 4077, Bd. 7, BAMA.
82. *Niederschrift Raeders über ein Ferngesprach zwischen ihm und Schultze: Gedanke, Levetzow als Militärbefehlshaber in Berlin einzusetzen [Berlin, 19 März 1920]*, Granier, *Levetzow*, 105–11, 231–32. Canaris told Raeder and other officers that Noske had resigned.
83. Bird, *Weimar*, 75–77.
84. Otto Gessler, *Reichswehrpolitik in der Weimar Zeit*, 146.
85. Bird, *Weimar*, 102–3.

86. Raeder, *ML*, I, 184.

87. Raeder to Levetzow, 1 July 1920, Levetzow, N 239/11.

88. Raeder anticipated a conservative government or dictator resulting from the "war criminal" crisis. Raeder to Levetzow, 30 December 1919, Levetzow N 239/26.

89. Levetzow to Ludendorff, 29 July 1923, Levetzow N 239/14. Levetzow hoped that a dictatorship would facilitate the restoration of the monarchy. Cf. *Levetzow an Ludendorff: Diktatur zur Rettung Deutschlands, Weimar, 29 Juli 1923*, Granier, *Levetzow*, 239–40

90. Gustav Noske, *Erlebtes*, 169–70.

91. Raeder, *ML*, I, 185.

92. *Reichsgericht, Äusserung des Käpitains z. See Raeder zur Vernehmung des Chefs der Admiralität, Vizeadmiral v. Trotha, Fasz.* 2028, BAMA.

93. Friedrich Forstmeier, "Zur Rolle der Marine im Kapp Putsch," *Seemacht und Geschichte*, 78.

94. *Erinnerungen*, Teil III, Michaelis N 164/5.

95. Cf. Michaelis's views of the putsch, *Fasz.* 4077, *Bd.* 7, BAMA, and *Richtlinien*, Admiral Michaelis, Michaelis N 164/5.

96. Raeder to Levetzow, 29 June 1920, Levetzow N 239/12.

97. Otto Gessler, *Reichswehrpolitik*, 135.

98. Raeder to Levetzow, 9 July 1920, Levetzow N 239/12, and *Levetzow an Raeder: Aufgaben des kunftigen Führers der Marine, 7 Juli 1920*. Granier, *Levetzow*, 233–36.

99. Raeder to Levetzow, 29 June 1920, Levetzow N 239/12. Cf. 9 July 1920, ibid.

100. Raeder to Levetzow, 1 July 1920, Levetzow N 239/12.

101. Rahn, *Reichsmarine*, 75–76, 83.

Chapter 3

1. Raeder had to be "pulled out" when it became apparent that the coup was going to fail (Admiral v. Mantey), Förste N 238/45.

2. Raeder's personal details are from the Raeder *Nachlass* guide and Ciliax, *Werdegangs*, 133. Raeder *ML*, I, 185–87.

3. Bird, *German Naval History*, 27–30 and 124–27.

4. Güth, *Die Marine des Deutschen Reiches*, 96.

5. Ibid., 95; Hubatsch, *Kaiserliche Marine*, 543–54.

6. War planning did not begin until the winter war games of 1921–1922. Gemzell, *Organization*, 257.

7. Tirpitz, *Erinnerungen*, 311–14; Bird, *Weimar*, 23–27; Dülffer, *Hitler und die Marine*, 184.

8. Rahn points out that most of the strategic interpretations were "incorrect, uncritical, and one-sided." *Reichsmarine*, 126.

9. Kurt Assmann, "Raeder und Zweite Weltkrieg," 3–8; Mantey to Keyserlingk, 7 October 1937, Keyserlingk N 161/10.

10. Widenmann N 158/7.

11. Erich Murawski, "Die amtliche deutsche Kriegsgeschichtsschreibung über den Ersten Weltkrieg," *Wehrwissenschaftliche Rundschau*, 586.

12. Raeder was also involved with the third volume, *Die deutschen Hilfskreuzer* (1937).

13. Paul Halperin, *Naval History*, 93.

14. Gemzell, *Organization*, 334–38. Cf. Groos and Michaelis papers, N 165/2 and N 164.

15. Raeder to Tirpitz, 10 July 1921, Tirpitz N 253/46.

16. Raeder to Tirpitz, 16 August 1921, Tirpitz N 253/46.

17. Raeder to Tirpitz, 13 November 1921. Mantey thanked Tirpitz for the "considerable support" provided to Raeder. Gemzell, *Organization*, 337; Raeder, *Kreuzerkrieg*, I, 538.

18. Siegfried Tägil, "Wegener, Raeder und die deutsche Marinestrategie," *Probleme deutscher Zeitgeschichte*, 89.
19. Schröder, "strategischen Konzeption," 46. Cf. Raeder, *Kreuzerkrieg*, I, 2.
20. Raoul Castex, *Strategic Theories*.
21. Raeder, *Kreuzerkrieg*, I, 3, 6, 8, 538.
22. Schröder, "strategischen Konzeption," 46–47. Tirpitz, noted Raeder, had supported the development of a cruiser squadron for "special purposes" before the war, but was not funded by the Reichstag.
23. Schröder, "strategischen Konzeption," 48.
24. Raeder, "Sind Kriegserklärungen von Beginn der Feindseligkeiten in heutigen Zeit notwendig?" *Marine Rundschau* 15: 291–311.
25. Steury, "Germany's Naval Renaissance," 200–201.
26. Schröder, "strategischen Konzeption," 46–47.
27. Halpern, *Naval History*, 93–94.
28. Raeder, *ML*, I, 94–95.
29. Schröder, "seestrategischen Konzeption," 46. Raeder's "Die deutsche und die britisch-japanische Strategie vor der Coronel- under Falklandschlacht," *Marine Rundschau* 26 (1921): 537, noted efforts to urge the Admiralstab to send the battle cruisers in the Atlantic to relieve the pressure on Spee.
30. Raeder, *ML*, I, 81–82.
31. Raeder, *Kreuzerkrieg*, I, 32, 246; Raeder, *ML*, I, 81.
32. Schröder, "seestrategischen Konzeption," 47.
33. Comments on Jacques de Prevaux's 1938 article on the strategic foundations of the German navy (*La Revue Maritime*), OKM Seekriegsleitung, K10–2/88, BAMA.
34. Capt. Lockhardheith, "Review of German Cruiser Warfare," Naval War Staff Study (1940).
35. Gemzell argues that Raeder never developed an independent strategic vision. *Raeder, Hitler und Skandinavien*, 150–51.
36. Raeder, *ML*, I, 212–13.
37. Raeder, *ML*, I, 187. Güth, *Erich Raeder*, 15 refers to Raeder as the "strict schoolmaster in the Prussian tradition."
38. Raeder, *ML*, I, 187–188, 193–96.
39. Raeder to Levetzow, 2 August 1922, Levetzow N 239/14.
40. Levetzow urged Raeder to get the navy to sea in order to train the core of the future fleet and provide the justification for its existence. 7 July 1920, Levetzow N 239/30.
41. Raeder, *ML*, I, 189.
42. Gordon Craig, "Reichswehr and Natural Socialism," 197.
43. Meerscheidt-Hüllessen, *Denkschrift*, III M 503/4, BAMA.
44. Michaelis N 164/6.
45. Wegener, *Die Seestrategie des Weltkriegs*, 80–84. The *Reichsmarine* was to serve as the "core" of a future High Seas Fleet, Michaelis N 164/5.
46. Rahn, "Die Ausbldung zum Marineoffizer zwischen den Weltkriegen 1920–1939," 123–25.
47. Raeder, *ML*, I, 192–93.
48. Güth, *Admiralstabausbildung*, 56.
49. Raeder, *ML*, I, 192–93.
50. Meerscheidt-Hüllessen, *Denkschrift*, III M 503/4, BAMA.
51. Raeder, *ML*, I, 189–207, 240. Previous regulations did not stress the leadership role of the officers. Captain Carl Claussen (Raeder's chief of staff in 1922), "Welche Vorschlage können gemacht werden um grosser Teilen des Offizierkorps zu Führern zu erziehen?" *Marineakademie*, II M 57/33, BAMA.

52. Meerscheidt-Hüllessen, *Denkschrift*, III M 503/4, BAMA.

53. Raeder, *ML*, I, 189, 204, 240–43; Meerscheidt-Hüllessen, *Denkschrift*, III M 503/4, BAMA. Salewski, "Selbsverständnis," 65–88, blames this "trauma" for contributing to the Kriegsmarine's harsh judicial system, which lay behind the leadership and camaraderie cultivated by Raeder.

54. Raeder, *ML*, I, 205; Klaus Müller, *Das Heer und Hitler*, 59.

55. Raeder, *ML*, I, 174–78. The engineering officers continued to regard themselves as "stepchildren." Werner Bräckow, Bräckow N 582.

56. Raeder, *ML*, I, 203; Siegfried Sorge, *Zeugenschrifttum* No. 1785, IfZ; interview with Admiral Ruge, spring 1970.

57. Raeder, *ML*, I, 190–91, 203; *Aktenstuck*, No. 5536 (15 February 1923), *Verhandlungen*, 376, 6255–65. For the navy's struggles with *Innenpolitik*, Bird, *Weimar*, 126–80.

58. Raeder, *ML*, I, 193–196, 275; Bird, *Weimar*, 152–53.

59. *Chef der Marineleitung*, 20 March 1926, *Innere Unruhen, Zeitfreiwillige W'haven (Reichstagsmaterial)*, 1926/27, II M 65/7, BAMA.

60. *IMT*, XIV, 74.

61. Dülffer, "Die Reichs- und Kriegsmarine 1918–1939," 371.

62. Salewski, "Menschenführung in der deutschen Kriegsmarine 1933–1945," 87.

63. *Gedanken über die Organisation der Marine*, July 1921, Schultze N 209/13, BAMA.

64. Raeder, *ML*, I, 188; Raeder to Levetzow, 31 October 1928, Levetzow N 239/30. Cf. Sorge, *Zeugenschrifttum* No. 1785, IfZ.

65. Raeder to Levetzow, 30 November 1923, Levetzow N 239/14.

66. Ibid.

67. Raeder to Levetzow, 28 January 1924, Levetzow N 239/15.

68. Scheck, *Tirpitz*, 144–63

69. Raeder to Levetzow, 18 and 28 January and 15 May 1924, Levetzow N 239/ 15, 16; Raffael Scheck, *Tirpitz*, 113.

70. Raeder to Levetzow, 15 May 1924, Dülffer, *Hitler und die Marine*, 103.

71. Raeder, *ML*, I, 197–198; Assmann, "*Raeder und Zweite Weltkrieg*," 5–6. Assmann argued that Raeder did not have the opportunity to "train his ships and himself at sea."

72. Interview with Admiral Ruge, spring 1970, and Admiral Wilhelm Meisel, *Zeugenschifttum* No. 1739, IfZ.

73. Raeder, *ML*, I, 198–207.

74. Gagern doubted whether any accommodation with Schleswig-Holstein's government was possible. 8 April 1921, Behncke N 173/8.

75. Raeder, *ML*, I, 207.

76. Bird, *Weimar*, 155–59.

77. *Vortrag betr. Artikel Eggerstaedt* [*sic*], *Beschuldigung betr. Vorfälle im KL. Yachtklub (KYC)* (August 1928–June 1933), II M 68/1 BAMA and Raeder to *Chef der Marineleitung*, 6 July 1926, II M 68/1, BAMA. Prince Heinrich involved Raeder in another controversy when the prince visited a ship that was leaving on a foreign cruise. See *ML*, I, 208, 210–11.

78. *Stellungnahme W [A] zu R.T.M. [Reichstagsmaterial]*, Nr. 447, *Einweihung des neuen Clubgebäudes des KYC*, II M 68/1, BAMA.

79. Groener to Begas, Nr. 2821/2W, 16 April 1928, II M 68/1, BAMA. Cf. *Schleswig-Holsteinische Volkszeitung*, No. 293, 15 December 1928, and *Ergebnis der Besprechung betr. Kaiserliche YC beim Herrn Reichswehrminister mit dem Vorstand des Klubs am 1.5.28*, II M 68/1, BAMA.

80. Raeder, *ML*, I, 208–10.

81. *Handbuch des Marine-Offizier-Verbandes* 1928, 248–49, and Vortrag, *5 February 1929, Betr. Marine-Offiziere-Verein*, II M 65/7, BAMA. The MOV ostracized Admiral (Ret.) Oskar von Truppel for joining the pro-Republican German Democratic Party. Truppel N 244.
82. Bird, *Weimar*, 162–67.
83. Document C-156, *Der Kampf der Marine* (Schüssler), *IMT*, XXXIV, 549–51; and *Ausug aus dem Protokoll der Ministerbesprechung vom 29 November 1926*, R 431/601.
84. Schleicher, *Notiz Für W*, II M 65/6, BAMA.
85. *Reichstagsmaterial*, NR. 159, March 1926, II M 65/6, BAMA; *Notiz für W., Vortrag beim Chef d. Marine, Betr. Abgeord. Hünlich/Zeitfreiwillege in Wilhelmshaven* (no date), II M 65/6, BAMA; *Vortragnotiz* (no date, handwritten by Schleicher), II M 65/6, BAMA.
86. *Schleswig-Holsteinische Volkszeitung*, No. 293, 16 December 1926. Seeckt was pressured by the right wing to take a more active role in dismantling the republican system. Claus Guske, *Das politische Denken des Generals von Seeckt*, 252–55, 261–63.
87. *Vorläufige Äusserung des Chefs der Marinestation der Ostsee zu dem Bericht des Reichstagsabgeordneten Eggerstedt* (no date, initialed by Zenker, 8 December 1926) II M 65/12, BAMA. For the extensive ties between Hermann Ehrhardt, his former men in the *Reichsmarine* and the NSDAP, see the Leutgebrune Papers, T 253, rolls 3–5, 11, 15, NARA, and "Innere Unruhen" *RWM/ML Handakten O.C.-Wiking (January 1926–August 1928)*, II M 65/12, BAMA.
88. *Vortrag beim Reichsgericht am 25. 2. 28, Betr.: Beschwerde der S. P. D. über unerlaubte Verbindungen von Offizierer der Station O zu rechtsradikalen Organisationen usw.*, II M 65/12, BAMA.
89. *Vorwärts*, No. 77, 15 February 1928; *Unterlagen für die Ausführungen im Haushaltausschuss (Marine) betr. Organisation Consul (O.C.) ca. 7 March 1928*, II M, 65/12, BAMA; 27 March 1928, *Verhandlungen*, 395, 13788.

Chapter 4

1. For the most recent analysis of Lohmann's activities, see Bernd Remmele's "Die maritime Geheimrüstung unter Kapitän z. S. Lohmann," *MGM* 56, no. 2 (1997): 313–76.
2. *Montag Morgen, Berliner Tageblatt*, 8 August 1927; *Vorwärts*, 9 August 1927; No. 4163, Anlage, *Bericht über Lohmann-Unternehmungen, Verhandlung*. 422.
3. Bird, *Weimar*, 189; Wolfgang Wacker, *Der Bau des Panzerschiff "A" und der Reichstag*, 127.
4. Remmele, "Lohmann," 330–43; Bird, *Weimar*, 187, 248.
5. Salewski points out that *Revisionismus* was not just limited to the military but reflected a broad consensus among the political parties, government, and public opinion. "Weimarer Revisionssyndrom," *Beilage zur Wochenzeitung "Das Parlament,"* Nr. 2/80.
6. Raeder, *ML*, I, 220.
7. Levetzow to Guidotto Donnersmarch, 19 March 1928, Levetzow N 239/29; Levetzow to Raeder, 22 April 1928, Levetzow N 239/29.
8. Raeder to Levetzow, 6 May 1928, Levetzow N 239/29.
9. Levetzow to Graf von der Schulenburg, 7 June 1928, Levetzow N 239/29. My emphasis.
10. Raeder to Levetzow, 22 August 1928, Levetzow N 239/29.
11. Albrecht *Erinnerungen*, III M 554/4, BAMA and Raeder, *ML*, I, 220–21.
12. Schleicher to Groener, 8 September 1928, Schleicher N 42/50.
13. No. 227, 22 September 1928. *Reichstagsmaterial (29 September 1928), Betr. Angriffe gegen Vizead. Raeder*, Raeder *Sammlung*, 2.
14. No. 228, 27 September 1928, and *Reichstagsmaterial*, Raeder *Sammlung*, 2.
15. Bird, *Weimar*, 209–10.

16. Raeder, *ML*, I, 220.

17. *Der Staatssekretär in der Reichskanzlei*, Raeder *Sammlung*, 2.

18. Pünder to the *Reichskanzler*, 22 September 1928, R43 I/954.

19. *Vortrag*, 22 March 1928, *Betr. Artikel Sch[leswig] von 13.3. 1928*, "Das System ist schuld." Raeder *Sammlung*, 2.

20. "Die Republik wieder einmal beliebt gemacht," No. 261, 5 June 1928.

21. *Vortrag*, 25 September, Raeder *Sammlung*, 2.

22. Rede für "Geschichtliche Woche," Schleicher N 42/50. My emphasis.

23. Carsten contends that this phrase, "Who holds . . . ," was deliberately omitted from copies of the speech sent to the Reichswehrminister. *Reichswehr and Politics*, 289. It was, however, in the copy sent to Schleicher.

24. Raeder to Götting, 24 September 1928, Raeder *Sammlung*, 2; *Vortrag*, 25 September 1928, ibid.; *Reichswehrminister*, Nr. 6975, Berlin, 31 August 1929, to Raeder, ibid.

25. *Reichstagsmaterial*, 24 September 1928, Raeder *Sammlung*, 2.

26. *Montag Morgen*, No. 40, 1 October 1928; the *Schleswig-Holsteinische Volkszeitung*, No. 230, 1 October 1928.

27. *8 Uhr Abendblatt*, No. 229, 29 September 1928.

28. Heinrich Brüning, *Memoiren 1918–1934*, 130; Gessler, *Reichswehrpolitik*, 553–56.

29. Raeder to Levetzow, 31 October 1928, Levetzow N 239/31.

30. Raeder to Tirpitz, 3 October 1928, Tirpitz N 253/235-K63. Cf. Albrecht *Erinnerungen*, II M 554/4.

31. Raeder, *ML*, I, 227; Raeder to Levetzow, 31 October 1928, Levetzow N 239/31.

32. Raeder to Tirpitz, 3 October 1928, Tirpitz N 253/235-K63.

33. Tirpitz to Raeder, 8 October 1928, Tirpitz N 253/235-K63.

34. Scheck, *Tirpitz*, 213–18.

35. Raeder, *ML*, I, 235. Cf. *Kampf der Marine*, C-156, IMT, XXIV, 600.

36. Klaus-Jürgen Müller, *Das Heer und Hitler*, 59.

37. Gemzell's *Organization* analyzes the role of personalities and group conflicts in strategic planning.

38. Albrecht, *Erinnerungen*, II M 554/4, BAMA; Raeder, *ML*, I, 220–21, 236.

39. Assmann, "Raeder und der Zweite Weltkrieg," 4, 11.

40. Güth, "Vor 40 Jahren: Grossadmiral Raeder nimmt seinen Abschied," *Marine Forum* LVIII (1/2, 1983): 23–26.

41. See Raeder, *ML*, I, 293 for his interpretation.

42. Assmann, "Raeder und der Zweite Weltkrieg," 5.

43. M.G. Saunders, "Hitler's Admirals, Reflections Inspired by Their Memoirs," *Journal of the Royal United Service Institution*, 325; Michael Salewski, *Seekriegsleitung*, I, 109–10.

44. Wülfing von Ditten to Schleicher, 15 November 1930, *Innere Unruhen*, RWM/ML, II M 65/4, BAMA.

45. Raeder, *ML*, I, 236–37.

46. Interview with Admiral Ruge, spring 1970.

47. Salewski, "Erich Raeder—Oberbefehlshaber 'seiner' Marine," *Die Militärelite des Dritten Reiches*, 406–22.

48. Güth, "Vor 40 Jahre," 23–26.

49. Raeder, *ML*, I, 206. According to Güth, Raeder's "stuffiness" led to comments that "Bei Onkel Erich und Tante Erika gab's nichts zu lachen!" *Raeder*, 21; Raeder, *ML*, I, 205–6.

50. Deist, "Die Aufrüstung der Wehrmacht," *DRZW*, I, 382–87; Raeder, *ML*, I, 205–6.

51. IMT, XIII, 621–22, and XIV, 252–53. Cf. Severing's account, *Lebensweg*, II, 137.

52. IMT, XIII, 622; *Kampf der Marine*, C-156, IMT, XXIV, 601.

53. Bird, *Weimar*, 233–34.

54. *Kampf der Marine*, C-156, *IMT*, 602.

55. *Beitrag von V.G.M. zür Führerbesprechung am 14 December 1928*, II M 62/I, BAMA.

56. Raeder, *ML*, I, 228; Severing, *Lebensweg*, II, 495–96; *IMT*, XIV, 254–55, 270. Severing later believed Raeder had deceived him.

57. Raeder, *ML*, I, 228, 233–34. Raeder to Levetzow, 6 May 1928, Levetzow N 239/30.

58. Raeder, *ML*, I, 222.

59. *Das Panzerschiff*, Groener N 46/147.

60. *Braucht Deutschland grosse Kriegsschiffe?* 28 May 1929, Rahn, *Reichsmarine*, 281–86.

61. *Das Panzerschiff*, Groener N 46/147; Salewski, "England, Hitler und die Marine," *Vom Sinn der Geschichte*, 165–66; Schreiber, *Weltmachtstreben*, 54–55.

62. Deist, *Wehrmacht and German Rearmament*, 11.

63. Wohfeil, "Heer und Republik," *Reichswehr und Republik (1918–1933)*, 6, 121–24; Schleicher to Groener, 19 August 1928, Schleicher N 42/20.

64. Schleicher to Groener, 8 September 1928 and 25 August 1928, Schleicher N 42/50.

65. For the Panzerschiff debate, see Gerhard Sandhofer's "Das Panzerschiff 'A' und die Vorentwürfe von 1920 bis 1928," *MGM*, no. 1 (1968): 35–62, and Rahn's *Reichsmarine*, 233–46. The memorandum of 2 October 1928, *Der militärische Wert der Panzerschiffs-neubauten*, noted that a failure to build the Panzerschiff would be the death of the navy!

66. Raeder, *ML*, I, 249; Assmann, *Deutsche Seestrategie in zwei Weltkriegen*, 110.

67. Rahn, *Reichsmarine*, 239. See Koop and Schmolke, *Pocket Battleships of the Deutschland Class* for technical details of the Panzerschiffe.

68. Rahn, *Reichsmarine*, 282.

69. Deist, Die Aufrüstung der Wehrmacht, DRZW, I, 386.

70. Schreiber, "Zur Kontinuität des Gross- und Weltmachtstrebens," 114.

71. Ibid. Hubatsch, *Admiralstab*, 188, characterizes the navy's conclusions from the 1925–1926 exercises as "phantastisch."

72. Gaines Post, The Civil-Military Fabric of Weimar Foreign Policy, 256, describes the navy's refusal to "conform naval strategy more closely to continental realities."

73. See Schreiber's "Thesen zur ideologischen Kontinuität."

74. *Braucht Deutschland grosse Kriegschiffe?* 28 May 1929, Rahn, *Reichsmarine*, 281–86.

75. Wacker, *Panzerschiffes "A,"* 53, argues that the Panzerschiff represented a "*Wechsel auf die Zukunft.*" Raeder, *ML*, I, 220–21; Albrecht *Erinnerungen*, III M 554/4.

76. Raeder, *ML*, I, 19, II, 221, 234, Wacker, *Panzerschiff "A,"* 130 n. 11; Raeder to Levetzow, 5 January 1927, Levetzow N 239/25.

77. This was an attitude shared by the officer corps in general. Gordon Craig, "Reichswehr and National Socialism," *Political Science Quarterly* 63 (June 1948): 197–98.

78. Bird, *Weimar*, 258.

79. *Amtschefvortrag*, 19 December 1928, PG/34464, *Innenpolitisches*, reel 43, Project No. 2, and Raeder to Tirpitz, 3 October 1928, Tirpitz N 253/235-K63.

80. The difference between the monarchy and the Republic represented "one of style." Interview with Admiral Ruge, spring 1970. Dülffer, *Hitler und die Marine*, 39, observes that the kaiser was still regarded as a legitimate leader by naval officers more than army officers.

81. Cf. Raeder to Levetzow, 28 October 1924, Levetzow *Nachlass*, N 239/15, BAMA.

82. Raeder, *ML*, I, 214; Raeder to Levetzow, 7 June 1927, Levetzow N 239/15.

83. Admiral Wilhelm Meisel, *Zeugenschrifttum* No. 1739, IfZ, Munich.

84. Raeder, *ML*, I, 240; II, 13–15.

85. Bird, *Weimar*, 198–201, 237–43; Thomas, *German Navy in the Nazi Era*, 58–64.

86. Raeder to Levetzow, 31 October 1928, Levetzow N 239/31; *Vortäufige Äusserung des Chef der Marineleitung*, II M 65/12, BAMA.

87. Admiral Freiwald, 8 August 1970.

88. *Vortrag*, 19 July 1929 and 37 April 1929, II M 65/13, BAMA.

89. Interview with Admiral Ruge, spring 1970.

90. Schleicher to Brüning, "Ein Brief," *Deutsche Rundschau* 53, no. 1 (1964): 86.

91. Admiral Leopold Bürkner, *Zeugenschiftum* No. 364, IfZ, Munich.

92. Heye to Schleicher, 17 January 1930, Schleicher N 42/42.

93. Wülfing von Ditten to Scheicher, 16 February 1931, II M 65/4, BAMA.

94. Meisel, *Zeugenschrifttum* No. 1739, IfZ, Munich.

95. Sorge, *Zeugenschrifttum* No. 1785, IfZ, Munich.

96. Goebbels, *Vom Kaiserhof zur Reichskanzler,* 102, 106, 292.

97. Baum, "Marine, Nationalsozialismus," 44.

98. Assmann, *Raeder und Zweite Weltkieg,* 4–5.

99. *Aufzeichnungen über eine Aussprache Admiral Raeders mit Reichskanzler Brüning am 21. 9. 1931* and *Konzept Admiral Raeders für einen Vortrag beim Reichskanzler,* undated (21 September 1931), Salewski, "Marineleitung und politische Führung 1931–1935," *MGM* 10, no. 2 (1971): 116–17, 150–52.

100. *Aufzeichungen über S.A.-Verbot und Beleitumstande,* Raeder *Sammlung, 3.*

101. No. 25, Memorandum of 10 June 1932 (Office of the Reich President), Vogelsang, *Reichswehr,* 462.

102. *Aufzeichnungen über S.A.–Verbot,* Raeder *Nachlass, 3,* BAMA.

103. *Aufzeichnungen des Reichswehrministers a. D. Groener (Auszug),* Vogelsang, *Reichswehr,* 450. Cf. Groener to Gero V. Gleich, 22 May 1932, Groener *Nachlass,* N 46/36, BAMA.

104. *Aufzeichnungen über S.A.–Verbot,* Raeder *Sammlung, 3,* BAMA; Raeder, *ML,* I, 270–71.

105. Groos *Nachlass,* N 165/2.

106. Raeder, *ML,* I, 270.

107. Ibid. Cf. Memorandum of 10 June 1932, Vogelsang, *Reichswehr,* 462.

108. Raeder to Levetzow, 15 May 1932, Levetzow N 239/35; Raeder, *ML,* I, 271–72.

109. Raeder to Levetzow, 15 May 1932, Levetzow N 239/35. Raeder asked Levetzow to burn his letter after reading it.

110. Dülffer, *Hitler und die Marine,* 129.

111. Ibid. and Raeder's 15 May 1932 letter to Levetzow, Levetzow N 239/35.

112. Dülffer, *Hitler und die Marine,* 129.

113. Raeder to Brüning, 13 May 1932 (copy), Schleicher *Nachlass,* N 42/91; Raeder, *ML,* I, 273.

114. Raeder, *ML,* I, 272; and *Aufzeichnungen über S.A.-Verbot,* Raeder *Sammlung, 3.*

115. 15 May 1932, Levetzow N 239/35.

116. Levetzow to Raeder, 14 May 1932, Levetzow N 239/35. Emphasis in the original.

117. Wülfing von Ditten's letter to Schleicher, 16 February 1931, II M 65/4, BAMA.

118. Levetzow's letters to Admiral Schmidt, 17 May 1932, and to Guter, 16 November 1931, Levetzow N 239/35.

119. Brüning, *Memoiren,* 228, 584; Groener to Richard Bahr, 22 May 1932, Groener N 46/152.

120. Raeder to Levetzow, 9 June 1932, Levetzow N 239/16. See Dülffer's description of the international negotiations and their impact on naval planning, *Hitler und die Marine,* 130–85.

121. Raeder, *ML,* I, 235; and *Chef der Marineleitung* to *Chef der Heeresleitung,* 18 November 1932, Raeder *Sammlung, 3.* Emphasis in the original.

122. Hubatsch, *Admiralstab,* 196, 197.

123. *Gedanken zum Umbau der Reichsmarine*, A II 20231/32, 23 November 1932, PG 34176, *Umbau der Wehrmacht*, reel 27, Project No. 2.

124. *Überlegungen über Offiziersvermehrung beim Umbau*, 13 December 1932, PG 34176, *Umbau der Wehrmacht*, reel 27, Project No. 2.

Chapter 5

1. *Innere Unruhen*, RWM, *Feinde der Marine*, II M 65/8.

2. Raeder, *ML*, II, 107.

3. Levetzow to Göring, 22 December 1930, Levetzow N 239/11; Levetzow to Donnersmarck, 6 October 1931, ibid.; Levetzow to Hitler, 5 October 1931, ibid.

4. Hitler to Levetzow, 24 August 1931, Levetzow N 239/11; Levetzow to Hitler, 5 October 1931, ibid.

5. Karl-Jesko von Puttkamer, *Die unheimliche See*, 11–12, for Hitler's knowledge of the technical details of warships. Fritz Wiedemann, Hitler's personal adjutant, 1934 to 1939, said that Hitler's knowledge of the British fleet often embarrassed Raeder. *Der Mann der Feldherr werden wollte*, 79, 211.

6. Hitler, *Mein Kampf*, 140, 247, 273–75; Hitler's *Secret Book* (published in 1961), 125–26 and 154–55; *Hitlers Zweites Buch*, 102, 108, 110, 163, 169, 218.

7. Schuster's comments to the foreign office, 9 December 1931, II FM *Marineangelegenheiten*, Bd. 2, AA.

8. *Völkischer Beobachter*, 12 October 1928.

9. Levetzow to Donnersmarck, 20 November 1931, Granier, *Levetzow*, 312.

10. Reproduction of the *Köln's* guest book in Fritz Otto Busch, *Das Buch von der Kriegsmarine* (following 184).

11. Paul Zieb, *Logistik-Probleme in der Marine*, 140. Dülffer sees Hitler's visit to the *Köln* as a "trial balloon" by Raeder to determine Hitler's intentions for the navy. *Hitler und die Marine*, 222.

12. *Völkischer Beobachter*, 21 October 1932.

13. Raeder to Levetzow, 23 October 1932, Levetzow N 239/35.

14. Raeder to Levetzow, 23 October 1932, Levetzow N 239/34; Götting to Schleicher, 9 December 1932, Schleicher N 42/23.

15. Levetzow to Raeder, 26 October 1932, Levetzow N 239/35.

16. Raeder to Levetzow, 7 January 1933, Levetzow *Nachlass*, General Admiral Raeder, *Innenpolitisches*, reel 49, Project No. 2.

17. Admiral Scheer, *Deutsche Marine Zeitung* (2 November 1924), Levetzow N 239/17. Levetzow had repeatedly cited the need for a "strong man" or "dictator." Levetzow to Ludendorff, 29 July 1923, ibid.

18. Levetzow to Raeder, 6 January 1932, Levetzow N 239/35.

19. Schmiedicke to Gregor Strasser, NSDAP, 9 April 1932, *Gau Brandenburg*, Abt. Sc/H, Wilhelm Busse Files, Berlin Document Center.

20. See Dülffer's description (*Hitler und die Marine*) of the domestic role of fleet-building. Rolf Bensel, *Die deutsche Flottenpolitik von 1933–1939*, 20, argued that naval rearmament was a means of solving the financial and unemployment crises. For the navy's ideological foundations, see Schreiber, particularly *Weltmachtstreben*. In 1969, Ruge claimed the *Volksgemeinschaft* "really existed." *In vier Marinen*, 115.

21. *Deutsche Allgemeine Zeitung* (16 April 1933), Kyserlingk N 161/12, *MOV-Nachrichten* XV (15 December 1933), 335; Admiral von Mantey to Admiral Kyserlingk, 27 April 1937, Kyserlingk N 161/10.

22. Trotha, *Erlass an die Marine*, 3 July 1919, *Volkstum und Staatsführung*, 184–86; Captain Schuster, *Vortrag von Führern der S.A., S.S., und des Stalhelm sowie Vertreten der Reichs-, Staats- Behörden in Kiel, Offizierheim Wik., am 5 Mai 1933*, II M 58/3, BAMA.

23. Salewski, "Menschenführung in der deutschen Kriegsmarine 1933–1945," 91.

24. *Deutsche Allgemeine Zeitung*, 2 April 1933.

25. Vogelsang, "Neue Dokumente zur Geschichte der Reichswehr," *VfZ*, 2 (1954): 434–35 (General a. D. Liebmann's notes). Raeder mistakenly dates this meeting as 2 February. *ML*, I, 280–81. Cf. the accounts by Otto Groos, *Groos* N 165/3, and Conrad Albrecht, RM 35 I/24, BAMA.

26. Dülffer, *Hitler und die Marine*, 204.

27. Wilhelm Treue, *Denkschriff über den Flottenbau 1926–1939* (ed. by Captain Bidlingmaier, December 1960), III M 151/1, BAMA.

28. *Konzept Admiral Raeders für einen Vortrag beim Reichskanzler undatiert (Ende März 1933)*, Salewski, "Marineleitung," 153–57. The date of this first meeting is not clear, although Raeder uses "February 1933" as the date of their first meeting. Raeder, *ML*, II, 108. Dülffer places the meeting as "probably" occurring between 16 March and 1 April 1933, *Hitler und die Marine*, 245.

29. *Konzept Admiral Raeders*, "Marineleitung," 153–57, and Dülffer, *Hitler und die Marine*, 245–47.

30. Raeder, *ML*, I, 284.

31. Kurt Fischer, "Grossadmiral Dr. h.c. Erich Raeder," *Hitlers militärische Elite*, 189.

32. Captain Schuster, *"Vortrag am 5 May 1933"* II M58/3, BAMA. Schuster was one of the few senior officers who identified openly with National Socialism. Salewski names Fricke, Boehm, and Carls as the exceptions to Raeder and the majority of officers who did not "readily" accept Hitler. Salewski, *Seekriegsleitung*, II, 443.

33. See Dülffer, *Hitler und die Marine*, 247.

34. Raeder, *ML*, II, 108. Raeder noted that Hitler kept copies of *Jane's Fighting Ships* and *Weyer's Flottentaschenbuch* "constantly at hand."

35. *Rede am 23.4.1933, Hitler's Wollen*, 52. Cf. London *Times*, 23 May 1933.

36. Wilfred Bade, *Deutschland erwacht*, 106.

37. *B. Nr. 1205*, 28 August 1933, RM 8/55, BAMA and *B. Nr. 1243*, 5 September 1933, RM 8/55, BAMA.

38. Groos N 165/2; Güth, *Erich Raeder*, 42, 44.

39. *Chef der Marineleitung, B. Nr. A II in 3762/33*, 22 September 1933, II M 100/2, BAMA.

40. Hans Guderian, *Panzer Leader*, 85; Friedrich Hossbach, *Zwischen Wehrmacht und Hitler*, 1, 3.

41. *Rede des Oberbefehlshabers der Kriegsmarine anlässlich des Staatsaktes in Laboe am 30. 5. 1936*, RM 8/58, BAMA. For the scale of this event, see the *Völkischer Beobachter*, 31 May/ 1 June 1936.

42. Raeder noted that the naval officers' handbook, Siegfried Sorge's *Der Marineoffizier als Führer und Erzieher*, was banned in 1944 for its "humanistic" overtones (Raeder ignored its decidedly National Socialist and pro-führer rhetoric). Raeder, *ML*, I, 242.

43. *Köhlers Flottenkalender 36* (1938): 30.

44. Dülffer, *Hitler und die Marine*, 248.

45. *Ansprache des Chef ML zum Abschluss der Gefechtsübungen der Flotte, September 1933*, Salewski. *Seekriegsleitung*, I, 3.

46. Raeder, *ML*, II, 114–15. See also Rear Admiral (Ret.) Helmut Neuss, *Soldaten für Hitler*, 154.

47. Salewski, "Erich Raeder," 414; Raeder, *Verhältnis zu Hitler*, Raeder N 391/3.

48. Raeder, *ML*, II, 106–7.
49. Messerschmidt, *Wehrmacht im NS-Staat*; Salewski, "Die bewaffnete Macht im Dritten Reich 1933–1939," *Handbuch zur deutsche Militärgeschichte.*
50. Ruge, *In vier Marinen*, 125, 134–35; *IMT*, XIV, 136.
51. *Verhaltnis*, Raeder N 391/3. Raeder, *ML*, 1, 288–89. Cf. *3. Buch: Unter der Diktatur*, Groos N 165/3.
52. Salewski, "Die bewaffnete Macht im Dritten Reich 1933–1939," 78. Cf. Schreiber, *Weltmachtstreben*, 11; Manfred Messerschmidt, *Wehrmacht im NS-Staat*, 47, 49–50.
53. For the Wehrmacht's integration, see Deist, "Die Aufrüstung der Wehrmacht," *DRZW*, 512–18; Raeder, *ML*, I, 290; Klaus-Jürgen Müller, *Heer und Hitler*, 133, 136–37.
54. Raeder, *Verhaltnis*, Raeder N 321/3.
55. Salewski, "Die bewaffnete Macht im Dritten Reich 1933–1939," 83–85; Heinz Höhne, *Canaris*, 133–37, 162–63, 173–74; Kahn, *Hitler's Spies*, 22–23, 226, 236. Raeder initially said it was impossible for him to work with Canaris.
56. Boehm, 25 October 1961, *Frankfurter Allgemeine Zeitung.*
57. Raeder, *ML*, II, 132–33, 338–39. Raeder recounted his efforts to help Jewish naval officers at Nuremberg (e.g., *Konteradmiral a.D.* Karl Kühlenthal's deposition, 28 October 1950), Raeder N 391/5. Raeder states he saved two officers. *ML*, II, 132. In June 1934, the official list of Jews in the navy included three officers (one "questionable"), four officer candidates, three NCOs, and four sailors. Messerschmidt, *Wehrmacht im NS-Staat*, 45–46.
58. Doc. 653-D, *IMT*, XXXV, 310–12; *IMT*, XIV, 73. Raeder "understood" that the government "took certain measures against them [Jews and communists] which were "excessive"; however, "That was the sense of my statements and I made no mention of any further steps which might come into question." This is consistent with the officers' identification of Jews as "Bolsheviks" in the naval mutinies and revolution and Raeder's concern for "communist infiltration" into the navy. *IMT*, XIV, 222. Salewski, "Erich Raeder," 414, notes Raeder's ability to assimilate Hitler's radical goals into his Weltanschauung.
59. *Ansprache an die Rekruten anlässlich der Veridigung am 1. May 6 1937 in Stralsund*, III M 503/3, BAMA. Speer did not regard Raeder as an anti-Semite. *Spandauer Tagebücher*, 401. Raeder's son-in-law allegedly qualified as a non-Aryan and lived in Guatemala before Hitler came to power. Thomas, *German Navy in the Nazi Era*, 103.
60. Raeder, *Meine religiöse Einstellung*, Raeder N 391/1; Raeder, *ML*, II, 141–42. Cf. Messerschmidt's *Wehrmacht in NS-Staat* for the issue of religion in the Wehrmacht (especially 171–99).
61. *Eideserklärung Dekan Friedrich Ronneberger*, 15 November 1950, Raeder N 391/5; Raeder, *ML*, II, 154.
62. Rear Admiral Helmut Neuss contended that Raeder was loyal to Hitler but that, because of his religious views, he was "in no way" a National Socialist. *Soldaten für Hitler*, 154. Raeder devotes an entire chapter in his memoirs to his support for the military chaplains, *ML*, II, 135–48.
63. Raeder, *ML*, II, 111, 116–25.
64. Harold Deutsch, *Hitler and His Generals: The Hidden Crisis, January–June 1938*, 93–96, for Raeder's role in Blomberg's scandal. Deutsch describes the Blomberg and Fritsch "episodes" as a virtual coup d'etat by Hitler to consolidate his control over the armed forces.
65. *Verhältnis*, Raeder N 391/3.
66. Deutsch, *Hitler and His Generals*, 236–37. Speer, *Erinnerungen*, describes Raeder as distraught as he left Hitler.
67. Raeder, *ML*, II, 120.

68. Deutsch, *Hitler and His Generals,* 237–38.
69. Raeder to Fritsch, 25 April 1938, Messerschmidt, *Wehrmacht im NS-Staat,* 186–87.
70. Deutsch, *Hitler and His Generals,* 238–39, 348–49, 387–88.
71. *Verhältnis,* Raeder N 321/3.
72. Deutsch, *Hitler and His Generals,* 387–88, and Raeder, *ML,* II, 123–24.
73. Raeder, *ML,* II, 121, 123 and *Verhältnis,* Raeder N 321/1.
74. Eberhard Weichold, "Die Bedeutung Grossadmirals Raeder in Vorgeschichte und Ablauf des 2. Weltkrieges durch Stellungnahme zu seinen Erinnerungsbuch '*Mein Leben,*'" MS in Wagner (August 1958) N 539/78.
75. Raeder, *ML,* II, 119, 128–31; *IMT,* XIV, 20. Raeder believed that Himmler (and other party leaders) intended to create a National Socialist Wehrmacht.
76. Raeder overestimated his ability to "prevent all sorts of friction, so that before long they rarely occurred." *IMT,* XIV, 70–71.
77. See Raeder's vacillation between his assessment of British psychology and politics on one side and his passivity toward Hitler's readiness to gamble (compare *ML,* II, 154–55, where Raeder notes the futility of war with England before 1945–1946, with 159, 172, where he notes the vulnerability of the British and the threat that even the small fleet posed to England. Weichold's "Die Bedeutung Grossadmirals Raeder," Wagner N 539/78.
78. Fritz Boie to Förste, February 1956, Förste N 328/42.
79. Erika Raeder declared later that they avoided every social interaction with party leaders and withdrew their son from the Hitler Youth. *Eidesstattliche Erklärung,* 13 November 1950. Raeder N 321/5. Cf. Salewski, *Seekriegsleitung,* II, 441.
80. Hanneli von Poser, the granddaughter of Admiral von Müller, Salewski, *Seekriegsleitung,* II, 441.
81. Bird, *Weimar,* 294–97.
82. *IMT,* XIV, 149.
83. Ibid., 75.
84. General Alfred Jodl testified that Hitler would refer to the Kriegsmarine as the "Imperial Navy" or the "Christian navy" and the army as "my reactionary army." *IMT,* XV, 294.
85. Dülffer, "Die Reichs- und Kriegsmarine 1918–1939," *Handbook zur deutschen Militärgeschichte 1918–1939,* 371.
86. Rahn, "Ausbildung zum Marineoffizier," 60, and Thomas, *German Navy in the Nazi Era,* 214.
87. *Verhältnis,* Raeder N 321/3.
88. Salewski, "Erich Raeder," 414.
89. *Auszahlungsliste der monatlichen Sonderzahlungen für April 1945,* Gerd Ueberschär and Winfried Vogel, *Dienen und Verdienen,* 245. Raeder stated that he had earlier turned down Hitler's offer to promote him to *Grossadmiral* because he did not want to be promoted to a rank superior to the army chief, Fritsch. He suggested instead that Hitler promote him to *Generaladmiral.* In 1939, he accepted the appointment as *Grossadmiral,* which he believed Hitler offered "in reaction" to Raeder's attempts to resign. *ML,* II, 129. His wife later wrote that he rejected any pay increases for his promotions. *Eidesstattliche Erklärung,* 13 Nov. 1950. Raeder N 321/5.
90. *Dotation an Grossadmiral Raeder über 250,000 RM, Schreiben von Staatssekretär im Reichsfinangministerium Fritz Reinhardt an Reichsminister Lammers v. 1. 4, 1942,* Ueberschär and Vogel, *Dienen und Verdienen,* 218–19. For Raeder's implication in the black market, see Lothar Gruchmann, "Korruption im Dritten Reich: Zur 'Lebensmittelversorgung' der NS-Führerschaft," *VfZG* (October 1994), 571–94.

91. *Verhältnis*, Raeder N 391/3. On 30 January 1937, the four senior Wehrmacht officers were honored with the Golden Party Badge. *Tagesbefehl Nr. 67, Marine-Verordnungsblatt*, 1937, 65.

Chapter 6

1. *Gedanken zum Umbau der Reichsmarine*, A II 20231/32, 23 November 1932, PG 34176, *Umbau der Wehrmacht*, reel 27, Project No. 2.
2. Dülffer, *Hitler und die Marine*, 275; Salewski, *Seekriegsleitung*, I, 13.
3. Dülffer, *Hitler und die Marine*, 283–84, 321–22; Salewski, *Seekriegsleitung*, I, 10.
4. Memorandum of mid-June 1934, Salewski, "Marineleitung." 139.
5. Documents 5, 6, and 7, Salewski, "Marineleitung," 156–58. Salewski demonstrates how both documents 5 and 6 were written later, probably 1944, as Raeder sought to defend himself against criticism that the navy had not been adequately prepared for war with England.
6. *Gespräch mit d. Führer bei Abmeldung [sic] des Kmdt. "Karlsruhe,"* Salewski, "Marineleitung," 156.
7. *Ausführung des Chefs der Marineleitung beim Besuch des englischen Marineattachés am 29, November 1933*, PA AA/II M FM, *Angelegeheiten*, Salewski, "Marineleitung," 131.
8. Deist, "Aufrüstung der Wehrmacht," *DRZW*, I, 454–56. See Raeder's vision of global war, *ML*, II, 32–33.
9. Deist, "Aufrüstung der Wehrmacht," *DRZW*, I, 454. Maiolo's *Royal Navy* argues that the Admiralty's readiness to sign a treaty was a response to a legitimate German threat.
10. Salewski, *Seekriegsleitung*, I, 9. Cf. Schreiber, "Zur Kontinuität des Gross- und Weltmachtstrebens," 121–23, who stresses the continuity of Raeder's anti-British policy.
11. Maiolo, *Royal Navy*, 25.
12. Deist, *Wehrmacht*, 76.
13. Raeder, *ML*, I, 308.
14. Salewski, "Marineleitung," 148.
15. Dülffer, *Hitler und die Marine*, 303–4. Raeder's 3 November 1934 meeting notes. Raeder Sammlung, 3.
16. Dülffer, *Hitler und die Marine*, 313–14, 383.
17. Ibid.; Thomas, *German Navy*, 107. The "fourfold" tonnage increase is based on the inability to reach the maximum 144,000 tons allowed under the Versailles treaty.
18. Dülffer, *Hitler und die Marine*, 346–47.
19. Otto Ciliax's lecture, January 1936, "Die militärpolitiche und seestrategische Lage Deutschlands," Dülffer, *Hitler und die Marine*, 347–48. See Donitz's rejection of the treaty, *Zehn Jahre und Zwanzig Tage*, 15.
20. Raeder's "guidelines," 22 January 1935, in Salewski, "Marineleitung," 147.
21. Dülffer, *Hitler und die Marine*, 313–14, 383; cf. Salewski, "Marineleitung," 146–47.
22. Salewski, "Marineleitung," 147–48.
23. Deist, "Aufrüstung der Wehrmacht," *DRZW*, I, 461; Maiolo, *Royal Navy*, 51–55.
24. Dülffer, *Hitler und die Marine*, 315.
25. See Raeder's attempts to justify these decisions in *ML*, II, 36–40, and Treue- *Denkschift, Deutsche Marinerüstung*, 41–121.
26. Raeder acknowledged the lack of clarification about Atlantic operations at the conclusion of the 1938 war games on 12 April 1938. Salewski, *Seekriegsleitung*, I, 65.
27. Raeder, *ML*, II, 147.

28. Raeder, *ML,*, II, 149, and Deist, *Wehrmacht,* 77, 79. Deist refers to Raeder's refusal to consider any conflict with England as an example of "autistic thinking" that prevented his discussing it for six months after he knew that it was a possibility.

29. Maiolo, *Royal Navy and Nazi Germany,* 134–38.

30. Raeder, *ML,* II, 150–51.

31. Deist, *Wehrmacht,* 77; Dülffer, "Reichs- und Kriegsmarine," 477.

32. Gemzell, *Organization,* 278; *Raeder, Hitler und Skandinavien,* 45–49.

33. Gemzell, *Raeder, Hitler und Skandinavien,* 45–48, 65–69. On 12 April 1938, Raeder openly admitted, for the first time outside of the OKM, that war with England was possible. Dülffer, *Hitler und die Marine,* 461.

34. Gemzell, *Raeder, Hitler und Skandinavien,* 46–49.

35. *Grundsätzliche Gedanken der Seekriegsführung. Vortrag ObdM gehalten am 3 February 1937,* RM 6/53, BAMA. In *Raeder, Hitler und Skandinavien,* 49–57, Gemzell extensively analyzes Raeder's dependence on Wegener, comparing side-by-side Wegener's words with Raeder's, arguing that Raeder was a "true 'student' of Wegener's."

36. See Steury, "Naval Renaissance," 189–203, for the development of post-Tirpitz and "post-Wegener" German naval theory.

37. *Grundsätzliche Gedanken,* RM 6/53, BAMA.

38. Ernst-Wilhelm Kruse, *Neutzeitliche Seekriegsführung,* 14.

39. *Grundsätzliche Gedanken,* RM 6/53, BAMA.

40. Steury, "Naval Renaissance," 190–98.

41. Gemzell, *Raeder, Hitler und Scandinavien,* 39.

42. *Grundsätzliche Gedanken,* RM 6/53, BAMA.

43. Gemzell, *Raeder, Hitler und Skandanvien,* 54–56.

44. *Grundsätzliche Gedanken,* RM 6/53, BAMA.

45. *Treue-Denkschrift, Deutsche Marinerüstung,* 157–58; Dülffer, *Hitler und die Marine,* 447.

46. Friedrich Hossbach, *Zwischen Wehrmacht und Hitler 1934–1938,* 207–217. Cf. Manfred Messerschmidt's "Hitlers Programm und das Kontinuitätsproblem," *DRZW* I, 626, which argues that "from this point onwards," Hitler was not pursuing a policy at the risk of war but a war policy, which he had thought out in advance and had been preparing since 1933.

47. Raeder acknowledged Hitler's "sharp tone." *ML,* II, 149–50.

48. Dülffer, *Hitler und die Marine,* was the first to place the 5 November 1937 meeting in the context of preparations for a war economy (see 446–51).

49. Hossbach memorandum, *ADAP,* Series D, I, 25–32; Dülffer, *Hitler und die Marine,* 447–51. Cf. Hildebrand, *Vom Reich zum Weltreich: Hitler, NSDAP und koloniale Frage 1919–1945,* 523–24, for Hitler's intent to develop a *Kolonialreich.*

50. *Ausführungen über England,* 1 October 1936, and *Studie über Aufgaben der Seekriegsführung 1937/38,* 18 June 1937, Salewski, *Seekriegsleitung,* I, 30–31; 33–34; Raeder, *ML,* II, 152.

51. Salewski, *Seekriegsleitung,* I, 40. These plans, he argued, were routine preparations "without consideration of the degree of probability." Cf. Raeder, *ML,* II, 152, 158.

52. Salewski, *Seekriegsleitung,* I, 41–42; Dülffer, *Hitler und die Marine,* 468–70.

53. Salewski, *Seekriegsleitung,* I, 44–45; Raeder, *ML,* II, 156. This was not a question of resistance to Hitler's foreign policy aims, but only to timing and tactics. For the army's resistance, see Geoffrey Megargee, *Inside Hitler's Command,* 50–55.

54. Raeder, *ML,* II, 155. He described this as "utopian."

55. Domarus, *Reden,* I, 868–70.

56. Deist, "Aufrüstung der Wehrmacht," *DRZW,* I, 465–470.

57. *Seekriegführung gegen England und die sich daraus ergebenden Forderungen für die strategisch Zielsetzung und den Aufbau der Kriegsmarine*, Salewski, *Seekriegsleitung*, III, 27–63. Cf. Salewski, *Seekriegsleitung*, I, 45–51.

58. Salewski, *Seekriegsleitung*, I, 45–46.

59. *Seekriegführung gegen England*, Salewski, *Seekriegsleitung*, III, 30–36. Maiolo points out that the senior planners in each navy conceptualized "essentially identical anti-British sea armaments strategies," *Royal Navy*, 71, 190.

60. *Seekriegführung gegen England*, Salewski, *Seekriegsleitung*, III, 37, 38–39, 41, 45–60, details the types of ships required for this "strategic offensive naval warfare." Emphasis in the original.

61. The committee chair was Vice Admiral Guse, chief of staff of the SKL. See Salewski's analysis of the final report to Raeder on 31 October 1938, *Seekriegsleitung*, I, 51–58, and Raeder, *ML*, II, 26.

62. Salewski, *Seekriegsleitung*, I, 48–49; Dülffer, *Hitler und die Marine*, 482–88. Dülffer argues that Raeder had to include the new "H" battleships since he had encouraged Hitler's preferences for these ships to gain his support.

63. NID translation, Carls, "Opinion on the Draft Study of Naval War against England," September 38, Box T-79, NHC, Washington Navy Yard. At Nuremberg, Raeder implied that this was a warning against war with England, but Carls clearly outlines the conditions under which preparations for war would occur as well as initiatives (occupying Denmark in the event of war with England in 1937 and Norway in September 1939). Dülffer, *Hitler und die Marine*, 486. Cf. Schreiber, *Weltmachtstreben*, 175–76.

64. *III. Bauplan (Vorläufiges Endziel), Seekriegsleitung*, III, 62–63.

65. Deist, *Wehrmacht*, 83.

66. Dülffer, *Hitler und die Marine*, 455–61, 491–96.

67. *Rede des Oberbefehlshabers der Kriegsmarine, Generaladmiral Dr. h.c. Raeder*, Raeder N 391/2. Emphasis in the original. Cf. *Treue-Denkschrift, Deutsche Marinerüstung*, 91–104.

68. SKL staff study, 17 November 1938, Deist, "Aufrüstung der Wehrmacht," *DRZW*, I, 470. Cf. Dülffer, *Hitler und die Marine*, 493, and Raeder, *ML*, II, 155.

69. Raeder, *ML*, II, 126.

70. Dülffer, *Weimar und die Marine*, 496. Puttkamer, *Die unheimliche See*, 15–16, points out Hitler's criticism of the navy's high-pressure steam turbines.

71. Raeder, *ML*, II, 126–27; *Verhältnis*, Raeder N 391/3.

72. See Dülffer, *Hitler und die Marine*, 497–99, and Salewski, *Seekriegsleitung*, I, 58–59, for the discussion of the alternative programs. Cf. *III. Bauplan (Vorläufiges Endziel)*, Salewski, *Seekriegsleitung*, III, 62–63.

73. Brennecke, *Schlachtschiff "Bismarck,"* 108.

74. *Treue-Denkschrift, Deutsche Marinerüstung*, 69.

75. Dülffer, *Hitler und die Marine*, 499–502; Salewski, *Seekriegsleitung*, I, 58, 253. For Raeder's version, see *ML*, II, 103–4.

76. In addition to shortages of ammunition, the Z-Plan's fuel oil demands would exceed total German oil consumption. Wilhelm Meier-Dörnberg, *Die Ölversorgung der Kriegsmarine 1935–1945*, 29–30.

77. Deist, *Wehrmacht*, 84.

78. Raeder, *ML*, II, 166.

79. For an evaluation of operational planning, see Salewski, *Seekriegsleitung*, I, 65–82, and Dülffer, *Hitler und die Marine*, 526–31.

80. Salewski, *Seekriegsleitung*, I, 75–76. See Gemzell's extensive analysis of the February-March war games, *Raeder, Hitler und Skandinavien*, 122–46.

81. Dülffer, *Hitler und die Marine*, 525–30. Dülffer points out that Raeder did not totally reject Norway, as Salewski argues (71), but regarded it as a second-best alternative and one that would have to be considered if war came earlier than expected. Ibid., 530.

82. Salewski, *Seekriegsleitung*, I, 77–78. Cf. NID translation, D771. G3913, 1940, NHC, Washington Navy Yard. *Fall Weiss*, "Directive No. 1 for the Conduct of the War," *Hitler's War Directives*, 31 August 1939, 3–5. For Hitler's foreign policy and the führer's vision of Weltmachtflotte, see Dülffer, *Hitler und die Marine*, 544–55, and Bird, *German Naval History*, 537–47.

83. Salewski, *Seekriegsleitung*, I, 59–63; 126–28.

84. Ruge, *Der Seekrieg*, 37.

85. Wegener, "Die deutsche Seekriegsleitung 1935–1945," *MOV-Nachrichten*, 211–15. Wegener accused Salewski of identifying too closely with the SKL.

86. Fuchs to Dönitz, 25 February 1961, Fuchs N 548.

87. Dönitz to Fuchs, 19 February 1961, Fuchs N 548.

88. Rosinski, *Naval Thought*, 66–67. Rosinski observes that Wegener regarded "command" as a struggle for command which could be localized—in effect, accepting the enemy's "command of its sea."

89. Hobson, *German School*, 61. The concept of a sea denial strategy had been repeatedly proposed in the 1930s; see Rahn's "German Naval Policy and Strategy from the Peace Treaty of Versailles to Hitler, 1919–1939," unpublished paper presented to the 13th Naval History Symposium, Annapolis.

90. Rosinski, *Naval Thought*, 53–100; Hobson, *German School*, 63.

91. Rosinski, *Naval Thought*, 94. Such a strategy, he argues, might have created "considerable disturbance and seriously impede[d]" the Allied command of the sea.

92. Rosinski, *Naval Thought*, 96. Rosinski points out that the navy continuously overestimated the diversionary effects of their strategy.

93. For the Admiralty's estimation of the German threat, see Maiolo's *Royal Navy*, 63–86.

94. Plans for the "H" class battleships were by no means the limit of the navy's (or Hitler's) ambitions to build even larger battleships. Dülffer, "Reichs- und Kriegsmarine," 485. Cf. Jochen Thies, *Architekt der Weltherrschaft*. Schreiber, "Zur Kontinuität des Gross- und Weltmachtstrebens," 126, describes this as the "beginning of the new period" of the navy's political ambitions—which eclipsed those of the High Seas Fleet.

95. Deist, *Wehrmacht*, 82–83.

96. See Bird, *German Naval History*, 550–52, for Raeder's apologists.

97. Ruge, *Der Seekrieg*, 49.

98. Salewski, "Das maritime Dritten Reich," 113–39.

99. Geoffrey Till, "The Battle of the Atlantic as History," in *The Battle of the Atlantic, 1939–1945*, ed. Stephen Howarth and Derek Law, 589–90; Graham Rhys-Jones, "The German System: A Staff Perspective, in *Battle of the Atlantic*, 142–46.

Chapter 7

1. Domarus, *Reden*, II, 1077–80.

2. DNB, 12 March 1939. On 31 May 1937, *Admiral Scheer* bombarded the Loyalist Spanish port of Almeria in retaliation for an earlier attack on the *Deutschland*.

3. Domarus, *Reden*, II, 1118–19.

4. Raeder, *ML*, II, 163.

5. Salewski, *Seekriegsleitung*, I, 38, 42, 63–64; Dülffer, *Hitler und die Marine*, 318, 513–16.

6. Maiolo, *Royal Navy*, 179.

7. 9 June 1939, *Deutsche Allgemeine Zeitung*, Dülffer, *Hitler und die Marine*, 518.
8. Salewski, *Seekriegleitung*, I, 92–94, and 15 August 1939, *KTB*.
9. *Bericht über die Besprechung am 23.5. 1939*, Domarus, *Reden*, II, 1196–1201.
10. Raeder, *ML*, II, 163. Raeder supported Hitler's view that timing and military superiority were in Germany's favor and that neutrality questions were "irrelevant in the case of victory." 25 November 1939, *Lagevorträge*, 56.
11. Raeder, *ML*, II. 164–65; Salewski, *Seekriegsleitung*, I, 82–94.
12. "Instructions in the Event of War for Commanders of Naval Ships and Vessels Abroad," Battle Instructions, NID translation, PG/33277, NHC, Washington, D.C.
13. Rust, *Naval Officers*, 72.
14. Raeder, *ML*, II, 165–68, 176. Hitler's address on 22 August 1939, Nos. 192 and 193, *DGFP*, D, VII, 167–72.
15. Franz Halder noted Hitler's comment that the "strengthening of the navy will not become effective before 1941/42." *Halder Diaries*, 28–32.
16. Salewski, "Erich Raeder und 'seine' Marine," *Hitler's Militärische Elite*, 414.
17. Raeder, *ML*, II, 167.
18. Directive No. 1 for the Conduct of the War, 31 August 1939, *Hitler's War Directives*, 3–5. Cf. Raeder, *ML*, II, 167, for the navy's "partial mobilization."
19. Bertil Stjernfelt and Klaus-Richard Böhme, *Westerplatte 1939*, 39–40, 79.
20. Raeder, *ML*, II, 167.
21. *Gedanken des Oberbefehlshabers der Kriegsmarine zum Kriegsausbruch 3.9. 1939. KTB*, 1.
22. *Weisung vom 23. Mai 1940, Ob.d.M*, Salewski, *Seekriegsleitung*, I, 522–24.
23. Hansjürgen Reinicke, "German Surface Forces Strategy in World War II," *USNP* (February, 1957), 185.
24. Raeder, *ML*, II, 176–77, 183; 7 September 1939, *KTB*, 1.
25. 10 October 1939, *Lagevorträge*, 27; Janet Manson, *Diplomatic Ramifications of Unrestricted Submarine Warfare, 1939–1941*, 94–118.
26. Raeder to Foreign Ministry, 3 September 1939, Doc. D-851, *IMT*, XXXV, 547; 23 September 1939, *Lagevorträge*, 24.
27. 7 September 1939, *Lagevorträge*, 23; Dönitz, *Zehn Jahre*, 59; and Blair, *Hitler's U-Boat War*, 68. Hitler directed Raeder to maintain strict secrecy and to alter both the U-boat command's war diary as well as *U-30*'s log. *IMT*, XIV, 78–80.
28. *Bericht über FdU Kriegspiel 1939* (Dönitz), Padfield, *Dönitz*, 176; *Gedanken über den Einsatz der deutschen U-bootswaffe*, 2 September 1939, Salewski, *Seekriegsleitung*, III, 64–69.
29. *Lagevorträge* entries for 23 September 1939, 10 October 1939, and 1 November 1939, 25–26, 27–35, and 47–48. Cf. Günter Hessler's *The U-Boat War in the Atlantic* (British Admiralty), 3 and Appendix I, 106–8, for a chronology of Raeder's requests and Hitler's responses. (Hessler was Dönitz's son-in-law.) Hitler rejected Raeder's attempts to obtain submarines from Russia and from Italy. Dönitz never recognized Raeder's efforts, although the documentation (*Lagevorträge*) reflects that Raeder tried "on no fewer than twenty-three occasions" to get Hitler's approval. Rhys-Jones, "The German System," *Battle of the Atlantic*, 145.
30. Raeder, *ML*, II, 179.
31. 23 October 1939, *Lagevorträge*, 37–42. Emphasis in the original.
32. Führer Order, 23 October 1939, *Fuehrer Conferences*, 53. The quote was Schuster's. Salewski, *Seekriegsleitung*, I, 140.
33. Puttkamer, *Die unheimliche See*, 24, *KTB*, 16 October 1939, 2, and 16 October 1939, *Lagevorträge*, 51.
34. Gerhard Bidlingmaier, *Einsatz der Schweren Kriegsmarineeinheiten im ozeanischen Zufuhrkrieg*, 67, and Salewski, *Seekriegsleitung*, I, 125.

35. Raeder actively pursued the use of Russian and Japanese ports, 23 September 1939, *Lagevorträge*, 26. See also Charles Burdick, "Moro: The Resupply of German Submarines in Spain, 1939–1942," *Central European History* 3 (September 1970): 256–84.

36. *Ansatz der Panzerschiffe* 29 September, *KTB*, 1; "Operational Orders," 4 August 1939, *Fuehrer Conferences on Naval Affairs*, 35.

37. Battle Instructions, NID translation, PG/33277, NHC, Washington, D.C. Cf. 29 September 1939, *KTB*, 1.

38. Raeder, *ML*, II, 182–83; 10 October 1939, *Lagevorträg*, 26–27; 1 November 1939, ibid., 42.

39. 12 November 1939, *KTB*, 3, 83; Salewski, *Seekriegseitung*, I, 159–62.

40. Stegemann, "Die erste Phase der Seekriegführung bis zum Frühjahr 1940," *DRZW*, II, 168–69.

41. Salewski, *Seekriegsleitung*, I, 162–63.

42. Puttkamer, *Die unheimliche See*, 26–27.

43. Marschall, "Stellungnahme," 60.

44. Raeder, *ML*, II, 196.

45. Boehm, *Die Vorgänge, die zu meiner Ablösung als Flottenchef auf eigenen Antrag führten*, PG71844, Microfilm T 1022/3407, NARA. Cf. Raeder, *ML*, II, 196–98. On 26 January 1940, Raeder argued that the escort of heavy ships to cover mining operations was "absolutely indispensable." *Lagevorträge*, 78.

46. Raeder, *ML*, II, 188.

47. 16 December 1939, *Lagevorträge*, 63–65; Raeder, *ML*, II, 187–88; 16 December 1939, *KTB*, 4; 30 December 1939, *Lagevorträge*, 66–67. Although the SKL had intelligence that British reinforcements were unlikely, Raeder deferred to Langsdorff's judgment. Eric Grove's *The Price of Disobedience: The Battle of the River Plate Reconsidered* argues that Langsdorff deliberately disobeyed his orders and sought to engage British naval forces.

48. Raeder, *ML*, II, 185–86. See Raeder's directive to all commands, 22 December 1939, Salewski, *Seekriegsleitung*, I, 164–65. For the role of the navy's tradition of never giving up without a fight—even if it meant the death of many of the crew—see Holger Afferbach's "Mit wehender Fahne untergehen," *VfZG*, 44 (2001), 595–612. Admiral Boehm criticized Raeder's treatment of Langsdorff, Boehm N 172. Raeder acknowledged Langsdorff's aggressiveness but noted that it contradicted the general directives issued by the SKL, *ML*, II, 187.

49. Salewski, *Seekriegsleitung*, I, 164–67, and 16 January 1940, *KTB*, 5.

50. 26 January 1940, *Lagevorträge*, 78–79.

51. 23 February 1940, *Lagevorträge*, 81.

52. Salewski, *Seekriegsleitung*, I, 162–63, 166–67. On 13 December 1939, the *Nürnberg* and *Leipzig* were heavily damaged by torpedo attacks while escorting destroyers on mining operations. Raeder now called the escorting of the destroyers with the cruisers "inexpedient and wrong." Cf. Cajus Bekker, *Hitler's Naval War*, 68–69.

53. 10 November 1939, *Lagevorträge*, 44; Klaus Maier, "Die deutsche Strategie," *DRZW*, II, 189–202; Dülffer, *Hitler und die Marine*, 521. Meeting notes (Raeder), 3 November 1934, Raeder *Sammlung*, 3 (Document 190-C, *IMT*, XXXIV, 375).

54. Salewski, *Seekriegsleitung*, II, 177–78.

55. 5 March 1940, *KTB*, 7. For Weser Exercise, see Bird, *German Naval History*, 629–32.

56. 2 April 1940, *KTB*, 8.

57. 8 December 1939, *Lagevorträge*, 57.

58. 11 and 12 December 1939, *Lagevorträge*, 59–61.

59. Directive 10A for "Case Weser-Exercise," 1 March 1940, *Hitler's War Directives*, 22–24. See Maier, "Die deutsche Strategie," *DRZW*, II, 198 and Raeder, *ML*, II, 209.

60. 26 March 1940, *Lagevorträge*, 86.

61. François Kersaudy, *Norway 1940*, 34; 2 April 1940, *KTB*, 8. See Hubatsch, *Weserübung*, 39–40, for the German operations plan.

62. Maier, "Die deutsche Strategie," *DRZW*, II, 200. Cf. Loock, *Quisling*, 258.

63. 4 April 1940 *KTB*, 8. See the Supplement to the *KTB*, *Zur "Weserübung*," 22 April 1940, *Lagevorträge*, 95–97. Raeder maintained that Weserübung was a "preventive measure." *ML*, II, 212–13.

64. 10 April 1940, *Lagevorträge*, 92–93.

65. Salewski, *Seekriegsleitung*, 186–87. See 11 April 1940, *KTB*, 8.

66. Bird, "Raeder," 57–58; *Erlass des ObdM zur Frage der Torpedoversager, MPA 2864 g v. 11. 6. 40*, III M 1005/2, BAMA. Wegener called Raeder's comparison of Weserübung with the Battle of Jutland "the pinnacle of Tirpitzean reasoning: he needs a battle in order to pass a naval budget or to build a fleet after the war." Wegener to Rear Admiral Donner, 3 November 1940, Wegener N 607/4.

67. Salewski, *Seekriegsleitung*, I, 212.

68. 4 June 1940, 20 June 1940, *Lagevorträge*, 105–7.

69. *Zur "Weserübung*," 22 April 1940, *Lagevorträge*, 97.

70. Raeder, *ML*, II, 218–20. Cf. 6 September 1940, *Lagevorträge*, 135, and 22 August 1941, ibid., 283.

71. 11 July 1940, *Lagevorträge*, 108.

72. Raeder, *ML*, II, 220.

73. Dönitz, *Zehn Jahre*, 86–89; 15 May 1940 *BdU KTB*, Hessler, *U-Boat War*, 26.

74. *Anlage 4, ObdM B. Nr. 83a/42 Gkdos, 9 Februar 1942*, Dönitz, *Zehn Jahre*, 499–501; Raeder's June 1940 memorandum in response to the torpedo failures (as well as his prewar ship-building program). *Erlass des ObdM zur Frage der Torpedoversager, MPA 2864 g v. 11. 6. 40*, III M 1005/2, BAMA.

75. 31 March 1940, *KTB*, 7. Cf. Salewski, *Seekriegsleitung*, I, 195.

76. *Weisung vom 18 May 1940*, Salewski, *Seekriegsleitung*, I, 519–22.

77. *Weisung vom 23 Mai 1940*, Salewski, *Seekriegsleitung*, I, 522–24.

78. Ibid.

79. Heinrich Schuur, "Auftragserteilung und Auftragsdurchführung beim Unternehmen 'Juno' vom 4. bis 10 Juni 1940," *Führungsprobleme der Marine im Zweiten Weltkrieg*, 20–22, 30–46; 4 June 19 1940, *Lagevorträge*, 105; Marschall, "Unternehmen 'Juno,'" *Atlantische Welt* 7/6 (1967): 4–7 and 7/7: 5–7. Boehm complained earlier of the lack of specifics in Raeder's instructions to him as commander of the naval forces in Spain (1936–1937). Boehm N 172, BAMA.

80. Compare the entries of 8 June 1940, *KTB*, 10 and 9 June 1940, *KTB*, 10.

81. In this case, Group West agreed with Marschall's decision to return, contrary to the SKL, who still saw operational opportunities. Schuur, "Unternehmung 'Juno,'" 46.

82. Schuur, "Unternehmung 'Juno,'" 28.

83. See Eberhardt Weichold to Boehm, 12 January 1960, Boehm N 172, for Raeder's "offensive drive"; *Erlass vom 16 Juli 1940*, Salewski, *Seekriegsleitung*, I, 527–33.

84. 22 June 1940, *KTB*, 10. For Raeder's intent to strengthen Trondheim's defenses, see 4 June 1940, *Lagevorträge*, 105

85. Salewski, *Seekriegsleitung*, I, 212.

86. Patzig Interrogation, NID 28/3/46, NHC, Washington, D.C. Marschall was unable, like Boehm, to meet with Raeder. In 1944 Marschall sent his documentation to the naval archives. Marschall, "Juno," 7. Boehm and Marschall were later both "rehabilitated" by Raeder—Boehm as naval commander of Norway (1940) and Marschall as commander of Group West (1942).

Chapter 8

1. 28 May 1940, *KTB*, 9; 21 May 1940, *Lagevorträge*, 103–4; and 24 May 1940, *Hitler's War Directives*, 27–30.

2. *Denkschrift des Referenten für operative Fragen der Seekriegführung auf dem Kriegschauplatz Mittelmeer, Fregettenkapitän Aschmann, vom 11. July 1940*, Schreiber, "Zur Kontinuität des Gross- und Weltmachtstrebens," 142–47.

3. 3 June 1940, *Raumerweiterungs- und Stützpunktfragen* (Admiral Fricke), Salewski, *Seekriegsleitung*, III, 106–8.

4. Salewski, *Seekriegsleitung*, I, 221–22; Hermann Böhme's *Entstehung und Grundlagen des Waffenstills von 1940*, 20–22, 47–48.

5. 20 June 1940, *Lagevorträge*, 106.

6. Ibid., 106–107. Cf. 11 July 1940, *Lagevorträge*, 110.

7. Puttkamer, *Die unheimliche See*, 38 and 5 July 1940, *KTB*.

8. Hillgruber, *Hitlers Strategie*, 159–61. Hitler stated on 31 July 1940 that U-boat and air warfare against England "may bring about a final decision, but this may be one or two years off." *Halder Diaries*, 244.

9. 21 May 1940, *Lagevorträge*, 104; 4 June 1940, ibid., 106; 11 July 1940, ibid., 109.

10. Salewski, *Seekriegsleitung*, I, 234–41, and "Selbsverständnis und historisches Bewusstsein der deutschen Kriegsmarine," *Marine Rundschau* 67 (1970): 82, minimizes the importance of these studies, arguing that it would be "completely false" to consider the "paper fleets" of 1940–1941 "in continuity with the Z-Plan or even the earlier building plans." See Schreiber's opposing interpretation and documentation in "Kontinuität des Gross- und Weltmachtstrebens" and "Theses zur ideologischen Kontinuität."

11. For interpretations of Hitler's ultimate goals, see Bird, *German Naval History*, 537–47.

12. *Raumerweiterungs- und Stützpunktfragen*, Salewski, *Seekriegsleitung*, III, 106–8.

13. *Beantwortung der gestellten Fragen von Carls, Generaladmiral Rolf Carls* (ca. early June 1940). Salewski, *Seekriegsleitung*, III, 108–114.

14. 11 July 1940, *Gedanken der Seekriegsleitung zum Aufbau der Flotte nach dem Kriege*, *Lagevorträge*, 113–20.

15. *Seekriegsleitung an Kolonialpolitisches Amt*, 4 August 1941, Salewski, *Seekriegsleitung*, III, 118–20.

16. *Gedanken zum Aufbau*, *Lagevorträge*, 115–16; *Betrachtungen über die Grundlagen des Flottenaufbaues* (ca. 1941), Salewski, *Seekriegsleitung*, III, 134.

17. Salewski, *Seekriegsleitung*, I, 238; *B. An M zur Unterrichtung des Ob. d. M.*, 31 July 1941 (Fricke), Salewski, *Seekriegsleitung* III, 135–36.

18. See Raeder's extensive comments on the Carls and Fricke documents. Salewski, *Seekriegsleitung*, III, 108–14, 122–37. Salewski argues that Raeder did not share the enthusiasm of his confidants and was more skeptical and objective. *Seekriegsleitung*, I, 239.

19. Hildebrand, *Aussenpolitik*, 96.

20. Halder, 30 June 1940, *Halder Diaries*, 219.

21. Raeder, *ML*, II, 227–28.

22. Salewski, *Seekriegsleitung*, I, 272–73. Hitler's ideas of "encircling" the British Isles persisted. 12 June 1940, *KTB*, 10.

23. 20 June 1940, *Lagevorträge*, 107; 3 December 1940, ibid., 165–66, 167–68. See Raeder's position on Sea Lion compared to Exercise Weser, 11 July 1940, *Lagevorträge*, 109.

24. Raeder, *ML*, II, 230.

25. 11 July 1940, *Lagevorträge*, 109; 13 July 1940, *Halder Diaries*, 227.

26. 16 July 1940, *Hitler's War Directives*, 34–37.

27. *Fuehrer Conferences*, 117–18, and 21 July 1940, *Lagevorträge*, 120–21. The army's demands are recorded in the *KTB*, 29 July 1940; Raeder's reports, 31 July 1940; and 13 August 1940, *Lagevorträge*, 126–29, 129. Cf. the navy and army's arguments, 10 August 1940, *Lagevorträge*, 131–34.

28. 31 July 1940, *Lagevorträge*, 126–128; Raeder, *ML*, II, 241.

29. *Fuehrer Conferences*, 128–30. OKW Operation Sea Lion, 3 September 1940, ibid., 131; Richard Overy, *Battle of Britain*, 87–88; 6 September 1940, *Lagevorträge*, 135–37, 138–41.

30. 14 September 1940, *Lagevorträge*, 142; *Halder Diaries*, 256–59.

31. 14 September 1940, *Lagevorträge*, 142.

32. See 17 September 1940, *KTB*, 13. Umbreit, "Deutsche Pläne und Vorbereitungen für eine Landung in England," *DRZW*, 2, 371; OKW, Operation Sea Lion, 19 September 1940, *Fuehrer Conferences*, 139.

33. OKW Order, 12 October 1940, *Fuehrer Conferences*, 139–40; 14 October 1940, *Lagevorträge*, 147.

34. Raeder, *ML*, II, 240–41.

35. Hitler told Raeder that Göring bragged about the Luftwaffe's superiority compared to U-boats. 26 September 1940, *Lagevorträge*, 145.

36. Hitler later said that he should never have allowed the navy to talk him out of any invasion. Walter Ansel, *Hitler Confronts England*, 161. Later, the navy documented its actions in *OKM SKL Stellungnahme Grossadmiral Raeder zu "Seelöwe" und "Barbarossa,"* 10 January 1944, K 10–2/94, BAMA.

37. See Norma Goda's well-researched *Tomorrow the World* for Hitler's attempts to incorporate Northwest Africa in summer 1940 as the first step in a future struggle against the United States.

38. Charles Cruickshank's *Greece 1940–1941* praises Raeder's strategy, as does Ruge, *Der Seekrieg*, and Lothar Gruchmann, "Die verpassten strategischen Chancen der Achsenmächte im Mittelmeerraum 1940/41," *VfZG*, XVIII (1970), 456–75.

39. Gerhard Schreiber's "Der Mittelmeerraum in Hitlers Strategic 1940," *MGM* 28, no. 2 (1980): 69–99.

40. Herwig, *Politics of Frustration*, 216.

41. Cf. Douglas Porch's new analysis of the Mediterranean theater in World War II, *The Path to Victory*.

42. 6 September 1940, *Lagevorträge*, 136–41.

43. 19 September 1940, *KTB*, 13.

44. 26 September 1940, *Lagevorträge*, 143–46.

45. Ibid. The navy had become alarmed that the French Colonies might secede from Vichy. 30 August 1940, *KTB*, 12.

46. Directive No. 18, 12 November 1940, *Hitler's War Directives*, 39–43.

47. 14 November 1940 (and attachments), *Lagevorträge*, 154–65.

48. Directive No. 19, "Undertaking Attila," 10 December 1940, *Hitler's War Directives*, 44–46.

49. Goda, *Tomorrow the World*, 136–50.

50. Directive No. 20, "Undertaking Marita," 13 December 1940, *Hitler's War Directives*, 46–48; Directive No. 21, "Case Barbarossa," 18 December 1940, ibid., 49–52.

51. *Niederschrift über Besprechungen beim Führer und Obersten Befehlshaber der Wehrmacht*, *Lagevorträge*, 181–84.

52. Directive No. 23, "Directions for Operations against the English War Economy, *Hitler's War Directives*, 56–58.

53. *Fragen und Antwort*, Güth, *Raeder*, 178–83; *OKM SKL Stellungnahme Grossadmiral Raeder zu "Seelöwe" und "Barbarossa,"* 10 January 1944, K 10–2/94, BAMA. Goebbels noted in

his diary on 30 December 1940, "Räder [*sic*] has a lot of no-hopers in his outfit, and could be one himself." *Goebbels Diaries, 1939–1941*, 222. *Die Seekriegsleitung und die Vorgeschichte des Feldzüges gegen Russland, September 1939—July 1941* is Kurt Assmann's two-part compendium of the naval background to the Russian campaign (T-1022, Reel 1820, PG32633 and 32625, NARA).

54. Raeder, *ML*, II, 245–46. Cf. 9 March 1940, *Lagevorträge*, 85.

55. *Besprechung beim Führer, Lagevorträge*, 49–55. Hitler refused to allow Raeder to obtain submarines from Russia. 23 September 1939, *Lagevorträge*, 26; 10 October 1939, *Lagevorträge*, 47.

56. 26 January 1940, *Lagevorträge*, 79.

57. Raeder, *ML*, II, 246. Cf. 6 September 1940, *Lagevorträge*, 137.

58. 31 July 1940, *Halder Diaries*, 243–46.

59. *Betrachtungen über Russland* (Fricke), Salewski, *Seekriegsleitung*, III, 138–44.

60. Raeder, *ML*, II, 247. Cf. *Verhältnis*, Raeder N 391/3. Fricke was concerned over the loss of the Russian aid, especially oil. *Betrachtungen*, Salewski, *Seekriegsleitung*, III, 144.

61. For the most recent summary of Nazi-Soviet naval relations 1939–1941, see Philbin, *The Lure of Neptune*.

62. 14 November 1940, *Lagevorträge*, 154–55; Raeder, *ML*, II, 248–49.

63. Raeder, *ML*, II, 249.

64. 31 July 1940, *Lagevorträge*, 128; 27 December 1940, *Lagevorträge*, 171–73. Hitler's order of 14 July 1941 gave priority both to the Luftwaffe and the U-boat program. Bernhard Kroener, "Die Personellen Ressourcen des Dritten Reiches im Spannungsfeld zwischen Wehrmacht, Bürokratie und Kriegswirtschaft 1937–1942," *DRZW*, 5/1, 928–32.

65. Salewski, *Seekriegsleitung*, I, 500.

66. 6 June 1941, *Lagevorträge*, 174; *Fragen und Antwort*, Güth, *Raeder*, 182–83.

67. Megargee, *Hitler's High Command*, 103–4.

68. Ueberschär, "Militärische Planung für den Angriff," 26–27. Cf. Hillgruber, *Hitlers Strategie*, 211, 227, 396, and Keitel, *Memoirs*, 134–35.

69. *Betrachtung über die strategischen Lage im östlichen Mittelmeer*, 6 June 1940, *Lagevorträge*, 258–62.

70. Salewski, *Seekriegsleitung*, I, 374. Cf. 19 June 1941, *KTB*, 22.

71. *Denkschift zum gegenwärtigen Stand der Seekriegführung gegen England* ("*Juli-Denkschrift*"), July 1941, Salewski, *Seekriegsleitung*, III, 189–210.

72. *Die strategischen Lage in Spätsommer 1941 als Grundlage für die weiteren politischen und Militärische Absichten* (OKW), Salewski, *Seekriegsleitung*, III, 210–14.

73. Raeder's handwritten notes, Salewski, *Seekriegsleitung*, I, 407–10, and the text, 411–412; 25 July 1941, *Lagevorträge*, 271–73.

74. 22 August 1941, *Lagevorträge*, 282.

75. 17 September 1941, *Lagevorträge*, 288.

76. *Lagebetrachtungen der Seekriegsleitung zur weiteren Kampfführung gegen England (Stand 20.10.1941)*, Salewski, *Seekriegsleitung*, III, 215–33.

77. 17 September 1941, *Lagevorträge*, 289; *SSD-Fernschreiben an: OKW/WFST, OKW/L*, *Transportlage Mittelmeer*, ibid., 298; *Verluste im Mittelmeer-Raum vom 1.7.—14.9.1941*, ibid., 299; *Schnellkurzbrief* (Puttkamer), 23 September 1941, ibid., 299–300. For OKW's objections, see Salewski, *Seekriegsleitung*, I, 475.

78. *Niederschrift der Besprechung des Führers mit dem Chef des Stabes der Seekriegsleitung, Vizeadmiral Fricke*, 27 October 1941, *Lagevorträge*, 301–4.

79. For Dönitz's reaction to the U-boat transfer to the Mediterranean, see Hessler's *U-boat War in the Atlantic*, 88–92.

80. Salewski, *Seekriegsleitung*, I, 407–10.

81. 7 December 1941, *KTB*, 27.

82. *Betrachtung der allgemein strategischen Lage nach Kriegseintritt Japan/USA, December 1941*, Salewski, *Seekriegsleitung*, III, 235–61; Salewski, *Seekriegsleitung*, I, 510.

83. Schreiber, *Weltmachtstreben*, 330, 334–36; *Betrachtungen der Seekriegsleitung zur Lage am 20.2.1942*, Salewski, *Seekriegsleitung*, III, 262–274.

84. *Welche strategischen Forderungen ergeben sich aus der gegenwärtigen Lage für die weitere Kriegführung?* 25 February 1942, Salewski, *Seekriegsleitung*, III, 266–73.

85. Fricke's comments to the Foreign Office on 18 January 1942, *KTB*, 28.

86. 13 February 1942, *Lagevorträge*, 355–56.

87. 25 February 1942, Salewski, *Seekriegsleitung*, III, 266–73; "Welche strategischen Forderungen," 25 February 1942, Salewski, *Seekriegsleitung*, III, 266–73.

88. Schreiber, *Weltmachtshreben*, 331.

89. Salewski, *Seekriegsleitung*, II, 85.

90. 15 June 1942, *Lagevorträge*, 397.

91. Krug et al., *Reluctant Allies*, 181–82 and footnote 6, 345.

92. *Lagebetrachtung der Seekriegsleitung*, 20 October 1942 and 1 December 1942, Salewski, *Seekriegsleitung*, III, 275–312 and 313–25.

93. "*Juli-Denkschrift*," July 1941, Salewski, *Seekriegsleitung*, III, 189–210; 13 April 1942, *Lagevorträge*, 381.

94. 12 June 1942, *Halder Diaries*, 623.

95. *Lagebetrachtung der Seekriegsleitung*, 1 December 1942, Salewski, *Seekriegsleitung*, III, 313–325; *Niederschrift aus Lagesprechung beim Chef SKL im kleinsten Kreis v. 30. 11. 1942*, Salewski, "Von Raeder zu Dönitz: Der Wechsel im Oberbefehl der Kriegsmarine 1943," *MGM 2* (1973): 104. For Raeder's efforts to colloborate with the French, see *Die Bemühungen der SKL um ein deut. Franz. Zusammengehen g. Eng.*, K 10–2/80, 81, 82, BAMA.

96. Rahn, "Alliierte Seetransportkapazität," *DRZW*, 6, 298–312; *Stand und Aussichten des U-Bootskrieges, Lagebetrachtung der Seekriegsleitung*, 20 October 1942, Salewski, *Seekreigsleitung*, III, 293–303. See 5 June 1942, *KTB*, 34, and 19 June 1942, *KTB*, 34, for the SKL's acknowledgment of the American building capacity in comparison to Germany's. 8 September 1942, *KTB*, 37. SKL warned that the "sharpest sword" was in danger of "being blunted against a hardening enemy shield," 8 September 1942, *KTB*, 37.

97. *Lagebetrachtung der Seekriegsleitung*, 20 October 1942, Salewski, *Seekriegsleitung*, III, 305.

98. 11 November 1942, *KTB*, 39/1; and 19 November 1942, *Lagevorträge*, 426–30.

99. 20 November 1942, *KTB*, 39; 22 December 1942, *Lagevorträge*, 436–45.

100. 22 December 1942, *Lagevorträge*, 436–45.

Chapter 9

1. 11 October 1940, *Lagevorträge*, 147. Cf. 10 October 1939, *KTB*, 2.

2. *Weisung vom 29 Juni 1940*, Salewski, *Seekriegsleitung*, I, 524–27.

3. 14 October 1940, *Lagevorträge*, 146–47.

4. 27 December 1940 *Lagevorträge*, 174.

5. *Besprechung beim Führer, Lagevorträge*, 49–55.

6. Salewski, *Seekriegsleitung*, I, 386–87.

7. *Unternehmung der Kampsfgruppe "Bismarck" zum Handelskrieg in Atlantik, Lagevorträge*, 240–42. Raeder credited Operation Berlin with having created the first strategic diversion between the Mediterranean and the Atlantic, enabling troops and supplies to reach Tripoli because the British Gibraltar forces were sent to the Atlantic.

8. 4 February 1941, *Lagevorträge*; 18 March 1941, *Lagevorträge*, 188, 202, and 206.

9. Hillgruber, *Hitlers Strategie*, 401; 10 and 20 March 1941, *KTB*, 19; 18 March 1941, *Lagevorträge*, 202–3.

10. Salewski, *Seekriegsleitung*, I, 380–82; the entries in *KTB* 19 (e.g., 12, 18, and 28 March 1941).

11. 20 April 1941, *Lagevorträge*, 218.

12. Schuur, "Juno," 16.

13. In Operation Berlin Lütjens avoided convoys escorted by battleships. 18 December 1940, *KTB*, 16.

14. *ObdM and Chef der SKL*, 2 April 1941, Burkard Freiherr Müllenheim-Rechberg, *Schlachtschiff Bismarck*, 383–89.

15. Raeder, *ML*, II, 265–67.

16. Salewski, *Seekriegsleitung*, I, 390.

17. On 11 July 1940, *Lagevorträge*, 110, Hitler urged the completion of the carrier *Graf Zeppelin* and cruisers with flight decks.

18. The British were reportedly concerned that the threat of the four battleships might force them to abandon the convoy system since "the English ships currently in service are utterly inferior to them." 2 January 1941, *KTB*, 17.

19. 11 April 1941, *KTB*, 20. Cf. Raeder, *ML*, II, 265, 267.

20. 18 May 1941, *KTB Prinz Eugen*; Bercuson and Herwig, *Bismarck*, 61. Hitler was apparently prepared to allow the *Bismarck* group to attack U.S. shipping. Cf. 20 April 1941, *Lagevorträge*, 219–20.

21. Raeder, *ML*, II, 266.

22. *Vortrag (Lütjens) bei Ob.D.M*, 26 April 1941, Salewski, *Seekriegsleitung*, I, 565–66.

23. Raeder, *ML*, II, 267.

24. Raeder first mentioned his plans for this operation to Hitler on 20 April 1941. *Lagevorträge*, 218.

25. Puttkamer, *Die unheimliche See*, 47.

26. Timothy Mulligan, "*Bismarck*: Not Ready for Action," *USNIP* 15 (February 2001), 20–26. In May 1937 the bombing of the *Deutschland* by the Spanish Republican Air Force had caused an irate Hitler to attack the commander of the Panzerschiff, Paul Fanger, for the failure to bring down a single aircraft. The captain was subsequently relieved. *The Hitler Book* (ed. by Henrik Eberle and Matthias Uhl, 2005), 21, 311.

27. Puttkamer, *Die unheimliche See*, 48.

28. 21 May 1941, *KTB*, 21, 308. Raeder concluded that "enemy agents in the Great Belt were responsible." Cf. *Unternehmung Bismarck*, *Lagevorträge*, 243. Müllenheim-Rechberg, *Bismarck*, 94–95, 98, notes that Lütjens had accepted the risk of early detection. He knew by early morning on 21 May that the British knew that his ships were in Norwegian waters. Bercuson and Herwig, *Bismarck*, 59–78.

29. Müllenheim-Rechberg, *Bismarck*, 77.

30. *Vermerk Schniewind*, Salewski, *Seekriegsletung*, I, 565–66, and Müllenheim-Rechberg, *Bismarck*, 77.

31. Marschall, "Juno," 7.

32. Lütjens made his "farewell" citing the superiority of the British forces he expected to pursue him and "was determined to carry out the task assigned to me honorably." Müllenheim-Rechberg, *Bismarck*, 80; Jochen Brennecke, *Bismarck*, 50.

33. Müllenheim-Rechberg, *Bismarck*, 78, 127.

34. The captain of the *Prinz Eugen*, Helmuth Brinkmann, complained about Lütjens's constant radio signals. Bercuson and Herwig, *Bismarck*, 167–68.

35. 6 June 1941, *Lagevorträge*, 239–40; Bird, *German Naval History*, 639.

36. Puttkamer, *Die unheimliche See*, 48; *Unternehmung der Kampfgruppe Bismarck, Lagevorträge*, 248.

37. *Unternehmung der Kampfgruppe Bismarck, Lagevorträge*, 240–57; *Betrachtungen zur Weiterführung des Atlantikhandelskrieges mit Überwasserstreitkräften, Lagevorträge*, 252–57. Emphasis in the original. German radar development focused on range measurements and not on reconnaissance. Ruge, Seekrieg, 174.

38. See Puttkamer, *Die unheimliche See*, 48, for Hitler's change in attitude toward Raeder.

39. Raeder, *ML*, II, 271.

40. For the role of code-breaking in the destruction of the navy's supply system, see F. H. Hinsley, *British Intelligence in the Second World War*, vol. 1, 345–46.

41. The loss of the *Bismarck* further reinforced the conviction that the surface war could not be fought without air support.

42. Hans-Jürgen Zetzsche, "Logistik and Operationen. Die Ölversorgung der Kriegsmarine," *Marine Forum*, 430–34.

43. Assmann, *Deutsche Seestrategie*, 147.

44. 9 July 1941, *Lagevorträge*, 264–68 and 25 July 1941, *Lagevorträge*, 271–75.

45. 25 July 1941, *Lagevorträge*, 271–72.

46. 17 September 1941, *Lagevorträge*, 288.

47. 13 November 1941, *Lagevorträge,*, 304–6.

48. 12 December 1941, *Lagevorträge,*, 325.

49. 29 December 1941, *Lagevorträge*, 334–37.

50. *Lagevorträge*, 336–39.

51. Raeder, *ML*, II, 274; 12 January 1942, *Lagevorträge*, 343–45.

52. 22 January 1942, *Lagevorträge*, 347–48.

53. Raeder, *ML*, II, 275. For Operation Cerberus, see Bird, *German Naval History*, 642–43.

54. Claasen, *Hitler's Northern War*, 194–95.

55. Salewski, *Seekriegsleitung*, II, 21–45.

56. 13 April 1942, *Lagevorträge*, 372–73.

57. Salewski, *Seekriegsleitung*, II, 25–27.

58. Zetzsche, "Logistik und Operationen," 430–34.

59. 12 March 1942, *Lagevorträge*, 359–60. Hitler considered it "entirely out of the question" for the fleet to operate without air cover. 13 and 14 May, *Lagevorträge*, 388–89.

60. Salewski, *Seekriegsleitung*, II, 29–30, refers to the navy's demands for the Luftwaffe to destroy the enemy's carriers and complete the *Graf Zeppelin* as "utopian and wishful thinking."

61. 5 July 1942, *KTB*, 35; F.W. Müller-Meinhard, "Der Einfluss der Feindelagebeurteilung auf Operationsplanung. Entschlussfassung und Operationsführung (Unternehmung "Rösselsprung")," *Marine Rundschau* 9–10 (1970): 513–30, 589–603.

62. Raeder to Carls (Group Command North), 5 July 1942, Salewski, *Seekriegsleitung*, II, 49.

63. 6 July 1942, *KTB*, 35. See the increasing references to the *Kernflotte* in *Lagevorträge* after March 1942.

64. Captain Reinicke (Scouting Forces) to Captain Heinz Assmann (SKL), Salewski, *Seekriegsleitung*, II, 50.

65. 15 June 1942, *Lagevorträge*, 397.

66. 6 July 1942, *KTB*, 35. Raeder's decision to withdraw was based on a report that British submarines had sighted his forces.

67. Salewski, *Seekriegsleitung*, II, 45, 47–49.

68. Raeder's *ML*, II, 283–84; Rahn, "Der Seekrieg im Atlantic und Nordmeer," *DRZW* 6: 413–14; 7 July 1942, *KTB*, 35. Salewski links the search for "new tasks" to concerns for discipline and battle readiness. *Seekriegsleitung*, II, 50–51, 186.

69. 26 August 1942, *Lagevorträge*, 405–6, and "Einsatz von Seestreitkräften in Nordmeer im Winter," *Lagevorträge*, 411–13.
70. 20 July 1942, *KTB*, 35.
71. 13 September 1942, 37, *KTB*.
72. Rahn, "Der Seekrieg im Atlantik und Nordmeer," *DRZW* 6:417–18.
73. Bekker, *Hitler's Naval War*, 278–79.
74. Wagner, 7 July 1942, *KTB*, 27.
75. Salewski, *Seekriegsleitung*, II, 194–96.
76. 19 November 1942, *Lagevorträge*, 427.
77. 30 December 1942, *KTB*, 40. Krancke, "30 December. Morning Situation Conference." ONI, Documents related to the Resignation of the German Commander in Chief, Navy, Grand Admiral Raeder and to the Decommissioning of the German High Seas Fleet from the Files of the German Naval Staff (December 1942-January 1943), NHC, Washington, D.C. (translated notes and *KTB* entries from Krancke's *Notiz über Ereignisse im Hauptquartier*, RM 7/259, BAMA).
78. Salewski, *Seekriegsleitung*, II, 196–97.
79. Salewski argues that Raeder's attempts to secure Hitler's approval (and share of responsibility) increased the stakes in the success or failure of this operation for both. Salewski, "Raeder zu Dönitz," 113. See chapter 10 for the Raeder-Göring conflict over control of shipping in the Mediterranean.
80. Krancke to Förste, 20 July 1957, Förste N 328/29. Cf. Salewski, "Raeder zu Dönitz," 101–46.
81. Rahn, "Der Seekrieg im Atlantik und Nordmeer," *DRZW* 6:419. The words "by Führer," missing from all the war diaries of the units involved, were added subsequently by hand at Raeder's direction.
82. For a description of the battle, see Rahn, "Der Seekrieg im Atlantik und Nordmeer," *DRZW* 6:418–23.
83. 31 December 1942, *KTB*, 40.
84. Raeder, *Verhältnis*, Raeder N 391/3.
85. Ibid. Cf. Raeder, *ML*, II, 285. Communication had also been a problem in the Spanish Civil War when the *Admiral Scheer* attacked Almeria in reprisal for the attack on the *Deutschland* that irritated Hitler. *ML*, II, 87.
86. ONI, Resignation of the German Commander, NHC, Washington, D.C. Raeder, *Verhältnis*, Raeder N 391/3. For the battle report, see 1 January 1943, *KTB*, 41.
87. 1 January 1943, *KTB*, 41. This is clear in Carls's directive of 6 January 1943, which called for offensive operational freedom on the tactical level. Salewski, "Raeder zu Dönitz," 116 and 129.
88. Raeder, *ML*, II, 284–85. Cf. Wagner, who asserts that the failure of Rainbow was a "direct result of Hitler's own orders to avoid risks"—which he later refused to admit. *Lagevorträge*, 455.
89. *Weisung des Oberbefehlshabers der Kriegsmarine vom 28. 1. 1943*, Salewski, "Raeder zu Dönitz," 136–37.
90. Salewski, "Raeder zu Dönitz," 116–17.
91. 26 February 1943, *Lagevorträge*, 471.

Chapter 10

1. Raeder, *ML*, II, 113.
2. Salewski, "Raeder zu Dönitz," 102–3.
3. Raeder, *ML*, II, 113, 288.

4. The SKL complained about its insufficient share of steel, which was not commensurate with its "tasks and position" in the total war effort. 15 December 1942, *KTB*, 40.

5. Raeder, *ML*, II, 288.

6. 23 July 1942, *Halder Diaries*, 646.

7. Goebbels *Diaries*, 163, 184.

8. Lothar Gruchmann, "Korruption im Dritten Reich: Zur 'Lebensmittelversorgung' der NS-Führerschaft," *VfZG* (October 1994), 571–94.

9. *Verhältnis*, Raeder N 321/3.

10. On 12 March 1942, Raeder unsuccessfully opposed appointing a commissioner of maritime shipping. *Lagevorträge*, 362. ONI, Resignation of the German Commander, NHC, Washington, D.C. For the Mediterranean crisis, see 10 December 1942, *KTB*, 40; Schreiber, *Weltmachtstreben*, 367–69, and Salewski, *Seekriegsleitung*, II, 114–15.

11. Gerhard Hümmelchen, *Die deutschen Seeflieger, 1935–1945*, 86.

12. *Verhältnis*, Raeder N 321/3 and Raeder, *ML*, II, 95–96, 103. Cf. Horst Boog, "Luftwaffe Support of the German Navy," *The Battle of the Atlantic*, 302–22.

13. Graham Rhys-Jones, "The German System: A Staff Perspective," *Battle of the Atlantic*, 141.

14. Raeder discussed these shortcomings with Hitler as early as 23 October 1939, *Lagevorträge*, 37. After Pearl Harbor, Hitler noted the value of torpedo planes and questioned the future of the battleship. *Lagevorträge*, 336–37.

15. The initial successes of the mine war far exceeded expectations. Raeder, *ML*, II, 189–90. Cf. Raeder's report to Hitler, 22 November 1939, *Lagevortrage*, 46–47, and 25 November 1939, *KTB*, 3.

16. 23 February 1940, *Lagevorträge*, 81. For Raeder's livid reaction see 26 February 1940, *KTB*, 6. Communication problems on both sides had led to the sinkings.

17. For the role of Special Intelligence ("Ultra"), see Patrick Beesly's *Very Special Intelligence: The Story of the Admiralty's Operational Intelligence Centre, 1939–1945*, and David Kahn's *Seizing the Enigma*.

18. Graham Rhys-Jones, "The German System: A Staff Perspective," *Battle of the Atlantic*, 141; Claasen, *Hitler's Northern War*, 258.

19. Kurt Assmann and Walther Gladisch, *Aspects of the German Naval War*, NID 24/T237/46.

20. See *Handmaterial Ob. d. M. Flugzeugträger Juni-Oktober 1942*, RM 68/86, BAMA, for the details of the carrier program.

21. Hümmelchen's *Die deutsche Seeflieger*, 62–66, 85–86. Göring told Dönitz in February 1941 that Raeder would never get a naval air force. Rhys-Jones, "The German System," 140.

22. 14 May 1942, *Lagevorträge*, 389.

23. *Unternehmung "Rösselsprung,"* 15 June 1942, *Lagevorträge*, 400–401.

24. 5 July 1942 and 7 July 1942, *KTB*, 35; Puttkamer, *Die unheimliche See*, 34.

25. Salewski, "Raeder zu Dönitz," 106–7. Raeder disliked Speer's "unconventional" methods that urged the navy to do anything necessary to seize necessary raw materials. 21 April 1942, *KTB*, 32; May 13, *Lagevorträge*, 388.

26. Speer, *Erinnerungen*, 284–85. Dönitz denied that his relationship with Speer was the cause of Raeder's ill will against him. *Meine Stellungsnahme zu den Schriftstuck "Der Wechsel im Oberbefehl der Kriegsmarine 1943,"* Wagner N 539/68.

27. *Meine Stellungsnahme*, Wagner N 539/68.

28. *Niederschrift über die Besprechung beim Führer in der Reichskanzlei am Montag dem 28.9.1942*, *Lagevorträge*, 420–24.

29. *Lagevorträge*, 145–46.

30. For the U.S. campaign, see Blair, *Hitler's Naval War*, I, 436–44, and Dönitz, *Zehn Jahre*, 193–203. See Eberhard Rössler's *The U-boat* for details of the U-boat construction program.

31. *Meine Stellungsnahme,* Wagner N 539/68.

32. 14 May and 28 September 1942, *Lagevorträge,* 388 and 420–24.

33. Salewski, "Raeder zu Dönitz," 109.

34. See Hessler, *U-boat War in the Atlantic,* 60–66, and 19 November 1942, *Lagevorträge,* 429–30, for the diversion of U-boat forces.

35. See Raeder's criticism of Dönitz, 28 August 1942, *KTB.*

36. Wolfgang Frank, Die *Wölfe und der Admiral,* 381.

37. Salewski, "Raeder zu Donitz," 111.

38. Frank, *Sea Wolves,* 506–509.

39. Padfield, *Dönitz,* 264.

40. For the "Commando Order," see Domarus, *Reden,* IV, 1928–1929. For the *Laconia* episode, see Blair, *Hitler's U-boat War,* II, 57–66. Raeder, responding to Hitler's insistence that the U-boats continue their operations, directed Dönitz to stop any rescue efforts. Raeder's *KTB* entry, *IMT,* XXXV, Document D-658, 325.

41. 14 May 1942, *Fuehrer Conferences,* 283. Dönitz's report is omitted from Wagner's edition of *Lagevorträge,* 388, and 28 September 1942, *Lagevorträge,* 420–422.

42. *Schlussansprache des Oberbefehlshabers der Kriegsmarine Grossadmiral Dr. h. c. Raeder auf der Tagung für Befehlshaber und Kommandeure der Kriegsmarine beim OKM, Berlin, 12 bis 15. January 1943, Sammlung Frühling,* MSg/297, BAMA.

43. Raeder's notes of 6 January (dated 11 January 1943). *Lagevorträge,* 453–55; *Verhältnis,* Raeder N 391/3.

44. *Verhältnis,* Raeder N 391/3; Raeder, *ML,* II, 287, 289.

45. *Verhältnis,* Raeder N 391/3.

46. *Schreiben Raeders an Hitler vom 14. 1. 1943 zur Wahl eines Nachfolgers,* Salewski, "Raeder zu Dönitz," 133.

47. *Verhältnis,* Raeder N 391/3.

48. Salewski questions whether Hitler requested two names. "Raeder zu Dönitz," 121.

49. Raeder to Hitler, 14 January 1943, *Lagevorträge,* 456.

50. *Die Bedeutung der deutschen Überwasserstreitkräfte für die Kriegführung der Driermächte, Lagevorträge,* 457–64. Emphasis in the original.

51. *Meldung des Ständigen Vertreters des ObdM beim Führer vom 17.1.1943, Grundlegende Fragen der Kriegführung,* "Raeder zu Dönitz," 133–35.

52. 21 January 1943, *KTB,* 41, and 26 January 1943, ibid., 41.

53. *Verfügung des Chefs des Stabes der Seekriegsleitung zu dem Befehl Hitlers über die Einstellung des Grossschiffbaues vom 27 January 1943,* Salewski, "Raeder zu Dönitz," 135–36. Cf. 26 January 1943, *KTB,* 41.

54. Keitel, *Memoirs,* 56. Dönitz purged some of Raeder's senior officers to prevent a "pernicious campaign" such as had occurred in the General Staff after the retirement of General Ludwig Beck. Raeder told Dönitz that he had intended to make personnel changes before his resignation.

55. *Befehl,* 30 January 1943, *KTB,* 41.

56. *Verlautbarung aus dem Führerhauptquartier über den Wechsel im Oberbefehl der Kriegsmarine vom 30.1.1943, Deutsches Nachrichtenbüro,* 30 January 1943, Salewski, "Raeder zu Dönitz," 137–38.

57. *Tagesbefehl Raeders vom 30.1.1943, Deutsche Nachrichtenbüro,* No. 30, 30 January 1943, Salewski, "Raeder zu Dönitz," 138.

58. *Ansprache Raeders von den Offizieren des Oberkommandos der Kriegsmarine zur Niederlegung des Oberbefehls am 30. Januar 1943,* III M 1005/7, BAMA.

59. Ibid.

Chapter 11

1. *Verhältnis,* Raeder N 391/3. The painting was valued at 37,793 RM.
2. Raeder, *ML,* II, 291.
3. *Verhältnis,* Raeder N 391/3.
4. Raeder, *ML,* II, 294–95.
5. 24 March 1959, Speer, *Spandau,* 334.
6. 27 February 1945, *Goebbels Diaries,* 1.
7. Raeder, *ML,* II, 299; *Verhältnis,* Raeder N 391/3. In *ML,* II, 302, he states he ground the badge to bits. At Nuremberg, he testified he threw it into the lake behind his house. *IMT,* XIV, 218.
8. *Verhältnis,* Raeder N 391/3; *ML,* II, 302. Raeder later claimed he had called to discuss Gessler's torture. *IMT,* XIV, 218.
9. *Verhältnis,* Raeder N 391/3.
10. Gilbert, *Nuremberg Diary,* 312. Göring hinted to Gilbert that the Russians "had better use" for Raeder.
11. *Verhältnis,* Raeder N 391/3.
12. Raeder Dossier, 920—Personnel, Intelligence Report, 9 June 1947, NHC, Washington, D.C.
13. Bradley F. Smith, *Reaching Judgment at Nuremberg,* 67, 247. Raeder was not added until 29 August 1945.
14. M. C. Vercel, *Les Rescapés de Nuremberg,* 25. The Raeders had been given poison pills. *Verhältnis,* Raeder N 391/3.
15. Raeder Dossier, 920—Personnel, Admiral Patzig, 28 March 1946, ONI Report, NHC, Washington, D.C.
16. Raeder Dossier, 920—Personnel, Admiral Patzig, 9 June 1947, ONI Report, NHC, Washington, D.C.
17. Peifer's *The Three German Navies* notes Soviet attempts to co-opt Raeder and others. See the correspondence regarding captured German officers in Russia. Ruge N 379/85.
18. Raeder, *ML,* II, 304-5.
19. *Verhältnis,* Raeder N 391/3. Keitel felt Raeder had "grievously smeared" him. Keitel, *Memoirs,* 236.
20. Dönitz to Wagner, 27 April 1957, Wagner N 539/67.
21. The Royal Navy and the U.S. Navy opposed the trial of the two admirals, largely because they respected the German conduct of the war but also because they knew that their own practices might receive unwelcome attention. Smith, *Reaching Judgement,* 248; John Bracken, "An Explanation at Nuremberg," *Naval History* 4 (1990): 16–17.
22. Pfeifer, *The Three German Navies,* cites the covert support provided by retired officers serving under British and American supervision as well as British naval officers who assisted in providing documents.
23. *IMT,* XIII, 625; *IMT,* XIV, 13, 19-23, 61-66.
24. Raeder, *ML,* II, 309.
25. *IMT,* V, 279–80.
26. Raeder, *ML,* II, 309.
27. *IMT,* vol. 13, 528, 597, 691.
28. *Der Kampf der Kriegsmarine gegen Versailles* 1919–1935, 156-C, *IMT,* XXXIV, 530–606.
29. *IMT,* XIV, 19–23.
30. *IMT,* XIII, 621, 631; *IMT,* XIV, 14, 31, 160–61.
31. *IMT,* XIV, 30–33. See Mulligan's study, "Ship-of-the-Line or Atlantic Raider? Battleship *Bismarck*: Between Design Limitations and Naval Strategy," *JMH* 4 (2005): 1013–44, for

266 ■ Notes to Pages 216–222

his documentation of the gap in the literature between the concept, design, and operational use of the *Bismarck* class.

32. *IMT,* XIV, 34–42, 46–48, 144–56, 161–201. Cf. Raeder, *ML,* II, 149–51, 163, 165–68.

33. *IMT,* XIV, 200, 207–9, 213–18; NCA II, 863–64. Kranzbühler and other counsels for the defense addressed Raeder as "Admiral." See Document 498-PS for the "Commando Order," *IMT,* XXVI, 100–101. For the execution of the British commandos in Bordeaux, see Document 176-C, *IMT,* XXXIV, 747–66. The *KTB* entry is reprinted in *IMT,* XXXV, Document D-658, 325.

34. *IMT,* XIV, 251–71, 277, 280–81, 298–351, especially 320 and 329.

35. *IMT,* XIV, 353–56. See the affidavits of support pleading for Raeder's release in Raeder N321/5, BAMA. Several of these were reprinted in *ML,* II, 337–40, 391–92.

36. *IMT,* XXII, 561–63; Raeder, *ML,* II, 306. See *IMT,* XIII and XIV, for the trial proceedings against Raeder. For the text of the indictment against Raeder, see *IMT,* I, Appendix A, 15 January 1946. *IMT,* V, 256–82. See Vol. XXII, 561–62, for the Tribunal's judgment (1 October 1946).

37. Raeder to Boehm, 24 July 1946, Boehm N 172/19.

38. *IMT,* XXII, 561–63.

39. Ibid. See Kranzbühler's defense, *IMT,* XVII, 378–81.

40. Telford Taylor, *Nuremberg Trials,* 566–68; Smith, *Judgment at Nuremberg,* 261–63; and Joe Heydecker and Johannes Leeb, *Der Nürnberger Prozess,* 482–83.

41. Gilbert, *Nuremberg,* 312, 394, 433; Raeder, *ML,* II, 319.

42. Raeder, *ML,* II, 321. Cf. 11 October 1946, *The Times,* 4.

43. Rolf-Dieter Müller and Hans-Erich Volkmann, eds., *Die Wehrmacht: Mythos und Realität.*

44. Hans-Erich Volkmann, "Von Blomberg zu Keitel—Die Wehrmachtführung und die Demontage des Rechtsstaates," *Die Wehrmacht: Mythos und Realität,* 60.

45. Hans-Erich Volkmann, "Zur Verantwortlichkeit der Wehrmacht," *Die Wehrmacht: Mythos und Realität,* 1198.

46. Steury, "German Naval Renaissance," 259. Carl Dreessen's 1999 *Die deutsche Flottenrüstung* argues that the navy was "totally inadequate for any large scale aggression."

47. Boie to Förste, February 1956, Förste N 328/42.

48. Raeder Dossier, 920—Personnel, Intelligence Report, 9 June 1947, NHC, Washington, D.C. See letter from Anita Diestel, Raeder's daughter, describing his prison routine in Nuremberg and her concern for her "Aunt's" disappearance (her stepmother) who was still held by the Russians. Raeder Dossier, 920—Personnel, 19 February 1947; 9 June 1947, ONI Report, NHC, Washington, D.C.

49. Raeder, *ML,* II, 323–24, 327–28. In a letter to his daughter, he describes the prison restrictions and his concern about the whereabouts of his wife. Raeder Dossier, 920—Personnel, ONI Report, 16 October 1947. NHC, Washington, D.C. See news clippings over Raeder's health problems and the loss of his son, Raeder N 391/27, and a report on his condition by his supporters seeking to free him. *Besprechungspunkte betr. Die Freilasssung der Grossadmirale Raeder und Dönitz,* 26 July 1955, Ruge N 379/85.

50. Speer, *Spandau,* 108, 111–12, 119, 199, 247. Speer notes Raeder's "fussiness" as the prison librarian.

51. See Raeder's glossing over of his relationship to Dönitz. *ML,* II, 326–27.

52. Dönitz, *Meine Stellungsnahme,* Wagner N 539/68, BAMA.

53. *ML,* II, 328. See the newspaper clippings (1954–1960) in Raeder N 391/26.

54. Wagner to Schulte-Mönting, 27 September 1955, Wagner N 539/67.

55. Rudolf Krohne to Wagner, 16 January 1956, Wagner N 539/67. For Förste's role, see N 328. Raeder already had begun writing a history of his early years, *Lebenserinnerungen eines deutschen Seeoffiziers.* Raeder N 321/8.

56. Raeder, *ML*, II, 328–30.

57. *Überlegung zur gegenwärtigen Situation in der Grossadmirals-Frage*, Wagner, 29 June 1956, Wagner N 539/67; *Besprechungspunkte betr. Die Freilassung der Grossadmirale Raeder und Dönitz*, 26 July 1955, Ruge N 379/85.

58. Hessler to Wagner, 26 December 1955, Wagner N 539/67; Wagner to Hessler, 17 December 1955, ibid.

59. Schubert to Raeder, 16 March 1956, Raeder N 391/14.

60. Ruge, *In vier Marinen*, 342–43, 359.

61. *Ansprache an die Marine-Lehrkompanie in Wilhelmshaven am 16. Januar 1956*, Jörg Duppler, *Germania auf dem Meere*, 203–4.

62. The 18 April 1956 Bundestag session sparked a debate over the relationship of the "old" navy to the "new." *Stenographische Berichte des Deutschen Bundestages, 2. Legislaturperiode, 140 Sitzung v. 18. 4.56.* 7208–7215.

63. Schubert to Raeder, 16 March 1956, Raeder N 391/14.

64. Raeder to Heuss, 5 April 1956, Raeder N 321/14; Ruge to Raeder, 12 April 1956, Ruge N 379/88

65. Raeder to the Kiel *Oberbürgermeister*, 14 April 1956, Raeder N 391/14. Cf. Heuss's delayed response to Raeder, 17 April 1956, Raeder N391/14.

66. "Guter Rat in den Wind geschlagen," *SPD-Pressedienst*, 23 July 1957, Wagner N 539/67.

67. The funeral program is reprinted in Düppler, *Germania auf dem Meere*, 142. See press clippings in the Ruge N 379/88 and Raeder N 321/6.

68. *Asprache des Inspekteurs der Bundesmarine, Vizeadmiral Ruge gelegentlich der Beisetzung des Grossadmiral a.D. Erich Raeder, Kiel, am 11 November 1960*, Ruge N 379/88.

69. "Staatsbegräbnis in Kiel," *Telegraf*, Berlin-Westsektor, 12 November 1960, and "War das Nötig?" *Bild*, 12 November 1960, Raeder N 391/26. Cf. Bird, "Civil-Military Relations in Postwar Germany," *Armed Forces and Society* (Spring, 1977), 517–26.

70. "Raeder als Vorbild der Bundesmarine," *Deutsche Woche* (Munich), Raeder N321/26. *Der Spiegel*'s obituary, 16 November 1960, 34, noted how the new navy regarded Raeder as a suitable model to legitimatize the "tradition-conscious" naval officer corps.

71. Raeder, *ML*, II, 334–35.

A NOTE
ON BIBLIOGRAPHY
AND SOURCES

Because of space limitations, complete bibliographic data could not be included in this volume. In the introduction I have acknowledged the key scholars who have contributed to our understanding of the history of the German navy and its leaders across two world wars. For publication information regarding specific sources, including works mentioned here, readers are referred to the selected bibliography on the website of the *International Journal of Naval History*, www.ijnhonline.org. I am indebted to Dr. Gary Weir of the Naval Historical Center, Washington, D.C., for arranging for this online bibliography.

The book's sources include my 1985 *German Naval History: A Guide to the Literature*, which provides an extensive analysis of the historiography of the Raeder era and summarizes the major studies and research issues. Since 1985, however, there have been a number of new monographs and published documentary collections.

Two recently published documentary sources have greatly enhanced access to the primary sources for the war years, 1914–1918 and 1939–1945. The first, *Kriegstagebuch der Seekriegsleitung 1939–1945*, published in sixty-eight volumes (Berlin, 1988–1997), represents *Teil A* of the SKL's War Diary. It is an indispensable tool for understanding the naval leadership's conduct of the war at sea and its rationale (the current reference of the original documents is RM 7). The second, *Die deutsche Seekriegsleitung im Ersten Weltkrieg: Documentation*, published in four volumes (Coblenz, 1999–2004), represents an attempt to duplicate the War Diary of World War II—a task made difficult by the lack of any centralized naval command (until the creation of the *Seekriegsleitung* in August 1918).

Other key documentary collections include Michael Salewski's 1973 *Denkschriften und Lagebetrachtungen 1938–1944*, volume III of his *Die deutsche Seekriegsleitung 1935–1945*, which provides significant records from the critical prewar years and the SKL over the course of the war.

Additional documents, especially those relating to the "continuity" debate of German naval history in the nineteenth and twentieth centuries, can be found in the studies of Gerhard Schreiber, notably his 1979 "Zur Kontinuität des Gross- und Weltmachtstrebens der deutschen Marineführung" and 1982 "Thesen zur ideologischen Kontinuität in den machtpolitischen Zielsetzungenden deutschen Marineführung 1897 bis 1945." The controversy over Schreiber's interpretation of the continuity of the ambitious fleet-building and expansionist planning of the naval leadership over the period 1897 to 1945 continues today, as the Militärgeschichtliches Forschungamt's June 2004 naval seminar at Potsdam demonstrated.

Two works that define the arguments over the assessment of the disputed documentation of the navy's revisionism and its attempts to establish a global naval power are the 1982 *Militärgeschichte,* edited by Klaus A. Meier, Werner Rahn, and Bruno Thoss, and the 1988 *Kiel, die Deutschen und die See,* edited by Jürgen Elvert, Jürgen Jensen, and Michael Salewski.

Another collection of essays that captures much of the literature and research trends in naval history since 1985 is the MGFA's 2005 *Deutsche Marinen im Wandel,* edited by Werner Rahn. The thirty contributions, primarily by German authors, document the historical roots of the German navy from the first German fleet (1848) to the period of the two world wars, through the Cold War and the navy's role in the world, 1991–2004. Rahn's "Twelve Theses" of the development of the navy in the nineteenth and twentieth centuries concludes the volume. Although it does not ignore the navy's two attempts to become a maritime power in the Wilhelmian and Nazi eras, its subtitle—*Vom Symbol nationaler Einheit sum Instrument internationaler Sicherheit* (From a Symbol of National Unity to an Instrument of International Security)—suggests a more politically acceptable "continuity thesis" connecting the democratic ideals of the mid-nineteenth-century *Bundesflotte* to today's *Deutsche Marine* than Tirpitz or Raeder would have acknowledged.

For archival research, this study relied extensively on the holdings of the German Federal Republic's *Bundesarchiv-Militärarchiv.* The *Bundesarchiv* has published additional guides to a number of its collections of private papers, and its website (www.bundesarchiv.de) provides an excellent oversight of its holdings. Over the last thirty years the *Bundesarchiv-Militärarchiv* has made some changes in the references of some of the documents. The PG classification used by the British in cataloguing the captured naval archives is still valuable in tying together the collections of the *Militärarchiv* and reconciling earlier evaluations of the documents. When the author was first studying in Freiburg, Germany, the Raeder collection (*Sammlung Grossadmiral Raeder,* RM 6) was in process of being compiled; today, it exists as N 391. Both references are utilized in this study.

The extensive microfilm collection of the German naval archives in the U.S. National Archives and Records Administration (NARA) remain invaluable, as Timothy Mulligan's excellent research demonstrates. Other significant and useful archives are the Institut für Zeitgeschichte, Munich; the Niedersächsisches Staatsarchiv, Bückeburg (Trotha Nachlass); the Politisches Archiv des Auswärtigen Amts; and the U.S. Department of the Navy–Operational Archives Section of the Division of Naval History, Naval Historical Center (NHC), Washington Navy Yard. Many U.S. Navy operational documents are also available through NARA.

The Internet has become indispensable to scholars and general readers alike for online access to countless articles and documents through such websites as the

Yale Law School's Avalon Project, which provides the proceedings of the International Military Tribunal at Nuremberg (www.yale.edu/lawweb). Finally, the MGFA's excellent multivolume *Das Deutsche Reich und der Zweite Weltkrieg* (six of seven volumes, 1979 to date) provides superb documentation and summary of the scholarship of World War II over the last thirty years. The publication of this series in English by Oxford University Press provides wider access to the works of the contributing scholars, many of whose works had not been previously translated.

INDEX

code breaking by, 183; colonial empire disposition after, 155–56; commerce war against, 138–42; declaration of war (September 1939), 137; French fleet attack at Mers el-Kebir, 154; in Operation Rhine Exercise, 178–84; planned invasion of, 157–60; plans for defeating, 168, 171–73; potential settlement with, 157; U-boat war against, 138–40; Z-plan and (*see* Z-plan of 1939)
English Memorandum of 1938, 123, 124
Ewers, Adm. Ernst, 45

Fatherland Party, 27
Felix, Operation, 163, 164, 167, 258n64
Finland: pressure on, 185; Soviet attack on, 146
Fischer, Fritz, on Germany's first bid for world power, xvii–xviii
flag, German naval, 38
Fliegerführer Atlantik, 198
Förste, Adm. Erich, xv, 222
Four Year Plan, 97
France: declaration of war (September 1939), 137; diplomatic deliberations with, 161, 162; fleet takeover from, 153, 154; naval bases in, 145, 154, 168, 175–77; occupation of, 153, 157, 164; Ruhr occupation by, 68, 81; sea parity with, 117
Franco, Francisco, Raeder's support for, 117
Fricke, Adm. Kurt, 155
Fritsch, Werner von, 106–8
Frost, Holloway H., on Battle of Jutland, 23
Fuchs, Adm. Werner, 130
Führer. See Hitler, Adolf

Gagern, Vice Adm. Ernst von, 63, 240n74
Geier, 51
Geneva Disarmament Conference, 90
German Faith Movement, 105
German National People's Party (DNVP), 62
German school of naval thought, xxiii, 11
German Sea Transportation Division, 190
Gesamtkrieg (total war), 54
Gessler, Otto, 69, 211
Gibraltar, occupation of, 154, 158, 161–63, 185
Gladisch, Vice Adm. Walter, 100
Gleichschaltung (enforced uniformity), 103
Gneisenau, 112, 149; in Atlantic, 176; in battle group, 54; in North Sea, 141–42; repair of, 177–78; torpedoing of, 151

Goebbels, Joseph, 257n53; anti-Christian view of, 105; on navy loyalty, 85; Raeder's relationship with, 196, 211
Golden Party badge, 211, 217, 220, 249n91, 265n7
Goldhagen, Daniel, on Holocaust, xxiv
Göring, Hermann, 88; anti-Christian view of, 105; as aviation chief, 97; in Fritsch scandal, 106–7; in Operation Rainbow, 190, 197; in Operation Sea Lion, 159–60; Raeder's criticism of, 184, 205; Raeder's relationship with, 103, 196–99; Z-Plan and, 127
Götting, Capt. Friedrich, 71–72
Graf Spee: deployment of, 136; in East Asia Cruiser Squadron, 28; Hitler's memory of, 176; rules of engagement for, 141–42; scuttling of, 131, 143–45, 151, 177, 193, 194, 254nn47–48
Graf Zeppelin, 184, 198, 260n17, 261n60
Great Britain. *See* England
"Great Plan," 170–73
Great Yarmouth bombardment, 20
Greece: Mussolini's attack on, 163; British naval bases in, 163
Grenfall, Capt. Russell, 230n5
Grille, 8
Groener, Wilhelm: as defense minister, 64, 69, 77; opposing *Sturmabteilung,* 87; Raeder's relationship with, 70–72, 75, 79–80, 86–87; replacement of, 87–88
Group North, 191
Group West, 142–43, 150–52, 255n81
Guse, Vice Adm. Günther, 251n61

Hague Peace Conference of 1907, 12
Hahn, Max, 27
Halder, Gen. Franz, 173, 253n15
Hambro, Carl, 146
Hamburg, 39, 63
"Heil Hitler" salute, 100, 109
Heinrich of Prussia, Prince, 6, 240n77; birthday cruise of, 72; cadet cruise of, 3; flagship of, 8, 18; as KYC officer, 64; Raeder serving under, 38; relationship with Raeder, 83
Heldengedenktag ceremonies (1939), 134
Helgoland Bight, 20, 29, 120
Hessler, Günter, 223, 253n29
Heuss, Theodor, 224
Heydrich, Heinrich, 103, 106
Heye, Gen. Hellmuth, 77, 123–24
Hillman, Jörg, on German navy, xx, 230n15

280 ■ Index

ABOUT THE AUTHOR

Keith W. Bird, an authority on German naval and military history, published *The German Naval Officers Corps and Hitler* in 1977 and the critically acclaimed *German Naval History: A Guide to the Literature* in 1985. A Fulbright and Duke University exchange scholar (1969–1970) at the Free University, Berlin, he held a fellowship to the Military History Research Office, Freiburg, in 1975. He is the Chancellor of the Kentucky Community and Technical College System.